NO APPLAUSE—JUST THROW MONEY

NO APPLAUSE—
JUST THROW MONEY

or

THE BOOK THAT MADE
VAUDEVILLE FAMOUS

A HIGH-CLASS, REFINED ENTERTAINMENT

BY TRAV S.D.

OVER 100,000 OF YOUR FAVORITE STARS

PROVIDING 2,500 YEARS OF ENTERTAINMENT

(ALSO EDUCATIONAL)

NINE MIND-BOGGLING ACTS!!!

ILLUSTRATED WITH 49 PHOTOGRAPHS

FOR YOUR VIEWING PLEASURE

FABER AND FABER, INC.

AN AFFILIATE OF FARRAR, STRAUS AND GIROUX

NEW YORK

Faber and Faber, Inc.
An affiliate of Farrar, Straus and Giroux
19 Union Square West, New York 10003

Distributed in Canada by Douglas & McIntyre Ltd.
Printed in the United States of America
First edition, 2005

Library of Congress Cataloging-in-Publication Data
Trav S.D., 1965–
No applause—just throw money, or, The book that made vaudeville famous : a high-class, refined entertainment / by Trav S.D.—1st ed.
p.   cm.
Includes bibliographical references and index.
ISBN-13: 978-0-571-21192-0 (alk. paper)
ISBN-10: 0-571-21192-5 (alk. paper)
1. Vaudeville—United States—History. I. Title: Book that made vaudeville famous.
II. Title.
PN1968.U5T73 2005
792.7'0973—dc22
2005009787

Designed by Jonathan D. Lippincott

www.fsgbooks.com

1   3   5   7   9   10   8   6   4   2

YOUR BILL OF FARE

THE OVERTURE

"Vaudeville is dead."

By the early days of talking pictures and coast-to-coast radio broadcasts, vaudeville's corpse hadn't even cooled, yet the phrase was already proverbial. But, as Poe observed, burials can be . . . premature. My contention is that this quintessentially American form of entertainment, which had been ubiquitous for half a century, only *seemed* to pass away in the early 1930s, yet in reality kept on kicking.

First, it lived on in the aesthetics and attitudes of its most successful veterans, some of whom (George Burns, Bob Hope, Milton Berle) continued to influence American pop culture into the 1980s. Certainly the first decade of talkies (as Henry Jenkins has observed in *What Made Pistachio Nuts?*) was dominated by the vaudevillian sensibility, as were USO shows in the Second World War, television variety shows from the 1940s through the seventies, and—eternally, it seems—stage shows in Las Vegas. But, second, vaudeville, like a phoenix, appears to be rising from the ashes, with scores, perhaps hundreds, of new variety venues popping up at alternative theaters and nightclubs throughout the nation. For a growing subculture of young people at least, vaudeville is back. So, while vaudeville as an institution may have passed away seventy years ago, its ghost has continued to haunt us thereafter, and has even possessed the souls of the living in order to walk the earth again. Not only do *Abbot and Costello Meet the Mummy* . . . but in a certain sense Abbot and Costello (and performers like them) *are* the mummy!

And yet as potent as this resurgence is among performers, I suspect that most people in the mainstream of society remain unaware of the historical importance—let alone the history—of vaudeville. Vaudeville utterly dominated American popular culture during its formative years at the turn of the last century. When Groucho Marx and Charlie Chaplin were born, vaudeville (in the form of its precursors, variety and music hall) had already been going strong for decades. Some of the most popular twentieth-century vaudevillians were alive until quite recently. One could make the argument that the story of American show business *is* the story of vaudeville . . . and yet that story is quite forgotten. (Just how utterly it has been covered by the sands of time is manifested to me in the blank and uncomprehending faces of some of the people to whom I have confided my work as master of ceremonies of my own vaudeville show. The telling and terrifying response—"Vaudeville? What's that?"— has chilled my blood on occasion, making me feel like Charlton Heston encountering the half-buried Statue of Liberty in the final scene of *Planet of the Apes*. "You fools!" I want to scream. "You blew it up!")

Despite our contemporary amnesia, the fact remains that for approximately fifty years—the period spanning 1881 to 1932—vaudeville was the heart of American show business. Its stars were America's first stars in the modern sense. People all over the country knew their names, read about them in magazines. Children collected their playing cards. If you were beyond the reach of vaudeville, then you were really in the sticks.

An illustration of just how influential vaudeville was in the popular culture may be obtained by tracing the evolution of a single stage and screen property and marking the number of vaudevillians attached to it. Because it was my favorite movie as a child, and the prime mover of the lifelong journey that led me to this book, I choose *The Wizard of Oz*. Two years after the publication of L. Frank Baum's children's book, the story was turned into a Broadway vehicle starring vaudeville's premier eccentric dance team, Dave Montgomery and Fred Stone (who played the Tin Man and the Scarecrow, respectively). The latter's performance inspired a young Ray Bolger both to become a dancer and to stop at nothing to play the same role someday. A 1925 film version starred one of the silent screen's biggest comedy stars, Larry Semon, a second-generation vaudevillian. (In this drastically rewritten version, Semon plays a farmhand who disguises himself as a scarecrow. The production also features a pre-Laurel Oliver Hardy.) The 1939 MGM version, however, is the mother lode. Every single principal cast member with the exceptions of Margaret Hamilton (the Wicked Witch of the West) and Clara Blandick (Aunt Em) had been in vaudeville: not only the aforementioned Bolger (who played Scarecrow), but also Jack Haley (Tin Man), Bert Lahr (Cowardly Lion), Judy Garland (Dorothy), Billie Burke (Glinda), Frank Morgan (the Wizard), Charley Grapewin (Uncle Henry), and even Singer's Midgets (the Munchkins, of course). Dancer Buddy Ebsen, cast first as the Scarecrow, then as the Tin Man, then released due to illness, was a vaudeville veteran, as was W. C. Fields, orginally up for the part of the Wizard. (A character who, incidentally, seems not a little based on P. T. Barnum and the many medicine-show hustlers L. Frank Baum no doubt encountered during the years he spent living out west. As we shall see, such "humbugs" would play a major role in the genesis of vaudeville.) Producer Mervyn LeRoy had been a singer in vaudeville. Edgar Allan Woolf, an important author of vaudeville playlets, was one of the principal screenwriters, and Harold Arlen, who co-wrote the songs, had played in vaudeville jazz bands. Over the years, many attempts have been made to recapture the magic of that 1939 film in sequels. All have failed miserably and the reason why should be obvious. The "school" that produced those incredible artist is no more.*

The watchword of vaudeville was variety. The opposite of a variety show, you might say, is a "monotony show." Twelve hours of monks chanting the same mantra over and over again—that's monotony. Twelve *minutes* of monks chanting the same mantra, clad in fabulous silken outfits, accompanied by "mysterious" dry-ice smoke and a very Chinese-sounding gong, preceded by a man who plays the vibes with his toes, and succeeded by a barbershop quartet . . . that's variety.

In this post-MTV, post-postmodern, attention-deficit-ridden age of electronics-induced schizophrenia, I make bold to suggest that few of us will have a problem with this "fractured" aesthetic. Most of us have not only grown comfortable with the idea of watching a singer-followed-by-a-dancer-followed-by a-stupid-pet-trick but can also somehow manage to

---

*A 1974 animated film called *Journey Back to Oz* deserves honorable mention, though. With show-biz vets Milton Berle, Herschel Bernardi, Paul Ford, Jack E. Leonard, Ethel Merman, Liza Minnelli, Mickey Rooney, and Danny Thomas providing the voices, the producers were at least in the right universe.

digest the inclusion of a car wreck, a baseball game, and a panel of old white men arguing about politics. Would it were ever thus. A hundred years ago, when variety entertainment was enjoying a golden age, some critics made the willfully blind error of deploring it for the very features for which it was so beloved. Typical are the observations of social scientist Michael Marks Davis, who wrote the following in a 1911 treatise, *The Exploitation of Pleasure: A Study of Commercial Recreations in New York City*:

> The humorous, sentimental, acrobatic and musical "acts" pass in succession like the grinning figures at a shooting gallery. Some are wholly crude, a few are decidedly clever; the majority are trite and empty; and as a whole there is no imagination behind their creation, and still less in the manager's mind to enforce their harmonious combination. . . . Vaudeville . . . may be described as a succession of acts whose stimulus depends usually upon an artificial rather than a natural, human, and developing interest; these acts having no necessary and as a rule no actual connection.

Davis makes the critical mistake, common for his day, of measuring the variety show against the "dramatic" theater, with its Aristotelian laws of structure and development. But vaudeville (and the other variety arts) never were, and never claimed to be, any such animal. It is its own form, with its own laws. One minute it is a concert; the next a freak show; the next a one-act play; the next a gymnastics display. Because of this, variety is much more like a parade, or a walk through a museum—or, as Marks puts it so disapprovingly, but without much comprehension, a shooting gallery.

Vaudeville has many relatives, near and distant, in the variety family, notably the medicine show, a small itinerant variety troupe whose performances served mainly to advertise alcohol-based quack remedies with whimsical names like Kickapoo Indian Sagwa; the circus, with its emphasis on clowns, acrobats, and trained animals, sawdust, the back lot, and popcorn and lemonade; the dime museum, precursor to the sideshow, with its freaks, junk science, and lurid displays of the stillborn; the minstrel show, a three-part performance hinged on the unifying element of its problematic impersonation of African-Americans; the English music hall, with its emphasis on bawdy and sentimental song;

and the Chautauqua, a sort of highbrow variety show, combining lectures, poetry, music recitals, and genteel humor. All of these various forms were performed in a wide range of venues, from taverns and inns to legitimate theaters, to riverboats, to saloons.

The common denominator among all of these forms was an aesthetic of constant surprise brought about through calculated novelty. In variety, incongruity is cheerfully, fragrantly flaunted. Its alphabet goes from K to Z to B to R to W—and therein lies its charm.

Of all the variants, vaudeville was the ultimate variety form, folding in elements of each of those others to create a spectacle that might justifiably be called "super-variety." Over the course of a couple of hours the vaudeville audience might encounter singers, comedians, musicians, dancers, trained animals, female-impersonators, acrobats, magicians, hypnotists, jugglers, contortionists, mind readers, and a wide variety of strange, uncategorizable performers usually lumped into the category of "nuts."

In a vaudeville show you could have everything: from the puritanical to the licentious, from the patriotic to the anarchistic; from idolaters of wealth to egalitarians; and on and on. It was a world where nightclub dancer Joe Frisco could meet opera singer Enrico Caruso backstage, and say, "Hey, Caruso, don't do 'Darktown Strutter's Ball.' That's my number and I follow you." High art, low art, and no art stood cheek by jowl. Like George Jessel's act of the same name, these disparate personalities were all sewn together like "patches from a crazy quilt."

The Greek philosopher Heraclitus said that all is change. Put your foot in a river twice and you will not have put your foot into the same river—the water is always new. Step out of a vaudeville theater to go to the bathroom, and you will return to an entirely different show. The vaudeville form suited a nation where nothing could be taken for granted.

The years of vaudeville's heyday coincided with the most dramatic period of growth and change this country has ever known. Subsequent generations can have little conception of what it was like to have lived that half-century from 1880 to 1930. In many fundamental respects the nation hadn't changed much in the century preceding vaudeville's advent. On the other hand, the America of 1930 was much more like life today, and this transformation took place during an average person's lifetime.

In 1880 all personal transportation (and some public transportation) was horse-powered. Manure was a serious problem in the big cities. In general, people lived with the aroma, and the mess beneath (and often above) their feet. Though the incandescent electric lightbulb had been invented in 1878, gas lights, lanterns, and candles were still the most common methods of illumination, both in the home and in the theater. Indoor plumbing was a rarity. Outhouses were still the norm. Telephones had been invented in 1871 but remained a luxury of the very rich. People communicated by post or by telegram. The phonograph had been invented in 1877, but it, too, would not become a common household convenience for years. Entertainment options consisted of live theater, social events, or family gatherings at home, centered around singing songs, playing games, or other parlor antics.

By 1930, only fifty years later, Henry Ford's autos had made horses an urban rarity. Cities like New York and Boston were crisscrossed with vast subway systems. Indoor plumbing and electric lighting were near universal, as was the telephone. Live theater was threatened by talkies and by new forms of home entertainment, such as the phonograph and radio.

Machines brought all sorts of emancipations, as well as new enslavements. Labor-saving devices for the farm and the kitchen created a new experience for some: leisure. Mechanization in factories brought greater productivity, but it also guaranteed low wages and long hours. Yet even the factory worker could partake of the unprecedented culture of leisure (and pleasure), whose institutions were affordable even to the poor: ball games, amusement parks, dance halls, and vaudeville.

All of this technological change brought social change. Improvements in transportation and the need for cheap labor to work the new factory machines brought millions of immigrants from abroad, and migrants north from the American South.

In 1840, New York City was home to 25,000 German and Austrian immigrants. By 1880, they numbered 370,000, over one-third of the population. By the turn of the century, there would be 800,000. The Irish came in even greater numbers. Poverty, war, oppression, and persecution in Europe caused 20 million people to emigrate to the United States between the years 1870 and 1910. Suddenly, America (New York, in particular) was flooded with Eastern Europeans (many of them Jews) from Russia, Poland, Hungary, and Lithuania, as well as Italians, Swedes,

Norwegians, and a second wave of Irish. This flood of immigration continued until the First World War, when it was curtailed and replaced by
a major wave of migration of southern blacks to northern cities, a trend
that continued until well after the Second World War.

The same technologies that moved all those people also made vaudeville possible, and would, ironically, eventually render it obsolete. Before
the days of film (a reproducible medium that made possible innumerable
copies of the same material for distribution nationwide) and broadcasting
(capable of beaming the same program to millions of people simultaneously), the performers themselves had to go on the road. Trains, steamships, and automobiles—new inventions a century and more ago—made
it possible for such a thing to happen with great efficiency. Telephones
and telegrams even made it possible to conduct business (e.g., book acts,
negotiate salaries) long-distance.

In this brief window of time before the innovations of media would
make traveling entertainment passé, vaudeville flourished, finding its own
unique niche. A parallel to vaudeville's curiously transitional role in history
may be found in the canal system that sprang up in the United States in
the 1830s. A revolutionary idea for its time, canals allowed for relatively
swift and painless overland transport during an era when intercity roads
were nearly impassable. The Erie Canal, for example, allowed New York
City to get a substantial jump on all other eastern ports, by connecting
the Hudson River with Lake Erie, thus making travel and trade with the
Midwest feasible on a large scale. As successful as canals were, however,
the same economic and technological forces that made them possible
quickly superseded them. Canals were almost immediately supplanted by
railroads, an even more efficient way to move people and goods across the
country. Likewise, vaudeville was a stepping stone beyond the rough-
and-tumble, vaguely criminal era of medicine shows, dime museums,
music halls, saloons, and so on, but it was rapidly overtaken by the mass-
production technologies of the recording, film, and broadcasting industries.

More enduring than vaudeville's own heyday at the forefront of
American consciousness was its contribution to the structure underpinning the entertainment industry. In essence, the science of American
show business—the complex distribution system for bringing performers
and performances to large numbers of Americans—begins with vaude-

ville. Some of its corporate management structure remains in place to this day (Loew's Theatres, for example) and some of our key movie companies (MGM, 20th Century Fox, Paramount, RKO) were founded by vaudeville producers. Vaudeville was the first attempt by entrepreneurs to standardize, quantify, and otherwise get a handle on mass entertainment, to manage it and efficiently bring it to people. Its "products" were a veritable Who's Who of twentieth-century American show business: Bob Hope, Jack Benny, the Marx Brothers, George Burns and Gracie Allen, Fred and Adele Astaire, W. C. Fields, Mae West, George M. Cohan, Buster Keaton, and ten thousand others. Though soon to be eclipsed by movies and radio, vaudeville was America's first star machine. But because film and broadcasting had yet to arrive, the stars had to be physically transported to their audiences. As we shall see, this incessant cross-country travel placed great demands on the performers, but it also left them uniquely disciplined, as well as responsive to the needs of their audience.

Vaudeville was also the first major American institution to offer serious opportunity for advancement no matter a person's race, sex, or religion, and thus had a liberalizing effect on the public. It was the instrument whereby new groups were introduced to the culture—initially demonized and ridiculed, later impersonated, then emulated . . . and eventually appreciated and loved. By thrusting all these groups together, vaudeville became an agent of assimilation.

Howard Patterson (better known as Ivan Karamazov, of the Flying Karamazov Brothers) has a healthy take on ethnic, gender, and race representation in vaudeville:

> To me it seems like a kind of group therapy that the country went through. Suddenly, the nation wasn't all white, Anglo-Saxon Protestant anymore. To us the humor of the time seems racist, bigoted and sexist, but I think what really was happening is that they were processing it. "This is my new neighbor, and he talks kind of like this . . ." So instead of one powerful group laughing at one particular other group, it was all of us laughing at how different we all were.

Furthermore, as time went on, the entertainment industry actually became an agent of change—a salvation from, not a cause of, bigotry.

As Joey Adams wrote, "In show business, for the most part, you are judged by your talent, ability and character, and not your race, creed or color." In 1911 Flo Ziegfeld hired the black performer Bert Williams to star in his *Follies*. The cast, in one voice, threatened to walk out of the production rather than appear onstage with him. Ziegfeld's response: "Go if you want to. I can replace every one of you, except the man you want me to fire."

Diversity, tolerance, democracy, the worth of the individual—all these could be learned within vaudeville's halls, even if the lessons were being absorbed unconsciously. But, like the complex country it so mirrored, vaudeville had its darker side. Its reigning principle was that of American market capitalism, best symbolized by Henry Clay Miner's most famous invention: the hook, that hilarious if insensitive device for dragging off an act that bombed.

And, with all this preaching, I sense that's what I'm about to get. So, enough persiflage.

But soft!

What's that I hear?

The scrape of a fiddle—the orchestra is beginning to tune up . . .

There go the other strings, the horns, the woodwinds. The drummer tests his trap, cowbell, wood block, slide whistle, duck call, kazoo, Jew's harp, ratchet, and washboard (this must be a vaudeville orchestra) . . .

Backstage the two-acts are running lines, the dancers and acrobats are limbering, the singers and actors are pampering their throats, the animal trainers are quieting their beasts, and the stage manager is calling "Two minutes to curtain."

And so, settle back . . .

You ladies, you gentlemen, you boys, you girls, you angels, you demons, you slobbering monsters, you men-made-in-God's-image, you freaks, you perverts, you paragons of virtue, you geniuses, you simpletons, you sophisticates, you farmers, you rich men, you peasants, you old-timers, you young 'uns, you manly manly men, you womanly womanly women, you he-she's, you she-he's, you anarchists, you flag-wavers, you with roots in darkest Africa, you whose ancestors came on the *Mayflower*, you Russians, you Irish, you Germans, you Swedes, you Hawaiians, you Alaskans, you Chinese, you Maoris, you Jews, Gentiles, Mohammedans, Hindus, Buddhists, Zoroastrians, and animists, you great sobbing, giggling, howling, gasping, chattering, gibbering, heaving, palpitating mass of smashed-together humanity that constitutes America, that characterizes the vaudeville audience, and that, I hope—Lord, I *hope*—represents the market for this book . . .

Siddown!

Shut up!

Take off yer hats!

This two-and-a-half-thousand-year vaudeville show is about to begin!

1

WHO PUT THE "DEVIL" IN VAUDEVILLE?

While the vaudevillian, as we commonly think of him, did not take the stage until the late nineteenth century, he carried with him a couple of dozen centuries' worth of baggage. To truly appreciate the revolutionary nature of his performance it behooves us to look at the long, hard road that led him there. And so we begin our journey with a detour—back . . . back . . . through the murky mists of time . . . back to the very dawn of creation . . . back to the first act of nonconformity by any sentient being . . .

Old Scratch was the first hoofer.

Milton depicts the universe's first slapstick moment in *Paradise Lost*. Not long after the world's creation, Satan took a wicked pratfall, tumbling earthward out of his privileged digs in the celestial vault, compelling him to toil thereafter amongst all sorts of lame clowns who were made (like him) all too imperfectly in God's image. Mae West said it best: "I'm No Angel."

Despite numerous tragic attempts to create a utopia in our midst, mankind in its weakness finds itself perennially veering from the high road to the trough of low amusements. Historically, that ditch has been a pretty crowded place, full of strange and unlikely company: on the one hand, clowns, jugglers, singers of sweet love songs, and others of their ilk; on the other, tavern-keepers, card sharks, prostitutes, and their brother (and sister) criminals. From the beginning of the Christian era until quite recently, these two groups have always gone hand in hoof: Entertainment and Evil, a double act spawned in the mind of a maniac. Entertainment feeds us punch lines; Evil, with his slow burn, is the straight man. And the dirty-minded maniac? Let's just call him "Reverend."

Ludicrous though it may seem to us to place jugglers, singers, and dancers in a caste with "Gypsies, Tramps, and Thieves," Christians (first Catholics and then Protestants) have done so for centuries. For moral support they need look no further than Saint Paul, who in his Epistle to the Ephesians (5:3–4) lumps "foolish talking" and "jesting" in with fornication, uncleanness, and covetousness. In his Epistle to the Galatians (5:21), "revellings" are in a class with "envyings," "murders," and "drunkenness." It is a litmus test that would sully the reputation of an Osmond.

To us, for whom Marilyn Manson is old hat, and who undoubtedly know at least one grandparent who can sing all the words to "Sympathy for the Devil," this is madness. Yet underneath the madness—at least initially—lay a method.

Theatrical performers, consciously or no, practice an art that began as a rite to honor the Greek god Dionysus, a deity principally associated with sexual abandon and intoxication. Aspects of the ceremony—even well after it had evolved into what we now call theater—were by most measures "obscene."

The shadow of Dionysus still darkens our fragmentary memories of antiquity. Thanks largely to the cinema's depictions of life under various caesars, the ancient world retains a distorted Bacchic patina. Say "Rome," and images out of *Caligula* and Fellini's *Satyricon* rage through the brain: public baths full of immodest sculptures, patronized by men, women, children, and livestock. Great, fat, oily courtiers in togas recline on silk couches munching pornographic pastries. Frolicking nymphs with grape leaves in their hair play leapfrog in the forest, pausing only to indulge their twin tastes in human sacrifice and lesbianism. Satyrs in outlandish codpieces swing their phalluses at one another, eventually coalescing into a great, heaving, perfumed, peach-colored daisy chain.

The early leaders of the Catholic Church apparently thought such images so horrible they couldn't stop thinking about them.

Come to think of it, neither can I.

Worldliness, materialism, sex, pleasure—all nicely integrated into the philosophies of the ancients—were now tarred with the broad brush of "evil." To turn the pagan Europeans from their wicked ways, some scholars feel that Dionysus was purposely equated with "Satan."

In decorative art and statuary, Dionysus and his cohorts (such as the demigod Pan) had been depicted as goatlike, possessing horns, hooves, and a tail, uncannily resembling what we now think of as the devil. Yet no such description of Satan exists in the Bible. There he is depicted only as a fallen angel, a serpent, or something called Leviathan. How astute (not to mention diabolical) of the Church Fathers to associate the nature-worship of Europe's oldest traditions with Evil Incarnate.

Fourteen or more centuries of official persecution of variety entertainers only make sense in this context—they have their roots in pagan antiquity. Among the first recorded variety performers were the Greek mimes, a motley lot who lumbered out of southern Italy during Greece's Golden Age to juggle, perform acrobatics, dance, and perform comical sketches for the vastly more dignified Athenians. These were very different from our modern mimes, in their whiteface and berets, who walk against the wind and scream-in-an-ever-shrinking-box (those mimes *are* satanic).

Rome, too, had its mimes; they begin to materialize in the Republic at about 300 B.C. Roman mimes were closely associated with the Atellan farce, ancestor to the Roman comedies of Plautus and Terence, the commedia dell'arte, the comic creations of Shakespeare and Molière, and all slapstick straight through the vaudeville era. The *fabula raciniata* was a form of early variety that incorporated tightrope walkers, trapeze artists, tumblers, jugglers, sword-swallowers, fire-eaters, dancers, operatic singers, and stilt-walkers. Tony Curtis proudly proclaimed himself among this performing clique in the 1960 film *Spartacus*: "I yam a magician and seengah of sawngs," he announces in ancient Brooklynese.

Throughout Euro-American history, the descendants of those mimes persisted. During the Middle Ages, itinerant bands of *jongleurs*, minstrels, troubadours, and similar entertainers would tramp from village to village with their exhibitions of juggling, fire-eating, magic tricks, little songs, and bits of clowning. In Elizabethan England, they came in from the cold and were incorporated into the presentation of great works of dramatic literature as preludes and entr'actes. That tradition was perpetuated in America into the late nineteenth century, when, as one historian put it, "all shows were variety shows."

Yet despite their deathless popularity in every land they roamed, these proto-vaudevillians always found public officials rabid to ring down the curtain.

"The condition of faith and the laws of Christian discipline forbid among other sins of the world the pleasures of the public shows," wrote Tertullian, a theologian of the second century A.D.

With a pitch like that, it's a wonder he made any converts at all. Yet the animus against pagan-derived spectacle by the early followers of Christ is understandable: some of those spectacles had involved the consumption of Christians by the creatures we in the business call "big cats." Siegfried and Roy meet *The Faces of Death* as staged by Cecil B. DeMille. A "light show" mounted by Nero might consist of hundreds of Christians tied to stakes, coated with tar and set afire. In the Atellan farce an unfortunate Christian named Laureolus is recorded to have been crucified during the show's climax and subsequently torn apart by wild animals. I repeat: this is in a *farce*. Not in a league with ritual murder, perhaps, but plenty appalling, was the attendant practice of presenting live sex acts as spectacle. In the case of slaves, many of whom were Christian, such performances would have been quite involuntary, and (for some, no doubt) a fate worse than death.

To enter another dangerous arena, drag, or female impersonation, has been a staple of theater since ancient times. This, too, had been a specialty of the Roman mimes, and one imagines a full range of possible transvestisms, from the silly and vulgar buffoonery associated with Milton Berle, all the way to the sort of feminine role-playing that takes place in maximum-security prisons. Ultimately, any lasting bad rep attached to drag would come from both kinds. Neither the shameless fool nor the sexual "deviant" had any place in the Christian order. By the early twentieth century, the feminine artistry of biological males like Julian Eltinge, Bert Savoy, Karyl Norman, and dozens of others would grace even the most conservative stages of America and Europe with little public furor. But they had a long road to walk (in high heels, no less) before they reached that coveted stage.

Fresh from the outrages of Rome, the rancor of early Church Fathers toward the theater is not surprising. But what of the lesser indictments that have haunted performers throughout history until the eve of our own era? What about the claims that the theater is a mere cesspool, a haven for prostitutes, con men, thieves, Satanists, ruffians, and drunkards?

"The participants of show business," wrote columnist Earl Wilson, "are rumpots, nymphomaniacs, prostitutes, fakes, liars, cheaters, pimps, hopheads, forgers, sodomists, slobs, absconders—but halt. I understate it horribly."

As late as 1904, clergyman J. M. Judy wrote in his treatise *Questionable Amusements and Worthy Substitutes*:

> With drunkenness, gambling and dancing, theater-going dates from the beginning of history, and with these it is not only questionable in morals, but it is positively bad . . . There you find the man . . . who has lost all love for his home, the careless, the profane, the spendthrift, the drunkard, and the lowest prostitute of the street.

The startling fact that emerges from these blanket pronouncements is not the extremity of the views; on the contrary, their assessments are right on the button.

"Cluck, cluck, surely this is an exaggeration," we sophisticated moderns are wont to respond. We laugh off such hyperbolic broadsides as the ravings of a lunatic. We hold this view because the past century has been a time of rehabilitation for the traveling player, not because the charges were ever discredited.

Tempting though it may be to scoff at the bugaboos of less enlightened times, these claims (despite their hysterical and intolerant tone) turn out to have been essentially true. Like Vivie in the Shaw play *Mrs. Warren's Profession*, vaudeville turns out to be the respectable, bourgeois daughter of a common whore. More accurately, a dynasty of whores stretching back to the Queen of Sheba. The only question has ever been: Do you have a problem with whores?

Throughout most of human history, ladies (and gentlemen) of the evening have been a featured amenity at nearly all theaters. In Rome, the world's oldest profession had developed into a fine art. There are three dozen words in Latin for as many types of prostitute. Four of them (cymbal players, singing girls, harpists, and mimes) have names that also qualify them for the Roman equivalent of the vaudeville stage. The Roman circuses and amphitheaters were handily equipped with special little enclaves called *fornices* where men could visit a sex worker during intermission. They were sort of like a concession stand, or those guys at the ball games ("Get yer red hots! Get 'em while they're red, get 'em while they're hot! And when we say hot, we mean *hot!*"). In medieval times, *jongleuresses* and lady minstrels entertained the populace, but also doubled as damsels-for-hire. Edward II himself was entertained by several of these charmers, who, with names like "Pearl-in-the-Egg" and "Maude Makejoy," were doubtless fingering more than lute frets.*

According to British historian Fergus Linnane's book *London: The Wicked City*, Elizabethan theaters were patrolled by girls called "orange sellers," who sold oranges, and were only too glad to peel it off. The Restoration stage gave us the actress-courtesan who accepted lavish gifts, jewels, dresses, an apartment—a living, basically—in exchange for being some admirer's girlfriend. One of the most famous actresses of the age, Nell Gwynn, even became the consort to Charles II. That this should be so is not surprising. Surely it's not nuclear physics to conclude that some of the men in the audience, inflamed by the beauties on stage, hearts thumping, minds racing, would fall all over themselves in a mad scramble back to the dressing room with boxes of chocolates, bundles of roses, bottles of champagne, wallets full of cash, family heirlooms, and probably deeds to property, in order to quiet the howling, libidinous demons inside them. Don't ask me why. I guess that's just how God made us.

Whether or not an actress was actually a prostitute was immaterial. By the late nineteenth century virtually none of them were, but the association remained. This is due to a peculiar phenomenon that still rears its ugly head, what specialists in rape law call "blaming the victim." Because the woman inspires lustful thoughts in a man (whether she purposes to do so or not) she becomes the source of evil. It's rather like the wolf blaming the sheep for looking delicious. So we find women becoming the Daughters of Eve, the Whores of Babylon, the Jezebels, the Delilahs

---

*While most famous for the homosexual liaison that brought down his monarchy, the pleasure-loving king was actually a switch-hitter.

and Salomes. To parade themselves in front of an audience is a brazen act of provocation inspired by Satan himself. Yet, as we shall see, at vaudeville's peak, in the first decade of the twentieth century, Salome would be very much in demand.

Esmerelda in Victor Hugo's *The Hunchback of Notre Dame* is the archetype of the nascent medieval variety artist: she dances, plays a tambourine, tells jokes, and performs a routine with a trained goat. That dance—that Middle Eastern, sexy Gypsy dance—proves the character's undoing. Ecstatic or "primitive" dancing in medieval and Reformation times was associated with witchcraft because it was believed that the dancer bewitched the male spectator by arousing impure thoughts. The anonymous pamphlet *A Pleasant Treatise of Witches* (1673) describes such a dance as "diabolical . . . they take one another by the arms and raise each other from the ground, then shake their heads to and fro like Anticks, and turn themselves as if they were mad." Hanging, stoning, burning, and drowning were the penalties for such behavior. But in the twentieth century, vaudeville dancers would teach America to shimmy, shake, cakewalk, and Toddle the Tolado.

Similarly reviled were the minstrels, or professional singers of secular love songs. In the Middle Ages, minstrels were particularly execrated by religious authorities, for they went about filling people's heads with seductive thoughts. As the medieval mystic Mechtild of Magdeburg wrote: "The miserable minstrel who with pride can arouse sinful vanity / weeps more tears in hell than there is water in the sea."

To bring the matter closer to home, think of most of the famous singers of the past century. Is there any doubt that the vast majority of them have made more than their fair share of "conquests"? Sinatra, Elvis, and the Beatles amongst them must have dispatched over a thousand women, plenty of them teenagers, most of them one-night stands, all of them somebody's daughter. This wasn't invented yesterday. The guy with the guitar always gets the chicks, even when the guitar is a mandolin and the love song is "Greensleeves."

One of these strolling Lotharios is most germane to our story, for (as tradition has it) he gave vaudeville its name. Some say the word is a corruption of *val de vire*, or *vau de vire*, meaning the valley of the Vire River, which is in Normandy, where a troubadour named Olivier Basselin made certain drinking songs popular in the fifteenth century. Thus was vaudeville, like the theater itself, born in a bottle. Imagine the setting: a wayside inn full of drunken, dirty peasants, Falstaff, Nym, and Pistol, feeling up the wenches and making lewd jokes. This would be the variety-arts setting for at least the next three centuries. But while the word "vaudeville" was coined in the Middle Ages, there will be much water (and more alcohol) under the bridge before we arrive at the unlikely destination known as American vaudeville.

Efforts to keep sex off the stage could sometimes backfire. The medieval English had banned women from the stage for fear of encouraging indecent displays. The female roles were all played by young boys in girlish costume. The result was that by Elizabethan times you had the unsettling situation of innocent children playing sensuous female roles like Juliet and Cleopatra, their hair long, their cheeks rouged, and their little eyelashes batting coquettishly. Ironically, an effort to suppress sexuality resulted in something uncomfortably skirting perversion. In this, perhaps, the Elizabethan theater had something in common with prisons, seminaries, English boarding schools, and the navy. Whether or not suspicions of pederasty had any real foundation, though, they added to the theater's stigmatization in some quarters. In 1629, the poet Francis Lenton labeled boy drag one of the "tempting baits of Hell / Which draw more youth unto the damned cell / Of furious lust." But we'll leave this tangent for the friends and enemies of NAMBLA to debate.

As that unregenerate sinner Oscar Wilde taught us, theater is, at bottom, the fine art of lying. Putting on a costume and claiming to be someone entirely different is a form of misrepresentation, or "false witness." As the temptation must have been great for the beautiful actress to capitalize on her advantages, so too must it have been for the artful, shape-shifting actor to cross the line from thespian to confidence man.

In medieval times, one sort of traveling entertainer embodied both sides of this wooden nickel. Performing his shows on moveable tables or "benches," the mountebank (literally "mount the bench" in Italian— as in "climb up on this improvised stage") was part businessman, part entertainer, making quack medicine his dodge. But he was also a showman, presenting a variety bill that might include clowning, slack-wire walking, juggling, conjuring, and feats of strength. The show was just bait, however. When the crowd reached critical mass, the mountebank would proceed with his real agenda: selling medicinal tonics, elixirs, and powders and performing simple medical services, such as corn cutting.

The mountebank was the ancestor of the pitchman, the carnival barker, and the circus spieler, not to mention our entire modern model of entertainment programming presented by advertising sponsors. Shakespeare "conjures" an unflattering image of a mountebank in *The Comedy of Errors*:

> . . . one Pinch; a hungry, lean-faced villain;
> A mere anatomy, a mountebank,
> A threadbare juggler, and a fortune-teller;
> A living-dead man. This pernicious slave,
> Forsooth, took on him as a conjurer;
> And, gazing in mine eyes, feeling my pulse,
> And with no face, as 'twere out-facing me,
> Cries out, I was posses'd.

Though such medicine shows (as they came to be known) have their origins in the Middle Ages, they persisted into the twentieth century and have come to be thought of as characteristically American. This is the "snake oil" patent medicine salesman of song and story, once a fact of life in rural America, and most prominently embodied in the character devised by W. C. Fields. Such shows were to coexist with and enrich vaudeville, sending forth such distinguished alumni as Buster Keaton, Harry Langdon, Eubie Blake, Jesse Lasky, Fred Stone, and Harry Houdini.

The mountebank was the prototypical theatrical entrepreneur. His brother in charms was the *ciarlatano* (Italian for "babbler"), whose bag of tricks was a little bigger, embracing not only medical cures, but magic and fortune-telling as well. Gypsies (more properly known as Roma, a people believed to have migrated to Europe from India), became associated with the latter line of work, which remains a staple at fairs, amusement parks, and carnivals to this day. The classic American charlatan is captured in the character of Professor Marvel from the 1939 film version of *The Wizard of Oz*, with his crystal ball, his turban, and his dubious ability to see into the future.

Unfortunately, mountebanks and charlatans have not faired well in the marketplace of history. Look the words up in the dictionary if you want to know how high their stock is these days. They are held in so little esteem that the terms have lost all theatrical association for the wider public and are now roughly synonymous with "crook." Of course, some of that discredit has been earned. Mediums, astrologers, and doctors with false credentials have been known to perpetrate swindles. These arts seem to fill some awkward middle ground between show business, on the one hand, and science and established religion, on the other. Because of the power wielded by the latter institutions in our society, laws against fortune-telling remain on the books practically everywhere. Yet, in America at least, those laws are rarely enforced, perhaps because life without magic—even pretend magic—is too cruel to contemplate. And just as television shows like *Crossing Over* and *The Psychic Friends Network* have held millions in their grip in recent times, vaudeville was rife with mind readers, mentalists, and second-sight artists. A need to believe in them is always there.

That didn't stop the authorities in less tolerant times, however, from trying to associate these people with the man downstairs. To make matters worse, the Romany word for "god" is *devel*, an unfortunate linguistic coincidence that must have led to some misunderstandings worthy of Abbot and Costello. Yet to be fair, the connection between magic and the guy with horns is an old one, and one probably only ever denied under threat of an Inquisitor's thumbscrew.

Only recently have magicians, for example, written off their sleight of hand as a question of mere dexterity. Pagan priests were the first magicians, a devious but socially expedient arrangement that may well go back to Neanderthal times. The writings of Egypt, Greece, Rome, Mesopotamia, and the ancient Jews are full of the doings of such characters who kept their flocks in line for fun and profit. Remember your Exodus. When Moses turns his rod into a serpent, what do Pharaoh's priests do? They turn *their* rods into serpents. When he turns the Nile into blood, what do the priests do? They turn *their* little bowls of water into "blood." Presto change-o! Miracles, in antiquity, were part of the apparatus of the state, much as a well-rehearsed press conference is today.

In the monotheistic order, however, magic, like the art of the actor, became *verboten*, inside the church and out. Catholicism, for example, relies on the subtler effects produced by music, poetry, wine, and incense to summon the spirit during its ceremonies—absent are the whistles, shadows, smoke, sparklers, mirrors, and black thread employed by pagan priests to make god appear, whether he wanted to or not. In medieval times, magic and its allied arts (e.g., mind reading, fortune-telling, hypnotism, and ventriloquism) went underground and became a dark cohort of alchemy, necromancy, and all manner of mountebankery. The conical-hatted wizard with stars and moons on his robe emerges from behind the curtain, inspiring Faust, Merlin, Gandalf, and Cookie Jarvis. Echoes of this former devilishness survived in the conjuring field until quite recently. Think of the archetypal magician, with his pointy goatee and mustache, his dark brow, his big, sweeping cape, magic wand, puffs of smoke, flashes of fire, and all of those Kabalistic words that have since become silly to us, but were once meant to call up demons from hell: *Hocus Pocus! Ali-kazam! Abracadabra!* Yet throughout most of the Christian era, such association with His Satanic Majesty, however great the financial rewards, has meant risking imprisonment, torture, and death at the hands of the authorities. As late as the 1780s, Cagliostro, who'd been the toast of Paris with his illusions, was sentenced to life in prison by the Inquisition; he perished within a year. A little over a century later, the vaudevillian Harry Houdini would escape from dozens of such jails and gain fame and fortune doing it.

Yet throughout most of the Christian era, the practitioner of magic needed to keep his bags packed. Another nickname for the Roma people is "Travelers." They lived right in the wagons that were their crucial mode of escape. But the Roma weren't the only travelers. Plenty of others hit the road, too, compelled by nothing more than the perverse imp inside them, that incessant siren song that made the plow and the spinning wheel seem a fate worse than death. Just as in the sideshow world there are many self-made freaks, in the wider performing arts, there are many self-made outsiders. Yet even they to a certain extent were handpicked by fate. Where is there a home for the butter-fingered farm boy who daydreams and drops all his tools? The peasant with an IQ of 160? The village idiot? The queer? The village trollop in a culture where allure was regarded as temptation and thus a hated product of Satan (cursed, as we still say, with a beautiful body)? For such people, the Island of Misfit Toys is the only logical destination.

Ironically these nonconformists were trapped in a no-win situation.

Forced by circumstances to keep moving, they were then often treated with fear and suspicion for being strangers. They were outsiders by definition, and remained so within living memory. Before the age of broadcasting, travel was the only way a performer could make his living. Once the townspeople have seen your show and tossed their pennies, it's time to move on. Like a farmer rotating his fields, when one area was fallow, you'd have to work another.

Yet since the dawn of civilization, civilization has been equated with stability. We like "pillars" of society and good "solid" citizens. We are distrustful of someone who "runs around." The person who comes and goes as he pleases is said to do so "like a thief in the night." Throughout most of Western history, one said "actor" the way one said "hobo." To become an actor was to throw your life away, leave your family (usually with a good deal of rancor), and live on the road. When you consider that Robin Hood, Billy the Kid, Jesse James, Bonnie and Clyde, and John Dillinger were also itinerant and that the definition of "highwayman" is "robber," it's no surprise that traveling performers were lumped in with more nefarious drifters. A 1545 English law expressed this association succinctly, grouping "players" together with "ruffians, vagabonds, masterless men and evil-disposed persons." In the 1940 Walt Disney film *Pinocchio* the title character is waylaid on the way to school by two evil creatures who teach him to sing "Heigh diddle dee-dee, the actor's life for me." The next thing you know, Pinocchio is smoking cigars and playing pool on Pleasure Island and literally making an ass of himself. Outsiders steal your laundry off the line. They sell you miracle cures that turn out to be turpentine, leaving nothing but a smoldering campfire as a customer-service desk. They entice your children, especially your daughters, down the primrose path. They leave no forwarding address.

Vagrancy and vagabondage were therefore serious crimes. In 1572 English law provided that all fencers, exhibitors of trained bears, players, or minstrels not specifically under the patronage of a nobleman be "grievously whipped and burned through the gristle of the right ear with a hot iron of the compass of an inch about." Variations of this law (albeit with diminishing severity) remained on the books until 1824.

"I must admit that there was some justification for the actor's unsavory social reputation," wrote Groucho Marx. "Most of us stole a little—

harmless little things like hotel towels and small rugs. There were a few actors who would swipe anything they could stuff in a trunk." Groucho came from several generations of show folk whose roots were in France and Germany. With little effort one can project such petty thievery among troupers backward across the centuries.

A well-known portrait of the American version of these ne'er-do-wells is provided by Mark Twain in *Huckleberry Finn*:

> DUKE: What's your line—mainly?
>
> DAUPHIN: Jour printer by trade; do a little in patent medicines; theater actor—tragedy, you know; take a turn to mesmerism and phrenology when there's a chance; teach singing—geography school for a change; sling a lecture sometimes—oh, I do lots of things—most anything that comes handy, so it ain't work. What's your lay?
>
> DUKE: I've done considerable in the doctoring way in my time. Layin' on o' hands is my best holt—for cancer and paralysis, and sich things; and I k'n tell a fortune pretty good when I got somebody to find out the facts for me. Preachin's my line, too, and workin' camp meetin's, and missionaryin' around.

After a typically heinous performance, the Duke and Dauphin exit the stage tarred and feathered, ridden out of town on a rail.

And yet I spy another crime in that fictional but realistic episode, one potentially far worse than that of our artless flimflam men. As some have commented, the lynch mob can be seen as a ghastly form of theater. Observers of the phenomenon have referred to its "carnival" or "festival" atmosphere. Spontaneous eruptions of civil unrest and mob violence often take theatrical forms, erupt in and around theaters, or have been harnessed by the authorities to serve as spectacles within the theater. The earliest religious ceremonies among tribal peoples often involved human sacrifice. In *The Bacchae* of Euripides, women possessed by Dionysus during his rites went off into the mountains together to get drunk on wine, dance, and tear live animals apart. Ritual reenactments of murder lay at the heart of every tragedy.

The Imperial Romans recognized this human propensity for blood sport and exploited it by extracting entertainment from their public executions. But more often such mob activity arises spontaneously, requiring no official encouragement. Seldom do such eruptions result in deaths . . . more often they serve as a simple (if enthusiastic) critique of those in power, and often with more hilarity than hysteria.

By definition, comedy is subversive. It is about defying expectations, turning things upside down, doing things wrong. It is antiauthoritarian. Note how, no matter how much pleasure comedy gives us, we don't speak of going to heaven but rather that "it's funny as hell." Many of us especially prize humor that is irreverent. But irreverence in a theocracy is risky business, as any Catholic-school wiseass knows from the welts on his forearm. Imagine that the entire universe is a Catholic school and instead of a ruler, the nun has a cat-o'-nine-tails.

The authorities attempting to Christianize Europe after the fall of Rome had a problem. They were trying to impose their values on a society steeped in centuries of pagan history prior to the spread of the Gospels. Among the hardest habits to break were the ancient holiday traditions, as witnessed by the mysterious intrusion of Christmas trees and Easter eggs in purportedly Christian celebrations. In point of fact the decorated trees and eggs had been cherished pagan symbols for millennia—Christmas and Easter were the Johnny-come-latelies. Christian festivals were scheduled so as to correspond to the old pagan calendar and to co-opt existing folk practices. One such festival was Saturnalia. Held annually in late December, the Roman Saturnalia gave license for a brief return to the "Golden Age of Saturn," an annual experiment in democracy when slaves were treated like kings and all underlings were given deferential treatment by their superiors. As we all know, kings behave like pigs. During Saturnalia, everyone else did too, and thousands of people from every walk of life were allowed to run amok through the streets.

In medieval Europe, the offspring of Saturnalia and similar festivals were officially proscribed at the highest levels but tolerated, and eventually facilitated, by the rank-and-file clergy at certain seasons. The reason is simple. Such an event, when practiced by the entire populace, is a difficult thing to control. Think of Woodstock. Half a million people are naked, doing drugs, and having public sex. What are you going to do, arrest them?

Prominent among the medieval festivals was the Feast of Fools, which fell between Christmas and Epiphany and has as its obvious descendant April Fool's Day. The Feast of Fools was a period (sometimes spanning several days) when the reigning values were overturned, when the sacred became profane, when the "Lords of Misrule" held sway, and when some lowly sap (a Quasimodo) would be elected "Pope of Fools." Travesty was the law of the land: a donkey said mass . . . feces was presented as a sacrament.

In these festivals, the emphasis on the "wrong" manifested itself in a celebration of the grotesque, the monstrous. Freaks, giants, dwarfs, and hunchbacks were mockingly elevated to positions of symbolic authority. Stilt-walking, masks, and puppetry allowed performers to be as outwardly strange as their imaginations permitted. Madness and mental retardation as comic material has its roots here; the fools were often literal idiots. The cruel flavor of this sensibility can be found in any good book of English nursery rhymes, the one about "Simple Simon" being only the most obvious example. Vaudevillian Ed Wynn was to play Simple Simon, and the list of his contemporaries who mined the comic possibilities of seeming mad or retarded is long indeed: the Marx Brothers, the Three Stooges, Joe Cook, Clark and McCullough—and so on.

These festivals are important to our history, for they enabled professional entertainers to perform for the public with relative impunity. Commedia dell'arte troupes, for example, flourished in the festival environment. Heirs to the vulgar Roman comedy, such clowns earned the people's affection by not shying away from the grossness of the human body or the liberal abuse of it. Then as now the kicking of someone's butt or balls was surefire laugh material. (Innocent as it sounds, that sort of comedy elicited numerous protest letters when it was performed in the films of Charlie Chaplin a scant eighty years ago.)

Another dangerous comic tradition that owes much to medieval fooling is the concept of the clown as truth-teller. During the time of festivals, the general public was granted the fool's license to tell it like it is. As we know from Shakespeare, the professional fool had this job as well (though he would do well to exercise a certain amount of caution despite his greater license). The most well-known real-life jester was Will Somers, who had the pluck to jibe the famously irascible Henry VIII, and lived to tell about it. In that tradition, a devastating honesty regarding the foibles of those in power would characterize many comedians of the vaudeville era—Will Rogers, Frank Fay, Bob Hope, and Groucho Marx among them.

Perhaps the most well-known medieval festival was Carnival, celebrated during the season just before the fasting-time of Lent. Its annual traditions of revelry, of abandon, and general joyous hedonism live on today in many European and South American cities, and (in the form of Mardi Gras) in New Orleans. The relationship in Carnival between the antinomian parody and the corporeal transgression it implies is the very reason our word "burlesque" can simultaneously signify a comical spoof, and six—count 'em, six—exotic dancing girls. It's all about living in our bodies . . . and crossing over the line.

For the most part, these festivals began to tone themselves down by the Renaissance . . . at which point the goitered, toothless, illiterate, lice-ridden hordes began to move indoors, where their admission price gave them the right to wreak their vociferous havoc on a nightly basis. Theaters—for centuries—were places where the inebriated audience ate in their seats, then threw their nut shells, orange peels, and apple cores at the performers. They talked throughout the performance, often shouting at the actors, and sometimes even joining them onstage. It would not be unheard of for a show to stop dead because of interference by the audience.

Much as most of us do today, the more refined inhabitants of past societies hated this aspect of theatergoing, which until the late nineteenth century was universal. By that time, of course, large contingents of both showfolk and the people who hated them had long since crossed the pond to Yankeeland, where the bulk of our story is set. And so now, to the relief of our Catholic readers, I'm sure, we can start to beat up on the Protestants.

In the 1620s and thirties, thousands of Puritans began colonizing the Plymouth, Massachusetts Bay, Rhode Island, and Connecticut colonies, laying the groundwork for what was to become one of the dominant forces in American culture for over three centuries. These Puritans felt that the Catholic and Anglican Churches had gotten too rich, fat, and sensuous and had strayed too far from the ascetic teachings of Saint Paul. For the Puritans, pleasure led to sin, and sin led to hellfire. For guidance on the proper tone of human conduct, the Puritans looked to such Biblical passages as Luke 6:25: "Woe unto you that laugh now! for ye shall mourn and weep." And James 4:9: "Let your laughter be turned to mourning and your joy to heaviness."

Puritan law was based on a literal interpretation of Deuteronomy. The Puritans did not believe in "lascivious dancing to wanton ditties," as John Cotton put it in 1625. For a man to dance with a woman was literally against the law. So was the celebration of Christmas, working on a Sunday, blasphemy, idolatry, cursing out your parents, adultery, and fornication.

And, of course, theater, also known as "the Devil's Synagogue," was not exempt from the list of punishable crimes. Well into the eighteenth century, laws forbidding stage plays and other theatrical amusements were still being passed in Massachusetts, Rhode Island, Pennsylvania, New Hampshire, and Connecticut, to name just some. A Boston ordinance from 1750 would "prevent and avoid the many mischiefs which arise from public stage plays, interludes and other theatrical entertainments, which not only occasion great and unnecessary expense, and discourage industry and frugality, but likewise tend greatly to increase impiety and contempt for religion."

In Rhode Island, the theater was referred to by one commentator as a "House of Satan." A Newport law forbid "plays, games, lotteries, music and dancing." In Connecticut, a 1773 Act for the Suppressing of Mountebanks forbade "any games, tricks, plays, juggling or feats of dexterity and agility of body . . . to the corruption of manners, promoting of idleness, and the detriment of good order and religion." In 1824, President Timothy Dwight of Yale College in his "Essay on the Stage" wrote that "to indulge a taste for playgoing means nothing more or less than the loss of that most valuable treasure the immortal soul." As late as 1872, the Methodists formally proscribed for their members "intoxicating liquors, dancing, playing at games of chance, attending theatres, horse races, circuses, dancing parties, or patronizing dancing schools." At the same time in New York, an Episcopal church refused Christian burial to a prominent actor.

Yet, the Thanksgiving myth notwithstanding, America was not exclusively colonized by, nor even founded by, Pilgrims. More to the purpose of our story is America's other origin myth, that of the founding of New York City. The Big Apple had been established not by Puritans or Quakers, but by Dutch merchants. Its storied beginning was not the creation of a City on a Hill, but the swindling of Indians for the purchase of Manhattan. Commerce—and commerce of a rather unsentimental sort—was setting up its tent across from the meeting house. The worshippers of the Real and the Ideal arrived on different boats, but at the same time. Much of American history seems to be about how these two groups learned to accommodate each other. But the Realists ultimately had an edge: men are real, not ideal.

Ships were the ruination of the Puritan Utopia. When cities reach a certain width and weight they must perforce tumble off their hills. Travel to Salt Lake City today and you will find ample reminder of the city's Mormon origins and the large number of Latter-Day Saints who still reside there. But the city is no longer exclusively Mormon. Barrooms, strip clubs, and pornographic video stores can be found within city limits, and there's not much the followers of Joseph Smith can do about it—they're outvoted. The early American theocracies underwent a similar process a couple of centuries earlier, as ever-improving modes of sea travel brought millions of non-Puritan immigrants to these shores. Thenceforward proceeds the steady but achingly slow weakening of the Calvinist headlock over the next three centuries.

For the first several decades, the American colonies couldn't support professional entertainment even if they had wanted to. In the crude frontier environment, every waking second had to be spent growing food, building shelter, and warding off hostile attacks from wild animals and the native inhabitants. Leisure simply did not exist. But by the mideighteenth century, cities like Boston, Williamsburg, New York, and Philadelphia had grown affluent and civilized, permitting free time and division of labor, both necessary conditions for the existence of an entertainment industry. Disputes over the taxation on that wealth were the reason the American Revolution was fought during this period. Indeed, the Revolution forced the closing of the handful of rudimentary theaters built prior to 1776, delaying the real birth of American theater until the eve of the nineteenth century.

As Christians might have predicted, the arrival of theater (that descendant of the old Dionysian rites) to American shores brought with it a whole host of familiar temptations. Variety took place in a wide array of venues in the nineteenth century, but most everywhere it flourished it was accompanied by the sale of alcohol and all the myriad sins that follow when inhibitions are relaxed. Variety confirmed all of the old prejudices that had been building up over the millennia. From the wine-drenched fertility cults of the Greeks . . . to the unspeakable indecencies of Rome . . . to the petty cons and thievery of the medieval vagabonds . . . to the prostitution that had always been part and parcel of the theatrical package. Fighting, robbery, gambling, whoring—these were among the pitfalls of attending a nineteenth-century American variety show. The association was so powerful that no one could imagine a variety show divorced from those related peccadilloes.

How appropriate that the process would largely take part in the city Washington Irving nicknamed Gotham (literally, "goat's town").

New York's first theater was the Park, built in 1798. The repertoire consisted mostly of Shakespeare and naughty Restoration sex comedies, with variety entertainment sprinkled fore, aft, and interstitially.

With only one theater to choose from, a complete cross-section of the population (apart from religious abstainers) would be in attendance at any show. The president of the United States or the mayor might be there with his retinue. So would mechanics, shopkeepers, dock workers, and, if they could scrape a few pennies together, the homeless. Washington Irving recorded his impressions of New York's first theater audience in 1803. The noise, he said, "is somewhat similar to that which prevailed in Noah's Ark." In addition to the hooting and whistling and yells, people were cracking and eating nuts, crunching apples, and throwing the left-over shells and cores at one another and at the people onstage. This element—this eternal element—is the stuff of which the American audience will be forged.

But the day when this one theater could serve the entire population of Gotham was to be short-lived. Technology, geography, and the opportunity to make the most of both, conspired to turn New York City into a permanent boomtown. The theater business would grow along with it. A series of historical developments, coming one atop the other, accounted for this unprecedented phenomenon. In 1820 regularly scheduled passenger service was offered for the first time on packet ships between Liverpool and New York, making transportation cheaper and hence available to larger numbers of poor and working-class immigrants. Then, with the opening of the Erie Canal in 1825, New York Harbor became the access point for the entire American Midwest. As a consequence, between 1820 and 1835, Manhattan's population more than doubled, from 124,000 to 270,000. The advent of transatlantic steamship service in 1838 meant travel was no longer quite as reliant on the vagaries of the weather. Famine in Ireland and social unrest in Germany in the 1840s brought large numbers from those countries on those steamships, and the influx continued into the twentieth century. By 1860, New York's population was over a million.

The explosion, the first of many, would catapult New York from a position of relative parity with its modest sister cities in the Americas to a world-class metropolis on a par with London, Paris, and Berlin. Ever-increasing growth and prosperity ensured an audience for, and a speculative market in, new and diverse entertainment venues. By 1840 there were twelve theaters; by 1860, thirty-two; and by 1880, sixty-two. Eight decades before, there had only been one.

Theatergoing changed to reflect these shifting demographics. The Bowery Theatre (built 1826), seated a thousand more patrons than the Park. To fill those seats, its manager increasingly reached out to a new audience, the emerging working class, composed largely of immigrants, who were now enjoying their unprecedented wages and leisure time. The lion's share of these new arrivals didn't care a fig for Puritan values—that was for the old-guard upper and middle classes. They wanted a rip-roaring good time.

To give them one, the Bowery Theatre managers, and their many imitators, stressed the more spectacular elements, producing blood-and-guts melodramas, truncated versions of Shakespeare ("da good parts"), swashbucklers, and bodice-rippers, calculated to get the Bowery b'hoys and g'hals worked into a lather. In America in the nineteenth century, as theater historian Robert M. Lewis put it, "*every* program in the theater was a variety show." An evening's entertainment, even a well-respected classical drama, was liable to be wrapped in a package of variety, with preshows, postshows, and entr'actes that could consist of anything from dancers to banjo players to opera singers to jugglers to opening prologues not so far removed from stand-up comedy. An 1838 bill featured

Shakespeare, ballet, sentimental ballads, and an exhibition of the "Science of Gymnastics." During her first American tour, Sarah Bernhardt was discomfited to find the acts of her *Camille* broken up by can-can dancers and a xylophone player.

Meanwhile, the drunken rabble in the audience would hoot, holler, throw firecrackers, coins, and spoiled fruit, have fistfights, and periodically get up onstage and join the show. One imagines the atmosphere of a pro wrestling match, mixed with a monster truck rally, a cockfight, and the bleachers at Yankee Stadium. The theater was no longer the sort of place where you might find George Washington and Alexander Hamilton. Instead, you met guys with names like "Spike" and "Crusher," and women with names like "Peaches."

By the 1830s, we have the first splitting of the American theatrical protozoa. At that time we can identify two separate entertainment markets, as the more discriminating theatergoers and hoi polloi start to peel apart, each group seeking a theatrical experience closer to its own tastes. The "legitimate" theater, of which the Park Theatre was for a time to be the principal exemplar, strove to differentiate itself from the raucous working-class entertainments offered by its principal competition on the Bowery. Within a few decades' time the stratification became so marked that vaudeville managers would have to haggle (and pay dearly) to convince stars like Sarah Bernhardt, Ethel Barrymore, and Mrs. Patrick Campbell to stoop to do a turn on their stages. "Legit" was the playground of cultured WASPs. Newer arrivals swam in the swamp of the "popular theater."

In the early-mid-nineteenth century the most important faction in this heaving *demos* was the outsized component of newly arrived Irish Catholics. Because of a peculiar set of historical circumstances, they at once constituted a hated Other in a manner reminiscent of the Jews and Gypsies back in Europe, yet they were also numerous enough to prove a decisive cultural force.

The performers of the variety stage were overwhelmingly Irish. Their dominance of early show business, of course, has to do with anti-Irish prejudice and a lack of other options for them to get ahead. When they first arrived, the Irish, it is well-known, were discriminated against, spat upon, and made the victims of what we would today call hate crimes.

"No Irish Need Apply." George Templeton Strong averred that "our Celtic fellow citizens are almost as remote from us in temperament and constitution as the Chinese." In 1855, after ten years of massive immigration in the wake of the Irish Potato Famine, 86 percent of New York's laborers were Irish, as were 74 percent of the city's domestics. Dig a ditch or dance a jig—which would you rather do?

Interestingly, the Irish first made their mark by impersonating yet another group of beleaguered Americans even lower than themselves on the social scale.

Around 1830, while touring the theaters of the Ohio valley, a performer named T. D. (Thomas Dartmouth) "Daddy" Rice blackened his face with burnt cork, took the stage, and impersonated a crippled slave he had seen working in a stable. The tune and the dance he performed (both appropriated from the slave, according to Rice) were called "Jim Crow"—hence the origin of the nickname for the South's old system of oppressive discriminatory laws.

> *Turn about and wheel about an' do just so*
> *Every time I turn about I jump Jim Crow!*

The act was wildly successful wherever Rice went—not just in the South and West, but also back in his hometown of New York, where, starting in 1832, he enjoyed a lengthy run at the Bowery Theatre. His debut was such a smash that (legend has it) the audience demanded he repeat the number twenty times in a row.

In *Love and Theft: Blackface Minstrelsy and the American Working Class*, author Eric Lott notes that most of the key performers and writers in minstrelsy were Irish-Americans: Stephen Foster, Dan Emmet, Dan Bryant, Joel Walker Sweeney, and George Christy among them. Their participation in a performance genre that degraded another race may well have had to do with their own feelings of inferiority relative to the native-born WASP Americans, who likewise looked down on them.

Blackface, some historians aver, has origins far older than American slavery. The practice can be traced, in fact, to those very same medieval festivals discussed earlier, where, in the atmosphere of general lawlessness, amateurs performed charivaris and mummers' plays with blacked-up faces, flitting from house to house through the night like grown-up trick-or-treaters. The tradition had always had more of the trick than the treat about it. Ironically, it stems from the same medievalist impulse that gave birth to the hoods and robes of the Ku Klux Klan. Masks are made for mischief—and sometimes dangerous mischief, at that.

Times change, though, and what offends us today about black-face—that it was a cruel and unfair misrepresentation of a group of Americans who were powerless to protest it—is actually the very opposite of what might have offended certain sensibilities in the nineteenth century. From a modern perspective, when we think of blackface comedy, or comedy demeaning to blacks (often portrayed by actual blacks), we are apt to conjure the most accessible examples available to us: old episodes of *Amos and Andy*, Stepin Fetchit movies, and so forth. This kind of comedy was without a doubt derogatory. Yet objections to black-face and minstrelsy on the basis of racism were few and far between until after the First World War, when enough political will was finally mustered to shame the practice. Instead, when minstrelsy arrived in the nineteenth century, observers were more concerned because the portrayals of African-Americans in minstrelsy seemed not false, but *truthful*, and thus vulgar. In other words, the manners and body language of Africans were considered so uncouth that to mimic them onstage was a sort of indecent display, not unlike that perpetrated by the exotic dancers down at your local strip club.

Just as women were said by some to be daughters of Eve, blacks were thought to be the sons and daughters of Ham, the cursed son of Noah, whose descendants according to Genesis were condemned to be the servants of the rest of mankind. Some did not even consider blacks to be human beings. But even those who conceded Africans membership in the human race—on a par with Native Americans, Pacific Islanders, and others—considered them part of some other, far more primitive, branch of humanity. Like women, blacks were viewed as simple, instinct-driven, childlike, and somehow closer to Satan.

This impression was enhanced by the nature of African religion, which to Christians resembled nothing so much as satanic ritual. From the lands of western Africa, where almost all of the American slaves originated, came the polytheistic religions that would evolve in the New

World into voodoo. With totems, drumming, and trance-inducing dances, these practices were shocking to Europeans encountering them for the first time. Traveler Alexander Hewatt wrote in 1779:

> . . . the Negroes of that country [South Carolina], a few only excepted, are to this day as great strangers to Christianity, and as much under the influence of Pagan darkness, idolatry and superstition, as they were at their first arrival from Africa . . . Holidays there are days of idleness, riot, wantonness and excess: in which the slaves assemble together in alarming crowds, for the purposes of dancing, feasting and merriment.

Sounds a lot like Carnival. No small wonder then, that in New Orleans, African voodoo culture would merge with French medieval festival traditions, resulting in Mardi Gras.

Music and dance were crucially important to all aspects of African society, pervading not only their religious customs but their social ones. In this realm, consequently, culture clash was at its greatest. Early Euro-American accounts of African dance are frank in their disdain and disgust, describing the movements as "savage," "lascivious," "sinuous," and "snakelike." After all, not long before, American Protestant zealots had banned all singing and dancing.

The musical tastes of the American middle class in the mid-nineteenth century ran to classical music and hymns. Suddenly a bunch of prominent stage performers—many of them Irish Catholics, no less—were undertaking to impersonate Africans onstage. These performances were part lampoon, part wish fulfillment. Masks are ideal enablers, and by impersonating blacks, these performers now had the freedom to engage in all manner of startling and liberating behavior that no self-respecting white man would ever dare to openly attempt.

It may be well to pause a moment and consider the cultural implications of the mass importation of vast numbers of Africans into this culture of White Anglo-Saxon Protestants. For, as much as integration between the two culturally polar groups moved with glacial slowness (indeed remains unfinished), the African-American made his cultural influence felt so keenly that it might rightly be said that it is the single most distinctive ingredient of American culture.

"The irony of the situation," wrote Alain Locke, "is that in folk-lore, folk-song, folk-dance, and popular music the things recognized as characteristically and uniquely American are products of the despised slave minority . . ." That such a thing has happened would have been deemed impossible by the whites of the nineteenth century.

In minstrelsy, black and white traditions merged in a sort of cultural miscegenation. Irish jigs, reels, and schottisches were intermixed with African shuffles and breakdowns. Popular, joyous, and nonsensical dialect tunes were written, ostensibly borrowed from plantation melodies but more often based on old English and Irish folk songs, made to serve the new form by spicing them up with recognizable "darky" lyrics full of slang and bad grammar and pronunciation. African musical instruments were pressed into service, bringing a new percussive element into the music. The most important of these had first been encountered by white men in Africa in the seventeenth and eighteenth centuries. A stringed instrument made out of a hollow gourd and a piece of wood, it was referred to variously as a banza, a banshaw, a banjar, a banjil, and a bangoe until posterity finally settled on "banjo." By 1819 it had evolved into a form familiar to us as that instrument, and was common on plantations until blackface minstrels like Rice, Dixon, and Sweeney began to popularize it on the American stage. Widespread too were the tambourine and the "bones," a pair of curved animal bones clicked together in the hand after the fashion of castanets.

Minstrelsy's cultural legacy makes the form extremely problematic for the vaudeville fan. On the one hand, its racial depictions are uniformly heinous. At its very best, it is merely patronizing. But, on the other hand, minstrelsy's songs, sketches, monologues, and overall format laid the foundation for the character of American show business for all time. American popular music of every conceivable type (ragtime, jazz, blues, bluegrass, country) owes something to it, as do all American solo, improv, and sketch comedy. Minstrelsy is like Hitler's Volkswagen—a very good car invented by and for Nazis.

For example, minstrelsy's pop tunes were so catchy that many of them are still "on the charts" 150 years later. Far and away the most successful minstrelsy songwriter was Stephen Foster, who wrote songs for both T. D. Rice and E. P. Christy. His hits (all of which are still in circulation) include "Old Folks at Home (Swannee River)," "Camptown Races," "My

Old Kentucky Home," and "Old Black Joe." Another important songwriter from the minstrelsy stage was James Bland (an African-American) who wrote "Carry Me Back to Old Virginny" and "O Dem Golden Slippers."

And then there is the invention of the comedy team. The minstrel songs would be interspersed with comic dialogue between a character known as Mr. Interlocutor (or, the "middle man") and his two "end men," Mr. Tambo and Mr. Bones. These stock characters were so called because the former played the tambourine, and the latter played the bones. Mr. Interlocutor was more subdued than the others, a sort of stiff, humorless master of ceremonies to bounce jokes off of. Some of the jokes they told, and the manner in which they told them, would be familiar to any child over the age of five:

> END MAN: Say, boss, why did the chicken cross the road?
> MIDDLE MAN: Why, I don't know, Mr. Tambo, why *did* the chicken cross the road?
> END MAN: To get to the other side!

This joke has become so well-known that it has ceased to be a joke. It is woven into our very cultural fiber. We know it as well as we know the Ten Commandments, and in some deplorable cases, better.

It would be hard to overstate how hugely influential the whole Tambo-Bones-Interlocutor comedy axis was. Any two-man comedy act (often called a "two-act") in the history of show business owes something to it. Mr. Interlocutor is the original straight man, Tambo and Bones the original stooges. The kind of rapid-fire interplay between them (known as crosstalk) would be perpetuated by everyone from Weber and Fields, to Smith and Dale, to Burns and Allen, to Abbot and Costello, to Lewis and Martin, to Rowan and Martin, to Ren and Stimpy.

Minstrelsy also exerted an influence on the format of American variety. The centerpiece of the minstrel show, called the "olio," was a pure variety show. The olio was very much like a crude form of vaudeville, featuring specialty acts like a banjo or fiddle player, a "stump speech" full of comic malapropisms, a drag act (known as the "wench"), Scotch and Irish jig dancers, and the like. So, while the minstrel show is American show business's original sin, it is also the ancestor of all we hold dear. Family histories are like that.

Ethnic lampoon by no means replaced the older, more traditional vices that had always been associated with the stage. For example, as had been the case for centuries in Europe, New York's theaters in the nineteenth century were as good as a street corner or a wharf for making assignations with ladies of the evening. John Jacob Astor had seen to that when he bought the Park Theatre in 1806 and outfitted it with special accommodations for hookers, giving them their own designated entrance and a section in the third-tier balconies where gentlemen could meet them and set up appointments. Though scandalous-sounding, this was a fairly pragmatic approach to take. His customers were bound to use his theater for such purposes anyway. (Yet how like the American businessman to devise a modern system to meet the needs of the oldest profession!) Not to be outdone, Astor's competitors at the Bowery, the Chatham, and the Olympic theaters all followed suit. For decades, no New York theater was without such a facility. Most opened an hour or two before showtime to allow the girls and their clients the opportunity to mix, mingle, make dates, and, most important, buy drinks at the bar. In time, particularly at the lower-class theaters, the girls grew more brazen, working the aisles, the bar, and the neighborhood around the theater. Scores of them—as much as a quarter of the audience—might be in attendance at any given performance. Brothels were built in the neighborhoods nearby, for the added convenience of men on the town, who generally made their dates right in the theaters.

As degenerate activities at the theater escalated, patronage by "respectable" people correspondingly dwindled. Partly to escape the mobs of the Bowery, Manhattan's upper crust moved uptown, far from the theater district. In so doing, they built themselves a sort of cocoon of virtue. The explosion of religious fervor in the late eighteenth and early nineteenth centuries known as the Second Great Awakening, along with the advent of Queen Victoria's reign, had made propriety and virtue fashionable with the upper class and the newly emergent middle class. "We are not amused," Victoria had famously pronounced—and she did her best to see that no one else was, either. Largely through her influence, a new "cult of domesticity" held sway, making it desirable for families to stay home in the evenings and console themselves with simple pleasures. For laughs, women might sit around in a circle embroidering pillows. Children were expected to play silently, perhaps with a toy

Noah's Ark, or a fragile ceramic doll. Men just sat in the corner grinding their teeth and watching the minute hand of the grandfather clock, praying, PRAYING for sleep to come . . .

Yet men had options that their wives did not. While the women remained the guardians of the hearth from dawn to dusk, the men toiled downtown, close to the theatrical district. This made it extremely convenient to stay out late on some pretext in order to behave less virtuously than they professed to be. The Bowery and lower Broadway provided an environment where a man could have intimate conversations with the sort of people he ordinarily wouldn't be caught dead talking to. In Victorian New York, it seems that every Jekyll had his Hyde. And the elixir that effected all those transformations was both ancient and plentiful: the active ingredient was alcohol.

Liquor had always been an integral feature of theatergoing, from the wine cult of Dionysus straight on through. Bibulousness began to reach new high (or lows), however, when advances in distillation made cheap whiskey widely available after the 1820s. Taverns, the relatively sedate and cozy institutions of yore, where a traveler could enjoy a meal, a mug of grog, a bowlful of tobacco, and a bed for the night, began to morph into a more specialized alcohol-delivery emporium, called a "salon" until ugly Americans began to mispronounce it, at which point it became a "saloon." By the 1850s, fairly elaborate variety shows were staged at the largest of these, which became known as "concert saloons."

In the post–Civil War economic boom, some three hundred such establishments existed in New York alone. Sections of Manhattan were like the Wild, Wild East.

In its rough-and-tumble heyday the Bowery was something like Times Square, Coney Island, Ripley's Believe It or Not Odditoriums, and Atlantic City all rolled into one, full of bars, gambling halls, whorehouses, dime museums, and plain old theaters. On the Bowery you could find Paddy Martin's basement saloon (with a Chinese opium den in the back); the Grand Duke's Concert Hall (a bar run by, and for, a gang of children and teenagers); Barney Flynn's saloon (a favorite of political hacks and similar crooks, with rooms upstairs for hanky-panky); the wonderfully named Paresis Hall; and countless others.

In nearby Chinatown, there was Nigger Mike's, conceivably a slur upon two races, as Mike was not an African-American. Of Maxine's, a similar joint, Jimmy Durante (who played there) commented, "If you took your hat off, you was a sissy." Harry Hill's, at the intersection of Houston and Crosby streets, was a major tourist attraction, with the flamboyant Hill making a great show of personally breaking up brawls and throwing out drunks, though such incidents were sometimes staged just to keep the place lively. Hill supplemented his variety programs with bouts of professional pugilism.

Farther west and uptown, in the region variously known as the Tenderloin, or Satan's Circus (roughly bounded by Fifth and Seventh avenues, from the Twenties through the low Forties), one could find dozens more such establishments, such as the famous Haymarket, the Aquarium, the Alhambra, and Koster and Bial's. Yet New York by no means held a monopoly on such shenanigans. Most of the major population centers had their own Bowery or Tenderloin equivalent.

In Chicago, so many booze joints popped up along Wells Street that for a time city leaders renamed it Fifth Avenue so as not to dishonor the name of the Indian fighter Captain Billy Wells. At John Ryan's Concert Saloon on South Clarke Street, "elegant and chaste performances" were promised; lewd burlesque shows were delivered. The major vice districts there were the Black Hole (the African-American section) and Hell's Half Acre. All of it was to burn down in the Great Chicago Fire of 1871, but within months new concert saloons were up and running, this time with "A Hot Time in the Old Town Tonight" on the orchestra's playlist. A major railway center strategically located in the middle of the country, Chicago was eventually to emerge as the second-most-important vaudeville town in the country.

In New Orleans, which had become even more famous for its sex industry, barrelhouses proliferated, so called because upon payment of his fee the patron drew his own booze from the tap. And concert saloons there were: the St. Nicholas, the Bismarck, and the New El Dorado; the Napoleon; the Gem, the Tivoli, the Eden, and the Royal Palace Beer Saloon & Concert Hall. At the Conclave, a tourist joint, the waiters were dressed as undertakers and the liquor bottles were kept in small coffins on marble slabs.

Because San Francisco was an international port, with ships coming in from the most exotic places in the world, it was reputed to have the very wildest dives and the sexiest shows. And yet, because it was without the uptight compunctions of the older eastern cities, women were as free as men to attend saloon performances. In Frisco's vice district, nicknamed the Barbary Coast after the pirate-ridden waters off of North Africa, one could sample the pleasures of the Cremonde, the Theatre Comique, the White Elephant, Eureka Hall, the Olympic, and the Belle Union. The latter establishment ran the following advertisement in the 1890s:

FULL GROWN PEOPLE
ARE INVITED TO VISIT THE
BELLE UNION
IF YOU WANT TO MAKE A NIGHT OF IT
THE SHOW IS NOT OF THE KINDERGARTEN CLASS
BUT JUST YOUR SIZE
IF YOU ARE INCLINED TO BE FRISKY AND SPORTY
IT'S RATHER RAPID, SPICY AND SPEEDY
AS SHARP AS A RAZOR
AND AS BLUNT AT TIMES AS THE BACK OF AN AXE

The Orpheum (founded in 1887) was the town's first variety theater (as opposed to saloon), but it most definitely had a bar attached. The Orpheum was to become the birthplace of a vast vaudeville circuit that would dominate the entire country west of Chicago.

Though New York, San Francisco, Chicago, and New Orleans were, without a doubt, the major centers, Cincinnati, St. Louis, Kansas City, and a whole range of similar towns also figured into the story. To get from place to place, troupers would take trains and riverboats as far as they could, then stagecoaches to get to the more remote dates. In the days before circuits, booking agents, and every other type of organization for support, actors were itinerants (literally), completely on their own and perpetually uncertain about what the next day would bring. Carpetbag in hand, they lived on the fringe in a work environment that could only be compared today to the exercise yard in a maximum-security prison.

These concert saloons were the very sum and summit of sinfulness—and proud of it. It was understood from the get-go that the prospective tippler needed to watch his back. Brawls were de rigueur, and there was the risk of being hit by a flying mug, chair, or knuckle sandwich. Pickpockets, swindlers, and out-and-out robbers worked the saloons as methodically as a butcher in a slaughterhouse.

In the "Rocky Raccoon"–like milieu, variety performers were by no means immune from the violence. John Ford nailed it in *My Darling Clementine* when a drunken actor is forced to do Hamlet's "To be or not to be" soliloquy while rowdy town folk shoot their six-guns around his feet for kicks. As Armond Fields relates in his biography of Eddie Foy, that comedian played an extended engagement in Dodge City, where he befriended Bat Masterson, Wyatt Earp, and the whole cast of characters from the Gunfight at the OK Corral. When he arrived, because he was dressed to the nines in the garb of a "dude" (then the slang for a high-tone, inexperienced easterner), a gang of enthusiastic fans dragged him through town on a rope and dunked him in a water trough. Foy took it without complaint and went on to become Dodge City's most beloved star, held over for months. But some chose not to grin and bear it. One performer named Sam Devere was reputed to have beaten a man to death with his banjo during an unwelcome brawl in Texas.

A likely source of friction, in addition to the gambling, drinking, and relative lawlessness, was the presence of available chippies. In the concert saloons, special hostesses called "waiter girls" worked the halls, socializing with the men and generally encouraging the purchase of more drinks. In addition to their own beverages, the men would buy drinks for the ladies, who usually only pretended to imbibe alcohol. Waiter girls wore distinctive short dresses and high boots, smoked cigars, and offered to sit in your lap. They were a cross between a hostess and a waitress, but many doubled as performers in the variety show and/or your "date" for the evening back at your hotel.

No less audacious were the gals onstage. Outraged commentators wrote about seeing female performers "almost entirely nude, in diverse lewd, lascivious, indecent and obscene postures and positions" or "gawdilly painted and scantily dressed." A particular sticking point among some was a dance called the can-can, an importation from the French music hall, or *café-concert*. This scandalous dance gave men a rare glimpse at women's legs. In the United States, where women's dresses were typically cut a yard or so below the soles of the feet, the can-can scored a bigger hit than heroin.

So this is the drill: you walk in off the muddy, horse-manure-strewn streets, through the swinging saloon doors into the wine room, concert saloon, music hall, melodeon, box house, or even "theater"—whatever this town or this neighborhood happens to call such establishments. The air is thick with cigar and pipe smoke (cigarettes didn't become universally popular until after World War I). Spittoons are available for those who prefer to chew. The floor is covered in sawdust to sop up the spilled alcohol, as well as any stray expectorations. The menu of beverages is limited: beer, whiskey, rum, perhaps wine or brandy if the place is highfalutin. The lighting is dim. Decoration is minimal, perhaps a few chromolithographs on the wall, pictures of naked women. You are surrounded almost entirely by rowdy, drunken men—some jolly to the point of singing, some sullen and murderous. Such women as are present are either trying to hustle you for drinks or sell you sexual favors.

Some accounts of saloon life make it sound like a scene out of Brueghel. Pantalooned harridans cackling into their mug of grog. Bibulous burghers tippling with tinhorns. Sordid assignations in the back room involving a goat, two Pacific Islanders, and a bowl of applesauce. Red-faced maniacs randomly gouging the odd face with the jagged end of a broken bottle, just for laughs. Gangs of unwashed, toothless freaks knock you on the head with a rock, take off all your clothes, set you on fire, and throw your body like a meatloaf into the East River. Somebody call the sheriff!

Yet variety culture can't always have been as bad as the most hyperbolic accounts. If it were, no one would have gone into a saloon. One went out for a good time, and perhaps that involved some risk to one's property and person. So does a ride on a roller coaster—but that doesn't mean everyone who rides one plunges eighty feet to his death. The concert saloon, too, sold thrills—intoxication, sex, and violence, whether it was an organized boxing match, rat-baiting in the basement, or a spontaneous brouhaha on the sidewalk out front. With all this going on, even I'm forced to admit that a variety show would rate pretty low as a diversion. In saloons, the performance was largely just an amenity, like a free bowl of peanuts. In those slow moments when no one was hitting or biting the fellow next to him, you could glance toward the stage. Nowadays in bars it's a TV with the game on. Back then it was a live variety show.

Depending on the resources of the establishment, the show could range from a single broken-down honky-tonk piano player to a full-on production. (In those days "honky-tonk" meant a low-down bar; it wouldn't come to be associated exclusively with country music for almost a hundred years.)

The show would usually start with an opening chorus sung by the ladies in the company (who, if the audience were lucky, might also oblige them with a can-can). There would then follow twelve to fifteen acts of a distinctively nineteenth-century sort: minstrels, jig dancers, banjo players, harmonizing quartets, acrobats, and so forth. Distinctive types of acts that have not survived the era include the sand jig (something like tap dancing, but the dancer would pour sand on the floor and make shuffling and sliding noises); playing the bones, as in minstrelsy; the egg dance (wildly dancing around several eggs on the stage without breaking any); "tidy tearing" (rapidly ripping and folding pieces of paper into recognizable shapes); and, with the Civil War fresh in everyone's minds, military acts, such as gun spinners and drill companies.

The olio, or variety portion, was generally followed by an afterpiece, a full-length comic sketch, frequently a parody of some other popular show and improvised around a set framework, as in commedia dell'arte.

As we have mentioned, the clientele of concert saloons were invariably male. A woman spotted going into a saloon was either a brazen hussy or bursting in to yank out her husband. The men who habituated saloons were of several types: (a) the completely criminal, i.e., thieves and gangsters; (b) the semicriminal: outcasts, drunks, ward politicians, street-brawlers, misfits, fallen women, and bums; (c) the workingman, who sometimes fell into one of the two preceding categories, but not necessarily—he might be perfectly law-abiding but coarse in his tastes, preferring beer and a leg show to buttermilk and tiddly-winks; and (d) slumming middle- and upper-class men out on a lark. After all, "men have needs." These might be parties of high-spirited college boys, businessmen entertaining out-of-town clients, or closeted thrill-seekers with less orthodox predilections. One big happy family. Actually, I think we have accounted for 98 percent of the male sex by now. Saloon-going was therefore mainstream and tolerated, although officially disreputable—something like recreational drug use is today in some quarters. The remaining 2 percent were unbelievably repressed prudes, eunuchs, theologians, and anti-vice crusaders.

Like the inaccurately named Moral Majority, these meddlers made a stink way out of proportion to their actual numbers. Thus, the spread of saloons was followed hard upon by the temperance movement. The Second Great Awakening, the huge religious revival that swept the nation in the 1830s, had specifically enjoined its converts to actively bring about social change. And so, even as wicked a city as New York in the mid-nineteenth century saw the formation of dozens of temperance societies and associations dedicated to the abolition of "demon rum" and the "dark beverage from hell."

Prodded along by such groups, New York's legislators passed the so-called Concert Bills of 1862 and 1872, which made life a little less hospitable for concert saloons. The laws decreed that no establishment could offer any two of the following at the same time: liquor, stage performances, or waiter girls. The waiter girls rapidly passed out of the picture (leaving can-can dancers and our old friend the theater prostitute as consolation prizes), but the saloon owners and their patrons remained quite attached to the booze-and-entertainment combo. The laws were flouted, as such silly laws usually are. Most saloon owners found ways to operate around these restrictions, through graft or trickery, and the laws went unenforced for the most part.

Saloons weren't the only venues presenting variety shows. The mid-to-late-nineteenth-century American entertainment landscape would include countless "music halls," "opera houses," "variety theaters," and "odeons"—and often the distinction between any two of them was blurry indeed. In this increasingly raucous environment, the concept of the full-length play was becoming ever less important in the theaters, while spectacle in the form of variety entertainment played a more privileged role. Bowery houses like the London, the Windsor, and the National devised a new formula of alternating full variety programs with their melodramas.

The London was started in 1875 by a man who would play an important role in the variety business as well as in early vaudeville: Henry Clay Miner. An ex-cop from the Bowery, Miner opened his first "museum and variety hall" in Baltimore in 1863. This was at the height of the Civil War, in a state technically occupied by a foreign army (a slave state, Maryland was occupied by Union troops), so it is not surprising that the venture was short-lived. Four years later, Miner was back on the Bowery, where he established the London Theatre, the success of which permitted him three years later to open the establishment that was his greatest legacy: Miner's Bowery Theatre. It is to Miner's that posterity owes the invention of "the hook" (as in "Give 'im da hook!"). The amateur night at Miner's was popular, the audience rowdy. A saloon and pool room adjoined the theater, helping fuel the rambunctious energy and necessitating the use of hired "policemen" to roam the place, ready to bust the heads of any troublemakers. Somewhere along the line, someone got the bright idea of yanking particularly clueless acts offstage with a shepherd's crook. The innovation lives on in popular memory, although Miner's does not.

Despite numerous hurdles, some truly remarkable performers came out of the early variety scene, many of whom would remain stars deep into the vaudeville age.

Lotta Crabtree was born in New York in 1847. In '51, her father, something of a drifter and a dreamer, split for San Francisco, to make his fortune in the Gold Rush. Mrs. Crabtree and the family followed him out there the following year. The old man had not found any gold, so, hoping to cash in on the national craze for "fairy stars" (child performers), Mrs. Crabtree enrolled her daughter in dancing school, and was soon pitting her against touring favorites as the local challenger. For several years, the family made the rounds of mining camps and rough settlements, presenting the singing and dancing Lotta for such pelf as they could wring from the drunken, riotous, and uncivilized audiences they found out in the wilderness. In 1862, a professional agent began to book her into San Francisco melodeons, where she did jigs, flings, polkas, and shuffles, played the banjo, sang songs, and acted "protean" (male) roles. By 1864, she had conquered Frisco, and from 1867 through '91 she was one of New York's top legitimate stage actresses.

As minstrel shows began to peter out in the years following the Civil War, the minstrels themselves began to work in variety. The most important of these were the team of McIntyre and Heath, a.k.a. the Georgia Minstrels. In the 1860s and early seventies, Jim McIntyre was a singer, actor, and clog dancer at various outfits throughout the American South. In 1874 he teamed up with Philadelphia native Tom Heath, forming a partnership that would last fifty years. McIntyre played "Alexander," the slow-witted stable boy; Heath played "Hennery," his pompous friend who tried to put on airs. Their most famous sketch (of many) was called "The Ham Tree"—and they rang various changes on it for decades. A 1905 full-length version provided W. C. Fields with his first speaking part.

While acts like McIntyre and Heath continued to be in demand through the end of the vaudeville era, the principle of ethnic masquerade based on a minstrelsy model found new modes of expression, following the major immigrant groups that continued to arrive on American shores.

The Irish, for example, turned their sights on a new target: themselves. The late-nineteenth-century stage saw no end of red-wigged, freckled, clay-pipe-smoking, lazy, alcoholic, jigging, swearing Irishmen. Acts like the Four Shamrocks and the Four Emeralds threw bricks at each other, talked about "the dhrink," said "bejaysus," and otherwise distinguished the sons of Erin. Harpo Marx was one of the last non-Irish to play such a role, known familiarly as the "Patsy Brannigan." In time, he stopped talking and left the ethnic outrage to his brother Chico. But he kept the curly red wig.

A team called the Russell Brothers presented an act that sounds like one of the most boldly audacious routines in show business history. They'd started with a blackface routine in 1877 . . . which evolved into a blackface wench (or drag) act . . . which evolved into the act that made them famous. Called "Maid to Order," the two men played bitchy, gossipy Irish servant girls. The stereotype was so broad, so outrageous, that the pair was frequently under attack by Irish antidefamation groups.

The vulgarity of the Irish stereotypes is best exemplified by Irish comedy teams like Needham and Kelly, and Harry and John Kernel, who wore padding under their clothes and beat each other up on stage in a rough-and-tumble manner that anticipates the Three Stooges. This is entertainment for people at the bottom of the heap. If you enjoy watching the Three Stooges, as I do, you've no doubt also undergone a small taste of the social stigma attached to this sort of theater. It's that sinking feeling when someone "above all that" walks into the TV room, rolls her eyes, shakes her head, and beats a retreat, tsk-tsk-tsking all the way. Something about the spectacle of semiretarded menials beating one another with pots and pans, speaking rude and substandard English

("Hiya, Toots!"), and demolishing the antiques brings out the snob in some people. Can you imagine the chagrin of the nineteenth-century WASP middle class when confronted with such stuff?

Eddie Foy (that victim of the Dodge City dunking) was another major variety utility man. From the early 1870s through the 1880s, Foy worked with a succession of partners (and occasionally solo) in old variety, touring every corner of the American show-biz universe at that time. His versatility stood him in good stead: he could sing; he did jigs, clogging, and eccentric dancing; performed in drag and blackface (sometimes simultaneously); did impressions; acted in sketches; and did acrobatics. His career was to take many a surprising turn over the next four decades, and we shall meet him and his substantial brood again ere long.

The two biggest Irish comedians to come out of the variety scene, becoming the most popular stars of the American theater of the seventies and eighties were the team of Edward ("Ned") Harrigan and Tony Hart. A New York native, Harrigan made his debut in San Francisco in 1867, singing (to his own banjo accompaniment) on some of the principal stages of the Barbary Coast. Clog dancing was another one of his specialties. From singing and dancing, he worked his way up to comedy sketches, playing an impressive range of character roles: blackface parts, a Swedish servant girl, Chinese laundrymen, Irish landlords, and so-called Dutch (or German) characters.

His first partner, Alex O'Brien, was such a drunk that Harrigan was forced to bring him to the "House for Inebriates" on a wagon. His next partner, Sam Rickey, worked with him clear across the continent, arriving in New York in 1871. Advertised as "the noted California comedians" they did their Dutch sketch "The Little Frauds" at the Globe Theatre on the Bowery. Unfortunately, Rickey was an even bigger drunk than O'Brien, and he too wound up in the gutter.

When Harrigan was twenty-six he hooked up with Tony Hart, then only sixteen years old and calling himself "Master Antonio." Born Anthony Cannon, in Worcester, Massachusetts, in 1855, Hart was placed in a reform school at age nine after announcing to his family that he wanted to go into the theater. He escaped and ran away to New York, where he found work singing, dancing, and doing odd jobs in circuses, saloons, and minstrel shows. By the time he and Harrigan joined forces, Hart had gained fame for one particular number, a tearjerker called

"Put Me in My Little Bed," which he sang dressed as a young girl. Audiences were crazy about him. Nat C. Goodwin, a prominent actor of the day and sometime vaudevillian, said: "Hart caused more joy and sunshine by his delightful gifts than any artist of his time. To refer to him as talented was an insult. Genius was the only word that could be applied. He sung like a nightingale, danced like a fairy, and acted like a master comedian."

Harrigan hired Hart to replace Rickey as "Fraulein" in his sketch. (This was when Cannon changed his name to Hart, reasoning that it sounded better with "Harrigan.") A regular gig at New York's Theatre Comique allowed the team to demonstrate their many talents. The variety show was three and a half hours long, followed by an afterpiece of forty minutes. Harrigan and Hart might do several different turns in the course of such a show—blackface routines, brief sketches interspersed with dancing, juggling, and singing. The team was so successful that by 1876 they assumed joint ownership of the Theatre Comique and had the whole show to themselves.

Besides the Irish, the other major immigrant group in the mid-nineteenth century was the Germans. Despite their equally large numbers in the population, the language barrier prevented them from being major players in variety and vaudeville. They were *represented* in vaudeville, however, for they were customarily mocked in absentia in the so-called Dutch acts. The fact that such a category as a "Dutch" comic even existed provides a real window into another world: a time when Germans were a significant faction in New York City.*

The premier Dutch act was a pair of Jewish kids from the Lower East Side named Joe Weber and Lew Fields. The casting was not as odd as it first sounds. Their roots were in western Poland, which was culturally more akin to its German neighbor than to the Slavic East, and they grew up speaking a version of Yiddish that was closer to German. Fur-

---

*Two early-twentieth-century disasters eviscerated this community and forced it into the woodwork. First, the 1904 burning of the ferryboat *General Slocum*, in which 1,030 German-American women and children were killed, took the heart out of Kleindeutschland, New York's "Little Germany." And then World War I and its jingoism prompted German-Americans to assimilate rather than endure the ire of their new countrymen. If not for these two occurrences, Germans might be as visible in New York today as, say, Italians, Russians, Poles, or Greeks, all of which have continued to maintain their own enclaves for many decades.

ther, having immigrated in the early 1870s, prior to the major influx of Eastern European Jews, Weber and Fields grew up in a Lower East Side that was still overwhelmingly German. Masquerading as two German immigrants, the boys would engage in outrageous wordplay, punctuated with slaps, kicks, punches, eye pokes, and choke holds—massacring the English language while making mincemeat of each other. Their two characters, "Mike" and "Meyer," wore loud checked suits and derby hats. Their violent spats generally arose from their misunderstandings of the subtleties of the English language.

The team's most frequently quoted exchange went like this:

MIKE: I am delightfulness to meet you.
MEYER: Der disgust is all mine.
MIKE: I receividid a letter for mein goil, but I don't know how to writtenin her back.
MEYER: Writtenin her back! Such an edumucation you got it? Writtenin her back! You mean rottenin her back. How can you answer her ven you don't know how to write?
MIKE: Dot makes no never mind. She don't know how to read.

Moses Schoenfeld (a.k.a. Lew Fields) and Morris ("Joe") Weber were born within six months of each other in 1867. They grew up on the Lower East Side, a densely populated, poverty-stricken neighborhood where kids ran the streets in packs. The boys met at age eight, while watching some clog-dancing buskers. The young Fields immediately bragged that he, too, could clog-dance—on a china plate without breaking it! In no time he succeeded in ruining much of his mother's good dinnerware, and received a drubbing for his efforts. From then on, Weber and Fields spent every spare minute (and many that were not-so-spare) practicing the skills that would later make them famous: tumbling, joke-telling, clog dancing. Like the leading Irish knockabout comedians of the day, they hid padding under their clothes and rehearsed smacking each another around for hours on end. An old mattress was used to break their falls.

By age nine or ten they had an act. Three acts, really: a blackface, an Irish, and a Dutch, in descending order of popularity with their audiences. Their first public performance was at a neighborhood benefit.

The boys did an act in blackface, wearing two special matching suits sewn by Lew's brother. Their mothers even turned out for the event. Everything went wrong in the performance, but the audience was gracious, and so the boys were bitten by the bug.

By 1882, Weber and Fields had been doing a sort of ethnic quick-change act, employing Irish, blackface, and Dutch characterizations up and down the Bowery for four years. Part of the act's appeal in these early years had to do with the fact that they were so ridiculously young. The sight of these mismatched boys (Lew was five-eleven, Joe was five-four) in heavy padding beating the tar out of each other with machine-like regularity must have been delightful.

The next few years were spent gaining valuable on-the-job experience in small-time theaters in New York and other cities in the Northeast, and very slowly climbing up the pecking order. Time spent in minstrel shows taught them the valuable skill of improvisation, which later would be a keystone of their act. There, too, the team learned the two-man byplay of the "endmen" Tambo and Bones that was to make the team so heavily imitated. The joke that begins "Who was that lady I saw you with last night?" is widely credited to Weber and Fields.

In 1885, the Adah Richmond Burlesque Company specifically requested a Dutch act, and the boys cooked up a new one, consisting of converted minstrel jokes padded out with knockabout business. The winning formula was Lew Fields's brainstorm: a knockabout act, but with a "Dutch" accent instead of an Irish one. To cement the illusion, the two glued on two phony little beards and smeared their faces with whiteface. To them the fractured dialect came easily—they'd heard it their entire lives.

This new routine slayed the audience. With all the vigor and enthusiasm of youth, they made every element more extreme than was customary—more and crazier malapropisms, and more slapstick mayhem. The fees Weber and Fields commanded, not to mention their prestige, continued to rise throughout the 1880s as they toured their "Teutonic Eccentricities" nationally, becoming the country's greatest comedy stars.

Weber and Fields may have been on top—but old-school variety was about to go bye-bye. In 1886 a major crackdown brought about by public pressure resulted in the closing of 900 concert saloons in New York, among them the leading establishments of the day.

Among the hardest hit by this sea change were two variety men who'd opened their first music hall at the corner of Sixth Avenue and Twenty-third Street in 1870. John Koster was in charge of the booze, and Adam Bial was in charge of the performers. They both did their jobs well—the place was satisfyingly boozey and burlesquey. For this reason, they were often in trouble with the law, eventually getting closed down for "encouraging prostitution." A February 1887 editorial in the *Spirit of the Times* illustrates the turning tide: "We have repeatedly pointed out that this establishment was violating the excise and the theatrical license laws by giving entertainments in a saloon where liquors were sold, and we are glad that the authorities have at last interfered."

Through various legal dodges, Koster and Bial's managed to reopen and hang on for a few more years, becoming one of the last of the concert saloons. On the occasion of its passing in 1901, Remold Wolf penned a scathing obituary in the *New York Morning Telegraph*. The headline itself is a mini epic poem:

Vulgar in Vaudeville Sped with its Sponsor—Passing of Koster and Bial's Begins Era of Cleanliness—Adult New Yorkers Tired of Indecency—Cyprian Display of Commonplace Lingerie Now Appeals Only to the Ultra Adolescent Rustic.

The piece goes on:

The days of vulgarity and salaciousness in vaudeville are of the past. Koster and Bial's was its home. Now Koster and Bial's is no more . . . no house in the city now caters to the offensive except the low priced Bowery burlesque houses. The present policy of vaudeville managers is to present only refined and worthy acts. Vulgarity means instant dismissal.

A bargain had been struck with the devil.

2

GOOD, CLEAN FUN

We are about to encounter a phenomenon unprecedented in history: a variety show acceptable to Christians.

Today, the phrase "good, clean fun" is idiomatic; we all know what it means. Little do we stop to think that someone would have had to invent the concept. The common misconception, I think, is to assume that innocence preceded worldliness, that men of the past were simpler and nobler, gradually becoming sophisticated (i.e., jaded) about sex and violence and the passions. Actually, something akin to the reverse happened. Mankind went from a wild state, all too knowledgeable about unbridled bodily urges, to, by Victorian times, a state of relative self-mastery. In the nineteenth century, one gentleman might upbraid another for smoking in a lady's presence; young people were chaperoned on dates; a woman might die an "old maid," unmarried, hence virginal. "Innocence," far from being humankind's default state, had instead been *achieved* through a lengthy process of refinement. Man having arrived at this highly controlled condition, "fun" was suspect. If you put even a single crack in a dam, won't it burst? For proof of that postulate, one needed to look no further than the corner saloon.

To convince the Victorians that entertainment was a moral and healthy activity would involve something of a hat trick. To dispel the centuries-old stink-cloud hovering over the theater (and the decades-old one over variety) would require someone born and bred for the role: an antic spirit, schooled from the bassinet in the art of the bait and switch, the shell game, and the sharp trade. In short, a modern mountebank.

Connecticut in 1810, the place and time of P. T. Barnum's birth, was one of the last, strongest holdouts of the original, undiluted strain of American puritanism. Founded shortly after Massachusetts, the state was to remain officially Congregationalist (as the Puritan denomination came to be known) until 1818. It was the last New England state with an established church, meaning that a portion of one's taxes went to the state religion, while all others were somehow penalized or banned. On Sundays, by state law, one couldn't travel, conduct business, or do much of anything outside of attending a Congregationalist church. The state had grown even more conservative than Massachusetts, which had become relatively cosmopolitan as Boston blossomed into a world-class city with a thriving commercial port. Connecticut had no comparable cities, least of all Bethel, which is the tiny hamlet where Barnum was born and raised.

Posterity can be grateful that Barnum enjoyed a more liberal upbringing than most. He had been raised in the Universalist church, which, in direct contrast to Congregationalism, preached the radical doctrine that man was *not* inherently evil and that *everyone* would someday go to heaven. This put him in the minority in conservative Connecticut, where Universalists were condemned as "deists."

While for a biblical literalist such a label carried derogatory connotations, certain Enlightenment-era Americans like Benjamin Franklin, Thomas Jefferson, and Thomas Paine had worn it with pride. These men, in turn, had been influenced by the so-called worldly philosophers, men like Smith, Locke, and Burlamaqui, who had introduced the revolutionary idea that people on earth deserve happiness in this life and that the best way to achieve it is to allow them some measure of personal freedom. The concept of "the Pursuit of Happiness" enshrined in our Declaration of Independence leads directly to another document cooked up in Philadelphia soon afterward, the 1789 "Statement of Rights" drafted by a group called the Dramatic Association.

Philadelphia's Quaker elders had fought the theater no less vigorously than their Puritan neighbors to the north. From 1700 to 1789, the assembly of Pennsylvania voted countless times to prohibit theatrical entertainment. By the late eighteenth century, some of America's most prominent citizens were forced to resort to a subterfuge to enjoy theater while in Philadelphia, claiming that such productions were "concerts" or "lectures." But theater fans (a group that included the likes of George Washington, who could not tell a lie) got tired of this pretense. The Dramatic Association's "Statement of Rights" argued for freedom of speech, introducing for the first time the phrase "rational amusement"—a coinage that would become common currency among the advocates of variety and its successor, vaudeville, in the coming century. Soon after the presentation of this petition, Philadelphia's last theater ban was lifted, permitting the erection of theaters on Chestnut Street, Walnut Street, and apparently any other street named for a nut.

The enlightened atmosphere of Philadelphia also fostered the birth of two related institutions that would play a crucial role in vaudeville's subsequent development. The first was the creation in 1786 of America's first museum by painter and natural historian Charles Willson Peale. In addition to an exhibition space for his own paintings, Peale's Philadelphia museum (the Peale Museum) was also a cross between what we think of as a natural history museum and a Ripley's Believe-It-or-Not Odditorium. Mineral specimens, taxidermically stuffed beasts, fossils, insects, and sea shells were displayed next to cannibal heads and a five-headed cow. Also to be found at Peale's were a menagerie, a collection of wax figures, historical artifacts, and an auditorium for lectures, concerts, scientific demonstrations, and magic-lantern shows. Art and culture sold the critics, but fun sold tickets. The lessons to be learned here would not be lost on Barnum.

Another sort of "education" was provided by the importation of a popular English fad known as a "riding school" by a man named John Bill Ricketts. The first such exhibition had been presented in England twenty-five years earlier and had as its centerpiece a large ring full of sawdust in which expert riders on horseback galloped around and did tricks. The presentation was enlivened by the addition of clowns, jugglers, tumblers, rope dancers, and trained animals. It was Ricketts who, in Philadelphia in 1793, first decided to call such an exhibition a *circus*, after the Latin word for "circle." The Romans had used that same word to denote their great outdoor theaters, the very ones in which gladiators fought to the death and Christian maidens became food for wild beasts. By 1797, another Philadelphia circus had sprouted, called Lailson's, and by the nineteenth century there were dozens.

Circuses, museums, and theater shows presented as "lectures," all bundled together and presented as "rational amusement"—this is the very boilerplate certain nineteenth-century impresarios would follow to convince mainstream society that the occasional laugh wouldn't cause the downfall of Western civilization. It is the quantum leap that would make vaudeville possible.

Barnum would take each one of those creations and make it his own, transforming America from a land of all work and no play into a place where people might learn to let their hair down. Through bluff, blarney, and a penchant for taking risks he was to take the foundering, run-down Scudder's Museum and in 1841 turn it into the premier American amusement institution. Christened Barnum's American Museum, his brainchild was a veritable palace of entertainment, the Disney World of its day, occupying several floors and, in its biggest incarnation, taking up nearly an entire city block. By turning that museum's Lecture Room over to the production of praiseworthy temperance melodramas, Barnum played an important role in redeeming the largely discredited art of theater in the eyes of many Americans. And, late in his career, when he put the full might of his pocketbook and reputation into the shady and semicriminal enterprise of the tented circus, he was able to create another American institution, the Ringling Brothers, Barnum and Bailey Circus, which at this writing has been going for 134 years and entertained millions of people.

How did he achieve these impossible feats? The same way such acts of suasion have been effected since the first mountebank sold a bundle of medicinal herbs from the back of a wagon. He talked a good line.

In addition to being the Father of American Show Business, Barnum is also in many ways the inventor of modern public relations. His penchant for exaggeration, and even outright lying, in the course of self-promotion is traceable to his Yankee upbringing in Bethel. In *Struggles and Triumphs*, Barnum's classic autobiography (which, in the nineteenth century, sold second only to the Bible in America), the showman describes two prevalent strains of socially sanctioned lying in Connecticut culture: practical jokes and sharp trading. The practical joke—the outlandish lie played on a gullible public—is the foundation of all American show business. Not despite but *because* of their very implausibility, there is a charm in "charms." The lie, the "unreal," the glimpse of an alternative universe is the building block of the magic castle. If for even an instant the universe becomes a more marvelous place, we are grateful. Who of us would give up the years spent believing in Santa Claus?

"Sharp trading," on the other hand, involves not only lying but stealing. Barnum justified it by framing it as a sort of game, one wherein the perpetrator is merely taking advantage of lapses in attentiveness on the part of the person with whom he is doing business. Giving a smaller amount of goods than what was promised for the amount paid is one sort of sharp trade. Another is to shortchange the customer through fast talk and sleight of hand (a common circus dodge). In both cases, the "sharp Yankee trader" would justify his actions by claiming that his victim should have counted the merchandise or his change, and so it was his own fault.

The practical joke and the sharp trade come together in the art of humbug. Essentially, one puts something over on the public in order to relieve them of their money. The trick is to do it in such a way that the people are so entertained by the lie that they feel they have gotten their money's worth. Barnum was (and remains) the undisputed master of this peculiar American art form, starting with his exhibition in 1835 of Joice Heth (the supposed 161-year-old nurse of George Washington), right through to his 1889 presentation in England of "supernatural illusions" including a creature with a woman's head and a peacock's body.

Among thousands of Barnum's whoppers, the mother of them all was the one that convinced conservative Victorians of the morality of amusement. Later, other showmen would pick up that baton; it was to be the principal drumbeat of vaudeville. Barnum's genius, and that of the vaudeville managers who would follow him a generation later, was to take two inimical audiences, the worldly and the godly, and fuse them together, much as he'd sewn together a monkey's head and a fish's tail and come up with the Feejee Mermaid. He wanted his productions to be "all things to all people." To bring it about he would convince half the people that fun could be wholesome, and the other half that wholesomeness did not spoil fun.

By the time he'd perpetrated this piebald confidence game, Barnum had long since outgrown the local yokels in his native village; he was now reaching out to the global village. This he did through one of the first instruments of the burgeoning mass culture: the newspaper. Barnum understood the power of the press thoroughly, having published and edited his own Jacksonian sheet, "The Herald of Freedom," back in Connecticut. The next step, once he became a showman, was to use that power to promote his own interests.

"I thoroughly understood the art of advertising," he wrote in *Struggles and Triumphs*, "not merely by printer's ink, which I have always used freely, and to which I confess myself so much indebted for my success, but by turning every possible circumstance to my account." The art of newspaper puffery used in this fashion would become a central tool of vaudeville (indeed, of all subsequent show business), for managers and artists alike.

Barnum had the good fortune to begin his enterprise just as the first "penny papers" were catching on. Earlier periodicals were expensive, subscription-based, and elitist, covering news that would mainly be of interest to the city's mercantile and governing classes. Beginning in the late 1830s and the early forties, papers like the *New York Sun* and the *New York Herald* hit the streets. Sold for only a penny, they were designed specifically to appeal to the interests of workingmen, replacing the staid shipping news with sports coverage and lurid crime stories. Circulation of these papers shot up into the tens of thousands, creating an unprecedented new marketing universe. In short, this was the first time in history a P. T. Barnum could have been possible.

Such was Barnum's genius that he could double- and even triple-dip his publicity. First, he would make bold and even preposterous claims for his attraction. An 1835 handbill for an exhibition of Joice Heth touted the wizened old granny as "The greatest natural & national curiosity in the world." Seven years later, his Feejee Mermaid was "decidedly the most stupendous curiosity ever submitted to the public for inspection. If it is artificial," the squib went on to claim, "the senses of sight and touch are ineffectual . . ." Next, Barnum would stage-manage the inevitable backlash, as irate critics and pundits published their protests about the deception. For example, scientists examined Joice

Heth and the Feejee Mermaid and pronounced them both impostures. By responding to the criticisms in print, Barnum got additional opportunities to plug his attractions, resulting in new bursts of box office as holdouts finally went to see what all the fuss was about, and folks who'd gone before went again in order to better make up their minds about Barnum's claims.

Then, as now, the public likes a good controversy. The fact that many of his attractions were obviously fabricated made it so much the better. Better a fake unicorn—and a spirited contretemps over its authenticity—than no unicorn at all. The sheer gall of the man was sport in and of itself. And besides, he only sold them what they themselves wanted to believe.

After years on the road with traveling exhibitions, circuses, and variety shows, in 1841 Barnum got the opportunity to acquire Scudder's Museum at Broadway and Ann Street in Manhattan, and he seized it. Like Peale's, Barnum's museum was not the specialized, academic, and impersonal institution we associate with museums today. It was a for-profit business combining elements of natural history museums, historical museums, zoos, sideshows, and fun houses.

While Barnum is famous for his "humbug," plenty of his exhibitions were genuinely educational, and the institution was eminently respectable in comparison with the later dime museums and sideshows it inspired. While Barnum's American Museum did showcase such whimsical whim-wham as the Feejee Mermaid, Zip the Pinhead, and the Wooly Horse, it also offered Americans their first glimpse of a hippopotamus, an orangutan, a giraffe, and a beluga whale.

This pose as an educator permitted him to do as Charles Willson Peale had done at his Philadelphia Museum. Taking a leaf from the Philadelphian's book, he gradually transformed his "Lecture Room" into a "theater," thus introducing the performing arts to a class of people who otherwise never would set foot in such a disreputable place—and creating a fiction not unlike the one of the medicine-show doctor: "Here, take this. It's good for you."

Initially, Barnum's Lecture Room was simply a place for talks on natural history, philosophy, and the like. But Barnum's experience as a variety producer told him that a steady turnover of entertaining acts would drive repeat business, and he was in need of cash. If the "lectures" began to consist of juggling exhibitions, magic, ventriloquism, and magic-lantern shows, he would sell more tickets.

But to get the families and the carriage trade (the fancy folks who lived uptown, away from the hustle and bustle of lower Manhattan and hence had to travel there) he had to keep it clean. Like the Philadelphia theater advocates, he promised "innocent and rational amusements." Unlike the theaters of his own day, his Lecture Room served no liquor. Objectionable people were thrown out. To attract women and children, he offered the first matinees in town. But Barnum's single greatest coup, and maybe his most important contribution to show business history, is, arguably, his highly successful promotion of Jenny Lind.

In 1850, Barnum hired a talented Swedish singer and turned her into the ideal of American womanhood. In *Struggles and Triumphs*, Barnum tells of his chagrin when, after committing huge sums of money to the enterprise, he learned that Lind was not as well-known in America as she was in Europe. His answer, as always, was an ad campaign. In his ads, Barnum called her "a lady whose vocal powers have never been approached by any other human being, and whose character is charity, simplicity, and goodness personified." In other words, she was both physically and morally perfect, a kind of supernatural being. By flogging, constantly, for months on end, the angelic purity of his "Swedish Nightingale," Barnum created a universal impression on the public that it was true. As a result, he sold thousands of tickets to God-fearing men and women who otherwise never would have gone anywhere near a theater. And because Ms. Lind was an excellent singer, with a fine, soulful quality, who in fact donated a large part of her income to charity, people did not feel deceived. Whether or not Jenny Lind actually was morally pure ended up being immaterial. Everyone had the impression that she was, and that was enough. Having gotten those holdouts in the door, Barnum set a precedent. He proved that a new audience was possible, one much larger than the debased market that then patronized theaters and saloons.

The squeaky-clean variety in Barnum's Lecture Room was an undeniable precursor to vaudeville. Variety acts presented there (not including the human oddities) included the trapeze artist H. W. Penny; the famous clown Dan Rice; the Chinese juggler Yan Zoo; the Swiss Bell Ringers; Professor Hutchings, the "Lightning Calculator"; the magician and ventriloquist Antonio Blitz; Benjamin Pelham, the "Great Paganini Whistler"; Bini the "Unrivaled Guitarist"; the clog dancer Tim Hayes; the Martinetti Family wrestlers; Young Nicolo, the Great Child Wonder (an eleven-year-old trapeze artist); Miss Darling (a lady magician); the monologist and impersonator Dr. Valentine; the ballad singer H. G. Sherman; and no end of Gypsy fortune-tellers, minstrels, contortionists, ventriloquists, trained animals, tattooed men, puppeteers, flea circuses, rope dancers, and "automatons"—literally hundreds of performers, presented in a chaste environment without the taint of alcohol or lasciviousness associated with the Bowery theaters.

Within decades, hundreds of upstanding variety theaters featuring thousands of unobjectionable acts would arise in every part of the country. But we are not there quite yet. When the last iteration of Barnum's American Museum burned to the ground in 1868, he went into the circus business. But that did not mean the death of Barnumism in the museum world. The vast fortunes accumulated by Barnum (and no doubt the fun he had in acquiring them) were inspirational to scores of younger entrepreneurs, and they would create an entire industry out of what had once been anathema to respectable businessmen. By the 1870s, all medium- and large-sized American cities had museums modeled after Barnum's. Some, like Kimball's Boston Museum, were similar to Barnum's in size and scope, but far more common were the small, fly-by-night affairs set up in storefronts, familiar to anyone who has seen the film *The Elephant Man*. A handful of curios would be on view—wax figures, oddities of nature, sideshow freaks—in combination, generally, with a variety show. In recognition of their popular prices, they were called "dime museums." For a time, New York's Bowery supported a veritable strip of them: Bunnell's (the largest and most respectable), Morris and Hickman's East Side Museum, the New York Museum, the Windsor Museum, Worth's Museum (which included a menagerie), the Grand Museum (owned by one "Broken Nose" Burke), and the Globe Museum (which was partly owned by George Middleton, who would later play a role in the evolution of the Orpheum vaudeville circuit).

The principal difference between this new crop of dime museums and Barnum's American Museum was that the gains in propriety and public trust (such as it was) won by Barnum eroded under the watch of these lesser showmen. For one thing, the dime museums tended to be more lurid and sleazy than Barnum's had been. While they often presented many of the same freaks that had graced Barnum's stage, such as Zip the Pinhead and Jo-Jo the Dog-Faced Boy, in the dark, underworld environment of the Bowery they seemed more like monsters than Astounding Miracles and Curiosities of Nature.

Hookers were reputed to work some of the dime museums, as well, but one gets the impression that they were a good deal more subtle than the ladies of the saloon and variety theater. The dime museums, as we've seen, were widely touted as a relatively wholesome alternative for a working-class family who wanted to take in a little entertainment, including a variety show. In the company of armless and legless wonders, skeleton dudes, bearded women, fat ladies, pickled embryos in jars, and mongoloid (i.e., Down's syndrome) children passed off as "Aztecs," many future vaudevillians got their start working on the variety stages of dime museums. Among them, comedians Weber and Fields, Harry Houdini, the Three Keatons, blackface comics McIntyre and Heath, acrobat Joe E. Brown, and singer Maggie Cline.

By the 1880s, straight, clean variety was an idea so ripe that it seemed to occur simultaneously to several different men working in different areas of show business. As true heirs and apostles of Barnum, each of these men had the habit of referring to himself as the "first" and "only," while in reality vaudeville was like the hub of a wheel and its creators like spokes converging from different directions. From saloons came Tony Pastor, Henry Clay Miner, Koster and Bial, Alexander Pantages, and John Considine; from dime museums B. F. Keith, Edward Franklin Albee, and Sylvester Poli; from variety theaters Hyde and Behman, and F. F. Proctor; from legit theater Percy Williams; from opera the Hammersteins. Significantly, Pastor, Keith, Albee, and Proctor had all worked for circuses (the first three for Barnum). All of them derived (consciously or not) the idea of harnessing what had been thought sordid and making it "clean"—sometimes by actually making it refined, often by merely saying it was so.

Circuses and dime museums had always been considered family entertainment. It is very likely these impresarios each independently had the inspiration to transplant the big top's relatively respectable atmosphere to variety. (No doubt, these former carnies also shared a natural desire to justify their chosen profession in the eyes of the prosperous classes they aspired to join; what's the point of making a bundle if you can't be a member of the country club?)

The managers' efforts were reinforced by elements from the culture at large. An important and surprising factor in this transformation from variety to vaudeville was the liberal urban clergy. After all, the managers' efforts would have been to little avail if their intended audiences continued to fear their theaters as portals to perdition. Freedom of religion had permitted a constant splintering of the Protestant denominations; those holding fast to old-style puritanism grew fewer and fewer in number. As we have seen, deism and Unitarianism had played a role in legalizing America's first theaters and inspired Barnum in his great crusade to amuse a nation. By mid-century, liberal theologians like Washington Gladden, Horace Bushnell, Mark Hopkins, and Frederick William Sawyer were publishing books and preaching from the pulpit about a great compromise. The old Calvinist line had been that pleasure of any sort was evil. The new thinking was a little more nuanced. It said that only evil pleasure was evil; yet some pleasure had to be a gift from God. The smile of gratitude on a person's face after we've done them a good turn, for example, produces a feeling of pleasure. Surely that is not the work of the devil. The idea was to identify the sources of wholesome pleasure and distinguish them, with great care, from base, sinful pleasures. These influential preachers did not know it, but they were cultivating a vast potential audience for the showmen of America. The vaudeville managers—sharp men, all of them—were not slow to take advantage of the new climate.

In the Victorian era, the forces of religion, government, and science seemed to conspire to sanitize everything once and for all: hearts, minds, streets, tenements . . . it was inevitable that it would happen to variety. This is the era when soda pop (or the "soft" drink) was invented as an alternative to liquor, when ice cream parlors were all the rage, when barbershop quartets had all the girls gaga, and songs like "And the Band Played On" and "Daisy Bell (A Bicycle Built for Two)" were burning up the charts (or rather, selling a lot of sheet music). A popular singer of the former song was one of the principal architects of vaudeville.

Antonio "Tony" Pastor was born in New York City in 1832. He first sang publicly at a temperance meeting at the age of nine. By the time he reached puberty, Pastor had already accumulated an impressive résumé, having sung at Barnum's museum as a "Child Prodigy," danced in a blackface act in the Raymond and Waring Menagerie, and performed juvenile roles and acrobatic turns with Welch's National Amphitheatre. A crucial break came his way when the ringmaster at the circus where he was working died suddenly, creating a vacancy that Pastor was ready to fill, though he was still a teenager. In those days, the job called for singing, dancing, and acting in the afterpiece, in addition to the customary announcing chores.

He began performing regularly at a music hall at 444 Broadway just after the Civil War broke out in 1861. The place was such a dive it never had a name; it was always called simply "444." The bar offered variety entertainment, with Pastor functioning in a role similar to that of the "chairman" in the English music hall. He doubled as master of ceremonies and a popular singer, presenting his own patriotic songs in support of the Union, as well as sentimental and humorous tunes about labor, a subject near and dear to the hearts of his working-class clientele. He claimed to have a repertoire of 1,500 songs. Favorite Pastor numbers included "Down in a Coal Mine," "The Great Atlantic Cable," "The Monitor and the Merrimac," and "The Irish Volunteers." The lyrics to these tunes were published in little "songsters" and distributed to the audience, who sang along music-hall-style and walked away with the book as a souvenir. Reportedly, Pastor had a terrible voice, but audiences loved him anyway, another tribute to his ability as a showman.

In 1865, he took over the Volks Garden at 201 Bowery and renamed it Tony Pastor's Opera House. Though his establishment was no less a bar, he set about making a number of improvements that would set it apart from garden-variety concert saloons. Rowdy patrons were expelled from the premises. Advertisements indicated in no uncertain terms the direction in which he was moving, insisting that his show was "unalloyed by any indelicate act or expression," offering the public "fun without vulgarity."

Part of the impulse to initiate the policy change may have been a genuine conviction on Pastor's part, he being a man of his times and all. A devout Catholic, he would eventually have a prayer room built in his theater, and a poor box installed in the lobby. His strongest profanity was said to have been "jiminetty."

But the times themselves must surely have played a role. A businessman with any instinct seeking to stay afloat in those years of high Victorianism must have been constantly mulling over the tirades of clergymen, temperance advocates, reformist politicians, and journalists railing against the saloon culture. The Concert Bills of 1862 and 1872 (mentioned in the previous chapter), while easy to evade, nonetheless existed on the books. As many a longtime New Yorker can tell you, such laws are like sleeping grizzly bears. All it takes is the election of a reformist mayor to jump-start their enforcement, and then the party's over. A savvy businessman tries to stay two steps ahead of this kind of development.

If Pastor's motives weren't pure as the driven snow, neither was his impulse to court families particularly original. German New Yorkers suggested a third way between the never-ending debauch . . . and a total abstention from all intoxicating beverages. It is impossible to imagine the Fourth of July (as we know it) had the Germans never arrived on these shores. It is to them we owe hamburgers, cold cuts, hot dogs, mustard, pickles, pretzels, brass bands, and, most important of all, beer.

For years, German and Austrian immigrants in New York had enjoyed their own imported style of drinking establishment, known as the beer garden. Beer, as Hogarth teaches in his famous engravings, is of a more benign genus of intoxicant than hard liquor. As depicted by Hogarth, the inhabitants of "Gin Lane" are a debauched and sordid collection of dregs. Meanwhile, on "Beer Street" life is sane, productive, and normal. Similarly, in contrast with the rowdy, whiskey-soaked concert saloons, beer gardens were genteel places where families went to listen to musical concerts together (and have a few lagers). Germans had a different relationship with alcohol. Beer and wine were served, but generally consumed in moderation. Relaxation for the Germans did not mean urinating outdoors, crying, fighting, singing dirty songs, and putting lampshades over their heads. One can picture transplanted burghers sedately sipping lager from personalized steins whilst their apple-cheeked *Kinder*, in lederhosen, frolicked in Der Garten, supervised by "mama." Nearby, a string quartet played music from the Old Country—a lullaby by Brahms. German families played together, stayed together, didn't break up the furniture—and surely brought in several times the proceeds.

Furthermore, Pastor's experience at Barnum's American Museum surely suggested the possibility that variety could and should be presented in a respectable environment. Above all, there hovered the lure of a vastly increased market. The concert-saloon clientele consisted of a mere percentage of men. If he could include *all* the men, *plus* their wives and children as his potential audience, think of the increased revenue.

By the 1870s, the overall environment was transitioning. "Variety theaters" and "music halls" had arrived and were gradually displacing concert saloons. For the most part, they were a cocktail containing the same ingredients, but mixed to a different formula. Instead of a bar with a theater attached, it was a theater with a bar attached. Still disreputable in some quarters, but marginally more genteel. Some were quite fancy, yet they remained men's joints. Here and there, however, these institutions began to sponsor special cleaned-up ladies' matinees, temporarily banishing the alcohol and cigars for a few hours. Pastor, more than any other saloon man, saw the potential in this trend and put himself at the center of the movement.

In 1875, Pastor moved "up" again, out of the ever-degenerating Bowery to 585 Broadway, near the present-day site of New York University. He still served liquor, but Pastor was now in a respectable neighborhood, in close proximity to New York's most popular theater, the Theatre Comique, where the Irish comedy team of Harrigan and Hart starred and would soon be proprietors. This stretch of Broadway had become one of the city's first official theater districts, thanks to the proliferation of nearby minstrel halls in the 1850s. Pastor's establishment was also now an easy distance from the Ladies' Mile, the city's main shopping district, and the emerging theatrical strip on Fourteenth Street, known as the Rialto.

Pastor made the leap to the Rialto itself in 1881, to a theater located right in Tammany Hall, on Union Square. At first he tried to follow in the footsteps of Harrigan and Hart, who had enjoyed major success by expanding to full-length form the comic afterpieces that still capped every variety bill. After the team assumed proprietorship of the Theatre Comique in 1876, a series of their sketches featuring a lovable character named Dan Mulligan became so popular that they became the whole show. Many regard them as forerunners of today's musical comedies. Their plays featured the so-called Mulligan Guards, a ragtag Irish militia mustered by the title character. Between 1878 and 1881 there appeared numerous sequels, including *The Mulligan Guards' Christmas, The Mulligan Guards' Picnic, The Mulligan Guards' Surprise, The Mulligan Guards' Ball, The Mulligan Guards' Chowder* (as a clambake was sometimes called), *The Mulligan Guards' Nominee,* and *The Mulligan's Silver Wedding.*

You can't argue with success. To Pastor, the expansion of the variety afterpiece seemed a winning formula. He had been presenting such afterpieces at his various venues since 1865, usually parodies of classics and popular shows of the day, as was the tradition since minstrel times. In 1881, he inaugurated his move into the Tammany location with *The Pie Rats of Pen Yan,* a parody of Gilbert and Sullivan's recent hit *The Pirates of Penzance.* But it didn't click. Within a few months, Pastor settled down to concentrate on what would prove to be his great contribution to American popular culture: straight, clean variety.

This is the common marker for the official genesis of vaudeville as a respectable institution. Recall that only men went to the variety theater at this time, and they only went when they were inclined to misbehave. Pastor instituted new policies: no drinking, no smoking, no vulgarity onstage, no mashers. The fact that there was a bar next door (in the Tammany building, but technically outside his own premises) helped him ease his customers into this frighteningly sober new establishment. Next, Pastor widely publicized his revolutionary new policies. To actively attract the better half, he started by making Friday ladies' night, offering door prizes to his female patrons: dishes, coal, bonnets, flour, dress patterns, sacks of potatoes. When he upgraded the prizes to sewing machines and silk dresses, what had been a trickle of estrogen into his theater became a flood.

One feature of that 1881 production of *Pie Rats* that Pastor retained was a by-product of his outreach to women: the singer Lillian Russell. Russell represented something new in variety. A more typical female singer in those days was one of Pastor's other stars, Maggie Cline, the "Irish Queen." Irish Mag's sentimental repertoire ranged from humorous ditties to tear-jerkers, but her fame rested largely on a single signature tune, a rowdy, raucous, crowd-pleasing number called "Throw Him Down, McClosky," a song about a pugilistic bout. At the refrain, the audience sang along, music-hall-style, and everyone backstage would throw whatever was at hand onto the stage. While there was nothing specifically "objectionable" about Cline or her song, this was clearly a saloon act. The fact that it was a crowd-pleaser was in its favor, but in no sense did it represent a break with the past.

The same could not be said of Russell, who, in the best vaudeville spirit, Pastor is said to have "created." In her day, she was the most famous woman in the world, the paragon of the age, the epitome of all that women aspired to be, and what all men aspired to possess—*and* one of vaudeville's, and the legitimate stage's, biggest stars. To generate this furor, Pastor relied largely on the template Barnum had used in promoting Jenny Lind, billing her as a young woman with the soul and voice of an angel. But Pastor went the old showman one better by starting from scratch with Russell. After all, Lind had already been a sensation in Europe when Barnum "discovered" her. When Pastor came upon Russell, she was merely Helen Louise Leonard, a classically trained singer from Clinton, Iowa. Bit parts in *H.M.S. Pinafore* and *Evangeline* at the Park Theatre in Brooklyn brought her to Pastor's attention. Captivated by her voice and her beauty, he booked her for his old Broadway Music Hall in 1880, then sent her out to San Francisco and a tour of western mining towns to give her a bit of seasoning.

When she returned, Pastor gave the girl her stage name (meant to sound like "Lily and Russell," two highly prized flowers in those days). He began to tout her as the most beautiful woman in the world. When she starred in *The Pie Rats of Pen Yan* in 1881, he billed her, in true Barnum fashion, as "the beautiful English ballad singer I've imported at great trouble and expense."

While Russell would appear in vaudeville from time to time over the decades, she grew to be primarily a star of operetta and the just-hatching musical comedy form. Many of Pastor's female singing stars—among them Russell, Fay Templeton, Blanche Ring, and May Irwin—moved gracefully between the two stages, thus enhancing the reputation of Pastor's theater. Far from the rough-and-tumble precincts of the Bowery, Pastor's new variety house was surrounded by legitimate theaters and starred legitimate stars.

Pastor's ladies were presented as ideals, as soulful and feminine—in touch with that higher realm wherein Beauty and Goodness were synonymous. "Airy, Fairy" Lillian Russell was known as "The American Beauty." Blanche Ring was called "radiant" by critics. Lottie Gilson was "The Little Magnet." The singers would be clad in elaborate costumes, often with an accessory prop such as a parasol or a fur muffler. Interestingly, these women were at the height of their fame in the 1880s and nineties, when the theater district stood at Union Square, just a dainty trot away from all the new department stores over on the stretch of Sixth Avenue known as the Ladies' Mile. As producer and author Robert Grau put it at the time, the theaters of Union Square were "distinctly popular with the class known as shoppers." After getting an eyeful of their ideal on the vaudeville stage, women in the audience could run over and plunder the dress and hat departments at A. T. Stewart's. As if the stage were not pedestal enough, for a while there was a vogue for singers to do their acts perched high atop a swing, evoking both the public gardens and amusement parks that were coming into existence at about that time.

At Pastor's there were other subtle hints of a changing dynamic on the variety stage. Some of his Irish acts began to explore the possibilities of a toned-down approach to their ethnic identity. John W. Kelly, known as "the Rolling Mill Man," would simply park himself on the stage on a chair and weave long, humorous, extemporaneous stories based on audience suggestions—an act that would never have been audible, let alone appreciated, in a concert saloon. Song-and-dance man Pat Rooney, while still dressed in the ridiculous leprechaun outfit that was the standard "Irish" costume of the day, is credited with bringing a more three-dimensional, sympathetic approach to his portrayals. Monologist George Fuller Golden rose to fame telling flowery, affectionate anecdotes about his friend Casey.

One of Pastor's acolytes became the premier producer of that wholesome vaudeville staple known as the kiddie act. German-born Gus

Edwards had been discovered by Pastor at age fourteen, when he was hired as a "balcony singer" (it was a convention of the time to occasionally surprise the audience by having a ringer rise from a seat in the house and join the onstage vocalist for a number). Edwards was to gain his first fame as a songwriter, penning such classics as "School Days" and "By the Light of the Silvery Moon." His first kiddie act, the "Newsboy Quintet," included himself as one of the cast members. As he outgrew that act, he went on to produce countless others featuring children hired from auditions: "The Kid Kabaret," "Nine Country Kids," "School Boys and School Girls," and "A Juvenile Frolic." Scores of children went through the Edwards machine, which is why he was able to boast such a distinguished roster of alumni: Groucho Marx, Eddie Cantor, George Jessel, Walter Winchell, Eleanor Powell, Mae Murray, Phil Silvers, Bert Wheeler, Jack Pearl, the Duncan Sisters, Sally Rand—these are just some of them. Edwards imitators (and there were many) included Ned Wayburn (who was later to start the premier "college" of vaudeville) and Minnie Marx, who employed not only her unruly sons but a company of ten others in some of their vaudeville acts. These are just some of the many acorns to fall from Tony Pastor's oak.

Pastor was a showman of the first water. A genial, hearty presence, he greeted every patron at his theater personally. He continued to dress like a ringmaster even after he had exchanged the sawdust of the ring for that of the barroom floor, and then he swept the sawdust up completely. With his silk top hat, handlebar mustache, swallowtail coat, and riding boots, he carried a bit of the magic of the big top around with him. He loved children and began throwing an annual Christmas party with prizes for the kiddies. He was also kind to his performers, never closing an act prior to the end of their contract, and never firing his veteran orchestra members long after old age had weakened their chops.

Interestingly, although he is often known as the "Father of Vaudeville," he never used the word "vaudeville" himself. For him it was always just variety. No frou-frou Gallicisms required. That Francophile designation would be contributed by a man whose prudery made Pastor look like an opium peddler.

Benjamin Franklin Keith was born in Hillsboro Bridge, New Hampshire, in 1846, the textbook definition of a Yankee, and he would prove himself appropriately tight-fisted. At age fourteen, he mustered enough imagination to run away and join the circus as a roustabout. From there, he worked his way into the world of dime museums.

Young Keith spent two formative years working at Bunnell's, learning the fundamentals of museum administration and management, then toured a bit with P. T. Barnum's circus, eventually settling in Boston, where he opened the Gaiety Museum in 1883. Here he displayed the likes of Baby Alice (a prematurely born infant), a stuffed mermaid, a tattooed man, a chicken with a human face, and the comedians Weber and Fields, whom he'd met whilst working at Bunnell's Museum.

Upstairs, as was common in dime museums, Keith set up a small theater for variety: a hundred or so folding chairs and a modest stage. He introduced the acts himself, more out of necessity than from any inclination or talent to perform. Keith was a plodding sort of character, colorless and surprisingly bereft of imagination for a circus man. Like Ringo, without "a little help from his friends" one suspects he would have been a mere footnote to this story instead of its most important player. From one sordid Boston museum, the Keith empire would come to embrace a continent, employ thousands of showpeople, and even form the groundwork for the entertainment institutions we enjoy today. The fact that your hometown probably had (and maybe still has) a Keith theater in it probably owes more to a man named Edward Franklin Albee (the grandfather—by adoption—of the playwright Edward Albee, who for reasons that may become obvious, never stresses the connection).

The elder Albee was born in Machias, Maine, in 1857. At age seventeen, he dismayed his well-to-do family by running off and joining the circus. From roustabout he was promoted to spieler ("Step right up! Right inside this tent!") and ticket man, where he was an expert in the art of short-changing customers. Within seven years he'd palmed his way up to circus executive.

At age twenty-six, Albee showed up at Keith's (whom he'd known from the circus) and made himself generally useful. He stayed for forty-seven years and ended up controlling the entire vaudeville industry.

Albee made Keith instantly successful by refining his whole operation. First he ditched the smelly animals that comprised the museum's menagerie. Then he proposed that they take advantage of the Gilbert and Sullivan craze that was still sweeping the country, by offering pirated productions of the plays at a fraction of what most opera companies charged, "embellished" by vaudeville acts. Interestingly, Keith was responding to the same operetta fad that had charmed Tony Pastor, but in the opposite way. Pastor had ennobled his enterprise by embracing operetta's chic associations, and raising his ticket prices accordingly. Keith presented *The Mikado*, but made it available for a quarter. Both were successful for decades, but we shall see which methodology won out in the end.

Keith's cut-rate operettas gave the organization enough profit to lease the much larger Bijou Theatre in 1885. Gone were the freaks and specimens in glass jars. Now they were presenting something called "vaudeville."

"How natural and appropriate it seems to use French words when treating of the vaudeville," wrote Episcopal clergyman Cyrus Townsend Brady in the late 1800s. The word "vaudeville" carried with it the sophistication and romance associated with Paris. Related Gallic borrowings include "salon," "café," "burlesque," "variety," "revue," "follies," "scandals," "cabaret," "matinee," and the French way of spelling "theatre." New York's most popular comedy theater in the late nineteenth century was the "Theatre Comique."

We have seen one theory for the word's origin, the troubadours of the Val-de-Vire region of France. Another theory is that it comes from *voix de ville*, meaning "voice of the city." Seen in this light, the phrase reminds us of vaudeville's identity as a folk form, an expression of the people's voice.

Whatever its etymology, the term came to signify little theatrical trifles of the sort that became a staple of the French Opera Comique. Used in this sense, Mozart called some of his operas vaudevilles, as did Chekhov some of his one-act plays. Paris had a Theatre du Vaudeville as early as 1792. Theater historian John DiMeglio says there was a "vaudeville theatre" in Boston in the 1840s. Benjamin Baker's 1848 play *A Glance at New York* mentions "vaudeville plays" at the Vauxhall Garden. As Baker's contemporary, the writer George Foster, describes this type of "vaudeville" it sounds not too different from the comedies of the Restoration and boulevard farces: "Intrigues with married women, elopements, seductions, bribery, cheating and fraud of every description—set off with a liberal allowance of double entendre."

The first specific application of its use to describe a variety show appears to have been in 1852 by one J. L. Robinson, who announced "the oldest established vaudeville company in the United States." The fact that the establishment was located in Portage City, Wisconsin, may account for its subsequent obscurity. In 1871 there was an outfit in Louisville calling itself "Sargeant's Great Vaudeville Company." Impresario M. B. Leavitt and "Dutchface" comedian John W. Ransom are also among those claiming to have first used the term in the early 1880s. In 1882, there was a "vaudeville theatre" in San Antonio.

It's clear that for decades the term was wielded rather loosely and indiscriminately. Soon it would be used by vaudeville managers to mean a highly specific cultural phenomenon. The word "vaudeville" as employed by these gentlemen distinguished the new business from "variety," which was used by some people like a curse word. "Vaudeville" had that Continental élan. It was a perfect choice to appeal to women who liked to stroll down "boulevards," shop at "boutiques," and eat at "restaurants" where they perused "menus."

The choice of this particular word to describe the new industry speaks volumes. After all, they didn't call it "Goody-Goody-Land" or "His Heavenly Kingdom on Earth, Inc." They attached this new industry to fashion. "Polite" became necessary because propriety was very much in vogue with the people in society who had the most disposable income. So the market chose politeness. The fact that powerful journalists and reformers could no longer plausibly object to it was an added gain. The managers were to become millionaires; the saloon-keepers would die small businessmen.

The genteel, the respectable, the proper: that was what this new audience wanted. Keith gave it to them and packed them in. One act that well illustrates the transition from rough-and-tumble variety to straight-and-narrow vaudeville on Keith's watch is the Four Cohans.

Boston, at the time Keith launched his vaudeville enterprise, was still one of America's biggest cities. With its excellent harbor and northern location, it became an immigration port of entry second only to New York. In the mid-nineteenth century, Irish streamed in by the hundreds of thousands. A creative ferment analogous to that in New York ensued. Those not cut out to dig ditches or lay bricks could—if they had the talent—earn their living singing, dancing, or telling stories.

One such fellow was Jerry Cohan. A happy-go-lucky song-and-dance man, Cohan had moved from Boston to Providence, where he began his working life as a saddle and harness maker. Jerry was good at Irish dancing, particularly the Irish clog, and he played both the harp and the fiddle. He started working the New England variety theaters and saloons in the 1870s. In 1874 he married Ellen ("Nellie") Costigan. Having no show-business background, nor, apparently, any inclinations in that direction, she worked first as a ticket seller where Jerry played. When an actress in the show walked out abruptly, however, Nellie joined the act. Though she'd never been onstage in her life, she'd seen the show many times from the wings.

The children arrived in short order. First Josephine ("Josie") in 1876, and then George, on July 4, 1878. Nellie had them in Providence but brought them both on the road as babies, parking them in drawers and trunks while the elder Cohans performed.

In 1883 they became regulars at Keith's, an organization with which they were to enjoy a close relationship for almost twenty years. In the safe and sane environment of Keith's theater, it was conceivable (in a way it would never have been in the saloon days) to put young children on the stage. In an atmosphere free of howling drunks, fistfights, gambling, and whoring, families could go to the theater and appreciate the odd spectacle of a performing family.

The kids crossed their theatrical Rubicons at ages seven and eight, Josie doing contortions, George playing violin. Soon the family emerged as a formidable quartet. The parents would do some crosstalk, Josie would do her artistic dancing, and George would sing and dance. George's traditional exit line said it all: "My mother thanks you, my father thanks you, my sister thanks you, and I thank you." Audiences were charmed by the wholesomeness of it all: the gentle paterfamilias, the loving, sacrificing mother, and the two precocious American children who followed in their footsteps. George (with the euphonious initial "M." now added) would later seize on this aesthetic of wholesome optimism and secure for himself a major place in American theatrical history.

Not all the early acts were quite so naturally domesticated as the Co-hans. Some would require a little training. The house bulldog in this department was Mrs. Keith (née Mary Catherine Branley), one of the great unsung proponents of American censorship. At her behest, all manner of blasphemy and lewdness was expunged from all of Mr. Keith's theaters. (Keith himself was a total stuffed shirt who doubtless was in complete harmony with the idea.) In Keith's Colonial (Boston, built in 1893), if performers wanted to smoke, they had to go into a small tin closet that was constructed especially for the purpose. That's a far cry from old-style variety, where they put you in a small tin closet if you *didn't* smoke, then locked the door and threw the closet into the East River.

Signs such as this oft-quoted "Notice to Performers" were a common backstage sight at Keith's theaters:

> Don't say "slob" or "son of gun" or "Holy Gee" on the stage un-less you want to be cancelled peremptorily . . . If you are guilty of uttering anything sacrilegious or even suggestive, you will be immediately closed and will never again be allowed in a theater where Mr. Keith is in authority.

Playwright Edwin Royce recalled a minor dustup over using a line about "the devil's own time" in one of his vaudeville sketches: "I had become so familiar with the devil, that I was not even aware of his presence," he wrote, "but the [Keith] management unmasked me and I received a po-lite request (which was a command) to cast out the devil. I finally got used to substituting the word 'dickens.'"

Some attribute the origin of the term "blue material" (which is what we call onstage vulgarity) to the fact that the Keith organization would send back its written suggestions to the performers in little blue en-velopes. Since then, we have come to call any sort of law that limits the time or place a producer may present a public entertainment a "blue law." Sundays, for example, were off-limits in many places until quite re-cently. The Keith organization would get over that hurdle by presenting programs of religious music on the Sabbath, one of many reasons why his outfit would come to be known as the "Sunday School Circuit."

Yet another Yankee circus man who helped invent the vaudeville business was Frederick Freeman ("F.F.") Proctor. Proctor began his career as one of America's most successful acrobats. Born in Maine in 1851, he started training at a young age in a gymnasium that his physician father had installed in the basement. Proctor was one of the first fitness freaks. As a young man, he spent his off hours at Boston's exclusive Tremont Gymnasium, where he not only worked out to build his muscles but also practiced juggling, trapeze, and similar arts. It was here that he was discovered by variety impresario M. B. Leavitt and encouraged to go professional. For years, Proctor traveled the United States and Europe with an act called the Levantine Brothers, before going solo as Fred Levantine, "the World's Champion Equilibrist." Because of his skill and knack for showmanship, Proctor stood out on the variety stage. He was one of the first acrobats, for example, to enhance his act by adding mirror inlays to props (such as barrels and boxes) to create a dazzling visual effect. With such gimmicks augmenting his own impressive abilities as a foot juggler, he was a hit at Tony Pastor's, Miner's, Hyde and Behman's, and the other major variety venues of his day.

Offstage, however, he was not a dazzler. In fact, he came across as a total drag, a kind of real-life Horatio Alger character, always lecturing his fellow performers on the value of thrift and temperance. While his colleagues spent a good deal of their earnings at the bars and theaters where they performed, Proctor, a teetotaler, saved every penny. Furthermore, he appeared to have no shame about how he made money. Whereas most of his colleagues—like nearly all show folk—would never condescend to do work that didn't involve performing, Proctor would buy concession rights and sell popcorn, candy, and drinks when not on stage. But the very performers who laughed at him would soon be crying in their beers.

By 1880, Proctor had saved up enough money to purchase his first theater, the Green Street in Albany, which he renamed Levantine's Novelty Theatre. It had been his original intention to make his theater booze-free, but advisers warned him against it—the real money came from bar sales, they said. Hence Levantine's was wet, and would only change after Pastor and Keith proved the efficacy of dry variety. Once the switch was made, however, not only was drinking prohibited in every Proctor theater, but if a Proctor employee was spotted in a saloon, even while off-duty, he would lose his engagement.

Proctor liked to call his product "polite vaudeville," which he prom-

ised was "kept scrupulously free of any gross or objectionable features." He performed his censorship personally, sitting in the front row
at Monday-morning rehearsals, ready to ax offending portions of the
week's acts. It's a no-brainer that you couldn't swear onstage; while
working at a Proctor house, you'd also be called into the dock for swearing *off*stage.

Like Pastor, Proctor at first performed in his own theater, but running the business rapidly became a full-time operation. At Levantine's
he turned the stage over to the best acts of a wholesome nature he could
attract to New York's relatively provincial state capital. A March 14,
1881, program lists

- The Renowned German team Mills and Warren in the Comedy entitled "Schneider, How You Vas?"
- Miss Josephine Shanley, the Empress of Song, whose Ballads
  and Operatic Selections "will be recognized"
- England's Greatest Musical Sensation Artist Luigi Del'Oro,
  famous for his ability to play two musical instruments at the
  same time
- Leonard and Flynn, the great Irish team and imitators, who
  are pronounced second to none
- The entire entertainment terminating with the laughable farce
  of the BABY ELEPHANT

For Albany in 1881 this was a pretty solid bill, notable for its lack of chorus girls and can-can dancers.

As cleanliness proved its draw at the box office, other variety men
began to jump on the bandwagon. Henry Miner, for example, inventor
of the hook and host of some of New York's unruliest audiences, began
to change his tune. By the 1880s, he was running ads that promised "A
first class family theatre, where ladies and children can enjoy with perfect
comfort a pure, wholesome and delightful entertainment." Even Koster
and Bial made an attempt, to the best of their limited abilities, to at least
appear proper. In 1893 they found themselves a beard. A Vandyke, to be
precise. The man who helped legitimize Koster and Bial was an eccentric
genius with a weakness for opera, and was, in fact, the grandfather of the

renowned lyricist of *Oklahoma*, *South Pacific*, *The King and I*, and *The Sound of Music*.

Born in Berlin in 1847, Oscar Hammerstein was trained in two areas of expertise, the construction business and music, which he eventually combined in his life's work, building opera houses. His father, quite the taskmaster, had taught Oscar the building trades because it was the family business. But nineteenth-century Germany was also the center of the music universe, and Oscar was taught to play piano, flute, and violin, on top of his scholarly studies (Latin, Greek, and Hebrew).

One night when he was sixteen, his father beat him for coming home late. Fed up, the boy ran away to America, where he found work as a cigar-maker's apprentice in New York. It was a tedious and repetitive job, much like working on an assembly line, only slower and more boring. Hammerstein set about doing what any wasted intellect would do who doesn't want to sit around rolling tobacco by hand all day: he invented a cigar-making machine. He then went on to make and patent numerous machines for the mass production of cigars and cigarettes, making hundreds of thousands of dollars in the process.

In 1889, with income from these patents, the *United States Tobacco Journal* (a trade magazine he'd founded in 1874), and some real estate holdings, he transformed himself into the archetypal opera impresario, augmenting the effect of his Vandyke with a silk top hat, opera cape and gloves, and a walking stick with a gilded head.

His first theater was the Harlem Opera House, which he built in 1889 in a then unpopulated Harlem. In 1890 he built the Columbia Theatre on 125th Street. While the real estate up there must have been cheap, it was still too far uptown to attract audiences, and he eventually ended up selling these theaters to F. F. Proctor. Next time out, the move uptown was more incremental. In 1893, he started building his Manhattan Opera House at Thirty-fourth and Broadway, the present location of Macy's Department Store. For various financial reasons, however, Hammerstein found himself needing a partner to bring the project to fruition, which is how he found himself in the vaudeville business with Koster and Bial.

In 1893, Hammerstein helped underwrite Koster and Bial's New Music Hall, which opened *sans* alcohol. The box seats, which had traditionally been used in the theaters and music halls as places for assignations with prostitutes, had glass doors so there was no hiding what occurred inside. What's more, unaccompanied ladies were not admitted to the theater. With these efforts at decorum firmly in place, Koster and Bial's became one of the premiere showplaces of variety entertainment in the late nineteenth century.

Success aside, the partnership was one of convenience. Koster and Bial benefited from Hammerstein's legitimacy; he benefited from their audiences. But the union lasted only a year. Hammerstein was a bit of an eccentric and could be difficult, even childish, on occasion. The break occurred when Hammerstein very publicly booed an act Koster and Bial had booked against his wishes. This was considered beyond the pale and the partners bought him out. Koster and Bial's remained a major venue for big-time variety through 1901. And Hammerstein would soon go on to open what many would consider the greatest vaudeville theater of all, the Victoria.

By the end of the 1880s, most new variety producers had come to realize that sanitized variety was not only more respectable but more profitable. Since polite vaudeville proved not incidentally a money-making enterprise, it is hard to know to what degree these avatars of purity were motivated by principle and to what degree by pocketbook. After all, there's cleaning up, and then there's *cleaning up*. Ultimately, "morality" was a quality that sold and by the turn of the twentieth century, vaudeville had completely supplanted saloon variety, leaving the more frankly roguish publicans to wipe their eyes with their bar rags.

In her 1969 memoir, *The Palace*, former Keith employee Marion Spitzer said that Keith vaudeville was "so clean it needs no Christian supervision." Indeed, industry-wide censorship was preemptively self-imposed, setting a precedent that would be emulated by others down the line, such as the Hayes Office for Hollywood films and the lawyerly standards and practices departments of network television. Such efforts, I have always thought, are like those signs in restaurant rest rooms that say "Employees Must Wash Hands Before Returning to Work." The sign is not meant to catch the eye of the employees but the customers and the authorities. It's all PR.

As we shall see, when they thought they could get away with it, the vaudeville managers were happy to make certain exceptions to their many strictures over the years. Late in vaudeville's life, some criticized it for having abandoned those earlier standards completely. Had Messrs. Pastor, Proctor, Keith, Albee, and company lived long enough to witness the birth of rock-and-roll, rap, and the "sick comedian," it is interesting to speculate whether they would have permitted such acts on their stages. There is reason to suspect they might have.

3

BIRTH OF AN INDUSTRY

THE MANAGERS

I am a businessman, and my business is to amuse people.
— *Vaudeville manager Martin Beck*

I am about to make a surprising assertion. Namely this: the indispensable ingredient of vaudeville was not the performers. Performers, as Jesus said of the poor, are always with us. Give a ham a half a chance and he'll do his thing anywhere—a street corner, a saloon, a nightclub, an opera house, a hotel lobby, or the back of a pickup truck. Ventriloquists, dancers, and corny comedians exist today, just as they had existed long before vaudeville came along.

Gather together some performers if you want to put on a show. But if you want to make show *business*—a paying operation that provides a living for the wide variety of professionals involved—that requires managers. The word "manager" in this context is old-style theater lingo, a holdover from the eighteenth and nineteenth centuries, loosely corresponding to today's "producer," "CEO," or "owner." These managers are not to be confused, by any stretch of the imagination, with the modern usage, in which an artist's manager is the guy who protects the performer, looks out for his interests, negotiates on his behalf. In most respects these managers were the polar opposite of that. The one exception to this rule was the great William Morris, founder of the agency named for him, who was an artists' rep but also briefly had his own vaudeville circuit. Agents like Morris spot talent, groom and cultivate performers, and, if both are lucky, nurse them along to stardom. An agent's job is to get the highest salary possible for his client. The manager's job, conversely, is to acquire the best talent for the lowest price. Being tight with a dollar ain't sexy, but in business—even a romantic business like vaudeville—it's necessary.

When people make reference to vaudeville (as in "back in vaudeville days" or "after vaudeville died"), it is really the business infrastructure they are talking about, the great network of famous circuits that stretched from Canada to America's southernmost precincts and brought the same high-quality professional entertainment to lobstermen in Maine, meatpackers in Chicago, miners in Scranton, ranchers in Texas, and garment workers in New York. This marvelous machine was devised by a motley, but mostly drab, crew of behind-the-scenes figures whose names today mean nothing to the general public, but without whom the Marx Brothers, Bill "Bojangles" Robinson, Sophie Tucker, and W. C. Fields might have been completely unknown outside their local taproom.

Unlike your average gin slinger, this new breed of manager was fiercely entrepreneurial. Entrepreneurs may be characterized as proactive dreamers. While everyone has dreams—of wealth, of happiness, of ease—the entrepreneur is the person who crosses the line. Not only does he brazenly conclude that his dream can come true, but he calculates how to go about doing it. As his enterprise, based on a dream, is necessarily new, an element of risk almost always exists, which can be thrilling. But the step-by-step, mind-numbing, soul-deadeningly humdrum process of realizing that dream is the deal-breaker for most dreamers, who by nature aren't cut out for such sacrifice. The peculiar hybrid of visionary and drudge—that's the entrepreneur.

The realization of worldly dreams also requires capital. Capital is surplus, and the only way to achieve that surplus with any certainty outside of a life of brigandage is to conform to the short list of rules found in *Poor Richard's Almanac*: (1) buy cheap and sell dear; (2) eliminate waste; and (3) organize, organize, organize. The so-called Gilded Age was rife with men who instinctively understood these principles: Andrew Carnegie, John D. Rockefeller, J. P. Morgan. Similarly, the time would arrive when men who had learned the ropes in circuses, dime museums, medicine shows, and saloons would bring these principles to bear in their own enterprises. We are talking about the invention of show business.

In the last two decades of the nineteenth century, a handful of crafty men invented certain revolutionary techniques for squeezing every last nickel out of what had heretofore been a notoriously sloppy and spontaneous art form. They pioneered morning-to-night, back-to-back performances of "continuous vaudeville"; they compartmentalized the anarchistic army of performers into useful categories and plugged them in and out of shows like car parts; then they shipped them around the country on rigid timetables on their nationwide theater circuits so as to get maximum play out of every single act under contract. The industry they created was as tightly run, hierarchical, closely monitored, and as epically complex as the Invasion of Normandy. Never, in the history of man, before or since, has there been so much in the way of live, constantly changing performance per capita, nor such a large audience for it. If vaudeville, as many have said, was all about laughter, the vaudeville managers were laughing all the way to the bank.

ALL VAUDEVILLE, ALL THE TIME

The revolution of the "double audience" (appealing to women and children now as well as men) added enormously to the profitability of variety production. It had been achieved chiefly through a public relations coup (courtesy of Barnum and his vaudeville acolytes) the likes of which may never be seen again. But several other innovations not only added to, but multiplied the growth of the vaudeville industry, making its expansion a foregone conclusion.

Variety, after all, had been small potatoes. Its producers were small businessmen whose dreams didn't extend any farther than their own saloon doors. Vaudeville, on the other hand, was big business. Following Adam Smith's principles of division of labor and mass production, its producers would come to control the entertainment of a nation. The difference is essentially the same as the one between the proprietor of your local greasy spoon . . . and Ray Kroc.

I make the comparison advisedly—one of the basic premises of industrialism is that the manufacturer is able to provide a standardized product of uniform quality. Such-and-such is always "a name you can count on." McDonald's hamburgers are not gourmet food, but the fact remains that a McDonald's hamburger you buy in Bohunkus, Iowa, is no worse than one you buy in Times Square, New York. It's not *steak frites*, but it is reliable. While this is an undeniable benefit to the consumer, it is really just a by-product of the producer's real agenda: minimizing expense and maximizing profits. Reinventing the wheel is expensive. You want to establish the most efficient system for creating the maximum amount of saleable product. The nineteenth century saw the birth of mass production and distribution of nearly everything: furniture, clothing, tools, appliances. It was inevitable that the techniques and the philosophy of industrialism would come to the theater.

"Continuous vaudeville" (that is, a constant turnover of back-to-back shows, dawn to dusk, so that a patron could enter or exit at any time she chose) was borrowed from dime museums and introduced by Keith and Albee at their Gaiety Museum in Boston in 1885. In the dime museums, acts might work a grind of fifteen shows a day, a tradition that was later maintained by the sideshows. Dime museum performances are more analogous to an exhibit or an installation. It's like those films at the natural history museum. You walk in or walk out whenever you like. In the dime museum or sideshow, the stage might be held by a fire-eater or geek; in the vaudeville house, it was a comedian or a tap dancer. As might be gleaned from the name, the main attraction in the museums, however, was the exhibits. Performances were "added value," and indeed many establishments did fine business without resorting to them. On the other hand, the vaudeville house was *all about* the show, with nary a calf's embryo or hairless cat in sight.

At the Gaiety, Keith began offering variety from ten-thirty in the morning till ten-thirty at night. An act like the Cohans would do five shows a day at Keith's. Jerry Cohan referred to it as a "machine shop." Yet, as Keith put it to him, "It's hard work, Jerry, but it's always there." And it was. While the Cohans would constantly drop out of vaudeville to take "legit" work during the dry periods, for a period of sixteen years they would (and could) always return to Keith. Job security—at least a much higher degree of security than in earlier times—was an important feature of this new industry. The loss of that security would be the most poignant aspect of vaudeville's demise fifty years later.

The move from legit to continuous vaud was a savvy one for managers, a way of maximizing the profit from their real estate. The payoff from a legit production, even with the addition of an afternoon matinee, isn't nearly as great as that of continuous vaudeville. Generally speaking, an ordinary theater just sits there racking up expenses 80 percent of the time, actually earning money only two to four hours a day. The peculiar properties of vaudeville allowed for the theater almost *never* to be dark. Furthermore, a play is a gamble, as likely to flop as to show a profit. The take from vaudeville was as steady and regular as that from a Las Vegas slot machine.

Like pop bottles or Colt pistols, variety performers now passed by continuously on an "assembly line." Not a minute would be wasted. As in manufacturing, "time" would now be king. Acts would be given strict limits on how long they could remain onstage. The time *between* acts was also compressed; unlike their British music-hall counterparts the American audience would brook no "stage waits," or dead spots, in the presentation. The show was structured in such a way that acts with minimal requirements, such as a comedian, a comedy team, or a solo musician, would alternate with acts that required more complicated scenery. The former would take place "in one," that is, in front of the closed curtain, while preparations were being made for the more complicated act (perhaps a magician with his apparatus). This made for a smoother, quicker presentation. Likewise, a simple system was worked out to avoid onstage traffic jams: all entrances were made from stage right; all exits stage left.

The afterpiece, a beloved part of minstrelsy, variety, and the vaudeville of most of Keith's early contemporaries, was here jettisoned to better streamline the process of one performance leading directly into the next. The "continuous" format dictated that the house would periodically need to be cleared out in order to maximize profit. This necessitated the inclusion of at least one unpalatable act, often called "the chaser." In continuous vaudeville the last act on the bill was usually boring (if not downright bad), thus driving out some of the audience to make room for new ticket-holders. Vaudeville sketch writer Edwin Milton Royle estimated that no more than 2 percent of the audience would stay for more than one complete show.

Other than that no one set formula existed for the arrangement of a vaudeville bill. It was a peculiar art form in and of itself, and how it manifested itself in the product varied from theater to theater, from booker to booker, from region to region. The running order depended on several factors: which acts were available; the need for contrast between acts; the need not to have two similar acts on the same bill; the need to alternate big productions and acts "in one"; and the need to be constantly ratcheting up excitement until the finale.

Eight or nine acts eventually became a sort of big-time standard, but the truth was, in vaud, the length of the bill varied wildly. Fred Allen recalled a theater in Maine that had one act plus a movie, technically the shortest variety bill possible, whereas a bill on the William Morris circuit typically ran an average of twenty-one acts. The more likely range in the big time was between seven and fifteen, depending on the theater.

That mythical "average" vaudeville bill would go something like this: first, the opener—usually a "dumb" act such as animals or acrobats to allow for latecomers. These acts were a sort of poor relation, a doormat. They existed for the same reason a prologue exists in Shakespeare, or the trailers at your local cineplex. A good part of the audience will be late; best to start the show with an act it matters little to miss. The act could be a large production since, being first, there was time to set the stage for whatever teeter boards, trapezes, slides, ramps, and platforms the performance might require.

Next followed the much maligned "deuce spot." The second act on the bill was generally "in one," and was typically a tryout spot for acts who weren't yet stars. In this slot you were likely to find a singing-sisters or dancing-brothers act, a male-female song-and-dance team, or maybe just an up-and-coming singer. The act's job was to settle the audience down a bit. It was the first act most of the audience would pay attention to, but not fully. For this reason, according to impressionist Elsie Janis, it was known as the "burying ground"—because so many performers "died" there.

Number three was usually a "flash" act—a large production with sets and a big cast, designed to finally snap the audience out of their stupor. Such an act might be a magician (with all of his apparatus) or a comedy sketch or one-act play with a full stage set.

Building upon the momentum of the third act, the fourth act was supposed to hit the audience between the eyes, to be the first in a series of numbers that would keep the audience mesmerized straight through to the headliner. As it was to take place in one, it would usually be either a popular singer or comedian or comedy team, a novelty act of some kind, or perhaps a hot dance act.

Five would be a headliner, so as to keep the audience buzzing during the intermission. Because the top headliner would get the next-to-closing slot, this position would belong to an act that was currently either rising to, or falling from, the peak of their fame. The type of act positioned here would depend on what sort of act had preceded it: if a comedy act had just gone on, then five might be a musical act or show-stopping dance number; if four had been a singer, then five would be a comedy headliner.

The act in the tricky sixth spot would have the job of settling the audience down again following intermission while matching the energy built up by the fifth act . . . yet without outclassing the acts in the seventh or eighth slots. The classiest dumb acts would work here—perhaps a top comedy juggler, a ballet dancer, or a musician.

A full-stage act would go on seventh, something on a scale to awe beyond the spectacles in the three and five slots. It could be a comic or dramatic sketch (if one had not gone on previously), or a large musical outfit, such as a novelty orchestra or hillbilly band.

The coveted next-to-closing slot would be the headliner, usually the most popular comedian, singer, or comedy team that could be secured for that particular performance.

Ninth and last came the "haircut act," or chaser. Usually something so appalling it would have the audience heading for the door, with all you would see being the back of their heads. It might be animals or acrobats, but it might also be just something intolerably strange and boring. Marcus Loew, dubbed the "King of Small Time," claimed to have the best chaser in the business; a bad sculptor who made inaccurate busts of famous people onstage. Another alternative for a chaser in later years would be a film. While films were often a great attraction, they

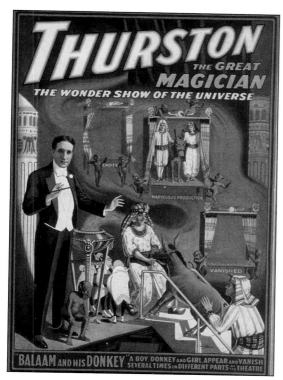

Who put the devil in vaudeville?
Magicians like Howard Thurston were part of a long line of conjurers who implied that their amazing feats were not mere sleight of hand, but performed with the aid of supernatural agents. (Library of Congress, Prints and Photographs Division)

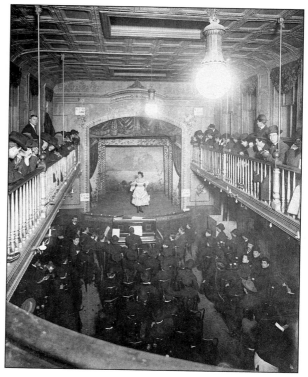

Cigareets and whiskey and wild, wild women were the constant companions of saloon-going males, American variety's first audience. A rare photograph of the interior of a Bowery concert saloon. (New-York Historical Society)

Der Schutzenfest. So-called Dutch comedians Joe Weber and Lew Fields made a career of slaughtering the English language (and each other) as two German immigrants named Mike and Meyer. After the Irish, Germans constituted America's second-largest immigrant group prior to the influx from Southern and Eastern Europe in the 1880s. (Billy Rose Theatre Collection, The New York Public Library for the Performing Arts, Astor, Lenox and Tilden Foundations)

BELOW: New York's **Tammany Hall** was home base to no less than two major vaudeville managers. Tony Pastor's theater was located right in the building (bottom left). Tammany politician "Big Tim" Sullivan was to start one of the premier circuits of the Pacific Northwest with his partner John Considine. (New-York Historical Society)

The Father of Vaudeville. Songster and saloon keeper Tony Pastor dared to dream of a variety theater fit for women and children. The resulting product was called "vaudeville" by everyone but him. (Billy Rose Theatre Collection, The New York Public Library for the Performing Arts, Astor, Lenox and Tilden Foundations)

Go figure. Lillian Russell was once considered the most beautiful woman in the world. Was it all just a PR put-up job? (Billy Rose Theatre Collection, The New York Public Library for the Performing Arts, Astor, Lenox and Tilden Foundations)

ABOVE: **My mother thanks you, my father thanks you, my sister thanks you, and I thank you.** The Four Cohans were a family act, a brand-new phenomenon made possible by the censorial strictures of the first generation of vaudeville managers. From left to right, the Cohans are George, Josie, Jerry, and Nellie. (Billy Rose Theatre Collection, The New York Public Library for the Performing Arts, Astor, Lenox and Tilden Foundations)

Never mind what the name sounds like: Proctor's Pleasure Palace at Fifty-eighth and Third was not a whorehouse, but quite the opposite—a temple of innocent amusements built to a scale that would dwarf many European cathedrals. (New-York Historical Society)

The Biddy Committee. Edward F. Albee gives a gaggle of society ladies the grand tour of one of his theaters, just to make sure it's all on the up-and-up. (Billy Rose Theatre Collection, The New York Public Library for the Performing Arts, Astor, Lenox and Tilden Foundations)

No bucks, no Buck Rogers. Without the organizational acumen of a handful of managers like Martin Beck (seated, center), work for thousands of vaudevillians would never have been so plentiful nor so lucrative. Never far from his side was a telephone—an indispensable tool of the trade and a fairly new invention at the time. (Billy Rose Theatre Collection, The New York Public Library for the Performing Arts, Astor, Lenox and Tilden Foundations)

"IN THE SCHOOLROOM."

As this *Variety* cartoon shows, the managers were widely regarded even in their own day as a gang of money-hungry robber barons. Such public opinion was a price they were willing to pay in return for the high profits to be got by banding together in a cartel. The cartoon is by the vaudevillian Leo Carrillo, better known to some as Pancho from the 1950s television series *The Cisco Kid*. (Billy Rose Theatre Collection, The New York Public Library for the Performing Arts, Astor, Lenox and Tilden Foundations)

Hammerstein's Victoria was the most cherished vaudeville house of its day. The sign in this photograph advertising Gertrude Hoffman as Salome suggests why: its manager Willie Hammerstein was a showman second to none. (New-York Historical Society)

Two of the most ripped-off flimflam men in the business. The magicians Ching Ling Foo and Harry Houdini were so successful at hoodwinking the public that each of them had dozens of imitators who deceived vaudeville audiences still more by stealing their acts and even (with minor alterations) their stage names. (Library of Congress, Rare Book and Special Collections Division)

BELOW: **You gotta love him, except you don't.** This *Variety* ad of Al Jolson's says it all. The successful vaudevillian could sometimes be so nakedly self-aggrandizing as to be repellent. I might pay money to hear this guy sing, but I don't think I'd send him a Christmas card. (Billy Rose Theatre Collection, The New York Public Library for the Performing Arts, Astor, Lenox and Tilden Foundations)

EVERYBODY LIKES ME

THOSE WHO DON'T ARE JEALOUS

ANYHOW, HERE'S WISHING THOSE WHO DO AND THOSE WHO DON'T

A MERRY CHRISTMAS
AND
A HAPPY NEW YEAR

Al Jolson

This nut with the tree branch on her head is Eva Tanguay, the quintessential vaudevillian. Her act was considered sexy in its day, and you have to admit those are some nice looking limbs. (Billy Rose Theatre Collection, The New York Public Library for the Performing Arts, Astor, Lenox and Tilden Foundations)

Unthinkably by today's standards, **Mae West** received nothing but bad press in her vaudeville days for having an act that was deemed too sexy. Here she is in her Theda Bara phase. (Billy Rose Theatre Collection, The New York Public Library for the Performing Arts, Astor, Lenox and Tilden Foundations)

also made a nice, clear signal that things had drawn to a close: when the film was done, so was the show.

Step ten: repeat.

The idea of "continuous" entertainment, where one may enter or exit at any time during the performance, could only work with variety. A straight stage play requires the curtain-to-curtain attention of the audience; further, it is difficult to imagine what play could ever be so successful as to fill the house several times a day every day. Time and money: the bottom line. Vaudeville cleared both of these hurdles neatly, thanks to the ingenuity of its founding managers.

THE CUSTOMER IS ALWAYS RIGHT

Later vaudevillians, who were apt to rhapsodize about their former participation in the then-defunct industry, were unanimous in their recollection of the manner in which content was shaped to fit their acts. Comedian and singer George Jessel said that in vaudeville "you lived by the reaction of the audience." Said vaudeville Renaissance man Eddie Cantor, "The audience is never wrong . . . If a performer failed to go across it was either the fault of the material or the manner of presentation." James Cagney, a former hoofer, concurred: "Audiences are the ones who determine material. It's only in their opinion that a thing is good or bad." Likewise, Jimmy Durante opined that "the customers are boss, and you have to please them, no matter how it hurts." According to Lew Fields of the comedy team of Weber and Fields, "Give the Public, who are the best judges, what they demand and you are apt to meet with success."

It is interesting that, although they expressed the sentiment in slightly different ways, all five of these gentlemen said exactly the same thing. It is as though each had been given the same mantra and muttered it over and over and over to himself, a mantra shared by ten thousand of their fellow vaudevillians, and the manager as well.

The words "the audience," coming from a vaudevillian, have a mystical, metaphysical ring to them. It's notable that these people mostly came of age in America's greatest patriotic period, encompassing the Spanish-American War, American Imperialism under Teddy Roosevelt, the liberation of Europe by American Forces during the Great War, and, perhaps most significant, the rapid assimilation of millions of foreign immigrants who were desperate to become Americans. The phrase "the People" as enshrined in the Constitution has the same kind of resonance, and, if one cares to step into the turgid waters of German mysticism (which was highly influential and not yet so dangerous in the years before Hitler), so does the word *Volk*. Emerson had written of an "Over-Soul," one great harmonious, transcendent flock of humanity. Whitman had heard America singing. Sandburg, inarticulate with awe, had merely moaned, "The People, Yes."

In the popular theater, the audience is "the people." The industry was full of "People's" theaters, at "popular" prices. The actress who cut the ribbon at the opening of Keith's Colonial had done so with the words "all are equals here." Vaudeville was an industry in which success could be measured scientifically and instantaneously using the world's most ancient form of marketing survey: applause. The vaudevillian was in the rare position of knowing how well he was doing financially coming right out of the gate. If something got over, he'd do well. If it didn't, it got cut (and so, maybe, did he). Every seat in the house was a throne, with its own caesar, poised to give the next act a thumbs-up or a thumbs-down. Vaudevillians emerged from the people, were a creation of the people, in a sense were elected by the people (in the case of amateur nights, quite literally). Like gods from the collective unconscious they had the privilege and the responsibility of enacting the people's dreams and fantasies. It was a rare vaudevillian who ever forgot that. Most felt like the comedienne and singer Fanny Brice, who, just before exiting the stage, would literally salute the crowd.

That the audience was composed of "customers" implies that they were being sold a "product." That product was the performers themselves, and pouring on the charm was called "selling it." Think of the word "showcase," a term still current among performers and producers to this day. A showcase is, after all, a piece of merchandising display furniture. The vaudeville show, in this respect, is not at all dissimilar from the dessert case in a diner, with cakes and pies slowly revolving before the patrons on a motorized lazy Susan. How fitting that during vaudeville's first decades, its audience would come directly from doing its shopping on the Ladies' Mile to catching the latest acts over at Union Square.

As Frederick Thompson, designer and co-owner of Coney Island's Luna Park, and of several important Broadway houses, put it: "We are coming to the age of the department store in theatricals." As if to underscore that point, none other than F. W. Woolworth dabbled in vaudeville, building a theater over one of his five-and-ten-cent stores in Lancaster, Pennsylvania. While you could buy farm implements, ladies' lingerie, children's toys, and furniture in a department store, in a vaudeville house you could sample the wares of entertainers from every known performance discipline, of every race, creed, age, sex, sexual orientation, and species. As Caroline Gaffin noted in her 1915 book *Vaudeville*, "we have every imaginable thing, animate or inanimate, keenly scrutinized with a view to their use for entertainment." Trained animals of every sort trod the stage: birds, dogs, simians, pigs, cows, horses, mules, seals, and eventually even elephants basked in the vaudeville limelight. Tumblers, strongmen, trapeze acts, cyclists (uni-, bi-, and tri-), and contortionists risked their necks upon the stage. Dancers demonstrated a broad terpsichorean spectrum, from the traditional jigs and clogs of the Irishman, to the cakewalk and breakdown of the African-American, to (in later years) ballroom, cooch, tango, tap, ballet, and even modern interpretive dance. Magicians, jugglers, mind-readers, hypnotists, and ventriloquists amazed audiences with their uncanny abilities. Musicians, singers, and comedians (in groups of one, two, three, or four) lightened the hearts of their fans. "Nuts" and "freaks"—comprising all those who would fit into no other large category (e.g., artistic whistlers, musical saw players, people who did birdcalls)—left people scratching their heads. Impressionists imitated all of the above. Soon, other categories would be added: pocket versions of stage dramas starring the top actors of the day, "tab shows" (abbreviated full-cast musicals), and, of course, the one attraction that would eventually replace all the rest: movies.

Because each act was a self-contained unit, it could be removed and replaced easily, like a spark plug, without affecting the rest of the machine. This meant that an act that flopped or swore or otherwise ran afoul of company regulations could be canned on the spot. (There might "always be work," as Keith put it, but you had to do your job well and play by the rules—necessary conditions for keeping a job in any occupation, incidentally.) The fact that acts could be so easily replaced is in stark contrast to the equivalent situation in a legit play, where the appropriate actor must be found, cast, and rehearsed in a part. Hence the cost-savings in the vaudeville approach. Pastor, Keith, Proctor, and many others had all at various times dabbled in legit production, but most came to the same conclusion: in vaudeville they had built a better mousetrap.

Furthermore, with the diverse array of talent at their disposal, they had a product in which the public would rarely be disappointed for longer than ten minutes. In a vaudeville show, chances were, every individual in the audience from every background would like at least *something*. Indeed, the genius of vaudeville is not only that it courts a double audience; it aims to please *everybody*. As this process began to gather steam, this "all things to all people" approach would enable the vaudeville industry to assemble America's first mass audience.

BARGAIN BASEMENT

Likewise, low ticket prices kept vaudeville accessible to people from all walks of life. As with the dime museum, at most vaudeville theaters, a ticket could be purchased with a few small coins. F. F. Proctor pioneered what was called the 10-20-30 scale of ticket prices, said to have been suggested by his sometime partner, dime-museum impresario H. R. Jacobs. The worst seat in the house cost one thin dime, the best just three of them. Keith, too, had made "popular prices" his watchword. The slogan of his pirated Gilbert and Sullivan productions had been "Why pay $1.50 when you can see our show for 25 cents?" As their product morphed from operetta to vaudeville, they retained the bargain-basement ticket prices that kept their houses packed.

The low ticket costs presented the managers with a problem, however. While a wholesome show would bring in middle-class folks, the 10-20-30 pricing scale also attracted the working classes, an element that was apt to be more, shall we say, vocally demonstrative in the theater. But the managers had an answer for even this potential difficulty. Like missionaries in some far-off Third World principality, they undertook to civilize the masses. Just as they had posted rules and regulations backstage to control their own employees, Keith and his cohorts took a similar approach in schooling their own customers. Consider it the *fin de siècle* version of

"Please Turn Off Your Cell Phones." Signs listing the rules were hung in the lobby. "No Smoking." "Take Off Your Hat." "No Foot Stomping." Small cards with a printed admonition were handed to offending patrons. Burly (if tuxedoed) ushers roamed the aisles, ready to pounce on especially nettlesome characters and toss them into the alley—in the most graceful, polite manner possible. In the early days, Keith himself was known to take the stage and lecture the assembled on the appropriate decorum. Oddly, this adversarial approach seems to have actually worked. The combined impression of the relatively tony theater and the refinement of the acts and the other theater employees seemed to inspire church behavior from the potentially rough characters in the cheapest seats. Just breathing the atmosphere here seemed to infect the classless with class. In a real sense, the lecturing and the hectoring were not acts of condescension or class warfare, but the opposite. On the contrary, by expecting that the audience behave like mature, civilized adults, the managers were showing them a form of respect, and they rose to the occasion.

A notable exception to the downward trend in ticket costs was Tony Pastor's Fourteenth Street Theatre. In an effort to differentiate himself from the free-and-easies, and to attract a higher class of New York audience (and to cover the costs of operating his comparatively small theater), Pastor had boosted his prices to $1.50, the going price of an operetta or other legitimate vehicle (although he, too, in his later years would switch to "continuous" and a cheaper ticket). In time the other managers would fine-tune their approach to appeal to different markets. Certain houses (generally the ones in the prime real estate) would take Pastor's original approach, offering the top acts in the country for a top ticket of one or two dollars, two shows a day. This became known as "big time." The lesser properties retained the 10-20-30 scale along with the five-a-day and were called "small time." And like the department-store magnates they so resembled, the managers would assemble these houses into large national chains.

CIRCUITS

A clean show, with a diverse sampling of product, presented cheaply at the customer's convenience. That's good business, but it's not yet big business. The success of the theaters presenting continuous vaudeville allowed the pioneering managers to expand. The recent development of the telegraph, the telephone, express mail, and regular, reliable rail travel made it possible to manage far-flung empires. Deals could be made instantly. Contracts could be turned around in a matter of days instead of weeks or months. If something needed personal attention in Scranton, to Scranton you now went.

Before trains, domestic travel was almost nonexistent. From 1869 on, you could get from one coast to another by rail. Never before had a reliable, efficient transportation network linked all of America's major towns and cities as it did now, creating a new scenario for performers. You got a show Tuesday at eight o'clock? We can get you there.

This mobility allowed the vaudeville circuits to take their place among the world's first corporate chains. Now that there are hundreds of such entities, it may be difficult to see how revolutionary this idea was at the time. Heretofore, only governments had ever had branch offices. In the nineteenth century, railroads, the telegraph, and freight carriers such as Wells Fargo and American Express, which provided government-like services, brought the idea into the private realm. Then grocery and department stores like A&P, Woolworth's, and Kroger's took advantage of those transportation and communications networks (and the organizational precedent they established) by creating the first retail chains. The vaudeville circuits were run on the same principle: a managerial staff at a corporate headquarters oversaw the affairs of a large number of "branch offices" (in this case theaters), hiring the staff, standardizing the product, and generally dictating operating procedures.

The idea of a theater chain is too radical and revolutionary to have been a deliberate innovation. What seems to have happened is that as the managers got fat with profits, they simply bought more theaters. As they expanded, it was only natural—in fact, necessary—to coordinate booking, establish uniform circuit-wide administrative guidelines, and develop a corporate identity.

Henry Miner, inventor of the hook, appears to have been the first to start a crude circuit in the 1880s, though his variety houses were few and mostly confined to New York City. Around the same time, M. B. Leavitt, working out of San Francisco, organized a small group of western theaters into a rudimentary circuit.

The first real inroads into the infant realm of vaudeville circuitry were made by F. F. Proctor. Enriched by "Levantine's," Proctor spent the early 1880s amassing an empire of small theaters in upstate New York: the Pearl Street in Albany (1882), the Theatorium in Genesee Falls (1884), and Martin's Opera House in Albany (1884). Before he was done, he also planted his flag in Rochester, Syracuse, Utica, Buffalo, Troy (New York), New Haven, Bridgeport, Hartford (Connecticut), and Lancaster, Worcester, Lynn, and Wilmington (Massachusetts). In the latter part of the decade, Proctor began to crack Brooklyn, with the opening there of Proctor's Novelty (1886) and Proctor's Criterion (1887). Before any of the other major managers had lifted a finger toward serious expansion, Proctor, with partner H. R. Jacobs, had his name on close to fifty theaters.

If his contemporaries were slower coming out of the gate, it must be remembered that the circuit model of expansion and management was completely new and untried; there didn't seem to be anything inevitable about it. A number of the early managers pursued a very different tack to take their vaudeville shows to the nation. Rather than buying numerous theaters and booking individual acts to perform in them, a manager could go the opposite way. He could put together a solid variety bill and tour the entire thing as a unit, booking the show into theaters around the country, much as "bus and truck" tours of Broadway musicals work today. If this sounds like a solid and lucrative strategy, it was, throughout the early years of the 1880s and nineties. Proctor's old mentor M. B. Leavitt toured such shows, as did Tony Pastor, Florenz Ziegfeld, Weber and Fields, Gus Hill (a former acrobat), and the Brooklyn-based firm of Hyde and Behman. Ziegfeld's (his first production, a decade before he was to launch his famous *Follies*) toured the country in the years 1896–99 under the name Trocadero Vaudevilles. Its star was America's premier strongman (what we would today call a body builder) and male sex symbol: Eugene Sandow. Sandow, Ziegfeld claimed, could lift a man up in each hand while two men stood on his back. He further boasted that he could hoist 750 pounds of dead weight with one finger and bear the weight of 3,200 pounds upon his body. While the Trocadero bill also featured comedian Billy Van, aerialists the Five Jordans, impressionist the Great Amann, and six other acts, the real attraction was Sandow.

In 1885 there were twenty such touring vaudeville companies in the country; in five years the number had tripled. In the mid-nineties, Weber and Fields alone had three separate units touring simultaneously in addition to their own New York–based show. These were all-star bills featuring some of the top stars of their day: singer Lottie Gilson, Dutch comic Sam Bernard, Hebrew comic David Warfield, and the Russell Brothers played these tours, with bills fleshed out by the likes of Draww (a juggler and equilibrist) and the trapeze act of Ramza and Arno. As former dime museum performers, Weber and Fields had no love for the five-a-day grind of continuous vaudeville. But as we shall soon see, the touring vaudeville show would soon bump up against a competing method of circulating talent. Its proponents would stop at nothing to win that competition.

FLAGSHIPS

While Proctor was dotting the map with vaudeville houses, the Keith organization was not exactly napping. Though Proctor's tendency was to grow his empire outward, Albee, as Keith's manager, preferred to grow his organization *up*. Albee was infatuated with the idea of building grand, palatial theaters, emphasizing quality over quantity. He followed up his Boston theater with two spectacular new houses in Providence and Philadelphia, both built in 1887. Any one of the Keith theaters during these years equaled several of Proctor's in terms of fame, scale, and prestige. In the years to come, such grandiosity would be the standard for all big-time vaudeville houses, and the managers would race to outdo one another in architectural phantasmagoria.

Keith's Colonial (Boston, 1893) set the standard. Dignitaries from around the globe were trucked in for its grand opening. Comparisons were made to the great structures of Europe. This new house set new standards for posh. Fireproof curtains, electric lights (then still a novelty), chandeliers, a Moorish dome. A veritable cathedral of entertainment, the Colonial was soon the international pride of Boston. The theater imitated the baroque palaces of southern Europe, smothered in a superfluity of wedding-cake detail: gargoyles, stained glass, marble pillars, hand-painted murals, gilded archways, red-carpeted floors, and fixtures of gleaming brass. Albee was especially proud of the whitewashed coal bin in the basement, which was adorned with an eighty-dollar red carpet. (The real doormats were the acts who tried to ask him for a raise.)

Consider that this cathedral was designed to showcase the labors of jugglers, clowns, singers, tumblers, and dancers—the very people who'd been barred from Europe's cathedrals and forced to do their shtick in the marketplace outdoors. Now they stood on the altar of their own temple, the architectural equal of history's most spectacular churches built for the glory of God. This was a revolutionary situation, a sort of institutionalization of the Feast of Fools. The crowning irony is that Keith's Colonial was made possible with underwriting from the Catholic Archdiocese of Boston. Call it an investment in public morality. Better for the flock to flock to Keith's than some low concert saloon.

As spectacular as Keith's Colonial was, however, it was far from the be-all and end-all. Even in the nineteenth century, America's true cultural capital was already New York, and anyone with ambitions of any sort would have to set his sights there eventually. More than ten years after the invention of vaudeville, Tony Pastor still had a lock on the business in the Big Apple (though alcoholic, risqué variety continued to flourish in countless New York theaters and music halls). The question, by the early 1890s, was: Who would be the first to compete with him, Keith or Proctor?

In this, as in all things, Proctor was the more nimble operator. By the mid-eighties he had made incursions into Brooklyn—in those days a completely different city, with its own government, its own culture, and its own audience, only recently linked to Manhattan by the Brooklyn Bridge, and not to be legally merged with it until 1898.

In 1889, Proctor bought his first Manhattan venue, the Twenty-third Street Theatre. In partnership with producer Charles Frohman, he at first presented legit plays there. But this precious "artistic" business did not suit a former acrobat like Proctor. In 1892, while Keith and Albee were dilly-dallying in an attempt to find just the right house for their announced New York expansion, Proctor played them a dirty trick. He switched his Twenty-third Street Theatre over to continuous vaudeville, introducing it to the New York public as his own invention. Essentially, just before Keith and Albee were to bring their revolutionary new

McDonald's to town, Proctor opened up a Burger King. With the catchy slogan "After Breakfast Go to Proctor's, After Proctor's Go to Bed," Proctor's Twenty-third Street offered shows six days a week, from noon to midnight.

Thereafter Keith and Albee vied with Proctor for the title of "Inventor of Continuous Vaudeville." Proctor certainly had justification for his claim. After all, he had planted his flag on the moon while Keith and Albee were still running simulations in Boston, Philadelphia, and Providence. But the die was cast. Keith and Albee never forgave Proctor for beating them to New York, setting the tone for the rest of the industry's history: a series of wars for dominance between competing fiefdoms. But while Keith and Albee were caught napping more than once, their unprepossessing start was most deceptive. As the tortoise said to the hare: "Slow and steady wins the race."

By the following year, Keith and Albee had established their own New York flagship literally across the street from Tony Pastor's: Keith's Union Square. After over a decade of unchallenged supremacy, Pastor was now confronted with two new cutthroat competitors in his own backyard. Determined to gain the edge over both Pastor and Proctor, Keith brought in a Boston newspaperman named J. Austin Fynes to manage the Union Square. Fynes's strategy was to attract the finest type of audience by getting stars of the legitimate stage to perform in short dramatic sketches. The theory was that the truly snooty vaudeville hold-outs would be lured in by the sort of entertainment they found respectable, and become attached to vaudeville in the process. And, essentially, this is what happened. By offering them more money than they received for straight theater, Fynes managed to secure the services of Maurice Barrymore, Mr. and Mrs. Sydney Drew, Charles Dickson and Lillian Burkhart, and many of the era's other most esteemed thespians. The short one-act melodrama with its penchant for the sensational plot culminating in a chest-beating climax, worked perfectly in vaudeville's environment of fast, hard-hitting punches. With Fynes at the helm, the Union Square Theatre soon outstripped both Proctor and Pastor. So Proctor hired Fynes away from Keith—and Fynes brought all those classy acts with him. Proctor, too, could now promise "High Class Vaudeville" with "First Class Artists."

Not coincidentally, in 1895 the *New York Dramatic Mirror*, the city's principal theatrical paper, deigned to add a vaudeville section to its pages, a condescension previously to be sniffed at. With the "Harolds and Arthurs" (as vaudevillians referred to legit dramatic actors) now in vaud, the industry was considered worthy of the paper's attention. Likewise, the first all-show-business trade periodical, *The Billboard,* had been founded the previous year, further validating the infant business. These magazines carried industry news, trade advertisements, and, more important, reviews, which acts could use to help leverage more and better bookings, and which audiences and bookers could rely on to help make informed choices. Such ancillary activity was a sign of the health of the burgeoning industry.

In 1895, Proctor stole Keith's thunder yet again. Since the Keith organization prided itself on having the most fabulous vaudeville houses, it must have been a trifle galling to hear of the opening of Proctor's Pleasure Palace, located at Fifty-eighth and Third. Despite having a name more suitable to a massage parlor, the "Triple P" was the most elaborate temple of entertainment built to date. Taking our department-store analogy one step further, the Pleasure Palace offered different departments—literally—with two theaters, a roof garden, a billiard room, and a Palm Garden in the lobby. What's more, the theater opened with one of the most incredible vaudeville bills ever assembled up to that time: Weber and Fields, comedian Sam Bernard, minstrel Lew Dockstader, singer Lottie Gilson, and a troupe of comedy elephants. (Eventually, the Pleasure Palace itself provided to be too elephantine, collapsing under the weight of its own expenses.)

Proctor was a bold risk-taker, while Keith and Albee were more cautious, and so it's not surprising that the challenge of matching Proctor's Pleasure Palace was not taken up by the Keith organization but by another manager, one who was Proctor's equal both in ambition and in rashness. With the profits from the sale of his share in Koster and Bial's, Oscar Hammerstein bought several lots on the east side of Broadway between Forty-fourth and Forty-fifth streets and there erected the Olympia Theatre, an undertaking that only his own operatic imagination could have hatched. Opened in 1895, it made the Pleasure Palace look like a popsicle stand. The mammoth multiplex contained several separate theaters: the Music Hall (seating 4,000), the Lyric Theatre (seating 1,800), a 600-seat concert hall, bowling alleys, a pool room, several lounges, smoking rooms, Turkish baths, plus a roof garden. His three sons (Willie, Arthur, and Harry) helped him run the place.

In the Olympia's Music Hall, where vaudeville was presented, the Hammersteins demonstrated a flair for promotion unmatched by any of their contemporaries. They managed to make a mint, for example, on an act that has gone down in theatrical lore as the most horrible ever seen on a vaudeville stage. Touted at the time as the "The Worst Act in America," the Cherry Sisters, as sheer spectacle, were about on par with a boating accident. To make matters still more entertaining, they had no idea that was the case.

Hailing from Marion, Iowa, the Cherry Sisters were five in number: Effie, Addie, Ella, Jessie, and Lizzie. They started performing to raise funds so that they could attend the Chicago World's Fair in 1893. Singers without charm or wit, they stood there, sang off key, and were under the mistaken impression that they were actually talented. "[Our] intertanement [sic]," wrote one of them later, "was as good as any that has been given . . ."

An enterprising and cynical genius spotted their act and realized he could make hay with it. As such, the Cherry Sisters were way ahead of their time, presaging, for example, David Letterman's presentation of the bizarre, talentless, former mailman Larry "Bud" Melman. The Cherry Sisters began to be booked widely throughout the Midwest. The cruelty underlying the act's appeal resembles that which accompanied gladiatorial spectacle. Its charm was akin to modern screenings of Ed Wood films. The difference is that the poor Cherry Sisters were live and had to endure the abuse of the audience, which not only hooted, howled, and hissed, but threw vegetables at them.

A review from the *Des Moines Leader* was not sparing in its bile:

Effie is an old jade of 50 summers, Jessie a frisky filly of 40, and Addie, the flower of the family, a capering monstrosity of 35. Their long skinny arms, equipped with talons at the extremities, swung mechanically, and anon waved frantically at the suffering audience. The mouths of their rancid features opened like caverns and sounds like the wailings of damned souls issued therefrom. They pranced around the stage with a motion that suggested a cross between a *danse du ventre* and fox-trot—

strange creatures with painted faces and hideous mein. Effie is spavined, Addie is string-halt, and Jessie, the only one who showed her stockings, has legs with calves as classic in their outlines as the curves of a broom handle.

Oscar Hammerstein, having read their notices, brought the sisters to the Olympia, confident that the sophisticated and cruel New York audience would relish this sort of entertainment.

The act the five Cherries performed in New York was called "Something Good, Something Sad." They never knew just how sad. The set consisted of moral melodrama, bad singing, and inept comic turns. Their repertoire included a song called "My First Cigar" (a cautionary tale), another titled "Fair Columbia" (with one of the sisters draped in a flag), and a tableau called "Clinging to the Cross" (in which one of them, dressed as Jesus, was crucified). And then there was their theme song. Dressed as Salvation Army recruits, they banged a drum, rattled a tambourine, and sang:

> *Cherries ripe, boom-de-ay!*
> *Cherries red, boom de-ay!*
> *The Cherry sisters have come to stay!*

Hammerstein actually encouraged the audience to throw vegetables at them, later explaining to the Cherries that the other acts, in their jealousy, had hired the hecklers for that purpose. Regardless, the girls' show sold out for ten weeks in 1896, helping to keep Hammerstein's outsized enterprise afloat.

FOREIGN IMPORTS

If all Hammerstein had to offer was cheese like the Cherry Sisters, he would have been rapidly laughed out of town, or at least down to the Bowery. But, lest we forget, the man was also an opera impresario. He had the rare know-how to offset his tastelessness with doses of taste. Such contradictory experiences in the same venue, in the same show, gave vaudeville its peculiar, rewarding tang—like the salting of an apple or the spiking of a soft drink.

One such pleasant surprise was Hammerstein's 1895 importation of French chanteuse Yvette Guilbert. A star of the Paris and London music halls, Guilbert was considered second to none in her ability to emotionally dramatize a song through the affecting use of facial expression and gesture. Despite the fact that almost the entire act was in French, Guilbert could connect with English-speaking audiences through that emotive power. People may not have understood the words, but they still knew when to cry. For this reason Guilbert was an extremely influential performer, inspiring an entire generation of American female singers who would seek to emulate her.*

Another quality import presented by Hammerstein at the Olympia Music Hall was England's greatest music-hall comedian Dan Leno (no relation to Jay). Billed as "The Funniest Man on Earth," Leno portrayed a wide variety of comic characters, with a minor costume change in between (much as some readers may remember Jonathan Winters doing on television in the 1960s). A Leno specialty was "pantomime dames," a species of drag act that would inform such later performers as Monty Python and Dame Edna. Leno stayed at the Olympia for four weeks.

Also appearing at the Olympia in the 1890s was the Italian quick-change artist Leopoldo Fregoli. Over the course of his performance Fregoli would change costume on average once a minute, playing an old woman, an ingénue, a magician, a juggler, a ballet dancer, and numerous other characters, all done in the blink of an eye.

In presenting Guilbert, Leno, and Fregoli, Hammerstein was capitalizing on a vogue at the time for burnishing vaudeville's glitter and gloss by importing foreign music-hall talent. The "Brits" joined the "legits" in bringing a classy veneer to what was, after all, popular entertainment. The Edwardian era was the peak of British imperialism, the English at the summit of their international influence. America was still more like Australia or Canada—another English-speaking country basking in the glory of the "mother country." The stars of the British music hall, then, had all the cachet of today's Hollywood stars.

---

*The most prominent of these would be vaudeville's biggest singing star, Nora Bayes, who was known by the singularly unfortunate billing "the Wurtzburger Girl."

Despite its marked predominance of singers (as might be deduced from the name), music hall resembled vaudeville in the wealth of diverse talents to be found on its stage. In his 1879 *Dictionary of London*, Charles Dickens, Jr., gave this account:

> Ballet, gymnastics, and so-called comic-singing, form the staple of the bill of fare, but nothing comes foreign to the music-hall proprietor. Performing animals, winners of walking matches, successful scullers, shipwrecked sailors, swimmers of the channel, conjurers, ventriloquists, tight-rope dancers, campanologists, clog-dancers, sword-swallowers, velocipedists, champion skaters, imitators, marionettes, decanter equilibrists, champion shots, "living models of marble gems," "statue marvels," fire princes, "mysterious youths," "spiral bicycle ascensionsists," flying children, empresses of the air, kings of the wire, "vital sparks," "Mexican boneless wonders," white-eyed musical Kaffirs, strong-jawed ladies, cannon-ball performers, illuminated fountains, and that remarkable musical eccentricity the orchestre militaire, all have had their turn on the music-hall stage.

In addition to the Olympia, other New York vaudeville houses jumped on the music-hall bandwagon. At Tony Pastor's in the late 1880s and nineties you could find Marie Loftus (a great beauty and one of music hall's first stars, billed as "the Sarah Bernhardt of the Halls"), Little Tich (a character comedian who stood four feet six inches tall and did a humorous routine with shoes that were nearly as tall as he was), Vesta Victoria (considered the British Guilbert), and Vesta Tilley (the era's greatest drag king). Not to be outdone, Hammerstein's former partners Koster and Bial booked Marie Loftus's daughter, Cissie (a.k.a. the "Mimetic Marvel," vaudeville's premier impressionist), Marie Lloyd, (who despite hideous buckteeth was music hall's biggest star), Ada Reeve (a dignified actress in musical comedies), Albert Chevalier (a popular talking-singer, similar to what actors like Richard Harris and Rex Harrison would later do in musicals), and Lottie Collins (whose signature number "Ta-ra-ra-boom-de-ay" is still sung in grammar schools and summer camps throughout the land). Charles Chaplin, Sr. (Charlie's father), a minor star, could be found at Keith's Union Square singing his hit song "Eh, Boys?"

Like vaudeville, British music hall was born in saloons. Unlike vaudeville, it had made no decisive break with the past. It still maintained its old sensibility from the days of tavern singalongs, despite the fact that the shows were now taking place in massive two-thousand-seat auditoriums. Consequently, a much bawdier product was tolerated in music halls, full of "wink-wink, nudge-nudge, say no more, say no more" double entendre, which had the advantage of delighting those who got it, while completely eluding those who didn't. A sterling example was a number popularized in 1897 by Marie Lloyd:

> *She arrived in Euston by the midnight train*
> *But when she got to the wicket*
> *There someone wanted to punch her ticket.*
> *The guards and porters came round her by the score*
> *And she told them all she'd never had her ticket punched before.*

American audiences accepted the clever innuendo of British music-hall talent because it was foreign and therefore "cultural" (much as for years, crime dramas and situation comedies that are as bad as any American commercial TV have been presented on PBS). Respectability rather than morality was always the managers' guiding principle. Being businessmen, they went with the market, and in that conservative era the market was conservative. The instant a market opened up for racier material (as happened countless times over the decades), managers were happy enough to exploit it.

MAINTAINING THE ORIGINAL CUSTOMER BASE

Sex, as we have seen, permeated every theater in every nation in every age prior to the invention of vaudeville. Indeed, it continued to flourish in other areas of show business in the vaudeville era. Burlesque, which had grown up exactly parallel to vaudeville (so much so that many continue to confuse the two), was hinged upon the presence of a chorus of semiclad cuties. While the burlesque of the nineties and aughts was a much tamer business than what came later (no striptease, for example, and certainly no foul language), the pantaloons and stockings freely on display in the burlesque house and the crude innuendo of its baggy-panted comics were far more scandalous than anything permitted on the vaudeville stage. While many performers continued to shuttle back and forth between the two arenas, they always knew what was allowable in each.

The rules against vulgarity in vaudeville remained as much in force as they ever had been. But a whore in a chastity belt doth not make a nun. Slowly, stealthily, sexuality made its way back into the variety business, but cleverly cloaked so as to follow the letter of the company codes, which was a necessary thing, because, as you will recall, a quarter of the audience or more had come from the concert saloons. There was a variety of covers under which racy material could be introduced. As we have seen, British music-hall performers were allowed to freely engage in double entendre, perhaps because the cleaner-minded folks in the audience had no idea what was being laughed at. Furthermore, it was "cultural"—the performers were foreigners from three thousand miles away. If one was so inclined, one could feel morally superior to them without thinking that American vaudeville was rotten to the core.

Exoticism—that was the key. The way forward was foreshadowed by three distinct displays at the 1893 World Columbian Exposition in Chicago (the same fair that had inspired the Cherry Sisters to go into show business). Designed to celebrate the four hundredth anniversary of Columbus's first voyage to America (they were a year late), it was the largest world's fair ever mounted up until that time. Among its many marvels were the world's first Ferris wheel, a dazzling display of lights by Edison, and a couple of his inventions that will return to bedevil us later, the Kinetoscope and the talking cylinder. One of the acts on view was Eugene Sandow, Ziegfeld's strongman. (The success of this exhibition was what led to the later, more ambitious tour of the Trocadero Vaudevilles.) Outfitted in Roman garb and compared by his promoter to anything from the gladiators of old to Hercules himself, in addition to his feats of strength Sandow was on deck to showcase his buff body, flexing, preening, making his muscles "dance." Before and after the perfor-

mances, titillated females were allowed to approach the hulking speci-
men of German manhood and feel his rippling pecs. To prove that they
were real, you understand. A 1902 review of Sandow's act in the *New
York Dramatic Mirror* said of the performance that "if [it had been] attempted by any woman, [it] would be promptly suppressed."

As in the dime museums and the medicine shows, science was providing a useful rationale for the display of human flesh. It was billed as
the "Greatest Physical Lesson of the Age." The physical-culture angle
was one that many vaudevillians would exploit. Athletics required freedom of movement, which in turn required near nakedness. Acrobats appeared in minuscule outfits named after the original "Man on the Flying
Trapeze," the French aerialist Jules Léotard.

Across the midway from the Sandow exhibition, you could encounter
a still more explicit diversion at a pavilion known as "The Streets of Cairo."
There, a dancer known as Little Egypt clad in harem pants and a sheer top
that left her midriff exposed did a sexy, snakelike dance, wiggling her ab-
domen and writhing her arms whilst beguiling the male patrons with a
look of "come hither." Not since the days of Rome had large audiences of
Caucasians beheld such a spectacle, for even the dance hall girls were attired in a manner far more modest. Initially presented with an anthropo-
logical rationale, the exhibition's baser charms became its selling point
almost instantly, much as an issue of *National Geographic* in the hands of
a teenage boy becomes pornography. Her act, which raised the brows of
many, became known variously as the "belly dance," the "cooch dance,"
or the "hootchy-cootchy." By the following year it had become a national
craze, with scores of Little Egypts to be found in carnivals, dime museums, and amusement parks all over the country.

Just as Sandow and Little Egypt had introduced sex appeal to visi-
tors at the '93 Columbian Exposition, a third seminal display would
have similar repercussions, if in a more roundabout way. For at that
world's fair there occurred the first major demonstration of a new type of
music known as ragtime. The process of "ragging," or syncopating, a
tune had been common practice among African-American musicians for
decades. In the years of Reconstruction, many gained their first access
to pianos and serious musical training, and experimented with their
"broken" or "ragged" rhythms on that instrument. Juxtaposing an "oom-
pah" bass line derived from the German march (the most popular in-

strumental music of the day) with a melody in a completely different beat, the music was at once intricate and sophisticated, but also free-spirited and strangely intoxicating. Its foremost proponent, Scott Joplin, performed in minstrelsy and vaudeville, but disliked those worlds; he had more serious ambitions as a composer.

At the same time, all-black minstrel companies were traversing the country, producing a new crop of African-American stage performers. Out of this new ferment arose popular new dances like the breakdown and the cakewalk, tailor-made to go with the scintillating rhythms of ragtime; and the period saw new artists like Walker and Williams, Cole and Johnson, Will Marion Cook, Miller and Lyles, and Ernest Hogan, nearly all of whom, despite *being* black, wore blackface.

Hogan, known to vaudeville fans as "the Unbleached American," set off a new craze of his own with his 1896 ditty, the unbelievably titled "All Coons Look Alike to Me." Like the hundreds of Irish who earned their corned beef and cabbage lampooning fellow Irishmen, and the similar number of Jews who would, likewise, mock the foibles of their own people, African-American performers of the day were among the chief purveyors of negative racial stereotypes. The "coon songs," which were to remain a major staple of vaudeville for the next two decades, were built upon minstrelsy's old nostalgia for the plantation, while adding a racy yet derogatory element: the comical lyrics depicted a culture of infidelity, gambling, fights with razors, unemployment, and general shiftlessness. Numbers like "Those Chicken-Stealing Coons" and the infamous "If the Man in the Moon Were a Coon" enjoyed immense popularity among audiences of all races. The sheet music to these songs was illustrated with inky black characters with bugged-out eyes and lips like inner tubes, invariably attired as farmers, lying down at the base of a tree and eating watermelon. There can be little doubt that they were performed with similar art direction.

The team of Walker and Williams cakewalked to fame performing such tunes, becoming vaudeville's first African-American stars as "Two Real Coons." The West Indian–born Egbert Austin Williams began performing in 1893 in an attempt to earn money for college. He started out in the rough-and-tumble world of Barbary Coast saloons, where his poise, dignity, and class were only handicaps. A subsequent tour of lumber camps, where he performed skits and songs fared hardly better. In these years, he gradually came to understand—to his horror—the racist expectations of his audience, and that, in order to be a success, he would have to stoop to portraying the sort of low stereotype that white people expected. While Williams was light-complected, African features predominated—to the audience he was a "black man," and in America, "black men" behaved a certain way. The problem was that Williams was well-educated, upper-middle-class, and sophisticated. To make a success in show business, he actually had to struggle to learn what was to him an alien dialect and mannerisms.

In these early years, Williams displayed few of the gifts for which he was later distinguished. No great shakes as a singer, dancer, musician (he played banjo), or comedian, his considerable intelligence managed to carry him through. With his evolving new "darky" persona, he started getting his first decent bookings, first a few months at the San Francisco Museum, then with Martin and Seig's Mastodon Minstrels.

It is at this early and embryonic juncture that Williams met George Walker, who though a year younger than Bert was already a veteran of minstrel and medicine shows. The two hit it off and worked up an act. George sang a song, "See Yer Colored Man," while Bert played banjo. Bert was the straight man in their first crude comedy routines. For nearly two years (1893–95) the two performed their songs and skits at Jack Halahan's Cramorne Theatre (later known as the Midway Plaisance).

The team next traveled to Chicago for a week's tryout in a show titled *The Octoroon*—but they flopped and were let go. The setback provided them with an opportunity to take stock of their act and make some improvements. In the next few months, they developed the basic characteristics that would make them world famous.

First, Williams decided to "black up." It was common for African-Americans to wear blackface in those days. In fact, that was how blacks broke into show business in the first place, by performing minstrel shows as "genuine coons." As with so many performers, the blackface seemed to work a miracle on the naturally shy and introverted Williams—it released his inhibitions and freed him up to be funny. He finally let go of his dignity (which is a fine thing for a man to possess, but a handicap for a clown) and started going for the belly laughs. The character he became known for was a loser, a sort of shabby, pessimistic Everyman in threadbare clothes, or as he sang in one of his more popular songs, "The Jonah Man"—the guy to whom everything bad happens. By contrast, Walker played a flashy dude in smart clothes, a ladies' man, a talker, a schemer, the eternal optimist, and the motivating force behind the plots of all their stories. The two characters were, of course, exaggerations of the men's actual personalities. The team is credited with introducing the cakewalk into mainstream America (evolved from the minstrel show walkaround, it would become a popular dance). Comical dancing became a highlight of their act, Walker high-stepping and lively, Williams, shuffling and clumsy.

So popular were the "Two Real Coons" that in 1898 they played every one of New York's major vaudeville houses: Koster and Bial's, Proctor's Twenty-third Street, Hammerstein's Olympia, Tony Pastor's Fourteenth Street, and Keith's Union Square. Successful as Walker and Williams were, however, it would be decades before African-Americans were a common sight on a vaudeville stage.

Just as the early blackface minstrels had copped their dances and vocal stylings from African-Americans, a new generation of white performers blacked up and started doing cakewalks and coon songs. Because the material was comic, and because the laughs came at the expense of a culture possessed of freer and franker attitudes toward sexuality than was the norm among the mostly white audience, sly references to the characters' sex lives could be permitted. Similarly, the high-stepping, fast-paced cakewalk was a crucial deviation from the previous tradition of genteel, almost rigid dance represented by the waltz and the even more stodgy steps it had displaced. Thus did the breach in the Puritan bulwark widen a little further.

One of the earliest white vaudevillians to strike out in this direction was a young girl from Chicago named Louise Josephine Kerlin. An aspiring singer, she chanced to meet Paul Dresser, a famous writer of coon songs and brother of the novelist Theodore Dreiser.* At age eighteen, Louise became Dresser's protégée and, at his instigation, changed her name to Dresser, pretending to be his sister. Throughout her vaudeville career, audiences and journalists believed this to be the case. The feigned relationship was to their mutual benefit; Louise sang all of his songs, helping to make them as famous as she was. The act was known

---

*See Dreiser's *Sister Carrie* for a wonderful snapshot of women's place in the theater and in society in the early twentieth century.

as Louise Dresser and Her Picks. The "picks" were "pickaninnies," actual black children with little pigtails and overalls who danced and backed her up on the numbers, a popular convention at the time. Some of the greatest African-American acts in vaudeville, such as Willie Covan, Florence Mills, and Bill "Bojangles" Robinson broke into the business as picks. Picks were supposed to be cute and they undoubtedly were, but the word "pickaninny" dates from slavery times and derives from the fact that those tiny children were put to work picking cotton from dawn to dusk. To the modern sensibility, the concept is more horrible than adorable.

Dresser was hardly the only young lady of her generation to stoop to such an act. In 1906, a young Sophie Tucker got one of her first breaks in the 125th Street Theatre. Because she was on the heavy side, a clever stage manager decided she ought to do her material in blackface. Thus did this nice Jewish girl from Hartford come to be billed variously as "the World-renowned Coon Shouter," "the Ginger Girl, Refined Coon Singer," and "Manipulator of Coon Melodies," performing a repertoire that included "Why Was I Ever Born Lazy?" and "Rosie, My Dusky Georgie Rosie."

Mae West also got her start as a blackface coon shouter. As a young girl in Greenpoint, Brooklyn, Mae had two favorite vaudeville performers: Eva Tanguay and Bert Williams. Her mother, who was to manage her early career, actually urged Mae to study Tanguay, whom they went to see at the theater many times, perhaps kindling the girl's latent sex instincts at a younger age than most people would think appropriate. And so great was Mae's regard for Williams that her father (a boxer with show-business connections), actually invited the famous performer to their house.

At age eight, Mae was already doing her impressions of Tanguay and Williams in neighborhood amateur nights. In her early teens, she merged the two and became a coon shouter, mixing blackface with a sexy Tanguay-esque approach, and performing tunes with titles like "Lovin' Honey Man."

The mania for coon songs was so terrific that for a while such stars of the legit and musical comedy stages as Fay Templeton, May Irwin, and Marie Dressler blacked up and performed them in vaudeville. But the vogue was short-lived. In the second decade of the twentieth-century, strong criticism from the newly formed National Association for the Advancement of Colored People (NAACP) and various other groups helped put an end to what is probably the most callously racist phase of American entertainment history. It would soon be replaced by a type of song that was musically identical, but with lyrics at once less racist and a good deal sexier.

MEASURES OF SUCCESS

The late nineteenth century saw vaudeville at the vanguard of a host of brand-new entertainment alternatives, which also included amusement parks, published sheet music and song recordings, dance crazes, nickelodeons, and professional sports. A bellwether for the spirit of the era was the extent to which vaudeville and the new national craze—major league baseball—cross-fertilized each other. In 1888, newspaperman Ernest Thayer wrote the immortal poem "Casey at the Bat." Later that year legit thespian DeWolf Hopper (husband of columnist Hedda Hopper) began performing it on vaudeville stages and was such a smash in his interpretation that he performed it more than ten thousand times over the next quarter-century. In 1908, vaudeville songwriters Jack Norworth and Albert von Tilzer wrote their most enduring song, "Take Me Out to the Ball Game," still sung every season in ballparks throughout the country, but once also a staple of the vaudeville stage. Certain performers were known to work in both arenas. In 1911, the New York Giants' feebleminded mascot Charlie Faust played vaudeville houses in New York with an act said to rank with the Cherry Sisters'. In 1922, after being suspended from the Yankees for throwing mud at an umpire, Babe Ruth toured the circuits. Conversely, between gigs as an acrobat, the young Joe E. Brown earned a living as a minor-league ballplayer. So hungry was the public for amusement that a man could maintain two separate careers in entirely different entertainment fields.

Yet all roads led to vaudeville. Music publisher Edward Marks observed that a show-business revolution occurred between 1896 and 1906, measurable in the concomitant explosion in his own business.

That rapid change, he said, was caused by the emergence of the vaudeville industry.

In the post–Civil War era, sheet music was sold primarily for what was then the most popular form of national entertainment among the middle class: domestic piano playing. The popularity of songs depended upon advertising and word of mouth. Vaudeville was a means of transmitting a popular song nationwide. The ditty usually credited with starting the song-publishing bonanza that was to become known as Tin Pan Alley was Charles K. Harris's 1892 composition "After the Ball." In the 1890s, a vaudeville act like the Manhattan Comedy Four (featuring the Marx Brothers' uncle, Al Shean) would take a number like "After the Ball" and perform it from coast to coast. If the act did two shows a day, six days a week, forty weeks a year (admittedly a best-case scenario) the tune might reach close to half a million people. Thousands of song sheets could be sold this way. So great were the profits to be made off this ancillary business that publishers began hiring "song pluggers"— that is, paying vaudeville singers to sing their songs onstage: and thus payola was born. The first performer to have taken this devil's bargain was one Lottie Gilson, "The Little Magnet," a popular rabble-rouser of the eighties and nineties. It soon became common practice throughout the industry.

Nearly two decades into its existence, vaudeville had evolved into a formidable business. By the turn of the twentieth century, vaudeville was already outstripping the very forms of entertainment that had played so large a role in its genesis. Traveling medicine shows (which in the nineteenth century were said to "abound like the locusts in Egypt") were now down to just over a hundred in number, and there were just ten traveling minstrel shows, a handful of dime museums, and virtually no concert saloons (although plenty of bars).

By 1900, there were two thousand vaudeville theaters in the United States, including all the small-time houses. This accounted for half the theaters in the country. New York had thirty-one, Chicago twenty-two, and Philadelphia thirty. Yet vaudeville was still in its chrysalis stage. And, in scale at least, what would emerge would be more Mothra than moth.

4

TOOTH AND NAIL

By the late nineteenth century, the relatively benign materialistic philosophy of Smith, Locke, Bacon, and America's Founding Fathers that had provided an argument for "rational amusement" had given way in the popular mind to a philosophy far less altruistic. The leading lights of the era were now Charles Darwin and Herbert Spencer. Spencer's watchword "survival of the fittest" was all too eagerly picked up by ambitious American entrepreneurs, grateful for the deterministic justification the Theory of Evolution gave them for behaving like animals. Just as in a state of nature the lion will pick off the weakest gazelle, in vaudeville, the hook would relieve the audience of the torture of sitting through a show's weakest act. The history of vaudeville (and its history is not so unique) is one of all-out war, pitting managers against managers, acts against acts, acts against managers, managers against agents, big time against small time, and vaudeville against competing modes of entertainment.

Such a situation made the old struggle of show business versus the powers of church and state seem quaint by comparison. That had merely been a battle for the right to exist. Now, the war, fought on a thousand fronts, would be to determine who of the countless competitors would be biggest, richest, most famous. As you might expect, there were many winners, but more losers. And there's only room for one in first place.

Like "vaudeville," the phrase "big time" has become generic and vague—essentially meaning "at the apex of one's field." It once meant something very specific: a circuit of high-prestige vaudeville theaters throughout the country where the nation's biggest stars played. It was, not surprisingly, controlled by a very small handful of men as a virtual monopoly. In a span of forty years, B. F. Keith's chain would grow from four to four hundred theaters, swallowing almost all of the other chains whole, eventually dominating the entire industry. Before that the Keith organization sat at the head of the cartel that dictated industry-wide policies. For most of vaudeville's existence, therefore, "big time" was, in many ways, Keith Time.

FORMING THE COMBINE, PHASE ONE

Keith and Albee—in the entire annals of the vaudeville industry, in the thousands of pages written on the subject, in hundreds of accounts and testimonies by as many people, no one ever said a kind word about either one of these New England circus hustlers whose veins ran with ice water. It would take a Dickens to delineate these characters. Like any good melodrama villains, they (and their many cohorts) hid their names behind initials, then hid their bodies behind enormous desks, in front of which a summoned performer was made to stand, cowering and fidgeting while the great manager meted out punishments and rewards. With very little imagination one can envision these mustachioed blackguards tying vaudevillians to railroad tracks and sending them down conveyor belts toward whirring buzz saws.

Keith, with his walrus mustache and capacious forehead, looked like the evil twin of a silent-film comedian. "I never trust a man I can't buy," he once said. Of the beady-eyed, narrow-skulled Albee, former employee Marion Spitzer recalled: "Scarcely anyone mentions E. F. Albee without intense bitterness . . . Mr. Albee, with his relentless air of holiness, was totally without humor and grim-visaged as he wielded his destructive power." Groucho Marx once called him "vaudeville's Torquemada," referencing one of the cruelest architects of the Spanish Inquisition.

Some of the things Keith and Albee said and did beggar belief, but there it is, time and time again, proof of their perverse, matter-of-fact villainy. And yet the product they made was vaudeville. How strange. It is as though Santa Claus were secretly Satan.

Take, for example, a famous conversation that took place in 1899 between the young George M. Cohan (by now the manager of the family's act), and B. F. Keith. As Cohan recorded it, when the family showed up at the theater, they found themselves way down on the billing on the sign out front. When Cohan went up to the office to protest, this is what he got:

KEITH: Well, I'm sorry. It's some mistake, some press agent's or sign painter's mistake, not mine.

COHAN: It isn't mine, either.

KEITH: What are you going to do?

COHAN: What would you do in my position?

KEITH: If I'd been associated with a man as long as you people have with me, I'd certainly go through for him.

COHAN: Well, Mr. Keith, I haven't any particularly fond memories of you. The only thing I can recall in the early days of Keith is a lot of hard work, a lot of extra performances, a lot of confinement, six and seven and eight shows a day, running up eighty and ninety steps to the dressing rooms, and a million rules and regulations hanging all over the place. Any time you wanted to smoke you had to go into a little tin closet. So the nice little speech you just made to me, inviting me to go through with the broken contractual conditions, doesn't mean much. Besides, Mr. Keith, I remember a little incident in Providence on a Saturday night. You didn't have enough to meet the payroll. And you came back to ask us if we'd mind waiting until the following Tuesday or Wednesday. And my father, Jerry, said, "Why, no, if you're short, and maybe we could lend you a little money, and how much do you want?" And you said about $600 and we let you have it.

KEITH: I don't remember it.

COHAN: Another thing you probably don't realize, Mr. Keith, is

> that we are getting a whole lot more money in outside book-
> ing than we did when we signed this contract three years ago.
>
> KEITH: Oh, that's the idea. You want more money.
>
> COHAN: Yes, a whole lot more.
>
> KEITH: I understand now; it's a shakedown.
>
> COHAN: Call it what you like, Mr. Keith, but just because of that
> crack, I'll make you a promise right now—that no member of
> the Cohan family will ever play for you again as long as you
> are in the theatrical business.

The Cohan family was fortunate to have its own built-in bulldog in the person of George. Plucky as he naturally was, conditions in 1899 permitted him to be still pluckier. When he vowed his family would never play a Keith theater again (and they never did), he could afford to make that threat. He knew he could take the act elsewhere.

In addition to the Keith and Proctor chains, a number of others had emerged to capitalize on the thriving new industry. Like prospectors staking out claims, aspiring managers began seizing territory in various parts of the country in which to build their vaudeville empires.

Sylvester Poli, an Italian sculptor of wax figures, immigrated to the United States to work at New York's Eden Musée in 1881. (Like Vincent Price's *House of Wax*, this was one of those "educational" institutions that edified the public with lifelike representations of famous murderers and historical tyrants.) Within the decade, Poli was ready to branch out on his own, opening his first dime museum in Toronto. Soon the variety shows he presented as an added attraction were more popular than the wax exhibitions. In 1892 he moved to New Haven, Connecticut. His first theater space there had been a free-and-easy concert saloon run by two veterans of the Kickapoo Medicine Shows. Poli cleaned the place up, switching it over to High Class Vaudeville (but not before presenting a dog-faced man, Siamese twins, and a giantess; old habits die hard, as we well know). Poli's New Haven became the base for a vaudeville empire that would extend throughout New England and New York State. Connecticut in particular became Poli's stomping grounds, with theaters in Hartford, New Haven, Bridgeport, and Waterbury.

Poli was a notorious skinflint who would respond to all monetary requests by whining. Yet although he didn't pay big-time salaries, his theaters often featured big-time talent because acts would take a Poli date at the last minute if they had nothing better. The proximity to New York made it convenient for such last-minute jaunts. As a result, Poli could never advertise specific artists in advance, yet audiences knew they could generally expect to see a high-caliber performer at his theaters. It was at Poli's Hartford house, for example, that a young Sophie Tucker had seen and been inspired by the likes of Willie and Eugene Howard, and the Empire City Quartette—big names at the time. Poli's New Haven, with its clique of inebriated Yale men, was notorious for rowdyism. This mob of young worthies once erupted into a show-stopping riot during a Mae West performance necessitating a call to the police. On another occasion, a pack of these fraternal mugs so annoyed Joe Keaton that he picked up Buster and threw him at them, clobbering three and breaking the nose of another. Buster, who was accustomed to being employed as a missile, was unhurt. If nothing else, Poli's Yale audience demonstrated that the sins of the old variety had less to do with class than everyone thought.

In Chicago, the firm of Kohl and Middleton began buying and building museums and vaudeville theaters at a great rate in the early 1880s. In 1900, C. E. Kohl bought out his partner, George Middleton, and went in with one of his theater managers, George Castle. Kohl and Castle would dominate the vaudeville business in Chicago, the Twin Cities, and the Midwest in general. Both men were taciturn and unapproachable—especially Kohl, who was hardly ever to be seen in one of his own theaters. Castle, the booker, on the other hand, communicated in one- and two-word sentences when he bothered to address his acts at all. Yet they were to build an impressive empire of Chicago vaud houses, comprising the Olympic, the Majestic, the Haymarket, the Chicago Opera House, the Academy of Music, and the Star. Of these, the Majestic was said to have been the most beloved. Comedian Jack Benny, a Waukegan, Illinois, native, described it as "the most beautiful, perhaps the most dignified theater in the world." A contemporary writer praised it for its "order, system, regularity, cleanliness and effectiveness"— highly prized traits in the culture of the day.

Meanwhile, a young Czech performer named Martin Beck had been touring the Americas with a German singing and juggling troupe. Stranded by his company in Chicago at the time of the World's Fair, he took a job as a waiter in music halls, working his way up to bartender, and finally to booker. (Thanks to his career trajectory he was sometimes referred derogatorily as "Two Beers" Beck.) By the late 1890s, Beck was managing Schiller's Vaudeville, a touring company, which brought him out to San Francisco, where he next began to manage the Orpheum for Morris Meyerfeld, playing Albee to Meyerfeld's Keith. (This same Orpheum is immortalized in the 1899 Frank Norris novel *McTeague*. It, and every other San Francisco theater, would be destroyed in the great 1906 earthquake.) Under the Orpheum rubric, Beck and Meyerfeld began snatching up theaters throughout the West at a pace that rivaled Proctor's.

Beck's technique was to partner with local businessmen in each new market. These collaborators would have important inside knowledge about the best local contractors, how to go about getting necessary permits, and which palms would need to be greased to move the enterprise forward.

Beck was an unusual character among the managers. In a field dominated by predictable men of reserve, Beck managed to become one of the most successful despite an erratic, volatile personality. He was known, simultaneously, for being insulting and cruel to those under him, as well as for his openness and generosity. The perfect example merging those two traits was an occasion when he learned an acrobatic trio booked for his circuit had accepted the paltry sum of $175 for a week at one of his theaters. Beck proceeded to berate the act, insisting that they ought to be ashamed of themselves and not take less than $350. It's an odd boss indeed who humiliates his employees for *not* asking him for a raise.

Beck's other major eccentricity was his highbrow pretensions. One of the best bookers in the business, the owl-like, multilingual Beck also stubbornly insisted on booking opera singers, classical musicians, and ballet dancers, even if sometimes he was the only one in the audience who appreciated them. He considered it his responsibility to educate the audience.

He nevertheless had a fine instinct for crowd-pleasing, as evidenced by two of his early major discoveries: Harry Houdini and W. C. Fields. In 1899, Houdini and his wife, Bess, were barely eking out a living in circuses and dime museums when Beck booked him for the Orpheum circuit. Under Beck's management, Houdini went from being a fairly run-of-the-mill magician to "the Handcuff King," vaudeville's premier escape artist, beloved by audiences for his uncanny ability to work his way out of handcuffs, shackles, knotted ropes, straitjackets, locked trunks, bank vaults, and jail cells. In a matter of months, Houdini's weekly salary went from $25 to $250 (and ere long would be ten times that).

The following year, a young W. C. Fields was still bumbling around small-time vaudeville and burlesque. In 1900, Fields was one of any number of "tramp jugglers," silent clownish entertainers in hobo garb who worked the circuits, keeping as many household objects aloft as they knew how. One of the best in the business, Fields would juggle hats, cigar boxes—anything he could get his hands on. Beck took him into the Orpheum at almost twice his previous salary and shipped him out to San Francisco, where he performed on a bill with the magician Howard Thurston and Mr. and Mrs. Sydney Drew. Fields's Orpheum travels brought him also to Denver, Omaha, and Kansas City—evidence of Beck's reach even at that early stage.

While Poli, Kohl and Castle, and Beck and Meyerfeld were building their local fiefdoms, new competition was also heating up in New York. In addition to Pastor's, Proctor's, Keith's, Koster and Bial's, and Hammerstein's major houses, the field was continuing to widen. In 1896, vaudeville's biggest comedy stars, Weber and Fields, started their own Music Hall (leased from Henry Miner) at the corner of Twenty-ninth Street and Broadway, not far from Proctor's Twenty-third Street and Koster and Bial's. No fans of continuous vaudeville, Weber and Fields put on all-star variety bills plus an afterpiece. In a few years, as Harrigan and Hart had done, the company would drop the olio and extend the afterpieces out to full-length Broadway vehicles. But at first, they were vaudeville competitors.

Meanwhile, F. F. Proctor had continued to expand at his usual muscular rate, adding two former Hammerstein opera houses, the Harlem and the Columbia (renamed the 125th Street Theatre) to his vaudeville holdings, as well as the Fifth Avenue Theatre (located, illogically, at Broadway and Twenty-eighth Street). The latter theater was to surpass the Twenty-third Street as Proctor's flagship, and indeed became one of the most important vaudeville houses in New York, providing big-time debuts for the likes of singer Nora Bayes, Fred and Adele Astaire, English actress Lily Langtry, trick cyclist Joe Jackson, Australian diver Annette Kellerman, and faux Russian singer-actress Olga Petrova, among countless others.

With all of these managers and theaters crowding the field, vaudeville was fast becoming a seller's market from the point of view of talent. Weekly salaries (which had been in the $50–$75 range) crept up into three figures and continued to surge upward. Because of the competition, the bold and aggressive vaudevillian stood to make unprecedented amounts of money. In this business climate, it became advantageous for talent to hire an entirely new species of show-business entrepreneur, a professional liaison between the acts and the vaudeville managers known as the "agent." Agents were in the business of spotting talent and bringing it to the attention of the vaudeville bookers. For their efforts, they got a 5 percent cut of an artist's salary. Like the busking performers before them, agents started out as itinerants, officeless, cutting their deals on the Rialto sidewalks or over lunch at nearby restaurants. But in due course, their profits allowed them the luxury of offices and staffs, another measure of the industry's magnitude. The atmosphere of these offices can be imagined: the waiting room packed with bizarre and eccentric performers anticipating their chance to see the Big Man, auditioning on the spot if they had to, whether they had the agent's permission or not.

Of the two dozen or so agents who worked in New York in the 1890s, the most prominent was William Morris, eponymous founder of the agency still thriving today. A German Jewish immigrant (born Zelman Moses), Morris sold advertising before prevailing on M. B. Leavitt, a distant relative, to provide him with an introduction to George Liman, then vaudeville's top agent. Morris clerked for him, quickly becoming his right-hand man. When Liman died in 1898, Morris hung out his own shingle, "William Morris: Vaudeville Agent," and went on to book acts for Poli, Hammerstein, Proctor, and, in the early years, even Keith. His stable would, at various times, include Al Jolson, Eddie Cantor, Sophie Tucker, the Marx Brothers, Sir Harry Lauder—nearly every big name in show business. As an advocate for these artists, Morris would grow to be a rich and powerful man—one in direct conflict with the interests of the vaudeville managers.

The emergence of all the new vaudeville circuits, the success of the big touring vaudeville shows, and the arrival of booking agents who negotiated better salaries on behalf of the performers were all thorns in the side of Keith and Albee. Thus far in our narrative, after seventeen years of vaudeville management, B. F. Keith and E. F. Albee have been but one partnership in a pack, possessing four showplace theaters in four key northeastern cities. But ah—beware the sleeping dragon! For this very blandness, this undistinguished quality has a notable analogue: the career of Joseph Stalin, that obscure party functionary who came to rule the Soviet Union through the lethal combination of careful, quiet plotting, and outward banality. So Keith had four houses and now competition was increasing for audiences, houses, and acts. Such moments are turning points; from this point on, had Keith not seized the initiative he may have been one of history's footnotes. But then the Grinch got a *wonderful, awful idea.*

It was the age of big combinations. John D. Rockefeller had formed Standard Oil, his oil-refining monopoly, back in 1882. U.S. Steel would soon be formed, a conglomeration formed out of Andrew Carnegie and Rockefeller interests, and overseen by J. P. Morgan. In Chicago, Armour and Swift combined to make up the Beef Trust. Then there was Bell Telephone, Western Union, and, of course, the railroads. Early in the twentieth century, it seemed as though the production and delivery of every major American good and service was monopolized by a trust. The Sherman Anti-Trust Act (1890) had theoretically made such activity illegal, but it would be years before Theodore Roosevelt would actually begin to enforce that legislation.

The pioneers of theatrical monopoly were Marc Klaw and Abraham Lincoln Erlanger. With evil-sounding names like "Klaw and Erlanger," they just had to be villains. Erlanger (who decorated his offices with portraits and busts of his hero Napoléon Bonaparte) had once been employed as an agent, PR man, and manager. Klaw had been a drama critic, a lawyer for the Frohman Brothers, and a theatrical booking agent. In 1896 they formed "the Syndicate" with four other producers, in an attempt to obtain the monopoly on legit theater throughout the United States. Any producer who wanted to put on a play, and any theater manager who wanted to book one, had to go through them, for they owned most of the theaters as well as the booking exchange that supplied the circuit with shows. In essence, by pooling their resources, the producers of the Syndicate had come up with an *Über*-circuit for the legitimate stage.

In 1900, Buffalo vaud manager Pat Shea got the idea that his industry ought to do something similar, and he brought the notion to Keith and Albee. In May of that year, they called together a meeting at their headquarters in Boston that would include Weber and Fields, Tony Pastor, Hyde and Behman (who ruled Brooklyn at the time), Kohl and Castle, Colonel J. D. Hopkins (who ran a string of vaudeville houses and amusement parks in the Midwest), and Orpheum's Meyerfeld and Beck. Conspicuously absent from this meeting was Keith's chief rival, F. F. Proctor, presumably a punishment for his many crimes against the Keith organization. The other managers wouldn't stand for Proctor's exclusion, however, forcing Keith and Albee to reschedule the meeting for New York.

The meeting resulted in the establishment of a cartel, the Vaudeville Managers Association. The VMA's formation was ostensibly to effect "the elimination of harmful competition." Specifically, this competition had come in two forms: bidding wars for popular acts (driving up the cost of talent for everybody and largely the handiwork of the agents) and turf wars where two or more organizations butted heads in order to grab the same audience.

At first, nearly every manager balked at the concept of joining. Co-operation would mean electing a president, and that president would almost certainly be B. F. Keith, thus forcing all of the other managers into subordinate positions. The ultimate lure for all of them, however, was undoubtedly the promise of greater profits to be gained by developing a brand-new revenue stream. In the present picture, the managers controlled the vaudeville houses—that was their reason for being in business. The talent was an unorganized outside element, contracted on an as-needed basis. A new angle was now proposed . . . to control not only the theaters but the performers as well.

Instead of working with an independent booking agent, the acts would have their entire routes laid out for them by a circuit's central booking office. For the privilege of the centralized booking service and steady work, the performers would kick back 5 percent of their pay to the VMA. The 5 percent was no more than they had paid to the agents, but with a crucial difference: the agents were working on behalf of the performers; the managers were working for themselves. The VMA could hardly be relied on, for example, to negotiate for better salaries and conditions for the performers. Indeed, Edward Albee expressed his real view of the matter at a meeting of his fellow managers in no uncertain terms: "Those damn actors have been sticking it into me for many years. Now I'm going to stick it into them—and harder!" Whether or not he twirled his mustache when he said this is not recorded. Acts were entitled to retain agents to negotiate with the bookers, but of course that would mean paying out an additional percentage of their salary. And certain major agents, such as William Morris, would gradually be blackballed.

This new system presupposed a certain model of vaudeville organization, one in which acts were booked as individual components. As we have seen, though, Tony Pastor, Weber and Fields, and Hyde and Behman preferred to tour whole companies of stars. That modus operandi was doomed under the new regime. Keith had fought the competing system for years, making his theaters unavailable to the popular Weber and Fields touring units. Such vaudeville companies tied up whole theaters for weeks. This was bound to foul up the lucrative new system of individual acts, each paying a 5 percent kickback. The existence of the VMA now assured that the member venues would be unavailable to touring shows. Managers would either adjust to the new system or lose out. And that's what happened. Hyde and Behman and Tony Pastor would soon pass into history. Weber and Fields would concentrate solely on the production of musical comedies. The VMA was now the preeminent power in the vaudeville industry.

The VMA divided the country into two spheres of influence: the Western Vaudeville Managers Association, overseen by Chicago-based manager J. J. Murdock, and consisting of the Orpheum Circuit, Kohl and Castle, and some smaller players; and the Eastern Vaudeville Managers Association, made up of everybody else, and overseen by Keith and Albee.

Murdock had proven his worth by making a success of the Masonic Temple Roof in Chicago. His masterpiece of promotion had been the furor he created over "The Girl with the Auburn Hair." She didn't do anything, she had no talent, no one knew who she was, she was just . . ."The Girl with the Auburn Hair." With no more description than this, Murdock managed to generate sufficient interest to sell thousands of tickets, largely by spilling countless tons of printer's ink in the form of newspaper ads and handbills. (Incidentally, the woman turned out to be his girlfriend, whom he presented onstage as a "living statue." Nice work if you can get it!)

Ostensibly an "Association" of equals, the VMA followed policies largely dictated by the coercive Keith and Albee. In the face of this inevitability, F. F. Proctor was a vocal dissenter. But he, like the other managers, saw the wisdom of banding together against the performers. He joined but could tolerate Keith's dominance only for about a year or so, before finally jumping ship. After his departure, Proctor would book his acts through independent agents like William Morris.

Another monkey wrench in the VMA machine was a troublesome newcomer by the name of Percy G. Williams. The son of a prosperous doctor, Williams had entered show business as an actor in melodramas, touring with his own production of *Uncle Tom's Cabin* and playing parts with various companies. His entrepreneurial bent emerged when he cooked up a medicine show to hawk herb bags prepared by his father. He started out busking with a spiel on the street, then began booking halls and mounting full variety shows to sell these hokey cures. The profits from the medicine bags enabled Williams, in partnership with chewing-gum magnate Thomas Adams, Jr., to build a Brooklyn amusement park in 1893 known as Bergen Beach. The addition of a casino (the word "casino" at the turn of the last century merely meant "pleasure resort" and didn't necessarily imply gambling) to the park three years later represents Williams's first experimentation with professional vaudeville, although his 1895 purchase of a plot of land in downtown Brooklyn shows he already had big plans. On that parcel, in 1901, he opened what was then considered to be the most beautiful theater in the world, the Orpheum, at Fulton Street and Broadway in Brooklyn. In the meantime, he had taken over the old Brooklyn Music Hall (later renamed the Gotham) and made it his own.

Williams was becoming a power. And he, too, was a VMA holdout. A naturally sweet and generous man, he infuriated Keith and Albee by paying large salaries (thus driving up the general cost of acts) and otherwise treating his performers like human beings.

Nor did the performers themselves take Keith's challenge lying down. They responded almost instantaneously by creating a union and negotiating for the retraction of the despised 5 percent commission. The vaudeville performers' union was founded by comedian and prize-fighter George Fuller Golden. Golden was one of the top stars of early American vaudeville. Joe Laurie, Jr., called him America's first intellectual monologist. His voracious reading in the classics (especially poetry) and biblical literature combined with his natural Irish blarney to produce a popular series of stories about an imaginary friend named Casey, whose adventures audiences followed with great delight. But Golden also had a serious side, a sense of fair play and justice that was bound to get him into trouble in a high-stakes arena like vaudeville. Part boxer, part idealist, he was just the sort of man to go down in a losing battle.

In 1899, Golden had been the beneficiary of the services of the Water Rats, England's music-hall performers' union, when his wife had fallen sick in London and he had gone without work for months. The Water Rats had paid his doctor bills and other expenses, and helped him and his wife get back to the States. Recalling his experience in England, when the managers formed the VMA, Golden knew just what to do. In short order he organized a leadership committee to form the White Rats, enlisting a large dues-paying membership and starting their own booking office. In early 1901, the performers, getting nowhere in negotiations with the managers, struck.

The Western managers folded almost immediately; in the East, Keith houses were without vaudeville for two weeks. Meantime, the sympathetic William Morris booked acts in non-VMA houses like Proctor's Fifth Avenue, Hammerstein's Victoria, and Percy Williams's Brooklyn houses. The VMA seemed to be over a barrel. But battles can be won or lost on the word "seem." When it came to giving performances, the actors of the White Rats had nothing on Messrs. Keith and Albee. Summoned into the august presence of Keith himself, a delegation of union reps was told that he was against the 5 percent commission, had been so all along, and that it had always been the idea of the other managers. In fact, said Keith, the managers had a meeting coming up in a few weeks. He would (he promised the performers) bring the matter up at that meeting as a formality, and the commission was sure to be abolished. The White Rats left the powwow convinced that they had won.

To seal the deal, Keith even announced as much to the papers, making the benevolence of the managers a matter of public record.

One of the lessons of history is that the audacious lie is the most potent kind. The well-meaning dupe on the short end tells himself, "This can't be a lie—no one could stoop *that* low." Sure they would.

Having announced a White Rat victory, the managers slowly, quietly, began to entice individual acts back into the fold with better contracts, though still very much on their own terms. The VMA could promise an act forty weeks of work, after all. Furthermore, the White Rats charged their own dues and booking commission and were administratively incompetent to boot. Despite his patronymic, Golden had little affinity for managing the precious metal. Big payouts were available to union members who were "in need." Lo and behold, money flew out of the White Rats treasury faster than it could be replaced by the dwindling membership. Golden's problem was that he was a pussycat and a dreamer. But running a union is a constant war. To win, the leader must be the equal (or superior) of management in ruthlessness. Someone who has a high opinion of human nature—an idealist—is lost, utterly lost. He'll get taken every time. Golden would later castigate himself for not seeing "the ridiculous futility of appealing with such sentiments as truth, justice or fair play, in this present age of Iron and Gold." The White Rats collapsed, and Golden became a laughingstock in the business, never working as a leader or an entertainer again. He died in 1912 of tuberculosis, a charity case.

Coincidentally, at around the time of the heroic White Rats debacle, the performers' other brave champion, William Morris, contracted tuberculosis. In 1900 he went into retirement (from which he would later emerge), leaving the VMA free to grow unhampered. Most of the managers joined the Association, but plenty continued to do their own thing, regardless.

Percy Williams, for example, followed up his membership in the VMA by building a chain of first-class vaudeville houses in the middle of Manhattan and continuing to pay top dollar for them, actions completely antagonistic to Keith's aims in founding the Association in the first place. In 1903, he built the Circle Theatre (on Columbus Circle), then purchased the nearby Colonial (built by Coney Island impresarios Frederic Thompson and Elmer S. Dundee, architects and owners of

Luna Park), and the Alhambra (an oriental-themed theater located in Harlem). This Proctor-like behavior drove Keith into a tizzy, and he threw Williams out of the VMA. Williams responded by building opposition houses in the Keith strongholds of Boston and Philadelphia. Keith caved in and invited Williams back. Williams's empire would eventually grow to thirty theaters, including, in addition to the ones previously mentioned, the Royal in the Bronx, and the Novelty, the Crescent, the Greenpoint, the Flatbush, and the Prospect in Brooklyn.

The most fondly remembered of all these was the Colonial. Like Tony Pastor's and the now-defunct Koster and Bial's, the Colonial was designed by Thompson and Dundee to resemble a British music hall. After only two months of management, the gentlemen sold the property to Williams, who proceeded to fulfill the promise of the place by engaging the era's top British music-hall talent: Vesta Victoria, Vesta Tilley, Charles Hawtrey (a legitimate stage actor later immortalized by John Lennon's reference to him on the Beatles' *Let It Be* album), Marie Lloyd and her sister Alice, and many others trod the stage of the Colonial, making Williams the first circuit-owning manager to venture into so costly an arena.

The Hell's Kitchen audience of the Colonial, perhaps egged on by the risqué songs of the London talent, became notorious for their unruly behavior. They invented the "Colonial Clap," an unnervingly slow clap delivered by the audience in unison in order to drive a performer from the stage. Only performers with an iron stomach or an irresistible charm could face this audience. Consequently, the Colonial presented some of the finest shows in the business. Only the spectacular could survive here.

VICTORIA REGIS

At the same time Williams was fast developing the most exciting chain in the early years of the twentieth century, oddly, New York's number one house belonged to Oscar Hammerstein. It was not, however, the previously discussed Olympia. Unfortunately, like Proctor's Pleasure Palace, that estimable enterprise collapsed under its own weight (not literally but financially) and folded after just three years of operation, its various theaters distributed amongst other producers.

Hammerstein was down but not out. Without a penny to his name, he began to work his way back, managing to patch together the funds to build a grand new theater on the other side of Broadway. It was a far cry from the scale of the Olympia, and was, in fact, done on the cheap, Hammerstein drawing on his experience as a builder to find innovative ways to cut corners. Secondhand materials were used, walls were unpainted, and the space between them was filled with building scraps to avoid hauling charges.

When he opened his new theater in 1898, he dubbed it the Victoria in commemoration of his victory over adverse circumstances. (The fact that it also happened to be the name of the century's most well-known human being couldn't have hurt.) For the first three seasons the Victoria showcased mostly legit plays and musicals. In 1902, under the management of Oscar's son Willie, the format switched to vaudeville, and the Victoria began to truly make its mark.

"If E. F. Albee owned the body of vaudeville," wrote Abel Green and Joe Laurie, Jr., in their book *Show Business*, "Willie Hammerstein owned its heart and soul." Will Rogers concurred. "We have never produced another showman like Willie Hammerstein," he said. Not for Willie the opera nonsense of his father. Willie's philosophy was "the best seats in a theater for a producer are seats with asses in them." To achieve that, he revived a bit of the old Barnumesque spirit, something ironically lacking in the theaters of circus protégés Proctor, Keith, and Albee. Unique among the big-time vaudeville theaters, a sideshow atmosphere prevailed at Hammerstein's Victoria.

From 1902 until shortly before its closing in 1915, the Victoria was the prime showplace of big-time vaudeville. Will Rogers called it "the greatest vaudeville theatre of that and all time." Buster Keaton praised the Victoria as "vaudeville at its all-time best."

Just as Barnum had used the penny papers (and reflected their spirit in his shows), Willie Hammerstein would garner publicity through the more sensational papers of his day, notably Joseph Pulitzer's *New York World* and W. R. Hearst's *Morning Journal*. Willie invented the freak act, which comprised not only obvious sideshow fare like Rahja the snake charmer from Coney Island, but a whole succession of tabloid headline acts as well, such as Nan Patterson "the Singing Murderess," and "Shooting Stars" Ethel Conrad and Lillian Graham, so called because together they'd shot up a dude named Web Stokes. In 1913 he booked Evelyn Nesbitt Thaw, one of the original Floradora girls, whose jealous husband, Harry K. Thaw, had shot and killed the famous architect Stanford White, throwing both press and public into an uproar. Fortuitously, during the run, Thaw escaped from prison, pushing the box office through the roof.*

In 1907, Hammerstein had Gertrude Hoffman, one of his own acts, arrested for indecency, just for the publicity. In 1908 in Philadelphia he came across a stone-faced woman dubbed "Sober Sue" and offered a cash prize to any comedian who could make her laugh. It remained a mysterious and impossible task for many years, though it later emerged that the woman's facial muscles were paralyzed, making laughter out of the question.

Willie loved to book famous people on the strength of their fame alone, for he understood that although their acts might be incredibly lame, their drawing power wouldn't be. As such, athletes like Babe Ruth, John L. Sullivan, and Jack Johnson; cartoonists like Windsor Mackay, Bud Fisher, and Rube Goldberg; explorers like Captain Cook; and Lady Hope and the Hope Diamond graced his stage. He presented Helen Keller as an act. (The famous deaf-mute lectured on her life and career with the aid of a sign-language interpreter.) He also presented Sadakichi Hartmann, who gave a "perfume concert" using a special machine that produced the scents of lilacs and other artificial aromas. He was canceled after one performance, which is a pity, for I feel certain his was the one act Ms. Keller could have appreciated.

Understand that these acts were just the icing on the cake; they gave the place its special flavor. When combined with the requisite assortment of singers, comedians, acrobats, magicians, and so forth, it was the best variety show in town. You got your money's worth at Hammerstein's. In fact, you got too much. The shows (two daily) were more than four hours long: a matinee from 1:45 to 6:00 p.m., and an evening show from 7:45 to midnight. Nobody with a life stayed for the whole show. In 1910, at their new Manhattan Opera House, the Hammersteins even attempted the first experiment with "twenty-four-hour vaudeville" and

---

*Incidentally, Thaw shot White at another of New York's famous theaters, Madison Square Garden. The play he interrupted so rudely was *Momzelle Champagne* by vaudeville playwright Edgar Allan Woolf.

"three-ring vaudeville," presenting three acts simultaneously in the fashion of the Ringling Brothers, Barnum and Bailey Circus. (One can only hope that the presentation was restricted to dumb acts, avoiding the avant-garde possibilities of macaronism.)

Another worthwhile amenity offered by the Victoria was the roof garden, which permitted the management to continue presenting vaudeville shows throughout the summer in those hellacious days before air-conditioning. The roof was advertised to be several degrees cooler than street level, though with the sun beating down up there, it was actually hotter. Willie overcame that problem by heating the elevator that brought the customers up, so that stepping out onto the roof actually felt like a relief.

So successful was the Hammerstein formula that a powerful group of the other managers forged a ten-year agreement with the Hammersteins that amounted to a sort of treaty: the VMA would agree to stay out of Hammerstein's Times Square territory, if Hammerstein would agree not to start a circuit. That agreement was to hold firm until 1913, when some unexpected treachery led to the Victoria's eclipse by a theater that was to become the most famous vaudeville theater of all: the Palace.

YOU GOTTA HAVE A GIMMICK

Willie Hammerstein's genius for showmanship and Percy Williams's penchant for building the most sumptuous theaters and assembling the most stellar bills can jointly be credited with uplifting the entire vaudeville industry. Around the time Williams and the younger Hammerstein come upon the scene, you can't help but notice a new competitive spirit emerging, with each of the major managers shaking off his own complacency and racing to discover and debut the next superlative act. Credit for the swelling talent pool, too, should be given to the new systemized talent recruitment of the VMA. In vaudeville's earliest years, its biggest stars had been imported, from the operetta and musical comedy, from the British music hall, from the legitimate drama. Now vaudeville was beginning to develop its own major stars.

The acts that came of age in the aughts were a new breed. For one thing, they had no compunctions about being thought pushy or competitive. That's what it took to survive. Interestingly, despite all the noise and all the rules about onstage propriety, the competition among these performers was not to see who could come up with the most "polite" or "edifying" act. Such a thing, then as now, was box-office death. When holier-than-thou acts like temperance advocate Carrie Nation or evangelist Aimee Semple McPherson were booked, they inevitably tanked. Rather, the pressure was on for novelty and showmanship.

As always, the most fruitful area for the managers and bookers to explore was sex, justified with the traditional pretexts.

Some followed Eugene Sandow's lead by exploiting the burgeoning physical-culture movement. Harry Houdini, for example, publicized his muscle measurements, said to be proportionally even bigger than Sandow's, and he frequently stripped down to his underwear to prove it. In 1908 Australian swimmer Annette Kellerman debuted an act at the Fifth Avenue theater in which she appeared in a scandalous one-piece bathing suit that showed off her trim arms and legs (instead of the gargantuan bloomers that were the preferred female swimming attire of the day) and performing a series of dives and other tricks into a water tank. She was to perform this act (and with this costume) with variations for decades, hailed as one of vaudeville's most popular attractions. Edward Albee, the public prude, had special mirrors installed for her act on one occasion, to be certain that the audience got a look at her caboose.

While Little Egypt's cooch dance had never quite made it to polite vaudeville (that was a realm better explored in burlesque), fifteen years after its introduction, an act using its same "exotic" rationale—with a new twist—finally brought its enticements to the vaudeville stage. This new phenomenon was able to break the "clean barrier" because it was based on biblical source material. However, its content was anything but uplifting. In 1905 Richard Strauss adopted Oscar Wilde's play *Salome* for the opera stage. The play climaxed with the title character's "Dance of the Seven Veils," performed for her leering stepfather, Herod, in exchange for the head of John the Baptist. A couple of years later, a British music-hall star named Maude Allen presented her own Dance of the Seven Veils at the Palace in London and was a smash success. Sensing opportunity, Willie Hammerstein sent interpretive dancer Gertrude Hoffman to London to study Allen's moves. The pirated Salome act opened at the Victoria in 1908 and played for twenty-two weeks. Critics sniffed at the crudity of the subterfuge ("a dignified cooch" was how Sime Silverman characterized it in *Variety*) but audiences flocked to see it. Like the Little Egypt craze before it, the Salome act inspired a hundred copycats.

Notable among these was Eva Tanguay, whose Salome has eclipsed Hoffman's in the popular memory, due to the fact that she stripped down to almost nothing and made love to John the Baptist's severed head.

As a teenager, Tanguay had worked as an acrobat and as a chorus girl. In the latter capacity she soon found herself in the employ of the likes of Hammerstein and Weber and Fields. She first gained notoriety in a Weber and Fields show where, in an overexaggerated attempt to stand out, she shimmied and shook and otherwise bounced around the stage out of control. Immediately she was recognized for her pep, and called by critics "cyclonic," "volcanic," "a dervish."

In the first years of the new century, she started working regularly at Hammerstein's Victoria, the perfect venue for her, as it was known as a showcase for freak acts. If anyone embodies the spirit of vaudevillianism, of the triumph of personality, originality, and sensationalism—not only over discipline and craft but even over beauty and talent—that person was Eva Tanguay. She was essentially a rock-and-roller (one would be hard pressed to identify many differences apart from the lack of amplification). Billed as an "eccentric comedienne," her act, at its heart, was that she was nuts. A bad singer and a graceless dancer, with hair like a rat's nest, the homely, overweight Tanguay would put on outrageous outfits, sing provocative, self-involved songs commissioned especially for her and fling herself around the stage in a suggestive manner. She was looked upon as a curiosity, like the "wild man" in a circus sideshow, evincing the same sort of appeal that Janis Joplin and Tina Turner later had in the rock era.

She first sang "I Don't Care" in the 1904 musical *The Sambo Girl*, and it quickly became her theme song, establishing her thereafter in the minds of audiences as the "I Don't Care Girl." The balance of her career was a sort of elaboration of the character she established with that song. It wasn't so much that she was sexy, it was that she didn't care; she flouted the conventions of polite society generally, and—much like the old woman in the nursing home—she didn't much care if her tits were inside her gown or if they happened to fall out.

Sure, sex was a big part of it. She did sing songs like "I Want Someone to Go Wild with Me" and "Go as Far as You Like." Writing contemporaneously, Freud's nephew and PR pioneer Edward Bernays called her "our first symbol of emergence from the Victorian age." But her racier numbers were deemed acceptable because her act was not really reducible to sex. She was just . . . crazy. Her costumes screamed as much. She once wore an outfit made of Lincoln pennies; another time she threw peanuts out to the audience. Too often for it to have been an accident, she wore conical, dunce-cap-looking hats that accented a "village idiot" impression. Once she dressed up in French flags and sang "La Marseillaise." That's not just crazy, that's vaudeville. Her suggestive gyrations were less like a sexy burlesque dancer's than a lunatic's. Her sexuality was an id sexuality, like Harpo Marx's, like that of a two-year-old. When Harpo chases a blonde, we have no idea what he'll do with her once he catches her; in the same vein, one imagines Tanguay shaking her ta-ta's and attracting men just so she can put them in a headlock and break a vase over their heads.

Still, her Salome turned heads, and it did give Gertrude Hoffman a run for her money. A rivalry of sorts arose, and in 1908 we find Hoffman issuing the following challenge in *Variety*: "Eva Tanguay! Stop four flushing and make good! If you think you are so extremely clever, appear on any bill with me. I will follow you and wager any amount . . . that I will receive just as much genuine applause as you do." One had to admire Ms. Hoffman's bravado. While she was to remain a respected interpretive dancer on the vaudeville stage for many years, Tanguay would reign as vaudeville's top act for a quarter of a century. (Hoffman outlasted her, though, and may be best known today for portraying Mrs. Odetts in the classic sitcom *My Little Margie*.)

Among the many dozens of competing Salomes in the 1908–9 season, yet another deserves our attention. This is because she was portrayed by a man.

The most famous female-impersonator of the vaudeville era (known in the business as a "he/she"), Julian Eltinge, often billed simply as "Eltinge," was a point of cultural reference as late as the early 1960s, when Lenny

Bruce dropped his name in a stand-up routine. With the excesses of Rome a distant memory, drag had become a staple of Anglo-American comedy: from the "pantomime dame" to the "wench" of American minstrelsy (when white men portrayed black women). The skilled variety comic not only had to handle his share of Irish, African, and Dutch characters, but he also had to be able to play a plausibly hilarious female. Eddie Foy, the Russell Brothers, Harrigan and Hart, and Dan Leno were all great character men who included females in their comic palette. The crucial difference with Eltinge was that he was not primarily comic. His goal was to be convincing . . . and beautiful. Jesse Lasky said that "neither men nor women could take their eyes off him." On the other hand, W. C. Fields once observed of Eltinge that "women went into ecstasies over him. Men went into the smoking room."

Born William Julian Dalton in Newtonville, Massachusetts, in 1883, he was already in drag by age ten, acting in an amateur stage production called *My Lady.* Soon he was getting national bookings. In 1904, he starred in the book musical *Mr. Wix of Wickham,* his first big break.

Next he tried vaudeville, where he generally received positive reviews. A typical turn had him coming out as a Gibson Girl, then emerging as a "dainty young miss in a pink party dress." Apparently his singing voice was far better than that of most other female-impersonators, as was his illusion of femininity. A stocky man, he had his Japanese male dresser, Shima, corset him up, and then he spent two hours on his makeup and dressing. His bag of tricks included face and body powder, eye makeup, rouge, painted nails, and numerous wigs. He even shaved his fingers. Graceful and classy, Eltinge was always said to be in good taste—"inoffensive."

The act went right to the big time: Keith's Union Square (1905), the London Palace (1906), and the New York Alhambra (1907), which is when and where he did his famous Salome turn. Eltinge always insisted that it was all just an act, an illusion, the same as might be accomplished by a magician or a ventriloquist. He made a point of distancing himself form the gay subculture and any hint of "perversion," overcompensating with macho behavior offstage—fistfights, beer drinking, boxing, horseback riding (western-style, natch). He circulated stories about himself beating up guys who had impugned his manhood. Above all, he claimed not even to like dressing in women's clothing—it was just something he did to make money. This is what permitted him to engage in an act as sexually adventurous as impersonating a beautiful woman.

As the vaudeville era came of age, drag became its own specialty. While it wasn't everyone's cup of tea, female impersonation had a good run of it, and a number of its practitioners became some of vaudeville's top stars: Savoy and Brennan, Bothwell Browne, Francis Renault, Rae Bourbon, Karyl Norman, Princess Ka, the Divine Dodson, and numerous others. One, "Barbette," was a drag trapeze artist! It just doesn't get more vaudevillian than that.

In addition to being vaudeville headliners, both Tanguay and Eltinge were also stars of a new theatrical form that was giving big-time vaudeville its first competition, and one that also had sex as its centerpiece. In 1907, Florenz Ziegfeld inaugurated his famous *Follies*, the first Broadway revue. He'd copped the format from the stage show of the French Folies Bergeres, which since 1869 had incorporated elaborate tableaux of beautiful young women as framing devices around the traditional music-hall talent. Ziegfeld's show combined elements of vaudeville and burlesque—and wrapped it in Broadway packaging. The vaudeville element was a bill of top variety acts from all fields. The burlesque element was a chorus of pretty, scantily clad girls. The Broadway element was an elaborate stage set, intricately choreographed routines, and a musical program distinguished by original scores from top composers like Irving Berlin. Initially created to showcase his wife, French chorine Anna Held, *Ziegfeld's Follies* eventually came to star all the major performers of the day. Early stars of the *Follies* included Nora Bayes and her husband, Jack Norworth (who co-wrote and presented "Shine On, Harvest Moon"); Fanny Brice (who would be closely identified with the *Follies* for thirty years); and the Dolly Sisters, a pair of gorgeous Hungarian twins who wore exotic costumes and were just as famous for their exciting love lives as for any song and dance they ever performed on the stage. Vaudeville and the *Follies* were to cross-fertilize each other for the next twenty-five years.

Ziegfeld's peculiar contribution to the mix was a legitimization of sexual objectification. He managed to present hundreds of beautifully draped females baring their long limbs to an audience that only a couple of decades before had never glimpsed a woman's ankle. He did so by scrubbing them clean, by removing any hint of sordidness, any suggestion of the actual sexual act. His corporate credo was "Glorifying the American Girl." Through his cold aesthetic, it was to become whole-some, natural, and all-American—patriotic, even—to ogle statuesque, if icy, females: half naked, but constitutionally virginal. This strange and uniquely American aesthetic lives on today in the Miss America pageant and the Radio City Rockettes, and it helped to make a small amount of nakedness possible on the vaudeville stage.

Thus, twenty-odd years after Pastor, Proctor, and Keith began prom-ising and delivering shows to which a man could bring his wife and chil-dren, the controls began to relax. A certain percentage of the audience and critics would complain, but the box office receipts told the man-agers all they really wanted to know. Censorship would continue as al-ways, but from here on, the Siegfried (or should I say Ziegfeld) line would forever be inching backward.

Sex wasn't the only thrill an act could use to set itself apart in vaude-ville. As in today's show-biz environment, sex's traditional counterpart vio-lence was also in demand. Weber and Fields and any number of so-called knockabout acts made vaudeville theaters resound with the rat-a-tat of their mutual skull-crackings. One of those acts deserves special mention, as the "he who gets slapped" was a mere boy.

Many people today are unaware that the great silent comedy star Buster Keaton started out as part of a family act with his parents, Joe and Myra. The Three Keatons' act would play as shocking and as dark today as it no doubt did then. The gist of the routine was that little Buster would torment Joe while he was busy doing something, until Joe proceeded to "discipline" him. "Father hates to be rough," he'd say just before slinging his five-year-old son around the stage like a sack of turnips. In a typical routine, Joe, dressed in a strange, grotesque outfit, would come out and sing a song. Buster, identically attired, would enter from behind and carefully select a broom from fifteen or so that were ar-rayed onstage, and then, taking careful aim, crack Joe over the skull with it. In another bit, Joe is shaving at a mirror with a straight razor. Unseen by Joe, Buster begins to swing a basketball attached to a rubber hose over his head, each pass getting closer and closer to Joe's head, until it finally smacks him. In response to these shenanigans, Joe "swings Buster around, bounces him off the scenery, throws him offstage," and otherwise exercises his fatherly prerogative.

As time went by, the act got progressively rougher. A suitcase handle was sewn onto the back of Buster's costume so he could be easily picked up and thrown. The elder Keaton regularly chucked the little guy into the orchestra just for laughs. Like a cat, Buster needed to become adept at taking falls, relaxing and tumbling into them, or risk broken bones, or worse. Nobody had ever seen anything like this before. It gave the act an edge, a gimmick that it had previously lacked, and the Three Keatons now became a big success. Offers flooded in, and although the Keatons never became major headliners, they were constantly booked and had a tremendous fan base. Will Rogers wrote of going to see them on his honeymoon—and preferring them to the Great Caruso.

The success of the act can be chalked up to two things. First, shock value: audiences could not believe what they were seeing. Second, and more important, Buster turned out to be a child prodigy, a sort of Mozart of physical comedy, with a gift for mimicry and improvisation that already outclassed most adults in the field, and the critics raved about the little guy.

J. Austin Fynes, F. F. Proctor's general manager, was one of the first to spot Buster's talent. At the turn of the century, the Keatons played Proctor's Albany, where they did so well that they were moved three times during the run to better spots on the bill. In 1901, they played Proctor's Pleasure Palace and remained a fixture on the big-time circuits for another fifteen years.

The matching getups worn by Joe and Buster were extremely weird, particularly the skull caps they sported, which had an odd, yarnlike fringe of hair that made the two of them look like Dr. Seuss characters. Vaudeville comedy (like most comedy since ancient times) derived much of its novelty from its grotesqueness. It was frequently close to what we consider "clowning," not only because of all the broad physical action (necessary to fill the big stage), but also thanks to the cartoonish appearance of the performers. Pants, coats, and vests mismatched—striped, polka-dotted, or plaid, take your pick. Battered top hats and derbies. Bodies frequently distorted with padding. And, especially strange by today's standards, the monstrous makeup. Some, to modern eyes, look more disturbing than amusing. Yet it served a purpose. The seasoned vaudeville comedian could get a laugh without uttering a word by just wiggling or flexing an artificially enhanced part of the face; think of Groucho's eyebrows, Chaplin's mustache, and the lips of the minstrels for some well-known examples.

W. C. Fields's makeup as a tramp juggler renders him unrecognizable. He may as well have become a bank robber. Weber and Fields were virtually spheroid with all their padding. And the added features of the glued-on pointy beards and derby hats, plus the fact that Joe Weber was five-foot-four, made them resemble the town fathers of Munchkinland.

The team of Bobby Clark and Paul McCullough started out as circus clowns, and their getup always retained something of the ring. Like Weber, Clark stood a mere five-foot-four. His trademarks were a pair of eyeglasses that he drew directly on his face with greasepaint, and a cane, apparently carried only to hook things with. Invariably with a cigar in his teeth, he would charge around the stage like a scene-chewing dynamo, devouring anything and everything in his path. A favorite trick of his was to spit his cigar up in the air and catch it a couple of feet in front of his face, and continue smoking. His partner, McCullough, was a sort of mixture of the straight man and the stooge role, and he came off as even more cartoonish. He wore an ankle-length fur coat, a top hat, and a tiny mustache.

In an age of grotesque comedians, Ed Wynn was one of the most outré. His egg-shaped body was covered in a too-tight jacket and baggy pants. A minuscule derby topped his head. His eyebrows were highly arched, like a cartoon's, and large round glasses framed his glassy, fish eyes. His quavery voice, lisp, and frequent use of the phrase "ya know" were almost certainly the basis of the vocal characterization of the McDonald's "Mayor McCheese" character. It can hardly be surprising that Wynn was quoted by his grandson as saying, "I never wanted to be a real person."

In keeping with the odd visual effect was a certain surreal verbal sensibility. The phrase "madcap" actually makes some sense when applied to the comedy of the vaudeville era. "Crazy" was often identified with "funny." The Marx Brothers are the most well-known of those who took this comic approach.

Joe Cook's most famous bit was his "Four Hawaiians" routine:

I will now give an imitation of three Hawaiians. This is one (*whistles*), this is another (*plays ukulele*), and this is the third (*marks time with his foot*). I could imitate four Hawaiians just as easily, but I will tell you the reason why I don't do it. You see, I

bought a horse for $50 and it turned out to be a running horse.
I was offered $15,000 for him and I took it. I built a house with
the $15,000 and when it was finished a neighbor offered me
$100,000 for it. He said my house stood right where he wanted
to dig a well. So I took the $100,000 to accommodate him. I in-
vested the $100,000 in peanuts and that year there was a peanut
famine, so I sold the peanuts for $350,000. Now why should a
man with $350,000 bother to imitate 4 Hawaiians?

Another bit cast Cook as a landlord arguing with a really tiny (imaginary)
tenant in a really tiny house. At the end of the argument, he picks up the
toy house and stalks off the stage in a huff.

Much vaudeville comedy seems to have been closely allied to the
comic strip. Broad, easily recognizable, larger-than-life cartoon characters inhabit a simplified world where anything can happen. This was especially valuable when performing for an audience made up largely of
recent immigrants. Not for nothing did Weber and Fields and their
brother performers physically resemble Mutt and Jeff. William Ran-
dolph Hearst even asked Joe and Myra Keaton to portray the cartoon
characters Maggie and Jiggs in a series of silent comedies based on the
comic strip *Life with Father*. (Joe, seeing no future in pictures, declined.
His son would prove to have better instincts.)

In an age when every comedian was trying to outdo the other in
strangeness, simplicity and honesty themselves became a novelty. This
was the niche that was to be exploited by a rope spinner (or "lariat artist")
from Wild West shows named Will Rogers. Debuting at the Union
Square Theatre in 1905, Rogers initially set out only to do rope tricks. On
those occasions when circumstances compelled him to speak (as when
he missed a trick), he found that his aw-shucks Oklahoma manner got
him a laugh, whether he sought it or not. Wisely, he went with the flow.

Further, while elocution, grammar, and propriety ruled the stage for
the monologist, Rogers, who said "ain't" and chewed gum publicly (considered rude by some), was something of a maverick. Rogers even worked
business with the gum into the act. If he missed a trick, he might pause
a moment, go upstage and stick the gum on the scenery, then go back and
try the trick again, as though the gum had hindered him somehow.
Another favorite lark of Rogers's was to rope a stagehand and drag him

onstage. The gesture was perfectly in keeping with his democratizing verbal humor—an impish way of saying, "Come on, buster, you're no better than the rest of us. I'm gonna see that you remember that." Such antics by Rogers and so many others endeared them to the common folks in the audience, who were thrilled and gratified by the spectacle of people "just like them" on the stage.

The performers' histrionic abilities onstage spilled over into a desire to spread their joyful noise into the wider world. The finest vaudevillians were also born publicists. Houdini was one of the greatest ever, up there with Barnum, Ziegfeld, and Billy Rose. Will Rogers called him "the greatest showman of our time by far." No other vaudevillian came close. While Martin Beck may have given him his first big opportunity, Houdini's career rapidly rocketed into the stratosphere as a result of his own ingenuity and exertions. The stage name young Erich Weiss devised for himself reveals his public-relations genius, having symbolic resonance for both professional magicians and the public at large. The name Harry Houdini conjures up three of his illustrious predecessors: first, the French father of modern magic, Robert-Houdin (1805–71); second, the "dean" of American magicians, Harry Kellar (1849–1922); and, third, an early Italian magician by the name of Pinetti (1750–1800) from whom the tradition of adding a final "i" to a magician's last name seems to derive. The public doesn't give a damn about any of that, of course. The name Harry Houdini works because it combines an earthy, American-sounding first name (adapted perhaps from "Ehrie," his Hungarian nickname) with a mysterious Eastern-sounding last name appropriate for a magician. Freighted with all that subconscious meaning, it may be the best stage name of all time. He then elaborated on his handle with the qualification "the Undisputed King of Handcuffs and the Monarch of Leg Shackles." To publicize his engagements, Houdini would visit the local police precincts in each town, summon the press, and arrange to break out of the town jail. Soon he had police, press, lock manufacturers—seemingly everybody—helping to publicize his appearances.

The magician Horace Goldin, who popularized the trick of sawing a woman in half, is famous for his PR stunt of driving through town in an ambulance with a sign that said "In Case the Saw Slips." When Will Rogers arrived at a town he would help publicize his performance by riding down the main street on his horse with a sign reading "Will Rogers, the Lariat King."

After 1905, if you had the scratch, you could take out your own ad in *Variety*, the new vaudeville trade publication founded by editor Sime Silverman. *Variety* was a godsend for this army of scrambling hams, providing a platform for publicity in the form of reviews, features, interviews, and, above all, advertisements. If an act wasn't getting any legitimate press of his own, or if he didn't like the sort of reviews he got, he could always puff himself up with a peppy ad, like this one of Jolson's: "Watch me—I'm a wow." Modern advertising was born at the very same time as vaudeville. Just as Coca-Cola, Burma Shave, and Nabisco were learning how to sear impressions of their products into the consumer's mind, vaudevillians began to apply the principle to their own market. The smart acts branded not only their act, but themselves. The big acts all had a catchy handle, to help the public remember them. In this light, "Last of the Red Hot Mamas," "the Perfect Fool," or "the Corkscrew Kid" are not too far conceptually from "Good to the Last Drop."

Some made their whole careers into PR stunts. Lillian Russell's offstage peccadilloes out west had preceded her in the pages of the New York papers, no doubt fueled by some of the scandalously revealing costumes she had worn. From that day forward, whispers about her private life were as much a part of her career as her singing voice. She was married four times (two divorces, one annulment), was engaged several times more, and was frequently spotted in the company of Diamond Jim Brady over a period of forty years.

Eva Tanguay billed herself as "The Girl Who Made Vaudeville Famous." If anyone embodies the spirit of vaudevillianism, of the triumph of personality, originality, and sensationalism, over craft, beauty, and talent, that person was Tanguay. Caroline Caffin called her a "Circe of the force of advertising."

Once, a fellow chorus girl in a show called *Hoodoo* had the temerity to criticize her for her showboating, so she choked her until her face turned blue and she lapsed into unconsciousness. In her next show, *My Lady*, with Eddie Foy, one of the girls threw back a bun tossed onstage by a heckler. Afterward, Tanguay knocked the girl's head into a brick wall. Tanguay was now all over the papers, and filling theater seats as a result. This led to headline roles and better salaries as befits someone the public recognizes—regardless of what for.

Bankable stars could risk such behavior despite the managers' strict behavioral codes for they knew the countermelody to their loud arias was a whispered dough-re-mi. In vaudeville, temperament was a sort of status symbol. It was something only the biggest stars could afford without being canned. A temperament was like a Rolls Royce, an entourage, a suite at the Waldorf, and a gown by Erté. This was a great unspoken. Managers forgave "attitude" in general because these people were stars . . . box office . . . money.

Olga Petrova was the very warp and woof of vaudeville flimflammery. Born a London cockney named Muriel Harding, she fobbed herself off to the public for her entire career as a Great Russian Actress. Never dropping character, to her dying day she kept up the accent, on and off the stage. Petrova was one of the highest-paid performers in vaudeville, at the peak of her career. The managers humored her every eccentric whim. In 1919 she was the toast of the industry with her combination of sentimental songs, dramatic monologues, and poetry recitations. Then, having hit the heights, she abruptly announced that she was saying goodbye to the stage. After tanking at the Folies Bergeres seven years previously, she had decided to stay in show business only long enough to find out what worked. And the lesson she had learned was "what made good was a noisy fake."

The art of theater—from masks to mountebanks—was founded on such fakery. The ability to shift identity is among the factors that made the general populace suspect show folk as criminals, or worse. As Shakespeare wrote, the devil "hath power to assume a pleasing shape." Melville's Confidence Man, morphing from one persona to the next, is generally adduced by readers to be a stand-in for Satan. America was the first nation in history that permitted—even invited—such reinvention, and even rewarded it. Founded by nonconformists and outcasts (religious, political, ethnic, philosophical, and economic), America put in place a system where anyone, from whatever background, could alter his name and appearance and become somebody completely different.

A person ashamed of past poverty or an alienating affiliation could make himself over and become part of the show-business aristocracy. Strange, unpronounceable foreign names became "Burns," "Tucker,"

"Cantor," "Berlin." Jack Benny (formerly Benjamin Kubelsky) was so good at his cover-up that today virtually no one realizes he was Jewish; his defining comical character trait—stinginess—and his dry, Midwestern manner say "WASP."

Like the vaudeville managers before them, who had laundered their identities as saloon-keepers and circus people by presenting clean variety, the performers, too, were achieving fame and fortune by shedding their old skins and growing new ones. As stage people, the vaudevillians took it to an entirely different level. The vaudevillian was not just creating an on-stage character; he was creating a persona that would appear to have a life of its own from performance to performance, and offstage as well. The most successfully wrought of these personae had an absolutely mythic power. The character W. C. Fields created, for example, was so irresistible that it seems to live on to this day, even without the living presence of the man who inhabited it. This uncanny quality was made manifest by the invention of an entirely new species of act, the celebrity impressionist. Assuming the well-known physical and verbal quirks of their fellow vaudeville stars, impressionists like Cissie Loftus and Elsie Janis seemed to conjure them onstage, seemingly affirming their magical potency.

But esoteric metaphysics was the furthest thing from the minds of vaudevillians (with the possible exception of Anna Eva Fay, the mind reader). The object in developing their personalities was practical. The fake was about business. The artist, as his own producer and press agent, knew that he had to be memorable, to create a bigger impression on the audience, and allow the act to stand out from his hundreds of competitors. Today there's not a major public figure of any sort in any field—entertainment, professional sports, politics, even religion—who does not understand this principle and exploit it, and they all have vaudeville to thank.

Some fakes were simple rip-offs and copycats. An act called the Rogers Brothers actually performed Weber and Fields's act line for line, wearing the same costumes. Houdini had tons of imitators, such as the Great *Bou*dini, perhaps the most shameless. One of his principal (friendly) rivals, however, was his brother, Dash, who performed many of Houdini's tricks as the Great Hardeen. The two orchestrated numerous challenges and competitions for publicity, the public never realizing that they were brothers.

After Houdini, perhaps the most ripped-off artist was another magician, Ching Ling Foo, "Court Conjurer to the Empress of China." Whether or not this was an accurate credential, Ching made a big splash at the Trans-Mississippi Exhibition in Omaha in 1898. He played the exhibition for four months, then took vaudeville bookings on the Keith circuit. Within the year, he was so wildly successful that countless imitators sprang up with similar names and acts. Among them were Tung Pin Soo, Long Talk Sam, Han Pin Chien, Li Ho Chang, Rush Ling Toy, Chin Sun Loo, and more than one of each of the following: Chung Ling Sen, Chung Ling Hee, and Chung Ling Fee.

Ching's success, and that of his many imitators, was ironic, given that Congress had passed a Chinese Exclusion Act in 1882 that kept the Chinese from immigrating to the United States. How odd that in a time when Chinese were being deported and turned away by the thousands from the United States (and when the ones allowed to remain were coolies working on the railroad for mere pennies) it was so fashionable to be a Chinese magician that numerous non-Chinese went to great lengths to seem so. The granddaddy of all these pretenders to the throne was Chung Ling Soo, "The Celestial Chinese Conjurer."

Chung was really William Elsworth Robinson. He might have been a footnote in Ching's biography but for one small detail: he was actually a better magician than Ching! Robinson had started performing magic at age fourteen and had apprenticed with Harry Kellar and Herrman the Great, before becoming Achmed Ben Ali with an act he'd stolen from a magician in Germany named Ben Ali Bey. In 1900, Robinson (as Ben Ali) lifted a page from Ching's book, and then, what the hell, lifted the whole book. In short order, Chung became better known than Ching, and Ching, whose business must have been affected, promptly issued a public challenge, offering $1,000 to any magician who could do his tricks. In his hubris, Ching hadn't counted on one thing . . . Chung could do Ching's tricks better, and demonstrated as much publicly during his act. When he went to collect at Keith's Union Square theater, where Ching was performing, Ching welshed on his offer and barred the door.

While Ching may have been the real McCoy, Chung was the superior showman, more "Chinese" than an actual Chinese person, because he knew just what the mostly white audience's biases were. He gave them the dime-store Chinaman they wanted, something an actual Chinese person would never dream of. For example, Chung made his entrance from the ceiling suspended by his Manchurian pigtail, a feat impossible for Ching for the simple reason that his pigtail was real. Chung even went so far as to speak only in mock Chinese and conducted press interviews through an "interpreter."

All vaudevillians were supreme individualists, in constant competition with their fellow performers. Unlike legit drama or musicals, where every actor needs to be a team player "for the good of the show," the principle of every man (or every act) for himself works just fine in vaudeville. In fact, it's to be encouraged. The stakes for the performers were high: the best booking, the best dressing rooms, the best salary, the best billing, the best everything.

An artist's place on the bill was in constant flux, depending not only on his level of celebrity, but also on those sharing the bill that night. It was an immediate signifier of how one stood in the business. In Joseph L. Mankiewicz's 1950 film *All About Eve*, a huffy Thelma Ritter rebuffs a slight from some character who belittles her vaudeville past: "I closed the first half for eleven years and you know it!" Almost no one alive today understands this line anymore. She's saying that her character once enjoyed the second-best spot on the vaudeville bill, the slot before the intermission. And twenty years after the death of vaudeville it remains a point of pride.

Jockeying for a top spot on a bill could be a nasty business. At a 1925 National Vaudeville Association benefit, Nora Bayes had a major dust-up with Sophie Tucker over the running order. She was so difficult that the Palace booker at the time, Eddie Darling, physically pushed her into the street and closed the door on her, stating, "Miss Bayes, you will never play a Keith theater again." She did not.

Rivalry was endemic. "I've always been an envious cuss," wrote George M. Cohan. "As a kid in vaudeville I was often on the same bill with a hoofer that I thought was the best in the world, so I spent all my time trying to match him. It was the same with songwriting, playwriting, and acting—there was always somebody a lot better than I was, and I worked to close the gap between us. My notion is the guy that thinks he's the tops isn't going to do much climbing."

Cohan's brand of competition was healthy. Would that it were ever thus. "Look out for the guy that pats you on the back. He's looking for a place to put the knife," wrote columnist Walter Winchell, himself a former vaudevillian. Mae West briefly teamed with song-and-dance man Harry Richman in 1922, scoring her one bona fide hit in vaudeville. But when it seemed that Richman was garnering more applause, she sent him packing. W. C. Fields, who'd started out copying the act of tramp juggler James Edward Harrigan, later sued anyone he thought was lifting his own jokes. On one occasion, when he thought Ed Wynn was upstaging him in the *Ziegfeld Follies*, he hit the offending competitor over the head with a pool cue, knocking him out cold. The audience, thinking it was all just part of the act, roared, and Fields went on coolly with his routine. Clearly competition still thrived in the vaudeville industry, on the boards as well as in the back office, and competition, from the audience's perspective, was a very good thing.

FORMING THE COMBINE, PHASE TWO

In 1905, a rather unlooked-for development promised to bring even more competition to the big time—and then backfired. Big-time agent William Morris (the "actor's friend"), having recovered from his TB and returned from his convalescence in upstate New York, started making overtures to F. F. Proctor for partnership. At around the same time, he ran an ad in the new vaudeville trade paper *Variety* announcing his return.

Unfortunately for both Morris and Proctor (and the many acts who might have benefited from such an arrangement), the latter had recently alienated his general manager, J. Austin Fynes, by pressuring him to book high-class acts at subpar salaries. Fynes quit and, as a parting gesture, informed B. F. Keith that the lease on Proctor's flagship Fifth Avenue Theatre was about to expire. Keith snatched it up. He now had a bargaining chip with which to coerce the manager who had been his primary nemesis in New York for over a decade. The surprising result was—of all things—a merger of the two competing organizations. Proctor and Keith became partners in all their New York and New Jersey holdings, although their properties elsewhere (largely their original empires) remained outside the terms of that arrangement. Proctor, who had been operating independently as a vaudeville manager for twenty-five years, was now in eclipse. The Keith machine was in high gear and ready to gobble up the entire industry.

Of still greater moment, Keith and Albee had engineered a mechanism for joint booking that applied to all the Proctor and Keith theaters. With Albee as general manager, the newly christened United Booking Office began operating in 1906. The UBO was a step toward consolidation beyond the VMA. Rather than a consortium of equals, the UBO was a B. F. Keith company providing a booking service for all of the circuits. The Western Vaudeville Managers, too, were soon on board to avail themselves of the new service. Martin Beck, now top dog of the Orpheum organization, moved his office from Chicago to New York, into the same building as Keith-Albee and UBO.

There were holdouts, but in each case, hatchet man Albee found a different screw to turn, a different button to push, a different ball to squeeze, to force each wayward manager into joining with them. In Connecticut, the independent-minded Sylvester Poli merely pretended to join, and then, when Keith's agent was a safe distance away, stopped payment on his initial dues check. Albee retaliated swiftly and decisively by announcing that he was building opposition houses in each and every town where Poli was planning to build a new theater. This caused the local banks to renege on their promised loans, stymieing Poli's hopes for any future growth. He quickly capitulated.

Percy Williams caved in, too, and joined the combine. Various explanations have been given for this: that pressure had been put on his stockholders (who in turn put pressure on him); that he needed to join in order to secure enough quality acts for his several properties; and that Keith simply cut him an extremely lucrative deal. All of these may have played a role. Or it could simply be that this nice guy simply weakened in the face of a more forceful opponent.

The Keith, Proctor, Orpheum, Poli, and Williams chains were now essentially one. The UBO's existence defines the heyday of what we think of as big-time vaudeville. This was the entity through which every major vaudevillian was discovered, hired, booked, presented, and promoted for the next several years (that is, until several mergers boiled the whole industry down to just Keith-Orpheum).

With the establishment of the UBO, William Morris suddenly found that he had lost all of his clients. With no business left, Morris went to the Syndicate leaders Klaw and Erlanger with a proposal for the creation of a vaudeville network to rival the VMA and the UBO. Morris would do the booking, the Shubert brothers (Sam, Lee, and J.J.) would build the houses, and Klaw and Erlanger would contribute some of their existing theaters and supply the backing. The result was called the United States Amusement Company. The wheels were set in motion, negotiations begun with acts, and so forth, but the enterprise was to last for only a few months.

When it came to pure ruthlessness, even Keith and Albee couldn't hold a candle to their Mephistophelean mentors, Klaw and Erlanger. Their next lesson would cost them plenty. The Syndicate had never intended to set up a rival circuit in the first place. Their only aim the whole time had been to get Keith to buy them out, which he did, for $1 million. So Keith-Albee kept their supremacy, Klaw and Erlanger pocketed the cash, and Morris was offered the management of the UBO, which he proudly turned down.

But Morris wasn't finished as a vaudeville manager. As part of the U.S. Amusement Company initiative (his short-lived adventure with Klaw and Erlanger), he had started his own William Morris Amusement Company to operate in towns where the larger venture had no plan to establish a theater. In 1908, he opened his own flagship for that circuit, the American Music Hall, at Forty-second Street and Eighth Avenue (on the east side of Eighth, across from the present site of the Port Authority Bus Terminal). "With this one house," he announced, "I can fight and whip the combined interests of vaudeville."

Morris was somewhat handicapped in that he could not hire UBO talent. Instead, like other managers before him, he looked to London for performers. Two of the acts he booked ended up being the most significant music-hall imports to cross the Atlantic, with a reach that would extend far beyond vaudeville. The first was Harry Lauder. Believe it or not, one of the top five vaudeville acts of all time, up there with Houdini and Eva Tanguay, was this token Scotsman with bushy eyebrows, who came onstage in full kilt regalia and sang sentimental songs in a thick burr. His biggest hit was a song called "Roamin' in the Gloamin'." To modern eyes and ears he seems a Warner Bros. cartoon's idea of a Scotsman. (Or perhaps I have it backwards—maybe Warner Bros. got its idea of a "Scotsman" from Lauder.)

Like the Great Caruso, Lauder was one of the first entertainers whose talents were widely appreciated before anyone had actually seen him live, thanks to the new invention of the phonograph. While Edison's cylinder phonograph had first become available in 1887, the technology's appeal had been enhanced by the invention of the gramophone in 1896 and the Victrola in 1906.

From the first, vaudeville performers were natural fodder for recording. The new machine was hungry for sounds, and vaudevillians made the sounds record buyers wanted to hear. In the very earliest days, each cylinder was a unique item, recorded one at a time, more like a painting than a print. But even then, brass bands like John Philip Sousa's were laying down tracks, the loud, brash horns best suited for a medium that could not yet convey auditory subtlety.

Vaudeville was such a major force in everyone's lives that the first records were often literally just the aural component of the vaudeville-going experience. For example, one early use of phonographs in the days before many consumers had them was as experimental advertising devises placed inside department stores. The primitive ads were structured like mini-vaudeville shows, the shopper supposedly halted in his tracks by a reading of that week's bargains alternating with the sound of some stage performer whistling the "Ode to Joy" theme from Beethoven's Ninth Symphony.

As soon as technology permitted and enough home units were sold, some of vaudeville's biggest stars started cutting records, selling thousands of them and proving, in the process, the viability of the new industry. Among the first major recording stars were Walker and Williams, who made history in 1901 by becoming the first black commercial recording artists. The cylinders they cut sold well enough to also put them among the first black bestsellers. The following year Enrico Caruso and Harry Lauder both became major recording stars.

Lauder's disks had been circulating in the United States for five years by the time Morris brought him here for the first time in 1907. Such was the power of the new medium that he was one of the most popular singers in the country without ever having set foot here. By the time he debuted at the New York Theatre he was so successful the audience of fans kept him onstage for over an hour. This would come to be the norm for a Lauder performance—this, in an era when seventeen minutes was a long time for an act to be on a vaudeville stage. Americans were so enthusiastic for Lauder that he toured the country twenty-five times, slaughtering the throngs with songs like "Wee Hoose 'Mang the Heather" and "It's a' Roon the Toon." The distribution of his records was therefore not only a great outlet for his talent, but a tremendous marketing tool for his live performance in the bargain.

The other major British act Morris can take credit for bringing to these shores was a knockabout panto group run by a gentleman named Fred Karno. One of the group's most successful sketches was called "Mumming Birds; or, A Night in an English Music Hall." It consisted of a vaudeville show within a vaudeville show, including members of the "audience" who would be played by Karno regulars out in the house itself. The centerpiece of the routine was a "drunk" who arrived late, causing a big commotion and calling a great deal of attention to himself. A version of this act can still be seen in the 1916 silent film *A Night in the Show*, made by the young man who played the drunk: Charlie Chaplin. While not a big star in either music hall or vaudeville, Chaplin went on very shortly to become the richest, most famous performer in the world through the medium of film, making him the most successful former vaudevillian. Not too shabby either was the subsequent career of Chaplin's understudy in this and other sketches, a kid named Stanley Jefferson, who later became known as Stan Laurel.

Chaplin and Laurel were at the crest of a flood tide of performers who would discover a new market for their talents on the silver screen. Just as singers and musicians could reach out to their audience through cylinders and discs, actors and clowns could now record their performances on film.

For many years, the preferred method of film viewing had been through peep machines called Kinetoscopes (later known as nickelodeons), which could be found (along with mechanical fortune-tellers and strength-testing machines) in penny arcades. The filmgoer popped a coin in a machine, turned a crank, and watched his own little movie privately through a viewfinder. If the format had never changed, cinema would never have posed a threat to vaudeville. But it did.

Ironically, the very first public projected film exhibition, a demonstration of Edison's Vitascope, was presented in a vaudeville house. The association of film with penny arcades and the lower classes had made movies seem déclassé to most of the vaudeville managers and their audiences. It fell to the earthier instincts of Koster and Bial to screen several short subjects at their music hall in 1896. Koster and Bial's gambit proved to be a box office bonanza, and Tony Pastor and Keith's Union Square rapidly swallowed their misgivings and followed in their footsteps. By 1897, there were already several hundred projectors across the country, many of them in dime museums and vaudeville houses. The first true American narrative film, for example, Edwin S. Porter's *The Great Train Robbery* (1903), was exhibited at Huber's Museum, Eden Musee, and Hammerstein's Victoria.

Scarcely halfway into its short existence, vaudeville was already being encroached upon by new technology. As a talent agent, William Morris was well situated to take maximum advantage of the shifting reality. In time, he would divest himself of his vaudeville circuit, and the acts he represented would increasingly be recording and film stars. The William Morris Agency represents such artists even today, giving Morris the last laugh in his battle against the managers of the UBO who'd made such trouble for him during the vaudeville years.

ORGANIZED SMALL TIME

Marcus Loew is the Henry Ford of Show Business.

—George M. Cohan

Meanwhile, the man to whom Morris sold his chain managed to outfox the big-time vaudeville managers with a two-pronged strategy that embraced both cinematic exhibition and a form of vaudeville that the UBO chose not to compete with. Cohan's epithet is telling, since Ford's chief contribution to society was, of course, the invention of the assembly line. In years to come, show business was to become just that—nakedly, even unapologetically, a mass producer of product. However, as Ford proved, the one unqualified good of an assembly line is that its creations are affordable for people who don't have much money. Before Ford, cars were custom-made items driven only by the well-to-do. After Ford, the automobile became the universal nuisance it is today. In vaudeville, something similar occurred. As big-time vaudeville grew in popularity and its stars started demanding higher salaries, ticket prices rose. Working-class people were being priced out of "popular entertainment."

Like Tom Mix at the climax of a one-reel oater, Marcus Loew rode to the rescue. Born and raised on New York's Lower East Side, Loew had worked his way through a succession of odd jobs, becoming a prosperous furrier by age thirty-five. Shortly after the turn of the century, he became friendly with his next-door neighbor, the ex-vaudeville actor David Warfield, a specialist in "Hebrew" characters who had been a company member at Weber and Fields's Music Hall. The two had been dabbling in real estate together when Loew noticed that one of his competitors in the fur trade, Adolph Zukor, was doing a booming business with a penny arcade. Loew and Warfield went in with Zukor, then branched off to form their own chain. In 1905, while Loew was in Cincinnati overseeing an arcade he'd just purchased, he ventured into a motion-picture exhibition in a nearby town. Entranced, Loew bought his own projector and started showing films on a movie screen. The screened movies were a success, and he soon began establishing special theaters just to show them. William Morris's chain, including the flagship American Music Hall, provided an ideal infrastructure for the infant business of motion-picture exhibition.

Cue the ominous organ music . . .

We are well aware what this new industry of Mr. Loew's portends, but it is a bit early in our tale to go there. Vaudeville would continue to thrive for at least two decades after these events we now relate, thanks, in part, to Loew's thriving movie houses. At the time, films were only ten minutes long, and Loew hired vaudeville performers to keep his audiences entertained during reel changes, ironically rendering Loew's establishments de facto vaudeville theaters.

Loew carved out his own niche by avoiding big-name acts and keeping ticket prices low. "I don't offer widely advertised top liners," Loew said. "I don't need Mrs. Thaw or Jim Corbett or performers of that class . . . I find girls who can dance with the best, and the writers of jokes turn out as good stuff for my artists as anybody else."

Dude look like a lady. Julian Eltinge made drag acceptable to most audiences by purging any suggestion of homosexuality from his act, presenting his portrayals of pretty little misses like the one on the left as illusions similar to those perpetrated by magicians and impressionists. For PR purposes, he staged macho offstage exhibitions like the one below—probably every bit as phony as the petticoats. (Billy Rose Theatre Collection, The New York Public Library for the Performing Arts, Astor, Lenox and Tilden Foundations)

Plus-size **Sophie Tucker** conjectured that she got away with a number of sexy double entendre songs—such as "There's Company in the Parlor, Girls, Come on Down"— because her wide girth and plain face made her a figure of fun and thus unthreatening. The fact that she had one of the most winning personalities in vaudeville couldn't have hurt. (Shubert Archive)

BELOW: **You snooze, you lose.** While Martin Beck (right) was in Paris booking the great actress Sarah Bernhardt (left) for his new Palace Theater, Edward F. Albee stole the whole enterprise out from under him. The Palace would become the best known and loved vaudeville house of all time. (Billy Rose Theatre Collection, The New York Public Library for the Performing Arts, Astor, Lenox and Tilden Foundations)

You can't get any more Scottish than this. In the vaudeville era, entertainers often exploited their own ethnic identity for maximum entertainment value. Scottish recording star Harry Lauder may have included songs like "Roamin' in the Gloamin'" in his repertoire, but to a vaudeville audience, the kilt, tweeds, and meerschaum pipe made all the difference. (Billy Rose Theatre Collection, The New York Public Library for the Performing Arts, Astor, Lenox and Tilden Foundations)

If that woman's Irish, I'll eat that hat. Leonora Goldberg ran away from her Orthodox Jewish parents, gave herself the Irish name Nora Bayes, and rose to a height of vaudeville fame that justified her billing as "The Greatest Single Woman Singing Comedienne in the World." She was one of the last in show business to feel such a need to bury her Jewish identity. (Billy Rose Theatre Collection, The New York Public Library for the Performing Arts, Astor, Lenox and Tilden Foundations)

Doing character songs in vaudeville about Lower East Side girls named Sadie, Becky, and Rose, there could be little doubt about **Fanny Brice**'s Jewish identity. The irony was, the Yiddish accent she often affected in performance was a put-on; her native tongue was English. (Billy Rose Theatre Collection, The New York Public Library for the Performing Arts, Astor, Lenox and Tilden Foundations)

One for the history books. Almost five decades before Jackie Robinson became the first African-American player in the major leagues, Bert Williams was a star of the American stage. He earned over $2,000 a week in an era when many people didn't make that in a year. In spite of such triumphs, and despite the fact that he was an actual African-American, he still felt the need to perform in blackface. (Library of Congress, Prints and Photographs Division)

Politically correct cork? The last major white star to achieve fame wearing burnt cork, the singer and comedian Eddie Cantor represented a sea change, performing a character who was nerdy, bespectacled, and bookish. He was playing against stereotype, but blackface is still blackface. By the eve of World War II, it was essentially a thing of the past. (Shubert Archive)

Vaudeville makeup could make comedians resemble grotesque cartoons. Here, **the Three Keatons** (featuring little Buster) look as though they just stepped out of the Sunday funnies. (Billy Rose Theatre Collection, The New York Public Library for the Performing Arts, Astor, Lenox and Tilden Foundations)

The unruly hair and the wild glint in their eyes should be the tip-off. These are the young Marx Brothers out of costume. Left to right, they are Julius (Groucho), Leonard (Chico), Adolph (Harpo), and Milton (Gummo). A fifth brother, Herbert (Zeppo), replaced Milton when he was drafted during World War I. (Billy Rose Theatre Collection, The New York Public Library for the Performing Arts, Astor, Lenox and Tilden Foundations)

There is a poignant significance to the title of this song associated with the jazz dancer **Joe Frisco.** Years earlier, in an attempt to discourage his show-business ambitions, Frisco's father had burned up his tap shoes in just such a stove. Despite the disapproval by reactionaries like Frisco's dad, the rhythms of jazz were about to make out-and-out Puritanism an ever-diminishing American subculture during the twentieth century. (Lilly Library, Indiana University)

A classy demeanor (counterbalanced with a certain amount of humble joviality) helped **Bill "Bojangles" Robinson** become vaudeville's first black solo act—sans blackface no less. (Billy Rose Theatre Collection, The New York Public Library for the Performing Arts, Astor, Lenox and Tilden Foundations)

Buddy and Vilma Ebsen, like most white dancers, rose to vaudeville success on a different path than their African-American counterparts, enjoying a genteel tradition of dance classes and chaperoned parties at social clubs, not to mention starring roles on television series like *The Beverly Hillbillies* and *Barnaby Jones*. Black colleagues like the Nicholas Brothers suffered more for their art, and reaped far less of the rewards. (Billy Rose Theatre Collection, The New York Public Library for the Performing Arts, Astor, Lenox and Tilden Foundations)

After outgrowing the kiddie act he formed with his partner Elizabeth Kennedy, but before becoming Uncle Miltie, this wiseacre was billed as **"Milton Berle, the Wayward Youth."** Having started in show business at age five in 1913, he remained a performer almost until his death in 2003, a career spanning some ninety years. (Billy Rose Theatre Collection, The New York Public Library for the Performing Arts, Astor, Lenox and Tilden Foundations)

In a nod back to continuous vaudeville, Loew (like those who used similar methods) made his profit by presenting several shows a day (four to six), as opposed to the now universal standard of just two. With multiple shows and off-price performers, Loew was able to lower ticket costs and bring back the working-class audience, a move in stark contrast to the big-time houses that catered to people with more money to spend. Essentially, Loew was able to do to Keith and Albee what they had done to Tony Pastor ten years before. Yet, because Loew didn't hire big-time stars, he wasn't perceived to be any sort of direct threat, and the two circuits managed to coexist on separate planes.

THE BATTLE FOR SEATTLE

It's two-a-day for Keith, and three-a-day for Loew;
Pantages plays us four-a-day, besides the supper show.

—*from* On Your Toes, *1936, Lorenz Hart*

Two other small-time managers emerged at around the same time to grow important empires in—of all places—Seattle. These two organizations, unmolested by the VMA thanks to their geographic remoteness, would join in a battle of supremacy reminiscent of the old-time land wars between cattle men and sheep men. Perhaps you will not be surprised to learn that in the 1890s, the concert-saloon scene in Seattle was every bit as wild as it had been in New York at mid-century. It takes a little time for modern developments to trickle out to the hinterlands. In 1889, an itinerant actor named John W. Considine blew into town and became a card dealer at Seattle's Theatre Comique, a so-called box house. (Concert saloons were sometimes called box houses because the theater boxes could be closed off for greater privacy.)

Within a few months, Considine was managing the People's Theatre, where he began to make improvements to the presentation of the show. Unlike his Bible-thumping contemporaries on the East Coast, he also supplemented his income by pimping, an important part of early variety entrepreneurship. The sign out front read "Come in and Pick One Out—They're Beautiful." At the height of the Alaskan gold rush, his "box house" flourished. A lot of marks blew through town, and Considine was out to get them both going and coming.

In 1894, the Seattle city fathers passed a law against selling liquor in theaters. Considine did what any self-respecting bar manager would do under the circumstances: he moved to Spokane. There he flourished with another People's Theatre until 1897, when the local city government passed an ordinance outlawing box houses. Fortunately, by that time they were making a comeback in Seattle. Considine returned there and brought with him the exotic dancer Little Egypt (who'd made a splash at the 1893 Chicago World's Fair). Little Egypt once again proved a big hit, and Considine used the profits to buy up saloons and other properties, including Edison's Unique Theatre (a movie and vaudeville house), making him one of the very earliest exhibitors of silent films. On a trip to New York to book acts, he hooked up with Tammany Hall machine politician and sometime theater producer Big Tim Sullivan. The two launched a new circuit together, with theaters in Spokane, Portland, Bellingham, and Everett in Washington, as well as Vancouver and Victoria in Canada. These were now respectable theaters—Considine, like his predecessors, had left the saloons behind for the bigger profits available through legitimacy. And things were going peachy, just peachy, until 1902, when a stranger walked into town . . .

The stranger could hardly have seemed much of a threat at first. He could neither read nor write, and barely spoke English. Born Pericles Pantages in the Greek Islands in 1871, he was later to change his first name, significantly, from that of the enlightened father of democracy to that of Western civilization's first imperialist conqueror: Alexander. In his late childhood, Pantages started working on freighters, becoming stranded at age twelve in Panama. He gradually worked his way north, and found himself in Alaska in time for the gold rush. Instead of prospecting, he swept barroom floors, which he had noticed contained large amounts of spilled gold dust. In this way, Pantages probably found more gold than 95 percent of the prospectors. Soon, Pantages, like Considine, had worked his way up to pimp, selling the services of one Klondike Kate. After stealing Kate's hard-earned money, he opened his first theater in Nome, where he was able to fetch $12.50 for a single ticket—*very* high for those days, but in line with prices in a boomtown economy. As the boom subsided and the miners left, Pantages relocated to Seattle, where his first move was to open a combination fruit store and shoeshine parlor across the street from a Sullivan and Considine house. Within a few months he opened his first Seattle theater, the Crystal, in a narrow storefront. He set up a few benches and showed movies alongside vaudeville acts, performing all the work himself, from booking the entertainment, to running the projector, to ripping tickets, to (his special expertise) sweeping the floor.

By 1904, he was able to build his first Pantages Theatre, and thereafter a fierce battle with Sullivan and Considine began. Pantages began to build more theaters, competing directly with every Sullivan and Considine house, and Considine did everything in his power to undermine him. Pantages paid him right back. They would trick each other, steal each other's acts, even foul up each other's deliveries at the train station.

Ultimately Pantages would prove the victor. The Sullivan and Considine chain was built on a flimsy foundation, each succeeding house bought by mortgaging an earlier one, and when bad luck hit, the dominoes began to topple. First, Big Tim Sullivan was declared legally insane in 1913. Then, the following year, the country experienced an economic downturn. Foreclosure proceedings were begun on Sullivan and Considine properties and the house of cards collapsed. Pantages and the Loew's chain (which by that time had gone national) picked up Considine's theaters for a song.

OTHER CHAINS

Numerous other small-time and regional circuits cropped up in the early years of the twentieth century, allowed to operate unmolested by both the big-time managers and the major small-time chains. Of the five thousand vaudeville theaters operating in the United States in 1912, an estimated four thousand of them were small time. Among the new chains were the Fox Circuit of vaud and movie houses throughout Manhattan, the Bronx, and Brooklyn; Fally Markus in New York State; Balaban and Katz in Chicago (owned and operated by the father and uncles of theater and film actor Bob Balaban); the Mozart Circuit (run by former fire-eater Fred Mozart) in Pennsylvania and New York; the Aborn Circuit of Polite Vaudeville Houses, concentrated in medium-sized Pennsylvania cities; the McLaughlin Circuit out of Pittsburgh; Mike Shea's in upstate New York; Bert Levey on the Pacific Coast; the Hathaway Circuit of Massachusetts; the Wells Circuit, which possessed eleven theaters in the South; the Delmar Circuit, which covered the Deep South; the Interstate Circuit, which served Arkansas, Louisiana, Oklahoma, Texas, Illinois, Kansas, Kentucky, and Missouri; and, last, and also least, the Gus Sun Circuit.

Gus Sun was synonymous with bottom-of-the-barrel small time. Actually named Klotz, Gus changed his name for professional reasons when he became a juggler (presumably, "Klotz" sounded too much like "Klutz"). He went from circus performer . . . to head of a medicine show . . . to opening his first movie and vaudeville theater in Springfield, Ohio, in 1904. His operation grew like wildfire: by 1907 he controlled seventy houses and oversaw the booking for a hundred others. By 1909, the number had leaped to two hundred. By 1926, three hundred. In addition to Ohio, his territory included Pennsylvania, Kentucky, Virginia, West Virginia, Michigan, Illinois, Indiana, New York, New England, and Canada, yet his enterprise remained too small to provoke the worry of Keith and the other big-time managers. In his relative poverty, Sun introduced all sorts of miserly innovations that were later picked up by larger organizations that had less of an excuse. Among these were the "split week," i.e., a three-day gig that forced an act to spend a sleepless night on the train getting to a town for their next three-day gig (the previous norm had been a full week's work, allowing for a more humane full day of travel and rest on Sunday); and the "cancellation clause," a contractual provision allowing managers to fire an act deemed unsatisfactory after the first performance, leaving the performers stranded.

MONOPOLY, PHASE ONE

I am Vaudeville.

—*Edward F. Albee*

Meanwhile, back in big time, Edward Albee was becoming a virtual dictator through a combination of luck, chutzpah, and ruthless guile. Challenges to his authority would still arise, but they were dispatched with increasing ease. Several factors contributed to Albee's consolidation of power. First, three of the most important vaud managers died: Tony Pastor (1910), B. F. Keith (1912), and Willie Hammerstein (1914), leaving a huge power vacuum for Albee to fill. Second, nearly all of Albee's major rivals began to cash out of the business, leaving him the last man standing in a war that had been raging for decades.

Since 1881, symbolically at least, Tony Pastor had been widely regarded as the benevolent grandfather of vaudeville. What must have been most galling of all to Albee and the managers of the VMA was the fact that Pastor, by never expanding beyond his one Tammany Hall location, had never appeared to be in it for the money. As *Billboard* eulogized him, he was "a grand and goodly soul crucified on the cross of commercialism." As the other managers fell all over themselves jostling for empires, Pastor had stayed put, doing what he had always done, by striving to present the best shows he could the best he knew how. But by the mid-aughts, Pastor's Music Hall was an anachronism. The theater district had continued to move farther uptown—from Union Square to Herald Square and now to Times Square. Pastor was getting long in the tooth and had no desire to go head to head with his younger competitors. By 1908, he could no longer make a go of it, and the man who gave birth to vaudeville closed his doors permanently. As most of the VMA managers were amassing fortunes amounting to millions, Pastor died in 1910, a few thousand dollars to his name. With him died the Mr. Fezziwig model of leadership; Scrooge now held dominion throughout the land.

Much like Pastor, B. F. Keith himself had long ago ceased to be engaged in the rough-and-tumble. At one time, Keith had been a true partner in Albee's campaign of avarice. ("I'll take any one of those birds on alone," said one manager of the two of them, "but God help me from sitting between them.") In time, Keith became more of a figurehead, allowing his younger and more ruthless agent to commit all manner of calumnies in his name. Though Keith never put a check on Albee, he had been, theoretically, the supreme power in the organization. As he gradually withdrew from the business in the late aughts, Albee became king. Keith officially retired in 1909. Then, in 1912, the man who once said, "I never trust a man who can't be bought," bought the farm. The B. F. Keith organization was willed to his son Paul, who continued to defer to Albee. And when Paul Keith died in 1918, he left Albee total control.

Also reaching his retirement years was Percy Williams, the man holding what were considered to be some of the best vaudeville houses in New York. In 1912, after only a half-dozen years of being one of the top players, Williams sold his twelve theaters to Keith-Albee, vastly increasing that organization's reach in the crucial market of New York.

As if on cue, another challenger sprang up to thwart Albee's plans of total domination. For a dozen years, Martin Beck had been content to run the Western Vaudeville Managers Association, out of Chicago. Now he was of a mind to expand. Not only were plans in the works for a grand new Chicago theater, called the Palace, that would act as an anchor for the Orpheum circuit, but Beck also decided to build an entire *new circuit* in the East. His flagship for that circuit, also to be called the Palace, could only be located in one place. Exploiting a loophole in the VMA agreement with Hammerstein to keep out of Times Square (Beck belonged only to the *Western* Vaudeville Managers Association), he set about building a grand new vaudeville temple right up the street from the Victoria.

Albee was beside himself with rage. The audaciousness of this incursion was on a par with Proctor's preemptive actions back in the 1890s. But just as he had with Proctor, Albee kept enough wits about him to definitively brake (and break) Beck. This time, he exploited his rival's own hubris. The highfalutin Beck (who reportedly spoke six or seven languages) would travel to Europe often to personally book high-level acts. While he was away in France, negotiating with Sarah Bernhardt for his new Palace, Albee took the opportunity to buy up every other house Beck had intended to include in his eastern wheel, among them certain Percy Williams properties in Florida. Beck returned to find himself over a barrel. For reasons that an accountant would probably understand best, he preferred to settle for the Williams theaters, which Albee sold to him, on the condition that Keith-Albee would now have a majority stake in the Palace. Beck would still be a prominent shareholder, and would be in charge of all the booking. Beck took the deal.

5

THE PALACE YEARS

The Palace opening, in 1913, laid an egg. At first, there was no reason to suspect the move was anything but a flop. An infuriated *Variety* headline read: "Palace $2 Vaudeville a Joke: Double Crossing Boomerang" (meaning the gambit backfired). The piece went on to state that the bill garnered "no praise and no attendance." The theater lost money for months, and it was widely predicted that it wouldn't last more than a season.

Two developments, however, would rescue this, the most famous of all vaudeville theaters, from early extinction: first, some of the highbrow acts Beck had booked (such as Sarah Bernhardt and Ethel Barrymore) were unprecedentedly successful, and gave the new theater an aura of class it was to retain until the end of its vaudeville days. These stars drew big crowds, who became habitual Palace audience members. And, second, as though on cue, Willie Hammerstein died the following year, at the relatively tender age of forty-two. Hammerstein had been the last (maybe the only) of the major vaudeville impresarios with anything like the old Barnumesque flair (indeed, in 1914, Hammerstein had even booked Mr. and Mrs. Tom Thumb). Henceforth, that spirit would be transferred to other industries: Broadway producers like Flo Ziegfeld, George White, and Billy Rose; rock-and-roll impresarios like Colonel Tom Parker and Malcolm McClaren; and independent film producers like William Castle, Roger Corman, and John Waters. Willie's brother, Arthur, tried to carry on the management in Willie's absence, but the magic was gone. The Victoria lasted until 1915, when it was converted to a movie house and dubbed the Rialto.

It was now the Palace's turn. Born of a swindle that turned into a counterswindle, the Palace was the perfect showplace for the biggest of big-time vaudeville during the years of near total monopoly for Edward F. Albee. After thirty years of production, the Keith organization was at last the owner of a theater that could honestly be called "the Valhalla of Vaudeville." The Palace became a show-business mecca. All the top acts would play there. The audience was peppered with bookers, scouts, agents, and fellow performers. Comedian Ed Lowry said opening day at the Palace was as exciting as the Kentucky Derby. The sidewalk out front, called the Palace "beach," was a popular hangout for industry professionals looking to network. For a vaudevillian, to have "played the Palace" was to have died and gone to heaven. Which is why that expression lives on in popular idiom, though its meaning has faded beyond memory. Jack Haley notes:

> Only a vaudevillian who has trod its stage can really tell you about it. Audiences can tell you about who they saw there and how they enjoyed them, but only a performer can describe the anxieties, the joys, the anticipation, and the exultation of a week's engagement at the Palace. The walk through the iron gate on 47th Street through the courtyard to the stage door, was the cum laude walk to a show business diploma. A feeling of ecstasy came with the knowledge that *this was the Palace*, the epitome of the more than 15,000 vaudeville theatres in America, and the realization that you have been selected to play it. Of all the thousands upon thousands of vaudeville performers in the business, you are there. This was a dream fulfilled; this was the pinnacle of variety success.

The advent of the Palace marks a new phase in our history. Key stars from the age of gaslight and hansom cabs would pass away or retire during these years: Ned Harrigan, Maggie Cline, McIntyre and Heath, and Lillian Russell, to name a few. With them went the spirit of Victorianism that had once been vaudeville's defining principle. Instead, the

Palace became the focal point of a new twentieth-century aesthetic of shazz and pizzazz, of (as *Variety* abbreviated it) "show biz." This quality permeated every aspect of the era's entertainment. The breezy new spirit was perhaps embodied most successfully in the personality of Bob Hope—wisecracking, confident, comfortable. Here was the future.

The Victoria had been a throwback to the age of dime museums and music halls. Nostalgia would always remain a strain in American variety, from the plantation fantasies of blackface minstrels, to the endless number of "tramp" clowns and medicine-man-style comedians, to the mysterious, ancient Eastern secrets put over on the public by magicians. But during the Palace years, a new zeitgeist prevailed. Here could be found the worshippers of the new, of sex, of jazz, of speed, of the modern, and of capitalism.

The 1920s may be the last time the latter notion would be considered a "progressive" value, but in an era when the entrenched power structure was ruled by religion, the "valueless, immoral" world of free enterprise was just as frowned upon by some as the criminal world, show business, and harlotry. This animus went back for centuries. In the medieval marketplace, right alongside the booths of the mountebanks were the first banks—the name for both sharing the same origin in the benches on which the individual did his work. In the Middle Ages, suspicion of profit-making was great. Loaning money at interest was considered theft, and consequently only Jews (such as Shakespeare's Shylock) were allowed to do so; Christians caught charging interest were excommunicated. Widespread suspicion and prejudice resulted, in particular the obviously false misconception that Jews were avaricious. These unenlightened attitudes persisted for centuries.

Not surprisingly, the influx of millions of Jews around the turn of the last century sparked dark, reactionary forces in the heartland of America. Indeed, as H. L. Mencken chronicled so well, a newly revitalized Ku Klux Klan decried the influence of Jews, Catholics, and other "foreigners" on the WASP population through the agency of show business. They could find common cause in the words of a certain Austrian malcontent, who wrote in his 1925 opus *Mein Kampf*: "Our whole public life today is like a hothouse for sexual ideas and simulations. Just look at the bill of fare served up in our movies, vaudeville and theaters, and you will hardly be able to deny that this is not the right kind of food, particularly for the youth." Meanwhile, America's homegrown anti-Semite Henry Ford penned and published a series of articles in the *Dearborn Independent* from 1920 to 1922 entitled *The International Jew: The World's Problem*. One installment, called "Jewish Control of the American Theater," informs us that

> the secret of the serious change which has occurred [in the theater] since 1885 is found in the Jewish tendency to commercialize everything it touches. The focus of attention has been shifted from the Stage [sic] to the box office. The banal policy of "give the public what they want" is the policy of the panderer, and it entered the American Theater with the first Jewish invasion.

Mr. Ford glosses over a fact that he himself states, however: the public did indeed want it. And of course he ignores completely that thousands of gentiles worked shoulder to shoulder with Jews to provide it. In the late nineteen-teens and the twenties, years of unprecedented economic expansion, it was becoming socially acceptable (indeed, one's patriotic duty) to celebrate America's newfound wealth and power. And in the cities, at least, this avalanche of sudden abundance was measurably connected to the contribution of millions of singing, dancing, sexy, joyous, non-WASP immigrants. The capitalist enterprise known as show business was therefore liberal in the precise way that all bigots despise.

Furthermore, vaudeville was modernist, in the same way Duchamp's much-ridiculed *Nude Descending a Staircase* was modernist. Vaudeville was the great Borg-form, a theatrical Frankenstein with parts taken from everywhere and thrust together in a sort of cubist pastiche. It achieved what Eugene O'Neill strove in vain for decades to accomplish: a uniquely American brand of theatrical experimentalism on the order of what Melville and Whitman had accomplished in literature: a form simultaneously fragmented, declarative, ambitious, cocky, poetic, scientific, romantic, and realistic. Vaudeville is the sight and sound of clash—the low comic's mismatched plaids, stripes, and polka dots, and the jazz snare, cowbell, and cymbal. It is the dramatic equivalent of a newspaper layout, the weather report butting up against a liver-pill ad, against an update from war-torn Cuba, against the Katzenjammer Kids. It is the skyscraped skyline in human scale, all glitter, tinsel, modernity, and optimism. (In a city where beautiful old buildings are routinely and constantly torn down to make way for less beautiful but more profitable new ones, a theatrical form in which every discreet act gets fifteen minutes of stage time before being booted to oblivion by the next act made sense.)

Vaudeville's very tempo was modern. Where old-style had represented American show business in its Edenic state, its Caliban-like denizens living in brutish but natural harmony, twentieth-century vaudeville blew forth a mechanical dissonance. Its rhythm was that of life lived at a full gallop—faster than a gallop, for this particular horse was made of iron and cut through mountains and over rivers and gorges as though God didn't even exist to put obstacles in its way.

"Things fall apart," Yeats had written; "the centre cannot hold." This centrifugal energy, so negative in society at large, was vaudeville's whole reason for being. Interestingly, it is a form in which the show itself is not the important thing. Try to analyze the show *as a show* and it crumbles in your hand like wet sand. As opposed to a revue, a musical, or a play, you don't walk away from a particular night of vaudeville remembering the *show* for the rest of your life. It is, rather, a form in which *individuals* can excel, and that's the point. For every ten thousand Joe Schmoes, there's one Joe Cook.

The ethnic variety of vaudeville made it the theatrical equivalent of the melting pot. Black, white, Jew, gentile, man, woman, child, Irish, Italian, Swedish, Chinese, Japanese, shoulder to shoulder, toe to toe, cue to cue. The hat rack in the dressing room had top hats, derbies, fedoras, turbans, sombreros, bejeweled headdresses, and Apache war bonnets. All were equally important. Vaudeville was like P. T. Barnum's "Happy Family," the caged menagerie that contained beasts of prey alongside grass-munching goats and exotic birds, all living in apparent harmony. The symbolic value of this mulligan stew of multifarious humanity—all combining to create a single, harmonious polyglot entity—cannot have failed to have an educative impact on the awkward, adolescent nation.

Fittingly, the tunesmiths of the day outfitted this era of transformation with the perfect sound track. With coon songs now phasing out, vaudeville audiences embraced a new type of song identified by the misleading label of "rag." Mostly written by white performers, and uniformly composed in a musical style quite different from true ragtime (of the sort we generally associate with the compositions of Scott Joplin), these songs nevertheless continued to draw their inspiration from African-American culture. But now the references tended to be celebratory rather than negative, and in fact their lyrics often made no reference to black life at all. Rather, they were often about "dancing," "feeling," "moving," and "doing it." Invariably performed to an up-tempo, electrifying beat, this new music seemed calculated to quicken the heart rate of even the coldest of listeners.

The primary exponent of the style was the runaway son of a Washington, D.C., cantor by the name of Asa Yoelson, a.k.a. Al Jolson. It was Jolson, more than any other, who transformed an industry drugged on saccharine, antiseptic renditions of songs like "Bicycle Built for Two" and "I Dream of Jeanie (with the Light Brown Hair)" and jazzed it up with finger-popping, hyperkinetic rags. Despite the incriminating and archaic blackface, he was at heart a Negrophile who played a central role in promoting the styles and sounds of black music to the mainstream white audience. His patented pathos, the hands on heart, down on one knee, crying out to his dead mammy, was show-stopping stuff in its day.

For years, this blackface performer had been shuttling back and forth between the last few remaining minstrel shows and small-time vaudeville. By 1909 he was a star with Lew Dockstader's Minstrels, the last of the big minstrel outfits. But the cocky Jolson chafed at Dockstader's old-fashioned, horse-and-buggy style. Though Dockstader wore blackface in performance, he made no effort to seem black; he simply sang the same old repertoire of sentimental nineteenth-century songs. For him, the blackface was no more than a convention.

For Jolson, it was a statement. He liked African-American music and wanted to emulate it. Consequently, he began working with songwriters to cook up a new kind of song for his act. One of these, a young kid named Izzy Baline, who'd started out as a song plugger at Tony Pastor's, supplied Jolson with "Alexander's Ragtime Band." The song swept the nation. Jolson eclipsed Dockstader in his own company and soon jumped into big-time vaudeville. (Baline was, of course, Irving Berlin, who quickly followed up

"Alexander" in a highly industrious fashion with "Stop That Rag [Keep on Playing, Honey]," "Play Some Ragtime," "Make-a-Rag-a-Time Dance Wid Me," "Draggy Rag," "That Opera Rag," "The Whistling Rag," "That Mysterious Rag," "The Ragtime Jockey Man," "Ragtime Soldier Man," and "Ragtime Violin.")

In December 1909, at the Colonial Theatre, Jolson introduced another of his early hits, "Hello, My Baby" (penned by Joe Howard and Ida Emerson), and it became a monster hit at the time for Jolson, and later for the WB frog:

Hello, my baby,
Hello, my honey,
Hello, my ragtime gal.
Send me a kiss by wire.
Honey, my heart's on fire . . .

This is surely history's first recorded phone sex. In this, perhaps the least romantic tune possible, one detects (or rather, is clobbered over the head by) a new twentieth-century spirit. Hurried, frantic even—Jolson sounds like he'd just had five cups of coffee and is telling his gal he loves her between bites of a sandwich—long distance, no less. In truth, the song is much more about the telephone than Jolson's love for his girl. Speed and distance, that's what this new kind of love affair was about. In the old days, the lover would pour his heart and soul into a lengthy, verbose letter . . . and give it to a postman, who would take a full month to deliver it. Not "My dearest" or "My own," Jolson addresses his girl as "Honey." One half suspects he doesn't know the girl's name.

Jolson's chutzpah was not to be believed. He once shouted his patented catchphrase "You ain't heard nothin' yet!" to the audience when his act followed Enrico Caruso's. Such brass had enormous sex appeal in 1910. Jolson seemed like he'd just arrived from some other planet. He and this new age—of electric light, of Model T Fords, nickelodeons, telephones, and, yes, vaudeville—were cut from the same synthetic cloth. So popular was Jolson's act that it effectively took him right out of vaudeville. After major dates at the Fifth Avenue and Victoria theaters, and a brief return to Lew Dockstader's Minstrels, he leapt, feet

first, into Broadway musical comedies, film, and radio, where he continued his string of crazy, raglike songs: "You Made Me Love You,"
"Mammy," "Swannee," "California, Here I Come," "Rockabye My Baby
with a Dixie Melody," "Toot, Toot, Tootsie," and "April Showers."

Back in vaudeville, plenty of others were on hand to pick up the
slack. In 1910 young Blossom Seeley, "the Queen of Syncopation," debuted "Put Your Arms Around Me, Honey" and "Toddlin' the Tolado"
(about which one critic swooned: ". . . you just have to hold on tight for
fear of getting up and toddling right along with her"). Dolly Connolly debuted the perennial hit "Waiting for the Robert E. Lee." Sophie Tucker
(now out of blackface) switched her set, too, and became known as "the
Mary Garden of Ragtime," a reference to a popular opera diva of the day.
Tucker's first double entendre song was the old whorehouse number
"There's Company in the Parlor, Girls, Come On Down." In the early
teens she started introducing songs to the vaudeville audience that
would become classics, including "Some of These Days," her theme
song, written by Shelton Brooks, who also wrote "The Darktown Strut-
ters' Ball," another hit for her (that's the song that starts "I'll be down to
get you in a taxi, honey"). She even had a couple of novelty numbers
about Rip Van Winkle: "Who Paid the Rent for Mrs. Rip Van Winkle?"
and "Where Was Rip Van Winkle When His Wife Went Away?" Such
numbers were to become a staple of her repertoire.

Meanwhile, Mae West (who also dropped the blackface of her early
career) was making her act increasingly outrageous and daring, presenting sexually suggestive songs accompanied by a low-down bump and
grind. She'd tone down the act in auditions for skittish managers, then
pull out all the stops in front of the audience. Critics decried her vulgarity. Nonetheless, she managed to get good notices after performing
"The Philadelphia Drag" at Jesse Lasky's shortlived Folies Bergeres club.
In 1912 she played in vaudeville as "Mae West and Her Boys," where
she did a "cooch dance" and performed a number called "Cuddle Up
and Cling to Me." Furthermore, in a move anticipating Janet Jackson at
the 2004 Superbowl, she wore an evening dress with a special break-
away shoulder strap. Sime Silverman and other critics of the day opined
that she belonged more in burlesque, being too suggestive for the more
refined audiences of vaudeville. Notwithstanding, she managed to get
booked at Hammerstein's Victoria, billed as the "Scintillating Singing

Comedienne," where she belted a few rags in tight-fitting costumes and played the bones, minstrel style.

Tucker had gotten away with doing risqué material, she believed, because her large size rendered her sexuality unthreatening. But West's approach to appropriating African-American culture for white audiences was a case of too much, too soon. As it happened, a "gradualist" approach was to put the movement on a more solid footing.

Vernon and Irene Castle were the catalysts and the center of a huge national craze for social dancing that hit America early in the last century. As impossible as it may seem, the fox-trot and similar dances represented a social revolution. (To put it in perspective, it was part of the larger pleasure revolution that included the invention of amusement parks, published sheet music and sound recordings, nickelodeons, and vaudeville itself. Truly, the dawn of the twentieth century was the birth of "fun.") Previous to this, the prejudice of the Puritan forefathers still prevailed. The socially acceptable dances were the waltz and the two-step, which in fact had been regarded as wicked by conservative forces in their day. One critic called the tango "the dance of the shameless savage and his squaw," and the turkey trot "a phenomenon closely analogous to those dancing manias of the Middles Ages . . . to which victims of a neurotic diathesis are susceptible." The Castles introduced the country to any number of these racy new dances, and because they were *so* eminently respectable, more conventional souls everywhere were emboldened to follow suit.

Vernon Castle had been a comedian with Lew Fields's stock company (Fields had broken up with Weber in 1904). Castle had a natural body for comedy, standing five-foot-eleven, weighing only 118 pounds, and with a prominent, hawklike beak sticking out from the top of it. Critics described him as an "attenuated green bean" and a "soda straw with legs."

Irene Foote was a child of privilege, born on a thirty-five-acre estate in New Rochelle. The town was at the time a summer resort for vaudevillians. The two met and married there, and Irene soon pestered him to get her a job in show business.* Their first public dance together was in

---

*Irene's parents were eccentric individualists (her father a homeopathic doctor who had once blown up the chemistry building at Cornell, and her mother the daughter of a circus PR man), so the fact that Vernon was in show business was not an obstacle.

a Lew Fields show called *The Hen Pecks*; their number was the hit of the production. A few months later, they were asked to perform for some Russian nobility who happened to be in town. Their impromptu concert brought the house down, and they were hired for a long-term engagement, which led also to gigs at private clubs and parties, quickly ingratiating them with the cream of society.

At a party for impressionist Elsie Janis in 1913, they improvised a new dance, which was subsequently known as "the Castle Walk." It caught on rapidly, and the Castles and their dances soon became a national craze on the order of Beatlemania. "The Castles," wrote the *New York Sun*, "are to terpsichore what Edison is to electricity." The team periodically came up with new dances to keep their routine fresh. In addition to the fox-trot, the turkey trot, the camel walk, the bear hug, and any other number of zoologically derived oscillations, they were now introducing the country to the Castle Innovation Waltz, the Castle Lame Duck Waltz, the Castle Half and Half, the Castle Innovation Tango, the Castle Maxixe, and the Castle House Rag. To teach these faddish movements they opened both the Castle School of Dance and Castle House, which was funded and patronized by society ladies and had marble floors, a fountain, a dedicated house orchestra, and a silver tea service. The idea was to create a safe haven where young people could learn to dance without exposing themselves to the dangers of nightclubs and dance halls.

Like Ethel Barrymore, the Castles only played vaudeville "when they needed the money," which, because of Vernon's profligacy, was constantly. The team headlined in vaudeville from 1914 to 1916, playing many dates at the Palace. In the mid-teens they embarked on a tour of thirty-two cities in twenty-eight days, something no one does who can afford to relax. Yet the pair were so popular that any little fashion innovation Irene made (including bobbing her hair) was immediately copied by hundreds of thousands of women.

In her memoir, *Castles in the Air*, Irene claimed that the team occupied a "middle ground" between the racy moves coming out of African-American dance halls and the deadly-dull ballroom dancing then considered proper for social occasions. In fact, the Castles can be said to have inspired two branches of vaudeville dance. One, the handsome, stylish, and thin white couple in fabulous evening clothes, gracefully dancing together as if floating on air, such as Fred Astaire and his sister, Adele (later replaced in films by Ginger Rogers); Buddy Ebsen (a.k.a. Jed Clampett from *The Beverly Hillbillies*) and his sister, Vilma; Pat Rooney, Jr., and Marion Bent; and the debonaire Clifton Webb with any number of partners. This sort of act was such a staple of the Palace years that one team, Paul and Grace Hartmann, made a career of *parodying* it. The second major branch enabled by the Castle revolution was the large number of African-American acts who were to break into vaudeville in the teens and twenties and would come to be regarded as classy themselves.

First among these black acts was the Castles' backup orchestra, organized and directed by James Reese Europe. As Irene Castle put it, "No inconsiderable part of our success was due to his wonderful playing." Europe can be thought of as the W.E.B. DuBois of American music—not just an accomplished musician, but a relentless teacher, theorist, and advocate for the cause of widespread acceptance of African-Americans as the equals of whites in the field of serious music. Not surprisingly, the Europe Orchestra and its alumni were among the first African-Americans to tread the vaudeville stage without the mask of burnt cork. Dressed in evening clothes, this crack ensemble of highly trained musicians infused their music with elements of ragtime and what was then coming to be known as jazz. Two of its more sophisticated alumni, Noble Sissle and Eubie Blake (writers of "I'm Just Wild About Harry"), would form their own team called the Dixie Duo and become Palace headliners themselves, in addition to creating the seminal Broadway musical *Shuffle Along*.

Sadly, both James Reese Europe and Vernon Castle were to become curious casualties of the First World War. When the United States entered the war in 1917, Europe had further distinguished himself by organizing an all-black regimental band. This patriotic group bravely entertained doughboys until the armistice, at which point they returned home for a triumphant U.S. tour. It was on the last performance of that tour in 1919 that one of his own musicians, incensed over some perceived slight, stabbed Europe to death. Meanwhile, Vernon Castle, who was British by birth, had enlisted in the Royal Canadian Flying Corps. He served bravely as a pilot, flying several missions over enemy territory, only to crash, fatally, in 1918 during a training exercise in Fort Worth, Texas.

Many remained behind to carry on their legacy, however. In New Orleans, a group of musicians rather unlike Europe's bunch were developing a completely new sort of black music. With no tuxedoes to their name, and far from the high-society cotillions, a generation of derby-hat-sporting, cigar-smoking, black-armband-vest-wearing musicians had grown up in Louisiana's fertile swamp of whorehouses, saloons, and dance halls. Musicians like Jelly Roll Morton, King Oliver, and Louis Armstrong mixed elements of the German march with the blues (itself derived from the African-American field holler) and every other musical style that had infiltrated the Crescent City's multiethnic precincts. The result was a highly original music known variously as "jass" or "jazz," that was about to turn the country upside down.

Vaudeville hoofer Joe Frisco and his partner, Loretta McDermott, heard their first jazz in a New Orleans nightclub one evening in the midteens. Inspired by the crazy crash of improvised sounds, they did what any spontaneous young dancers would do on the dance floor, venturing their own crazy moves to match the music. This brought the house down, so they built an act around it.

Frisco turned out to be a crucial figure in the history of jazz. In 1915, he hired the Dixieland Five to come back to Chicago with the team as their accompanists, making him among the first to bring the intoxicating new music to the attention of mainstream audiences in the North. When Joe caught McDermott fooling around with the band's singer, he left the lucrative scene in Chicago for solo stardom in New York. Billing himself as the "World's First Jazz Dancer," he soon made "the Frisco dance," or "Frisco shuffle," the most widely imitated step in the country. There is even a reference to it in *The Great Gatsby*. A picture of Frisco, once formed in the mind, is indelible: in a sharp business suit, with a derby and spats, and a cigar in his mouth, he performs a compulsive series of motions, pelvic thrusts, bunny hops, and contortions, all the while incorporating the derby and cigar as props. Decades later, choreographer Bob Fosse (*Cabaret, Chicago, All That Jazz*) would cop much of his vocabulary from the Frisco lexicon.

The timing of Frisco's trip to New Orleans is significant. At this stage of American history, approximately 90 percent of African-Americans (most of them the children and grandchildren of slaves) still lived in the South. This may be the reason why you can count the number of early black vaudevillians on two hands: vaudeville evolved in the North, where there were few people of color at that time.

When World War I began, the immigration spigots were turned off, producing a dire need in the North for the cheap labor previously provided by workers from eastern and southern Europe. This change made it practical, for the first time, for poor blacks in the South to pack their bags and move. For most southern blacks, the end of slavery had merely meant another sort of servitude: tenant farming, or sharecropping, slaving away for a pittance, getting deeper and deeper in debt on somebody else's property. Harsh Jim Crow laws forced blacks into the role of second-class citizens. Around the turn of the twentieth century, the frequency of lynchings began to increase. (Seven hundred fifty-four were recorded between 1900 and 1910. Surely many more went unrecorded.) Given these details, perhaps the question should be not why blacks moved north, but why any stayed behind at all.

Thus, starting in 1914, large numbers of African-Americans began to settle in New York, Chicago, Detroit, Philadelphia, Newark, and other northern cities. This population shift, which lasted for decades, is known to American historians as the Great Migration. In Harlem and Chicago, where the black populations doubled between 1920 and 1930, a flourishing scene of nightclubs and dance halls began to evolve, and the music that had so excited Frisco began to excite his fellow vaudevillians.

In 1916, Sophie Tucker, by now a Palace regular, introduced her new backup band, the Kings of Syncopation. Calling herself "the Queen of Jazz," she started emulating many of the African-American acts she had seen in nightclubs. She claimed to have been the first major act to introduce the dance known as the "shimmy," and there may be some justice to that claim, as in 1916 she was already performing an act called "Ev'ry-body Shimmies Now." More than any other dance that had made its way to the vaudeville stage previously, the shimmy raised eyebrows, for there was technically little to distinguish it from those tribal gyrations earlier whites had called "satanic." Predictably, Mae West, too, started doing the shimmy, which she performed to great acclaim in a show called *Sometime* and then brought to the staider precincts of vaudeville, where she received a tepid reaction. Mae, who was said to shake so hard when she performed that the powder flew off her body, was simply too overtly sexual for vaudeville.

In addition to jazz, both Tucker and West inflected their acts with large amounts of another form of African-American music. The blues, with its deceptively simple chord structure (but all too sophisticated rhythms) and its risqué, downright raunchy lyrics, was known by some as "the devil's music." It would be nearly forty years before that sort of music would start to mainstream in the form of rock-and-roll. Indeed, the African-American singers who developed it, such as Mamie Smith, Bessie Smith (no relation), Ida Cox, and Ma Rainey, performed for a segregated, all-black audience. In 1920, Mamie Smith cut the first "race record" ("Crazy Blues") for Okeh Records, and throughout the twenties and early thirties she and her colleagues would make and sell millions of disks in the classic blues style. These blues women, whom Tucker and West so loved to emulate, developed larger-than-life personas that were nonetheless based on their own lives, telling tales of hard drinking, sex outside of marriage, and shooting faithless lovers.

Also in 1920, a separate but unequal all-black vaudeville circuit was established. The organization's initials, TOBA, stood for the Theater Owners Booking Association, or, according to the acts who played that circuit, "Tough On Black Asses." In addition to the aforementioned blues singers, TOBA showcased the talents of dancers like Leonard Reed (inventor of the Shim Sham Shimmy), the Nicholas Brothers, and the Will Mastin Trio (featuring a very young Sammy Davis, Jr.), and comedians like Stepin Fetchit, Eddie "Rochester" Anderson, "Pigmeat" Markham, "Moms" Mably, Stump and Stumpy, and Mantan Moreland. In addition to the forty-five theaters of the TOBA circuit, which was focused in the South and Midwest, there were other, smaller, all-black circuits in the Northeast and mid-Atlantic states. Blacks were now so great a factor in show business that in 1920, *Billboard* magazine launched the first-ever column devoted to black entertainment.

But if the big time had a problem with Mae West, they certainly weren't going to make room for authentic blues artists. Rather, the African-American acts who made it to the big-time "white" vaudeville tended to do so by following the James Reese Europe model: dignity, class, and sharp, sharp dress—tuxedoes, top hats, and carnations on the lapel.

The first to make it to big time and the Palace was Bill "Bojangles" Robinson. After decades of performing, by the late teens, Robinson had risen to become one of America's best-loved entertainers as vaudeville's first solo African-American act, billed as the "Chocolate Nijinsky, Undisputed Dean of the Darktown Steppers." His act was an amalgam of little steps and moves he had copped from others, then stitched together into a whole that was far greater than the sum of its parts. He worked his alchemy by rehearsing and performing the act so much that he could do it in his sleep, and then "selling it" through the sheer force of his infectious personality. He would intersperse his routines with little jokes and remarks, such as the famous "Everything's copasetic!" (a word, incidentally, that Robinson invented). His smile and his exuberant spirit were remarked upon by many a critic, if often in terms that today we would consider patronizing and racist; still, Robinson found it useful to cultivate the image, frequently billing himself as "The Dark Cloud of Joy."

In 1918, Robinson introduced what was to become his signature bit, "the stair dance." Versions of this dance can be seen today in numerous films, from the Wheeler and Woolsey vehicle *Dixiana* (1930), to what is probably Robinson's most famous screen role, opposite Shirley Temple, in *The Little Colonel* (1934). As effortlessly as if his feet had wings, he tapped his way up and down a staircase, playing the steps with his feet as if they were they keys of a piano. By 1923, Robinson had reached the second best spot on the bill at the Palace (or next to "next to closing")—the highest spot to which he could aspire, given the prejudice of the times.

In Robinson's wake came a whole host of others to big time and the Palace, most of whom also had done some time on the all-black circuits: Peg Leg Bates, Leonard Reed, Buck and Bubbles, Willie Covan, and the Nicholas Brothers. Bates's act was particularly noteworthy, and not just because he was that rarest of birds, a one-legged tap dancer. What kept his act from being a "freak act" was that, by any measure, Bates was an extraordinary dancer. He began at age five on the South Carolina cotton plantation where his family sharecropped, dancing barefoot and with no music, just the rhythm of hand claps. When his father abandoned the family, the twelve-year-old Bates went to work at a cotton gin, which is where he lost the bottom of his right leg in an accident. But he loved dancing so much he simply never stopped. It took him eighteen months to get the hang of the broom-handle-like contraption at the end of his knee, and then he went right on dancing, horseback riding, bicycling, and playing baseball, never realizing that it was completely remarkable. By age fifteen he was quite the professional. Burning with ambition, he surpassed many two-legged tap dancers, developing a unique sound with a special wooden leg, the tip of which was half rubber and half leather, allowing him to achieve a variety of rhythmic effects. The consummate showman, he even had numerous colored pegs, which he would coordinate with his costumes.

Fayard and Harold Nicholas were all of sixteen and nine when they made their debut in 1930, but they were already so dazzling that they stopped the show wherever they went. Self-taught though they were, the boys were clearly prodigies. Leaping head-high into the air, landing in a full split, and then coming up out of the split as though yanked by a giant unseen cable, and all in less time than it takes to type this—such was the stuff of the Nicholas Brothers.

Dance, of course, is the vaudeville specialty to which African-Americans made the greatest contribution and where they made the greatest inroads. Yet despite their success on the stage, the conditions of black performers' lives offstage were drastically different from those of their white counterparts. White dancers tended to come out of a genteel tradition, involving formal instruction at dancing academies and chaperoned parties at social clubs. On the other side of the equation, some of the African-American dancers had gone without shoes, let alone lessons, during their formative years. Theirs, like the Irish of early variety, was a folk tradition, transmitted from one unprivileged person to another unprivileged person. This is not to impugn the excellence of the white dancers, which, in the highly competitive environment of vaudeville, had to be extraordinary. African-Americans had tremendous regard for some of their white colleagues, and the cross-fertilization between the two traditions is largely responsible for the richness of American popular dance. Both groups served the same God. But the black dancers, as great as (and often greater than) their lighter-skinned contemporaries, deserved the same lucrative movie deals and the concomitant national fame into which their Caucasian counterparts literally waltzed. It was not until several decades later that African-American dancers such as Ben Vereen and Gregory Hines were afforded the sort of prominence their talent warranted.

Certain African-American singers, however, *did* receive the accolades and the remuneration they deserved. In 1925, Florence Mills, star of such Broadway shows as *Shuffle Along, The Plantation Revue*, and *Dixie to Broadway*, headlined vaudeville engagements at the Hippodrome and the Palace. More major shows followed, but she was to die, essentially of overwork, two years later, at age thirty-one. She was succeeded as the top African-American singer by Ethel Waters, who had come up through TOBA and the nightclub circuits to headline in the late twenties at the New York and Chicago Palaces for the astronomical salary of $3,000 a week. Like Bill Robinson, Ms. Waters was one of the few black vaudevillians to go on to a successful film career.

As touched on previously, vaudeville is often unfairly portrayed as being a uniquely bigoted endeavor, but such was not the case. The most racially derisive feature of vaudeville, blackface, for example, is often discussed as though it were part of an organized propaganda instrument of some secret racist cabal, when it was, in fact, the opposite. Vaudeville was market-driven. The *society* was racist; its entertainment was only a reflection of that fact. Furthermore, a case can be made that, compared to nearly every other American institution of that era (the military, the hospitality industry, retail, manufacturing, academia, medicine, government, law), show business was the peak of progressive liberalism for its day. Indignities and injustices there were, but in show business change came faster and more visibly than anywhere else in society.

The African-American acts mentioned above were a pretty compelling argument for the genius of a people, alongside which blackface minstrelsy could not long survive. In mainstream vaudeville, the few remaining whites in blackface started to be replaced by the genuine article (except in the South, where African-Americans continued to be barred from theaters). Many of these artists, through a combination of their brilliance as performers and the class they exhibited onstage, became a new source of pride for African-Americans and obtained great measures of respect from those whites who were not utterly blinded by racism. Vaudeville was a showcase for black heroes fifty years before the Brooklyn Dodgers hired Jackie Robinson. In an era when blacks couldn't stay at the same hotels, eat in the same restaurants, use the same bathrooms, or even walk in the front door, vaudeville was significantly ahead of the curve on race relations.

As Hitler and Henry Ford were good enough to remind us, the other ethnic group to make a major impact on vaudeville and the culture at large during the Palace years were the Jews of Central and Eastern Europe. Interestingly, they didn't even arrive at the party until it was nearly half over. Yet, in some respects it feels like until the Jews arrived all in vaudeville is mere prologue. Somehow or other, this group seemed to arrive, take a look around, roll up their sleeves, and then say, "Okay, you people are amateurs. We'll show you how it's done."

The "Hebrew" comic type had been a staple of variety and early vaudeville, although one less important than the Ethiopian, Teutonic, and Hibernian delineators. The most famous of this early type was Joe Welch, whose character made Shylock look like Gregory Peck in *Gentlemen's Agreement*. "Zo! You t'ink I'm heppy?" he'd ask the audience with a sigh and a shrug. Weber and Fields, David Warfield, Willie and Eugene Howard, Eddie Cantor, Gummo Marx, and Harry Jolson (Al's brother) all played such Hebrews early in their careers. Shemp Howard played a straightman to a Hebrew comic.

Interestingly, for a non-Jew to play the Hebrew was rare, but there were some. The Nazis, who later banned the films of Charlie Chaplin on the erroneous assumption that he was Jewish, were probably unaware that as a young performer he had once billed himself as "Sam Cohen, the Jewish Comedian," wearing a false nose, whiskers, and the whole nine yards. Chaplin was not Jewish, and his characterization got him booed off a London stage (he'd made the mistake of booking himself into a music hall in a Jewish neighborhood).

DOCTOR: On what side are you Jewish?
EDDIE: On the East Side.
(From the Eddie Cantor sketch "Insurance")

Around 1880, a series of vicious pogroms beset the Jews of Russia. Between that year and the start of the First World War, two million Jews, most of them from Eastern Europe, found refuge in America. Over 325,000 of them settled in New York's Lower East Side. On some blocks there were a thousand people per acre, the highest population density in the city. Between 1880 and 1890, three out of four Jewish immigrants settled in the Lower East Side. Out of this deceptively small bit of geography came the vaudevillians Weber and Fields, Eddie Cantor, Irving Berlin, George Burns, Molly Picon, Smith and Dale, Willie and Eugene Howard, and Belle Baker. By 1920, a third of New York City was Jewish.

Jews were by far the largest ethnic group in vaudeville, overwhelmingly comprising the lion's share of comedians and singers (i.e., the biggest stars). At the turn of the century, most of them were just starting out. By the late teens and twenties they had climbed sufficiently far up the show-business ladder to storm the Palace.

Thanks to the participation of so many Jews, Yiddish became an important part of the language of vaudeville. A bit of comedy business is known as "shtick." To "schlepp" (as one does with one's costume, trunk, and props) is an important Yiddish verb, as is to "schmooze" (as one did on the sidewalk in front of the Palace). And—very important for comedy—the language is unusually rich in names to hurl at a pathetic loser: nebbish, klutz, schnook, schmo, schmendrick, schlemiel, schlimazel . . .

Like African-Americans, Jews had their own segregated vaudeville circuit, although on a much smaller scale. On New York's Lower East Side you could find a thriving Yiddish theater scene, a component of which was Yiddish vaudeville. Echoing the nickname for New York's uptown theater district, Second Avenue became known as the Jewish Rialto. According to cinema historian Judith Thissen, in a Houston Street theater (known to New Yorkers today as the Sunshine Cinema), audiences could go to see a Yiddish-language vaudeville show featuring "the prophet Elijah," Hilda the Swedish Handcuff Queen, jugglers, one-act plays, songs and dances, and klezmer music, all on the same bill. Although Weber and Fields, Al Jolson, Sophie Tucker, and singer Nora Bayes were the first Jews to attain the very highest levels of stardom, none of these acts originally did so explicitly as Jews (although they all later incorporated their Jewishness into their public personae). America's first entertainer to make Jewishness a part of her act (without re-sorting to a grotesque "Hebrew" caricature) was Fanny Brice.

Born Fanny Borach, a daughter of Alsatian and Hungarian Jews, the aspiring entertainer commissioned a then-unknown Irving Berlin to write her a character song in 1909. He gave her "Sadie Salome, Go Home." Throughout her career, Brice was well-known for singing such character songs involving the names "Sadie" and "Rose." Today she is best remembered via Barbra Streisand's portrayal of her in the musical films *Funny Girl* and *Funny Lady*. Brice was actually rather unlike Streisand in appearance. Tall and gangly like Olive Oyl, with two bright crescent-shaped eyes on either side of her parrot-like nose, Brice was always using her mug for low-comedy effect. Her shtick was frequently to cast herself ironically in the roles of cinematic vamps and high-class society dames with English accents, playing humorously against her obviously ethnic style and physiognomy. To smack the point home, she often spoke in performance with a strong Yiddish accent—an accent she did not evince offstage.

Even more explicitly Jewish was another Palace star, the incomparable Belle Baker. A Russian Jew whose real name was Bella Becker, she had her first hit in 1913 with the Berlin song "Cohen Owes Me $97." A few years later, she started doing a song given to her by the great Sophie Tucker (whose real name was Kalish, also from Russia). The song was the ultimate vaudeville tearjerker, "My Yiddische Mama," and so popular that Sophie started doing it herself, making it one of her signature numbers.

Although these singers could be comical (especially Brice), they also brought with them to the stage an intensely histrionic sensibility, the awareness that even the slightest song was a dramatic presentation. The audience had the understanding that the person onstage was going to take them on a journey through the peaks and depths of sensible possibility, leaving no emotional stone unturned. In the course of eighteen minutes they would be transported to Elysium, hurled into an abyss of despair, sob for their dead mothers, root for the boys overseas, and piss their pants at the wit of the character right there in front of them.

In the Chaplin film *A Dog's Life*, the Little Tramp ducks into a variety house and finds on the stage a performer singing what appears to be a very sad song. The film of course is silent, but we know the song is sad because of the singer's outward manner (hand over heart, eyes gazing heavenward), and because there isn't a dry eye in the house. The audience is heaving, convulsed with sobs. One man's walrus-style mustache is completely soaked with tears. Chaplin was exaggerating for the sake of humor, but he was exaggerating a truth. People used to like to go to the theater to hear sad songs that made them cry. Joe Franklin likes to describe the "throb" in Belle Baker's voice and how, when she sang "My Yiddische Mama," all of the women in the audience would not only be crying but howling, screaming, and falling into the aisles, clutching their handkerchiefs. When was the last time you, or anyone you know, had—or sought—an experience like that?

Working-class women could identify with such performers, who were, like Shakespeare's Richard III, "not shaped for sportive tricks" but could sport a few tricks nonetheless, by developing an irresistible inner spirit, a fire in the belly, a white lightning of the solar plexus that churned and throbbed and tumbled until it overflowed the vessel containing it and streamed out the performers' eyes and fingertips and engulfed the audience in crackling bolts of electric plasma. Performance technique as devised by Nikola Tesla.

Sophie Tucker was the essence of what made vaudeville and subsequent American show business great. She was hardly the best singer in the world, but she had "it," a terrific ability to sell a song, along with a terrific sense of humor and a knack for picking out appropriate character songs for herself, so that you felt that you knew her. You got a powerful sense of who she was. A hearty and honest presence, she suggested everything that was good and bad about life itself. A Tucker set, sung in her trademark husky voice, would evoke laughter, tears, and a healthy, Rabelaisian contemplation of sex. Eddie Cantor once said of Sophie Tucker that she would cry at a card trick. Emotions were her stock in trade.

Cantor himself was vaudeville's first male "out" Jew. In his heyday, there were few bigger stars than Eddie Cantor, almost forgotten today. Born Israel Iskowitz, the son of Belarussian immigrants, his act was in some ways a spin-off of Jolson's. A sometime blackface performer (indeed, he was one of the last major stars to come of age burning cork), Cantor was a sort of combination stand-up comedian, sketch comedian, singer, and dancer. He sang and recorded several amusingly suggestive (and sometimes nonsensical) songs that were the very soul of the 1920s, among them "If You Knew Susie," "Yes, We Have No Bananas," "Yes, Sir, That's My Baby," and "Ma! He's Making Eyes at Me." His style of delivering a song was kinetic and eye-catching. He was famous for doing a strange little dance while he sang, sort of marching around the stage with high steps, while he patted his hands together in rhythm to the music. He even had a signature exit device—a little hankie he waved at the audience.

Yet unlike Jolson (who was also Jewish), Cantor incorporated his Jewishness into his act, acknowledging it in one-liners and lines interpolated into songs, and throwing in Yiddish words and references to his "Russian" origins. He was a new sort of American character, impudent and familiar, fast-talking, urban, breezy, assertive. The persona he developed anticipates Bob Hope and Woody Allen by decades, with its intriguing and contradictory qualities of chutzpah and matter-of-fact hilarious cowardice. Scrawny and bug-eyed (or "banjo-eyed," as the scribblers put it), Cantor was light years away from the cursing, fighting, drunken "Irishmen" who'd convulsed audiences only a few years before.

In the late teens and twenties, a whole crop of similar Jewish singer-comedians came up. So gifted a performer was Lou Holtz that he was hired by the Shuberts as an understudy for Jolson, to remind Jolie that he could always be let go. But in vaudeville, Holtz was also a popular comedian. He created a character named Mr. Lapidus, a stereotypical Jew who said things like "In shoes I take a size eight, but size nine feels so comfortable I wear size ten." George Jessel was best known for a humorous routine he did involving a telephone conversation with his mother. ("Hello, Ma? It's me, Georgie. Georgie. You know, the one from the checks?") A Boston hoofer and comedian named Benny Rubin did comic Jewish monologues, a tap dance, and a trombone solo. The Jewish routine brought him great popularity, although less so among more sensitive Jews. His character was a broad (and to many, offensive) stereotype. A photo of one of his characters tells it all: a greasepaint vandyke and skull cap accentuate his prominent proboscis and too-narrow eyes. Eventually, public pressure caused Rubin to abandon the character completely.

Perhaps the archetypical vaudeville male two-act was a Jewish team known as Smith and Dale. They were born Joe Sultzer (Smith) and Charles Marks (Dale) on the Lower East Side in the early 1880s. They met as teenagers when their bicycles collided. The boys' ensuing argument was thought by bystanders to be "as funny as Weber and Fields," and they began to cultivate an act in Bowery saloons doing song-and-dance bits in blackface. When a deal came their way on some unclaimed business cards, they adopted the names "Smith and Dale." But it would be another two decades (during which time they also performed with an act called the Avon Comedy Four) before they would permanently adopt the pseudonyms, going on from there to become a familiar fixture at the Palace.

When one thinks of a "vaudeville comedy team," one thinks of something like Smith and Dale. Neil Simon based his play *The Sunshine Boys* on their act, although their offstage relationship wasn't as dire as Simon wrote it—that part was based on another team, Gallagher and Shean. Smith and Dale may have had another sort of influence on Simon, as the originators of the "whattayou" joke construction. For example, a line from Smith and Dale's doctor sketch:

DALE (as doctor): What kind of dishes do you eat?
SMITH (as patient): Dishes? What am I, a crocodile?

From Simon's *The Odd Couple*:

OSCAR (to Murray): What are you, Bulldog Drummond?

The kind of jokes Smith and Dale told later became staples on the Borscht Belt. From their "Dr. Kronkite" sketch:

DOCTOR: Did you have this pain before?
PATIENT: Yes.
DOCTOR: Well, you got it again.

This type of humor would inform the work of comedians like Milton Berle and Soupy Sales for the remainder of the twentieth century.

There is an unsentimental utilitarianism about Smith and Dale.

How far their intentions were from "art" can be seen in the way their sketches tended to go untitled and are merely tagged with the situation that allows them to spin off a barrage of site-specific jokes: the "doctor" sketch, the "school" sketch, the "bank" sketch, the "restaurant" sketch. In fact, the sketches are *all joke*, zipping along from punch line to punch line (as in early Marx Brothers films) with gleeful disregard for plot and character. The very crudity of it has a distinctive vaudevillian charm.

The rapid-fire pace at which Smith and Dale performed has much to do with the particular parameters of the vaudeville medium. The vaudevillian was constantly squeezed for time. He had a certain number of minutes for his slot. If he went over, he could be fined, even fired. Getting onstage and offstage had to be done at a breakneck clip. One can hear Phil Silvers as the theater manager: "Bing! Boom! Bam! Chop-chop! Get goin'! What is this, a staring contest?" Comedy naturally evolved to suit the new twentieth-century speed limit. Comedians be-came "fast-talking." The ultimate distiller of this process, the king of comic economy, was the great Henny Youngman, who started out just as vaud was in its last gasps, in the early 1930s. Youngman was the Samuel Beckett of funnymen: setup, punch line, laugh, setup, punch line, laugh. Not an ounce of fat (and sometimes no meat) on that act. A more recent example of this kind of pared-down act would be Steven Wright, who adds a surrealistic sensibility and a broad (if subdued) character choice that is similarly reminiscent of vaudeville.

The traditional monologist's approach had been somewhat differ-ent. Incubated in Chautauquas (the pseudo-vaudeville education circuit that specialized in lectures and recitals and grew up at the same time as vaudeville), the style was literary, formal, and verbose. A prime example of an early vaudeville monologist who came out of Chautauquas is the hunchbacked humorist Marsall P. Wilder, who might begin an anecdote like this: "I am a good-natured man, and purpose to be cheerful on all occasions. But once in a while, I meet someone whom I have to sit down upon . . ." In the time it took Wilder to spit all that out, Henny Young-man could have told three jokes.

At the Palace another approach to solo comedy was developing, snappy and spontaneous, witty and often completely improvised—in short, the forerunner to modern stand-up comedy. The man who originated this style is an unjustly forgotten innovator by the name of Frank Fay (the "Great Faysie").

There was much to set Fay apart. Unlike most vaudevillians, Fay was no populist. He cultivated the aloof arrogance of the aristocrat—his trademark was the barbed put-down delivered on the spot with predictable lethalness. When one of his many foils, Patsy Kelly, announced she had just come back from the beauty parlor, Fay would ask, "And they didn't wait on you?" Audiences prized him for his comic ruthlessness. He was also one of the first comedians to make no gesture whatsoever toward clownishness—no plaid jacket, no derby, no greasepaint for him. Rather, he was charismatic, dashing, and impeccably dressed, with a broad handsome Irish face (something like that of actor Ralph Fiennes). One gets the feeling that Fay sold his jokes through *charm*.

By 1918 he had established himself as a monologist, and by 1919 he played the Palace. This was, of course, the very highest aspiration of most vaudevillians. A select handful ran a week there. In 1925, Fay ran *ten* weeks. He was so successful, in fact, that he helped change the entire format of vaudeville. Unlike the British music hall, which had its proceedings orchestrated by a "chairman," for most of its existence vaudeville had no such creature as a master of ceremonies. Performers were announced by a placard ("Petunia and Her Performing Poodles") placed on an easel, which was changed between acts by a stagehand. While there had been tentative experiments with emcees by such performers as James C. Morton and Loney Haskell in earlier years, such was the force of Fay's talent that in the 1920s it became a permanent fixture at the Palace. The emcee position called for someone who could think on his feet, who could kid around with the acts on their entrances and exits, could improvise clever introductions, and pad the show if there was some emergency backstage. Fay was the sort of performer who could rise to that occasion, and an entire generation of stand-up comedians would follow his lead.

Anthropologically speaking, Fay is the "Lucy" of stand-up; all stand-up bloodlines lead back to him. For a botanical analogy, he is the trunk from which two main branches of comedy would grow. On the one hand, he originated the stand-up comedy style we associate with Hope, Benny, Carson, Leno, and Letterman, the extremely polished "American institution" style, an unspoken confidence that says "an army of people made me possible." This type of comedian specializes in telling America the jokes that will be repeated around the water cooler at work the next day. On the other hand, with his flip irreverence, Fay is also the father of the more burlesquey style that was to be identified with Ted Healy, Milton Berle, Ken Murray, and such aggressive late-twentieth-century comedians as Don Rickles, Alan King, and Jackie Mason. Of all of these, Fay's foremost successor was Lester Townes ("Bob") Hope.

As a teenager, Hope had seen Frank Fay perform at Keith's 195th Street in Cleveland. Bitten by the bug, he quit school at age sixteen, took dancing lessons, and started singing with a quartet. For most of the twenties, Hope worked as a hoofer, with a succession of partners (including, amazingly, the joined-at-the-hip Hilton Sisters) until 1927, when at a gig in New Castle, Pennsylvania, he was asked to announce upcoming shows. This was his first true assignment as a comedian. He moved to Chicago that year, and, after several weeks without work, began a successful run as emcee at the Stratford Theatre, where he went over big.

Making the leap to New York, Hope got himself booked at Proctor's Fifty-fourth Street, in a conscious attempt to impress the Keith booker. He soon learned that this was the toughest house in the city and that his turn there would be a make-or-break moment. With typical resourcefulness, he devised a show-stopping opening line while waiting in the wings to go on. Prior to his entrance, the stage was occupied by a performer named Leatrice Joy, who was then living down her divorce from the actor John Gilbert. As Joy walked off, Hope walked on and quipped to a woman in the audience, "No, lady, I am *not* John Gilbert." Hope's chutzpah in exploiting the personal life of a fellow performer for the sake of a joke slayed the audience and for the rest of the set they were eating out of Hope's hand. He got several curtain calls, and William Morris promptly signed him to a three-year contract with the Keith organization.

Hope's strength was his comic manner, not necessarily his material. Something about his face, the arched eyebrows, the devilish glint in his eyes just before he delivered a punch line, helped him sell it. His personality was brash and bold and he instinctively knew how to get a joke over, no matter how lame it was. Often the material was so weak in the early days that in 1930 he hired the consummate vaudeville gag man Al Boasberg to write jokes for him. Boasberg also wrote for Burns and Allen, the Marx Brothers, and others before one corned-beef sandwich too many summoned him prematurely to that one layover from which no vaudevillian ever returns.

Hope started in show business at just the right time. He came to vaudeville late in its evolution, and although his ascent coincided with its demise, he managed to get a foothold elsewhere before it winked out. While there was still a vaudeville he was glad to work there, but by the time it died he didn't need it anymore. He stepped from his dates at the Palace into book musicals and radio as one might step off a ship that is going under. Vaudeville was his training ground, though. "Being successful in vaudeville is the only true measure of a comedian's ability," he once said. Hope spent the better part of a decade on the vaudeville stage, learning timing and improvisation, and developing a stage presence that would take him through another seven decades of performing.

Hope's branch of the Fay family also includes Jack Benny, who is said to have adapted his pregnant silences and icy glares from Fay. Benny, like Hope, also literally stole Fay's gait. Those of you of a certain age will remember that Hope and Benny would sashay onstage with a certain "swishy" energy, arms akimbo, with the hands upturned so the palms were parallel to the floor. They walked almost like fashion models. In delivering their monologues they'd adopt coy mannerisms, study their fingernails, fold their arms across their chest, adjust their hair. Hope and Benny copped these moves (as did many other comedians of their generation) from Fay. These humorous gestures helped telegraph character, communicating vanity, pride, and a whole host of other potential comic foibles.

At the base of the other branch of Fay's descendants is another unjustly forgotten comedian by the name of Ted Healy. Healy broke into burlesque while still a teenager, doing minstrel routines in blackface. With partner Betty Brown (who became his wife), he went into vaudeville, telling jokes in his loose conversational style, and singing a couple of songs. He first hit it big at the Keith Theatre in Jersey City, and was strictly a big-time act after that. He began writing sketches that called for interruptions by stooges, plants from the audience, something Fay had done with confederates like Patsy Kelly. But Healy was more down-to-earth, a little more "low" than Fay. His stooges would seem to be hecklers at first, or stagehands, or messenger boys, or something similar, and Healy would cut them down to size with a humorous ballet of slapstick. Right from the first, a rude or dumb line from a stooge would earn him an instant slap in the face.

By now you may have gleaned who these stooges were. (Hint: there were three of them.) Healy, standing over six feet tall, towered over Moe, Larry, and Shemp (Curly did not join until the team went into pictures). Healy was never the straight man, as might be assumed; he was the star of the act. The bald-headed, shiny faced, red-nosed, and genial Irishman would come out and sing songs as a solo, until interrupted by the stooges, whereupon he would start to get violent. The act, one imagines, relied a good deal on shock and surprise for its humor. The sound of the slaps in the theater must have been something. Healy invented much that one associates with the stooges; the whole rhythm of slapping, the whole audacious trope of slapping as a form of "communication" is his, as is even the vaunted "triple slap." (Credit for the finger poke, not to mention their own bizarre characterizations, must be given to Messrs. Howard and Fine, however.)

One young comedian who patterned his walk, talk, tempo, and flippancy on Ted Healy's was a former child star named Milton Berle. After a few years of bombing as an awkward adolescent, Berle hit his stride in the late 1920s as "Milton Berle, the Wayward Youth." He had discovered that supreme necessity of the vaudevillian: personality. For Berle, the gags may be hoary and stale, but a good comic could get over on the strength of his verve alone. He developed a brash quality that one associates with burlesque, although he never worked the girlie shows. He'd pick on people in the audience, ad-lib, and get as close to risqué as he could without actually crossing the line. When, late in its life, vaudeville evolved the role of a master of ceremonies to helm the proceedings, Berle was one of the few naturally prepared to take on the job. In 1932, he got an opportunity to emcee at the Palace, when Benny Rubin came down with appendicitis. For a comedian, hosting at the Palace was a dream gig. Instead of the standard twelve minutes, the whole show was yours. Berle was a smash hit, staying on eight weeks. He had a similar gig at the Chicago Palace the following year, and it was around this time that columnist Walter Winchell famously dubbed him "the Thief of Bad Gags."

This author's first exposure to Milton Berle was in the 1970s, when he was principally one of a seemingly limitless crop of septuagenarian, cigar-smoking comedians who still dominated television at that time. The disparity between Berle's legend and the codger I saw onscreen had me scratching my head for years. *This* was Mr. Television? This dirty old man who was constantly apologizing for his Joe Miller–style jokes was once such a phenomenon that he quadrupled the sale of TV sets? Restaurants emptied out on Tuesdays because of this man?

The mystery was cleared up when I finally got around to watching kinescopes of his old shows, *The Texaco Star Theater*. The answer is, that the middle-aged Berle (as opposed to the elderly Berle) was a ball of fire. The man had so much energy, and was given to such crazy spontaneity that it seemed as though he would jump out of the TV screen. Hilarious, kinetic, and uninhibited—the sort of comedian who would run into the audience, snatch a woman's fur coat out of her hands, and put it on. It seems like ancient history to see Berle so young; and yet at that point Berle had already been in show business for over forty years.

A contemporary of Berle's was Ken Murray, who was known for being the "bluest" of vaudeville's comics. Murray claimed to have been the first comedian to make smoking a cigar a part of his act, which he adopted on account of being the youngest big-time comic (he was in his early twenties) and wanting to add some "experience" to his persona. But surely Groucho Marx and Bobby Clark were puffing their cheroots long before Murray came along. As time went on, more and more of them became associated with the vice: Milton Berle, George Burns, George Jessel. Why a cigar? Let's just skip over the more lurid implications and examine what the unassuming observer might make of all this. To my mind, the vice humanized the performers, which made the audience relate to them all the better.

There were no stand-up comediennes in the vaudeville era. Even today, it is a male-dominated field. Then, as now, the woman stand-up was demonized as aggressively unfeminine. Funny women abounded, though, in ways that generally reaffirmed popular ideas of appropriate female behavior. The solo funny women in vaudeville were all "singing comediennes" in the tradition of British music-hall stars. Prominent examples included Nora Bayes, Trixie Friganza, Marie Dressler, Irene Franklin, Fanny Brice, and Beatrice Lillie. Music was considered a reasonably acceptable realm for women to express themselves in. Amateur singing and piano playing in parlors by women and girls was probably the nation's leading form of home entertainment for many decades. But for a woman to go on stage and start making smart cracks about everything under the sun would have seemed seditious, and carried with it a vague whiff of the suffragette and anarchism. Not until the 1960s were women commonly seen prowling around the stages of comedy clubs spouting one-liners.

Much as African-Americans had been forced to put on blackface, overalls, and straw hats, pretend to love watermelon, and so forth, women comedians were forced into the role of the "Dumb Dora." Male-female comedy teams almost all followed the same formula: ditzy, impractical, doe-eyed female delivers the laugh lines, with the straight lines fed to her by a solid, normal, increasingly impatient male who shares with the audience an eye-winking "Am I right, fellas?" sort of attitude. Burns and Allen were of course the best and most famous of these, but there was also Block and Sully, and countless others. Bob Hope worked with his own Dumb Dora named Honey Chile. Jack Benny's Dumb Dora was Dorothy Maguire.* The stereotype was that women couldn't drive, manage money, or understand important "man" things like politics. Eve Sully's lines were so influential they have long outlasted her memory: "Some nerve!"; "I'll say!"; and "I'll bet you tell that to all the girls!" This is from the Burns and Allen sketch "Dizzy":

(A man comes out, puts his arms around Gracie, and kisses her, and she kisses him. They wave to each other as he backs offstage. Gracie returns to George at center stage.)

GRACIE: Who was that?
GEORGE: You don't know?

---

*Naturally, this was before he teamed up with his wife, Mary Livingston, a cousin of the Marx Brothers, who wasn't dumb at all.

GRACIE: No, my mother told me never to talk to strangers.

GEORGE: That makes sense.

GRACIE: This always happens to me. On my way in, a man
stopped me at the stage door and said, "Hiya, cutie, how
about a bite tonight after the show?"

GEORGE: And you said?

GRACIE: I said, "I'll be busy after the show, but I'm not doing
anything right now." So I bit him.

Another top male-female comedy team of the Palace era was actually
composed of two men: Savoy and Brennan. Bert Savoy, the first modern
drag queen, was the complete opposite of Julian Eltinge. He established
the pattern for drag performance that obtains to this day, creating a
character who was campy, mean, and brassy and who inspired both
pathos and rude guffaws. Arch and cutting, he was a true artist in di-
recting his satire inward, making no attempt to seem graceful and glamorous like Eltinge, preferring to accentuate his hairy arms, awkward,
manly size, and male voice for comic effect. He called everyone "dearie"
and referred to gay men as "she."

After years as a boy cooch dancer and a fortune-teller, he served an
apprenticeship with the Russell Brothers, stepping in when one of the
brothers passed away. In the mid-teens, he created a new act with Jay
Brennan, whom he'd met on a streetcar the previous year. Brennan
turned out to be one of the best straight men in the business, feeding
lines to Savoy, who played a loud-mouthed, overdressed woman who
rambled on constantly about her friend "Margie." Savoy based his character on a lady he and Brennan met in a bar. (Edmund Wilson described
her—i.e., Savoy—as "a gigantic red-haired harlot . . . reeking of corro-
sive cocktails . . . One felt oneself in the presence of the vast vulgarity of
New York incarnate and made heroic.")

BRENNAN: Is Margie married?

SAVOY: No, she's a widow.

BRENNAN: Where did she bury her husband?

SAVOY: She said his last wish was to be buried in San Francisco, but Margie buried him over in Brooklyn.

BRENNAN: But she should have carried out his wish.

SAVOY: That's what his sister said: "If you don't he's liable to come back and *haunt* you." I thought I'd die! Margie said, "We'll try him over in Brooklyn. If he bothers me, I will send him to 'Frisco."

But all depictions of women in vaudeville weren't so derogatory as the Dumb Dora characters or Savoy's vulgar broad. Singing comediennes and the era's great actresses ruled the vaudeville stage. Indeed, proportionally, they were the industry's highest-paid and best-loved stars, not to mention some of the best-compensated, most powerful women in America. Far from being the helpmeet and masseuse of some man, these women called the shots wherever they went, spent their money how they liked, got quoted in the newspaper, and, in short, proved—on the world stage—that they were nobody's inferior.

While the women's movement of the 1960s and seventies gets the lion's share of attention historically, much greater leaps forward had been made two and three generations earlier. In 1880, women were expected to defer to their husband in *all* matters. Recall the plight of Nora in Henrik Ibsen's *A Doll's House* (1879). Women were expected to be mindless and obedient pets, fawned upon, spoiled, and perhaps loved . . . but powerless to make decisions. Women *were* children, even in the eyes of the law, and plenty seemed to like it just fine. Change in America was so slow that it was not until 1920 that the Nineteenth Amendment extended to women the right to vote.

In the wake of Ibsen, and in the political context of the women's suffrage movement, some, like Alla Nazimova and Olga Petrova, used the drama as a platform for broadcasting a feminist message. One-act plays and monologues pleading for more equitable laws for women actually played a small but integral part of vaudeville—a good half-century before the advent of political performance art. The fact that these plays dealt with racy topics like marital relations under the cover of high art may have helped justify their bookings, however.

Russian-born Nazimova studied and acted with the Moscow Art Theater (and splinter groups therefrom) before coming to the United States on tour in 1905. Her 1906 performance as Hedda Gabler was such a hit that she went on to star in most of Ibsen's major plays over the next few years. She almost always did "important" naturalistic plays, usually with progressive political themes. A gorgeous woman with enormous eyes and a sensuous mouth, she reinforced the sensationalism of her feminist forays by giving them sex appeal. This is what made her a hit in vaudeville.

In 1914 she debuted a one-act play at the Palace titled *An Unknown Woman* that made the case for more sensible divorce laws. A querulous Edward Albee canceled the act at the urging of a Roman Catholic clergyman, although Nazimova was paid in full for her services. In 1915 she returned with the pacifist playlet *War Brides*, which was especially timely, given the conflict overseas. This turn was such a hit she toured the Orpheum circuit with it, and then adopted it into a 1916 movie. After a movie career with many ups and downs she went back to the Palace for several vaudeville engagements through the 1920s. One of the playlets she introduced was another feminist drama called *India*, cowritten by Edgar Allen Woolf, who was probably vaudeville's most prolific playwright.

Olga Petrova, the phony Russian actress, was taken quite seriously by audiences. Apparently, she was so moving in her dramatic portrayals, and so serious about the content of her art, that she had to be taken seriously. An ardent feminist, she always chose strong, independent female roles in plays and monologues that offered a moral. In the 1920s she wrote and starred in three plays: *The White Peacock* (1921), *Hurricane* (1923), which dealt with the issue of birth control, and *What Do We Know?* (1927), which was about spiritualism.

Yet what is most impressive about Petrova is the strength of will she displayed offstage. Once, booked at Proctor's Fifth Avenue, she accepted the gig only on the condition that for the first week she would receive no money and no billing. Perplexed, the booker agreed. During the week, she slayed the audience. The next week, English performer R. A. Roberts joined the bill, at which point Petrova abruptly insisted on top billing. The request was granted. Roberts, who'd been hired as the headliner, made a stink and quit the engagement. Petrova years earlier had done a tour of South Africa with his company. It was the opinion of some that Roberts had once been a beast to her, and that this was her way of getting even.

That sort of deliberateness and calculation was characteristic of

Petrova, who often germinated and hatched such schemes across a period of several years. For example, she once told her booker that she wanted vaudeville engagements in the following towns: Providence, Oklahoma City, Columbus, Indianapolis, Fort Worth, and Houston—a preposterous tour if you stop and think about it—extensive travel, and all to small towns. Furthermore, she asked to be paid one dollar more than the previous highest-paid performer at each theater. Her strange demands met, Petrova went off to conquer each town, even breaking Sarah Bernhardt's previous attendance record in several cities. It turned out that the strange itinerary was her attempt to disprove a taunt made years earlier that she would flop in all of those venues. Now she could show that not only was she a hit, but she was the highest-paid performer at each stop.

If Olga Petrova, with her delusion of Russian heritage and her whimsical plots of revenge, sounds a little bit "out there," she had plenty of company in vaudeville. One of the beauties of vaudeville was that its appreciation for diversity extended in all directions. If it was new, different, or strange, chances are it could find a home in vaudeville. There was an entire subgenre of acts called "nuts" featuring performers who couldn't otherwise be categorized.

Examples: Chaz Chase (who ate things) and Hadji Ali (who spit things up). Chase earned his living downing all sorts of crap that mommies and daddies tell babies not to swallow: pins, needles, lit cigarettes, and the like. Hadji Ali was a practitioner of an actual vaudeville subcategory called a "regurgitation act." At the climax of his performance, he would swallow some turpentine, then some water; then somehow manage to spit the turpentine up first, all over a lit flame, which he would then extinguish by regurgitating the water. There is an element of *Ripley's Believe It or Not* to these acts, as there was to "Willard, the Man Who Grows," who had the ability to add as much as seven and a half inches to his height at will.

Another act, Singer's Midgets, was a vaudeville staple and is actually well-known to modern audiences thanks to their prominent casting as the Munchkins in *The Wizard of Oz*. Let's face it, when you're a midget singing group, *The Wizard of Oz* is your dream gig. In fact, one might have thought it'd be your *only* gig, but apparently there was some measure of demand for this chorus of little people—even without the meringue wigs and George Hamilton tans.

Other nuts of the Palace years included: A. Robbins, "The Banana Man," a silent character who removed an astonishing number of items from his coat, including pieces of furniture; Doc Rockwell "Quack Quack Quack," a comical double-talk lecturer on human anatomy; Professor Backwards, a man who could write anything in reverse; and Will Ferry, "The Frog Man," a contortionist dressed in a frog costume.

Thousands of musicians tried to distinguish themselves with nutty gimmicks—the harmonica kings, musical saw players, accordionists, ukulele orchestras, and concert harpists—a gambit with a limited shelf life, but peculiarly vaudevillian nonetheless. No less than two characters, for example (Will Mahoney and Dave Monihan, and there were probably others), played the xylophone with their feet. A gentleman named Orville Stam climaxed his act by continuing to sing while his piano was placed on his chest. John Carl alternated his banjo interludes with recitations of Shakespeare. A kid named Ernie Forest played his banjo blindfolded. Borrah Minevitch had a small orchestra of harmonica players, "His Harmonica Rascals."

William Demarest (best known as "Uncle Charlie" from TV's *My Three Sons*) is the only one of these "nuts" to become more than a footnote. In the late teens he developed an act that is best described by Demarest himself:

> The audience settles back and says, "Here comes another straight musical act." I could play the hell out of that cello, and I get going good on "Zigeunerweisen." All of a sudden I stop, put the cello down, lie down on the floor and try to do a nip-up [flip into a standing position from a supine pose on the floor]. It looks like I'm going to make it, but I don't. I snap way up in the air and come down flat on my back like a sack of cement. You'd think I'd broke my neck. I don't say a damn thing, just pick up the cello, sit down and go on with "Zigeunerweisen" where I left off.

Music? Comedy? Acrobatics? Anyway, it worked for Demarest. In 1927, Warner Bros. signed him; he appeared in *The Jazz Singer* and several Vitaphone shorts. By 1932, he was a master of ceremonies at the Palace. (In fact, he hosted their very last two-a-day.)

The annexation of Hawaii in 1898 seems to have fueled a vogue in vaudeville for that territory's native instrument, the ukulele. The uke was ubiquitous in vaud at least through the twenties, and any number of peppy warblers with a modicum of musicality accompanied themselves on said micro-instrument. One, Cliff Edwards (best known as the voice of Jiminy Cricket in Walt Disney's *Pinocchio*), rode to fame in radio and vaudeville as "Ukulele Ike." But for the most part, the uke was a dilet-tante's instrument—you didn't really have to play to "play," if you know what I mean.

Not until late in vaudeville's life did musical outfits become big at-tractions in and of themselves. People probably thought such a thing was redundant—after all, every theater already had its own house musicians. And plenty of singers could accompany themselves, on banjo, piano, or guitar. A musician who was just a musician was sort of like an acrobat or animal act—stardom for the mute artists, however brilliant, was rare. The musicians who did become big names on their own did so in the same way acrobats did: by becoming comedians, or singers, or at the very least songwriters. Musicians who graduated in this way included Olsen and Johnson, Jimmy Durante, Chico and Harpo Marx, Jack Benny, and Harry Richman. Conversely, just as many other sorts of acts had dancing in their bag of tricks, so, too, did many excel at an instrument. Many co-medians would add on a gratuitous musical turn at the end of their act for their big finish. Ken Murray would throw a clarinet solo into his act. Frank Tinney played the bagpipes. Comic lecturer Doc Rockwell ("Quack Quack Quack") topped his act off with a pennywhistle tune.

In the twenties, big bands started to come into play, and they be-came such a strong draw on their own that they would merit the coveted fifth slot on the bill, just before intermission. Vaudeville bandleaders were not the bland characters we sometimes associate with the big band era, essentially just standing there with their backs to you, blocking the view of the orchestra. In vaudeville, the bandleader had a huge person-ality. They made a visual impression. Paul "Pops" Whiteman was an enormous man with a pencil-thin mustache and a dashing flair for dress. He looked a combination of Oliver Hardy and Sydney Greenstreet. Ted Lewis wore a battered top hat and would frequently entertain the audi-ence by rolling it down his arm and catching it. Rudy Vallee and His

Connecticut Yankees had a Joe College thing going, with everybody dressed in cute letterman sweaters. Vallee himself sang into a megaphone like a varsity cheerleader. The band leaders all had their familiar catch phrases—most of them outliving the memory of those who made them famous. Ben Bernie's was "Yowsah, yowsah, yowsah." Ted Lewis: "Is ev'rybody happy?" Rudy Vallee: "Heigh ho, everybody!" Vallee was to become quite the heartthrob. He, like all of the other bandleaders, enjoyed great stardom in radio, as well, which helped fuel the popularity of his vaudeville appearances. So great a star was Vallee, recalls Joe Franklin, that he needed a police escort, with sirens blaring, to get to his engagements, and, says Franklin, "He was bigger than Britney Spears, Michael Jackson, and the Rolling Stones combined."

CHIPS OFF THE OLD BLOCK

The Palace was to become the jewel in Albee's crown. Not only was it the principal showplace for vaudeville performers, but shortly after it opened, the United Booking Office headquarters were moved there. Big-time acts were booked on the sixth floor, small time on the fifth. Martin Beck (and his successors Eddie Darling and George Godfrey) ran the show there, presiding over regular Wednesday meetings wherein the fates of thousands of performers were decided. An assistant would read a list of acts, and Beck would give his verdicts, either "pick up" or "no interest," along with the number of weeks, salary, and so on. The bookers made these decisions based on reviews, weekly reports by the various theater managers around the country, and secret reports filed by hired snitches, fellow performers who were also spies on the Keith-Albee payroll. It was show business as conceived by George Orwell.

With so much power concentrated in so few hands, the managers felt they could take any measure they wished to control performers with impunity. In 1913, for example, a decree went out declaring that any act that advertised in, or was even caught reading, *Variety* would be canned. Sime Silverman's vaudeville trade publication was a perpetual thorn in management's side, never hesitating to trumpet its abuses. Now it was banned from all major vaudeville theaters.

In the mid-teens, waves of bad luck arrived. World War I hurt international trade, resulting in a bad economic slump in 1914. The war had the equally devastating effect (to vaudevillians) of closing Europe to American performers, creating a glut of talent at home. On top of that, feature films had just caught on, and their greater length meant fewer slots for entertainers on the vaudeville bill. Managers were feeling the pinch themselves. They solved the problem by cutting performers' salaries across the board by 15 percent.

This draconian step brought the White Rats, the vaudeville performers' union, out of hibernation. The organization had been slowly regaining momentum since about 1910, under the more experienced leadership of British music-hall performer and agitator Harry Mountford. Among Mountford's contributions was the creation of a new charter for the White Rats through the American Federation of Labor and the acquisition of a large building for the group's headquarters on West Forty-sixth Street. Mountford vigorously hammered the vaudeville bosses to obtain better contracts for performers, greater accountability from management, and a closed shop. Over ten thousand (which translates to "virtually all") vaudevillians were members.

In 1916, Albee exacerbated tensions by forcing all of his acts to sign statements that said they were not members of the White Rats. Furthermore, he enforced mandatory membership in a new "union" called National Vaudeville Artists—created and run of course by the Vaudeville Managers Association.

In 1916 and 1917, the White Rats attempted another strike. This one was even less successful than the one in 1901. All the White Rats were blacklisted, membership dropped drastically, and the union was forced to sell its building. In a quintessential act of symbolic pettiness, Albee bought the building in 1917 and made it the headquarters for his new NVA. No one ever heard a squeak from the White Rats again. (Although variety performers would continue to organize: in 1932, with vaudeville in a shambles, the American Federation of Actors was founded with Eddie Cantor as president. After a series of corruption scandals, it was reorganized in 1939 as the American Guild of Variety Artists [AGVA], which still exists today, though some critics charge it does little to protect its members beyond the annual bestowing of a "Georgie"

Award, named after George Jessel. But, to be fair to the union, there isn't much of a variety industry today for it to police.)

But in the heyday of vaudeville, a vaudeville union might have been a useful counterweight to some of the UBO's more egregious abuses. So why weren't the performers successful at organizing?

It's simple. Vaudevillians were more like entrepreneurs than "workers." As opposed to factory hands, these people were professional individualists, the descendents of those antisocial medieval minstrels, each of whom produced his own act. The vaudevillians bought their own costumes, they paid their own staff, and, as befits materialists, they commissioned their own material. They wanted to be rich and they liked to be their own bosses. None of which makes for solidarity. Sure, they loved clubs and associations such as the Friars and the Lambs, mostly so they could sit around, play cards, drink scotch, and swap show-biz anecdotes. But a union? You can measure the vaudevillian's antipathy to the concept in Willie Howard's sketch "Come the Revolution":

> WILLIE (as a leftist agitator): Come the revolution, you'll eat strawberries and cream.
> LISTENER: But I don't like strawberries and cream.
> WILLIE (scowling): Tomorrow, come the revolution, you'll eat strawberries and cream, and you'll like it!

Who'd want to substitute B. F. Keith for a union boss who extorts dues? By cooperating with management one stood a chance of climbing the ladder to that coveted $2,500 weekly salary. Going against management ran you the risk of having to go out and get a real job, and the trials and tribulations most performers endured in the industry were naught compared to what they'd left back home. The personnel of vaudeville were drawn almost entirely from the ambitious underclass. Many began their working lives as children, selling newspapers, shining shoes, and even working in factories. Since show folk were imaginative enough to envision themselves as the wide variety of characters they were called upon to play, it should be no surprise that they first had also been imaginative enough to envision *themselves* in roles other than the factory hands, farmers, and grocery clerks society was asking them to play. Some went right to the streets and sang and danced for coins. Anyone with a brain—and they all had brains—could see that such a life was for the birds. With nothing to lose, they went into vaudeville.

Most vaudevillians had the souls of businessmen and lived to wheel and deal. In Waukegan, Illinois, magician Harry Kellar showed his true mettle as a conjurer by materializing an entire engagement with nothing more than his wits. Using charm, cunning, and pathos, he managed to bum a coat and the use of a hall for two nights, as well as handbills and props. The profit from the two nights' performances enabled him to pay off everyone he owed, to buy proper new props, and to extend his tour for a few more weeks. Houdini struck deals with various manufacturers in order to get in-kind donations of products and free publicity. Such deals had Houdini escaping from donated packing crates, hampers, barrels, bank safes, a glass box, a boiler, a rolltop desk, and a canvas mail pouch. The companies, of course, got free advertising out of it.

George Burns said, "You needed three things to work in vaudeville: glossy pictures, business cards, and an act." Eddie Cantor diligently saved his money from his early gigs and invested it in a new suit and business cards, so he could make the rounds with agents. Worn down by Cantor's persistence, small-time agent Joe Wood finally sent him out to Gain's Manhattan Theatre (a venue famous for sending acts packing) just to be rid of him. Shockingly, Cantor did so well that he ended up being retained by the theater, and the impressed Wood began booking him in upstate theaters as well.

Each performer was, in essence, the producer of his own act. Like a theatrical producer, he bought scripts and songs (unless he himself was a writer), bought costumes and props, and hired personnel if he needed them. He made the act pay however he could. While still a performer, Walter Winchell earned extra money slipping backstage stories to show-business columnists. Eventually, trading in such gossip became his entire career, making him one of the most powerful men in the country.

"No applause, folks, just throw money," Joe Frisco famously quipped. "We are out for the shekels," said Lew Fields, "and come pretty near getting our share." Yet beneath the humor, one finds a kernel of insight about the vaudevillian's psychology. Ed Wynn once said, "When you cry, it's easier if your tears fall on Persian carpets." "I've been rich and I've been poor," said Sophie Tucker. "Believe me, honey, rich is better." As we have noted, the people who went into vaudeville were not only poor but also largely restricted from more traditional avenues of acquiring wealth. Their goal was not perfection as an end in itself, but a perfection that would allow them to retire to the proverbial chicken farm in New Jersey.

A typical VMA dispute centered around the fact that Percy Williams paid Marie Dressler $1,000 when Keith only wanted to pay her $650. Yet either way, it's a little hard to get around the fact that without the vaudeville system, Ms. Dressler's salary would have been less than 10 percent of either of those amounts. Even at that, in variety the top pay had been $40 a week, but that was already three times what the average workingman was making at the time. Before vaudeville was finished, the top figure had grown to a hundred times that. Big earners included: Lillian Russell ($3,000), Eva Tanguay ($3,500), Sir Harry Lauder ($3,500), Al Jolson ($2,500), Belle Baker ($2,500), and Joe Frisco ($2,500). And that $2,500 equaled over $40,000 in today's money. Per week. The big-time vaudevillian could count on forty weeks of employment on the circuits, with summers off to spend at one of the vaudeville resort colonies. Plus applause. Where do I sign? As San Francisco journalist Bert Lowry so aptly put it in 1927, "In the days when variety was variety, actors and actresses were poorly paid and uncertain . . . Today the men and women of the vaudeville circuits have little to complain of."

Eva Tanguay sang entire songs celebrating her salary. Some performers had their own private train cars, ate only at the best restaurants, and could take a suite of rooms at the fanciest hotels. At the height of her fame, Nora Bayes traveled in a private railroad car in which she carried a full entourage consisting of her two children, their governess, her maid, her piano player, and the piano player's wife.

Vaudeville stars epitomized the Horatio Alger drama known as the American Dream. In recent decades, skeptics from many fields have prided themselves on pointing out the illusory nature of that dream, referring to it instead as "the success myth." Yet this book is filled with hundreds of examples of people for whom American success was hardly a myth—it was the literal, empirical truth. Were there thousands of people who never achieved that success? Sure. But no one ever said that *everyone* in America would become a millionaire. The American Dream is not that one *would*, but that one *could* achieve success.

It's hard to make a union in a field where the object is to get filthy rich. The White Rats had largely failed for this very reason. As hard as life was for them, vaudevillians were not "workers," they were "capitalists." The difference between them and the managers was one of degree, not one of kind. Their assumptions were the same. The business of show business is business. Nazimova, one of the greatest actresses of the age, bemoaned the fact that she was not as famous as Mickey Mouse! None of these people chose a career on the stage because it *wouldn't* make them rich. No one was trying to do "an honest day's work for an honest day's pay," as a worker does. The goal of the vaudevillian was to do fifteen minutes' work for the equivalent of several month's worth of the salary they otherwise would have made working in a factory. The girls who weren't in vaudeville worked in the Triangle Shirtwaist Factory. They were the people in Upton Sinclair's best-selling exposé *The Jungle*. They had calluses on their hands. They lost their looks and shape and teeth by thirty. Beside them, the trials and travails of a handful of entertainers is mere kvetching. To properly "exploit" a vaudevillian in the sense that workers of the period were exploited, you would need to force him to repeat his act twelve hours a day, six days straight, in a back room—with no audience. Looked at another way, what if every tool-and-die worker operated his machine onstage for twelve minutes three times a day and received audience adulation on top of his $800 weekly salary? I'd take that job. In fact, I think I will. I'm sure there's one like it over in Europe.

Some performers rose through the ranks to become the Boss: Tony Pastor, F. F. Proctor, Martin Beck, Harrigan and Hart, Fanchon and Marco, Eddie Dowling, Weber and Fields, and George M. Cohan, to name just a few. A tiny percentage—a few dozen at most—eventually became wealthy as headliners. A few hundred made the big time. And the rest, several thousand of them, slogged around the small-time circuits their whole lives, just barely earning a precarious living. Some weren't able to grab the brass ring themselves but created a foundation that allowed the next generation to achieve their goals. Most never even had that satisfaction. Still, they had beaten the system. They never had to work a lathe or a sewing machine, a plow or a cash register. They were songbirds, not dray horses. They were free. They were in show business.

FINISHING TOUCHES

In some ways, Albee's previous victories were minuscule compared to the things he was to accomplish in the 1920s. Starting in 1919, he fought a major war with Marcus Loew, whose chain was growing at an alarming rate. In 1921, Loew even went so far as to build an enormous, glittering theater down the street from the Palace, the 3,500-seat State Theatre. Albee was able to compete by hiring the biggest stars in the country (and *paying* for them), and by adding more movies to his bills—a harbinger of things to come.

In 1920, the Shuberts attempted once again to set up a rival circuit, called Shubert Advanced Vaudeville. Their plan was to outbid Albee for all his major acts until he went broke—at which point, presumably, they would buy out his theaters and then pay the acts whatever they wanted. But Albee was not to be so easily cowed. He called the Shuberts' bluff by matching all their bids, no matter how high, and threatening to black-list all those who went to their circuit. Strapped for acts, Advanced Vaudeville hung on for a few years by switching to touring revues and musicals as entire companies (as Weber and Fields and others had done in the 1880s and nineties), a move that was feasible since they owned all of their theaters. Weber and Fields themselves traveled with one of these Shubert units, as did the Marx Brothers, Ed Wynn, James Cagney, and Fred Allen. But this strenuous gambit defeated the whole purpose of switching to vaudeville, which was its increased cost-effectiveness. The Shuberts caved and went back to producing regular Broadway musicals, and Albee showed uncharacteristic grace toward the acts that had defected. He only blacklisted them for a year, after which they were allowed back on his circuit for a smaller salary if they would take out an advertisement in *Variety* apologizing for their foolish transgression.

As often happened with efforts to unseat Albee, the old fox only grew more powerful. Just as talk of a Morris-Proctor partnership had resulted in a Keith-Proctor partnership and the formation of the UBO, and as

Beck's scheme to infiltrate Times Square ended up with the Keith organization owning the Palace, in his struggle to keep up with the deep-pocketed Shuberts, Albee was forced to drastically expand his empire.

In 1920, the year Shubert Advanced Vaudeville was launched, Albee picked up the B. S. Moss chain of New York theaters and added it to his growing constellation. In 1923, he purchased New York's enormous Hippodrome Theatre (colloquially known as the Hip), located between Forty-third and Forty-fourth streets on Sixth Avenue (one block from Bryant Park). Built in 1905 by Luna Park's Thompson and Dundee to showcase mammoth fantasy spectacles like *A Yankee Circus on Mars* and *Neptune's Daughter*, the Brobdingnagian Hip was outfitted with a retractable hydraulic floor and swimming pools for water shows of the sort film fans now associate with Busby Berkeley and Esther Williams.

The Hippodrome was the most fabulous theater ever built in the United States. Its stage—twelve times the size of that of an ordinary Broadway house—could accommodate up to a thousand performers, and the audience sat 4,500–5,200 depending on how the space was configured. Despite these selling points, Thompson and Dundee failed to make a go of it, and sold the house, which changed hands a number of times before Albee sunk his talons in.

Needless to say, the Hippodrome was a unique space in which to present vaudeville. In order to fill its cavernous stage, acts were booked that were presentationally "big," such as the comic trick horseback rider Poodles Hanneford, Bobe Pender's Knockabout Comedians (the outfit that brought young Archibald Leach a.k.a. Cary Grant to American shores), Houdini with his large escape contraptions, Powers Elephants (an act that could fit in no other vaudeville venue), and ballerina Anna Pavlova, who now had unprecedented distances across which to *sauter.*

By 1925, the Keith-Albee circuit had 350 theaters and employed 20,000 people. In 1927, the circuit merged with Orpheum, which itself had acquired Kohl and Castle in 1919. Albee's empire had reached dizzying proportions, yet the corporate entity was still not done growing. Keith-Albee-Orpheum theaters (as the circuit was now called) could be found from California to Montreal and from Vancouver to Florida. They were in virtually every state capital; some cities had half a dozen. Four hundred and fifty theaters were owned by the concern; 750 were booked by its affiliate, the UBO. Yet within this Leviathan lived an equally monstrous parasite, a tapeworm made of real tape: celluloid, fed through projectors with interlocking gears and sprockets, and very soon it would strangle the very life out of vaudeville.

6

TROUPERS

We are about to take one last look at a way of life that has vanished. In point of fact, there is almost no one alive who remembers it the way it was. (Of the big-time stars, two remain that I know of: Rose Marie and Fayard Nicholas of the Nicholas Brothers.) It has been over seventy years since vaudevillians crisscrossed the country, bringing their live shenanigans to a public that would ultimately forsake them, almost overnight.

Yet, in a way, the vaudevillians had turned away first. After all, these were people too impatient, restless, vain, and arrogant to confine themselves to the desk, the sales counter, or the assembly line. Men too proud to suffer silently the indignities of being told what to do by some boss. Women too beautiful and charming for the butter churn. These were characters out to beat the system. So much did they hate the prospect of the "humdrum" existence lived by 98 percent of humanity (including their family and friends) that they were willing to suffer untold humiliations and inconveniences to escape.

What lives on a circuit? Electrons. Kinetic, frenetic, ungovernable, unmeasurable, ephemeral. No less than Edison, the inventors of vaudeville were harnessing the power of electricity to run the machine they had built. We have seen what unruly misfits show people are. Minstrels have always been, by definition, wandering. "An actor's home," wrote Joey Adams, "is where he hangs his hat." Chaplin's tramp, W. C. Fields's

Eustace McGarrigle, the Marx Brothers' anarchic gate-crashers, Mae West's semicriminal scarlet woman. These vaudevillians romanticized the runaway because they themselves were runaways. One symbol of vaudeville is the hat and cane; but another is the steamer trunk, covered with labels marking points of embarkation. Perhaps this is why vaude-villians so loved to play the tramp character, the lovable ne'er-do-wells who hopped freight trains, stole meals, or begged from strangers. The experience of the hobo was not so far from their own formative (and in some unhappy cases, ongoing) experiences.

America has always romanced runaways. The country was founded by them. Escape from the tyranny of the majority and the "settled life" has been a major American theme since the days of Natty Bumpo. At age five, when I fantasized about running away from home (inspired by the examples of Huckleberry Finn and Dorothy in *The Wizard of Oz*), I imag-ined carrying a bindle over my shoulder, one of those little hankie bundles tied to the end of a stick. Children's literature had provided me with a template for how to accoutre myself. Road movies, westerns, and prison-break films constitute entire cinematic genres filled with vagabonds. Books like *On the Road* and *The Electric Kool-Aid Acid Test* inspired a generation of upper- and middle-class kids to drop out and hitchhike around the country. Countless pop songs celebrate restless-ness and rootlessness, such as Del Shannon's "Runaway," Dion's "The Wanderer," the Grateful Dead's "Truckin'," and Willie Nelson's "On the Road Again."

All classes, all psychological types, all races, creeds, and religions were represented in vaudeville. Broken homes, stable families, rural, ur-ban—they're all accounted for in some measure, and what they had in common was a refusal to be settled.

Some vaudevillians ran from a tyrannical upbringing, usually stern, old-fashioned parents. Al Jolson's father was a strict, religious man, a cantor. It was he who had taught his wayward progeny to sing, with the understanding that they would follow in his footsteps. Al and his brother Harry ran away from home so many times their house became like an-other stop on the vaudeville circuit. Jolson's real-life story is effectively replicated in his 1927 film *The Jazz Singer*. When Jolson's character chooses the stage instead of the life of a cantor, his father wails, "I have no son!" Singer Nora Bayes was born Leonora Goldberg, the daughter of devout Orthodox Jews. She told her parents her singing lessons were for religious purposes, then hit the road as soon as she turned eighteen. Joe Weber's father had been a kosher butcher. His son was unable to tell him he'd become a performer until he had become well established.

Ed Wynn's father wanted his son to follow him into the hat business. Instead, Wynn worked up a comedy act called "The Boy with the Funny Hats." W. C. Fields's father made him work alongside him at the family fruit stand. Many a brawl erupted owing to the younger Fields's propensity to bruise the merchandise while attempting to juggle it. According to his own account, Fields tapped his old man on the sconce with a shovel before beating a hasty departure.

Many saw in the big-city lights of vaudeville a chance to escape from farms, rural boredom, and dawn-to-dusk hard work. Joe Frisco started out performing Lancashire clogs and soft shoes outside of Dubuque theaters not far from his family's Iowa farm. His father, who was determined to see him succeed as a plowboy, threw his tap shoes in the stove. Joe hopped a freight train and never saw his father again until he came home for the old man's funeral. Numerous others from America's breadbasket similarly rejected the bucolic existence, including Harry Langdon, Joe Cook, and Chic Sale.

Others ran from urban poverty. Eddie Cantor, an orphan, grew up in a Lower East Side basement with his grandmother, dressed literally in rags. Like nearly all children on the Lower East Side at that time, he stole to get by and hung out with street gangs. (Bert Lahr, Fanny Brice, and the Marx Brothers were other performers with sticky-fingered youths.) Cantor had been funny from early childhood, getting laughs on street corners (as Richard Pryor would later do) to keep the tough guys from terrorizing him. When Cantor took the plunge into professionalism by performing at a Miner's Bowery Theatre amateur night in 1908, he was so poor he had to borrow a friend's pants in order to go on. Despite a rough crowd, Cantor won the amateur contest and took home $12.

Jimmy Cagney, Fanny Brice, and Charlie Chaplin were the latchkey children of dissolute drunks. When they were very young teenagers, Joe Weber and Lew Fields were earning more at entry-level vaudeville gigs than their fathers made working in a factory.

Sophie Tucker grew up working at her family's restaurant in Hartford, Connecticut. The inexpensive but good food attracted a lot of traveling types, such as salesmen and *show people*. When in town, folks like Willie and Eugene Howard and Jacob Adler ate there. If the glamorous and romantic presence of real live show people wasn't incentive enough to make her want to run off and seek a life on the stage, her surroundings were. She wasn't starving or poor, and her family gave her plenty of love . . . but they also gave her plenty of work. Sophie, her two brothers, and her sister were all slaves of the family restaurant. Sophie was up at three a.m. every day, chopping and peeling vegetables before school. At night she was bussing and waiting tables and washing dishes. At school, she used to fall asleep at her desk.

Immigrants ran away from the Old Country. And then their children ran away from *them*. Harry Houdini, Al Jolson, the Marx Brothers, the Dolly Sisters, Belle Baker, Sophie Tucker, Eddie Cantor, George Jessel, Jimmy Durante—you could fill a phone book with the names of immigrants and children of immigrants who went into vaudeville.

There is a definite skew in the direction of ethnicity (first- or second-generation immigrant, or black); poverty; and absent, mentally ill, or alcoholic parents. For every Irene Castle (native, white, upper-middle-class) there are a thousand Eddie Cantors (Jewish, poor, orphaned). So the personnel (and consequently much of the material) in vaudeville were that of the ambitious underclass. And for them the vaudeville industry provided opportunity. If you wanted to get in on the ground floor, it was plenty accessible. Getting to the higher floors was the tricky part . . .

The first thing you needed to do was work up an act. This is not as easy as it sounds. All of vaudeville's great stars started out as something vastly different from the personae that made them famous, only slowly groping their way toward the acts and the identities that would define them for all time. The process could take ten, fifteen, twenty years. George Burns, for example, fumbled around for over two decades. He performed with perhaps dozens of failed acts prior to teaming up with Gracie Allen: comedy acts, song-and-dance acts, even a trained-seal act. He was performing impressions with Billy Lorraine in 1923 when Burns decided he wanted to do a Dumb Dora act after copping a bunch of good jokes from a college humor magazine. Only then did he partner with Gracie.

The Marx Brothers' act evolved over fifteen long years of research and development. As children, Groucho and Gummo appeared with a third boy in a singing act called the Three Nightingales. Then, in order to secure a booking for a quartet, their mother, Minnie, drafted Harpo, whose only experience had been playing piano in honky-tonks. For a short time Minnie and her sister were also in the act, and they were known as the Six Mascots. The act went from being a singing ensemble to a sketch comedy troupe. The brothers each tried on various other characters before settling on the ones they would eventually play: Gummo a Hebrew, Groucho a German, and Harpo an Irishman. Chico, who'd already established his Italian bit with another act, joined up in 1912. As we saw earlier, Harpo would eventually stop talking and started playing the harp. Chico started playing piano in the act. World War I forced Groucho to drop his "Dutch" character and caused Gummo to be drafted and replaced by Zeppo. Having begun in 1906, the familiar Marx Brothers don't emerge until the late teens.

"Everybody had to double in vaudeville," said Donald O'Connor. "If you went out and were just a singer, that didn't mean too much. Or just a dancer, that didn't mean too much. But if you could sing, dance, tell jokes, and what have you, that would mean that you were really outstanding." In a business as competitive as this, someone with only one skill would be dead in the water. Unless that skill was completely unique, you had to have more than one talent. Many comedians had been something else first: W. C. Fields and Fred Allen had both been jugglers; Joe E. Brown had been an acrobat; Will Rogers did rope tricks; Bob Hope had been a song-and-dance man; Jack Benny had been a violinist; George Burns had tried everything. Even Daisy and Violet Hilton, the Siamese twins immortalized in the 1997 musical *Side Show*, sang and played musical instruments. Eddie Cantor conquered more fields than perhaps anybody—you could not pigeonhole him. Stand-up comedian? Sketch comedian? Singer? He'd even done time as a juggler. He went on to enjoy success in book musicals and revues, radio, TV, Hollywood, and the music recording industry. He even dabbled as a songwriter, penning, most notably, the theme music to Warner Bros. Merrie Melodies cartoons.

Over the years the Marx Brothers managed to cook up the most perfect act in show business, encompassing all the comedy genres then in vogue, plus music. They had a first-rate pantomimist and harp player (Harpo), a top-notch dialect comedian and piano player (Chico), a "talker" (Groucho), and a romantic light comedian (successively, Gummo and Zeppo). Gummo had the intriguing added feature of being a great dancer. They were like several acts in one, combining the appeal of Charlie Chaplin, Weber and Fields, and Milton Berle. W. C. Fields called them "the one act I could never follow."

Similarly, Joe Cook was known as the "One Man Vaudeville Show" and the "Master of All Trades." His skills were listed as "juggling, unicycle riding, magic, hand balancing, ragtime piano and violin, dancing, globe rolling, wirewalking, talking and cartooning." Critic Brooks Atkinson once described Cook as nothing less than "the greatest man in the world."

Fred Allen, taking the opposite tack, billed himself as the "Worst Juggler in the World." His act was a sort of parody of vaudeville. He would mock other acts by doing bad ventriloquism, a bad song on banjo, and, of course, bad juggling.

There were some who managed to become reasonably well-known without changing or expanding their shtick. The most notorious were Moore and Littlefield, whose sketch called "Change Your Act" was about a vaudeville team in need of new material. Moore and Littlefield did this act for twenty-three years—and never changed a word of it! Gallagher and Shean built an act around a single song: "Oh! Mister Gallagher and Mister Shean." Joe Penner worked a bit for years where he came onstage with a duck in a basket, looked around, and asked the audience, "Hey, you wanna buy a duck?" After a few years, no one did. That was the downside of becoming known for a single routine.

Having come up with some kind of act, you would have to find a place to present it. One of the most popular platforms for breaking in an act was the "amateur night." Theaters like Miner's on the Bowery and the Columbia in Boston devoted one night a week to a tryout for fledgling performers, who competed for a cash prize. This was no cakewalk.

"The amateur night is primitive," said Fanny Brice. "It is a thing of large proportions. It is either terribly cruel or vastly appreciative, leaping like a wild animal on the weak, praising to the skies those who please it, and always admiring a fighter. I learned to watch its every move and to beat it to that move. When it wanted sentiment, I gave it tears by the bucketful. When it wanted funny stuff, I clowned to the best of my ability."

The amateur night was indeed a tough gauntlet. Because the performers were inexperienced, it was a case of "guilty until proven innocent." The audience, expecting you to be bad from the outset, was out for blood. To provoke a reaction, they would hoot, stamp their feet, clap their hands, and throw rotten vegetables, and sometimes pennies (as if to say, "Dis is all dis crummy act is woith"). The act dare not show the slightest hint of fear or hurt, lest the mob of motleys out front tear them apart like dogs. And the management was *very* helpful. If an act was going badly at the Circle (in New York, at Columbus Avenue and Fifty-ninth Street), the stage manager would hold up a big sign that said "Beat It." At Boston's Columbia, the emcee would bonk you over the head with a clown's inflated bladder. Your only hope under such circumstances was to pack the audience with a gang of your buddies, pay off the clique that caused most of the commotion in the house (usually a single gang), or murderize them with the spectacle of your genius (that is, if you could get them to hear you). Miraculously, a fair number of them did just that. Mae West, Eddie Cantor, Milton Berle, Fanny Brice, and Bob Hope are a few of the hundreds who got their start this way.

Another way to get your foot in the door was to start at the lowest type of dive, such as a storefront museum or medicine show, and claw your way up. But this alternative came with the harshest of lifestyles. In the medicine show you were a complete itinerant traveling in a wagon, dependent on the takings from a passed hat in an often hostile small town—just a wagon away from being a hobo. Dime museums were more stable, but were also the worst of all possible grinds, with acts performing anywhere from twelve to fifteen shows a day. A magician like Houdini would become ever more skilled from such repetition, but an acrobat like Joe Keaton would practically kill himself.

Another sort of venue that afforded opportunity for the aspiring vaudevillian was the burlesque show. Burlesque, which developed as an institution parallel to vaudeville, became a sort of bush league for broad comedians. Like vaudeville, burlesque had grown up out of variety. But unlike "polite" vaudeville, burlesque had accentuated the racier aspects, betting all of its chips on the all-male adult audience. Variety acts continued to be part of the show, but now they were broken up by a chorus of scantily-clad females. In burlesque, comedians had the freedom to work a little bluer. Bert Lahr, Fanny Brice, Clark and McCullough, Jimmy Savo, Phil Silvers, and many, many others first achieved success on the burlesque circuits (informally known as "wheels") before making the jump to vaudeville. Burlesque conditions were a little shabbier, and the audience a lot less genteel. But it offered experience, a paycheck, and a place to make a name for oneself—and that was all that was required.

Others resorted to crazy stunts to get themselves noticed. Weber and Fields did this at least twice: once they did their act for Tony Pastor right on the sidewalk as he walked into his theater, and another time they swore to museum owner George B. Bunnell that they could introduce him to a Chinese man with a third eye growing out of his forehead. By the time Bunnell realized he'd been duped, the boys had already made a hit at the theater and so couldn't be fired! One actor even had himself delivered to Martin Beck in a box.

Truth to tell, there were all sorts of ways in. Sophie Tucker started out singing in restaurants (beginning with her family's). Others, like Al Jolson and Eugene Howard, broke in as "balcony singers," stooges hired to surprise the audience by joining in song with the performers onstage. The point was to get in *someplace*. Getting to the *right* place could be finessed later.

Making it to the next level was not only a function of innate talent and charm but of how hard one was willing to work. If you worked harder than the next guy, you stood a chance of being noticed in your field, thus increasing your chances of getting booked. The adolescent W. C. Fields, for example, practiced juggling for several hours daily, enduring bruising physical pain, boredom, and frustration in order to become first-rate at his skill. For her New York debut, the young Eleanor Powell applied herself with rare, almost masochistic, rigor, tying sandbags to her feet to learn to tap dance. Houdini put himself through the tortures of the damned. Not only was it necessary for him to learn to dislocate his joints to wriggle out of straitjackets, and to regurgitate picks or hide them in his orifices but he also had to study long hours in order to make himself familiar with the inner workings of every sort of lock made around the world. He never slept more than five hours a night and worked almost every waking moment.

Like all the top vaudevillians, dancer Bill Robinson was an obsessive workaholic, either practicing or performing constantly, sometimes doing five shows a day. He said that he danced best when totally exhausted; it took the edginess off his performance. He wore out twenty to thirty pairs of tap shoes a year—roughly one pair every two weeks. The Reverend Adam Clayton Powell, in his eulogy for Robinson in 1949, said that he "died from a heart that had become weakened because he had danced so much."

That's the kind of single-mindedness it took to cut the mustard. And having attained the highest levels of skill, you would then have to invest the act with showmanship. Hoofer Hal Leroy famously claimed that it took "twenty years to learn to walk on with class, twenty years to talk with class, and twenty years to walk off with class." (At that point you're dead, but boy do you have class!)

In a field where enthusiasm was everything, Jimmy Durante wrote the book. If somebody laughed at one of his jokes, "I got a million of 'em" was his gleefully shouted reply. Blessed with a physiognomy that practically dictated a career in show business (that or a life of crime), the man radiated exuberance like sunbeams. Born with an extremely large proboscis (the famous "schnozzola"), he was also afflicted with tiny "piggy" eyes, a diminutive chin, a very small body (five-four, 135 pounds), and premature baldness. Added to that was a peculiar hoarse voice, a "dese and dem" Bowery accent, and a natural disinclination to book-learning that led him to check out of school in the seventh grade.

Durante was to make assets out of all of these seeming drawbacks. The physique (well, the nose, really) became his material, and he exaggerated the lack of education by peppering his speech with a beguiling combination of malapropisms and jazz-age slang ("hot-cha-cha" was one of his). Listening to him tell any anecdote is like a window into another culture: "So I goes into de jernt and I says to de guy . . ." He was such a "character" that he actually had *two* straight men, Clayton and Jackson, who patronizingly fed him lines as though he were a child, an animal, or a sideshow freak. On top of this, he was a top-notch ragtime and jazz piano player. While it wasn't unheard of to be loved for your personality alone in vaudeville, superlative skill helped. Durante had both.

Some acts were such hams, you literally couldn't turn them off. Eddie Leonard's habit of overstaying his welcome onstage was legendary. He took seemingly endless encores, and when he felt it was time to retire, he took seemingly endless farewell tours. When told that his client would have to confine his act to ten minutes one time, Leonard's manager exploded, "My God! It takes Eddie Leonard ten minutes just to bow!" Jack Lair called him "the Chinese Philosopher, On Too Long, Bow Too Long."

This is not to say that some naturally subdued people didn't go into vaudeville and rise to the highest heights. There were plenty, but all found elements of themselves to exaggerate when creating their onstage personae. Many comedians fit this profile: bookish and reticent in real life; insane, extravagant, and surreal onstage with a bit of greasepaint, burnt cork, or clownwhite to hide behind. Such were Bert Williams, Groucho Marx, and Charlie Chaplin.

Having broken into an entry-level gig and made a hit, an act would next be seen by some scout, agent, booker, or manager. Then he would be contacted, given a contract, and given a series of dates. The series that was laid out for him was known as a "route." ("I got a route!" the vaudevillian would happily proclaim.) The specific circuit he was booked on would be his "time." Besides the "big time" and the "small time," vaudevillians also referred to "Keith time," "Proctor time," and even "Pan [Pantages] time."

Travel was the very essence of the vaudevillian's life. One had to go where the jobs were. Engagements in any one place were not for very long (three to six days) owing to the never-ending demand for "variety." A good deal of the vaudevillian's life was spent moving from place to place, and by today's standards *all* travel was unpleasant. Distances between gigs were known as "jumps," perhaps in the ironic recognition that unlike a flea or a jackrabbit, one would be traversing the long miles in a slow and eminently uncomfortable manner—less like a jump than a trudge through a tar pit.

Trains were the most common means of long-distance domestic travel in those days, but this isn't Amtrak we're talking about. If it was hot and the window was open, soot and smoke from the steam locomotive would make its way to your seat, onto your clothes, into your face. If you couldn't afford a berth, or if there were none available, you spent the overnight jumps in your seat and tried to steal a few winks upright—that is, if you could ignore the deafening clackety-clack, the periodic ear-splitting whistles, the smell of soot, and the idiotic conversations struck up by fellow passengers bored out of their wits. Many performers whiled away the long hours by getting up card games, drinking, and striking up idiotic conversations. (If you can't beat 'em, join 'em!)

If you were playing split weeks or one-night stands, your ordeal was worse: no time to take a breather before the hop to the next town. The far West, with its epic distances, was known as the "Death Trail." There were no big-time theaters (and thus no layovers for a Keith-Orpheum act) between San Francisco and Omaha. That's 1,500 miles. Hundreds of small-time theaters dotted the landscape in between, but to take an engagement at one risked banishment from the UBO, essentially ruining one's prospects for future or continuing stardom.

When a performer's career reached a certain level, it was thought necessary to make a jump to Europe to enhance his résumé. As inconceivable as it may seem now, London and Paris were the real show-business centers of the world until the First World War heralded the shift of focus to New York and Hollywood. All trips abroad in those days necessitated voyages by ship and commitments of many months. The crossing itself took about a week, and after having made it, you were hardly about to turn around and come right back if you could help it. If you had a problem with seasickness, like Harry Houdini, that was just tough luck. And if a shipwreck destroyed all of your expensive props and costumes, in addition to a fortune in gems and coins amassed during your South American tour (as happened to magician Harry Kellar) that was even tougher luck.

Sometimes a European jump backfired. A 1909 tour of England proved disastrous for the Three Keatons when the bookers and audiences there were appalled and offended by the onstage abuse of Buster. In 1922, the Marx Brothers toured England, a move that was doubly disastrous. First, the Brits did not get the team's humor at all. Upon returning to the States with their tails between their legs, they learned that they were now blacklisted from the big time, having neglected to clear the English tour with Keith-Albee.

Olsen and Johnson also had some bad luck in London that season. Hours after docking, Ole Olsen fell sick. The entire time they were in England, he was confined to his bed. The team had to return to the United States, having missed every one of their engagements.

Some, however, like Sophie Tucker, Arthur Tracy, and Harry Houdini, found a second home in England. Central and Eastern Europe could be tougher. In countries like Germany and Russia, with their authoritarian legal systems and strict laws against "trickery," Houdini sometimes found himself in hot water. In Berlin, Will Rogers was nearly run out of town on a rail when he playfully lassoed an offstage character who turned out to be a minor public official (with an outsized sense of his own importance).

Many from Europe made the reverse journey. As we have seen, vaudeville was enriched by stock from the "Mother Country," through importations from English music halls: Albert Chevalier, Vesta Victoria, Vesta Tilley, Dan Leno, Cissie Loftus, Gracie Fields, Charlie Chaplin, Stan Laurel, Beatrice Lillie, and Cary Grant. France supplied us with the talents of Yvette Guilbert, Sarah Bernhardt, Jules Léotard ("The Man on the Flying Trapeze"), Anna Held, Little Tisch, Irene Bordoni, Mlle. Dazie, Gaby Deslys, Maurice Chevalier, and Polaire, "The Ugliest Woman in the World" (who had a fifteen-inch waist and a nose ring).

The wars that erupted during the vaudeville era (the Boer War, the Spanish-American War, and World War I) all resulted in stranded performers and canceled bookings, minor hardships in the larger scheme of things, but unpleasant enough for those who had to endure them. Nora Bayes was a cancer patient at a German sanatorium when the outbreak of World War I required her to flee the country. Meanwhile, the press had accidentally reported that she had died. The twin whammy of the false death report and the "dramatic escape" from Germany splashed her all over the front pages, with the result that she was more popular than ever.

W. C. Fields was the ultimate international act. From 1900 to 1914, Fields crisscrossed the globe numerous times, performing not only in Europe but also in such far-flung places as Australia and South Africa. During these tours, he became a dumb act, to avoid the difficulties of the language barrier in non-English-speaking countries.

That steamer trunk mentioned at the top of this chapter was no mere symbol but a vital piece of equipment for the traveling vaudevillian. Manufactured by the firm Herkert and Meisel, it was typically equipped with hanger space on one side and drawers on the other. Every performer had one, proudly covered in stickers proclaiming his every port of call: Paris, New York, London, Berlin, Sydney, Singapore, and so on. Known affectionately as "H & M trunks," these massive pieces of luggage were considered indispensable.

Because the very nature of the business necessitated travel, performers were unable to hold down a day job, even if they'd wanted to. Their entire living had to be earned from bookings. Hunger and worry were frequent companions. Who knew where the next dollar was coming from? Many is the actor who was left high and dry in some remote spot by an unscrupulous partner. This happened to Groucho Marx several times as a boy. His name comes not from his demeanor, but from the fact that his "grouch bag" (the little satchel in which vaudevillians commonly kept their money) had been stolen by fellow actors on so many occasions. Likewise, magician Harry Kellar had been robbed by his first manager and was briefly reduced to hoboing.

In such circumstances, the vaudevillians had to eat crow, as in, "Dear Mom and Dad, I'm stranded in Altoona and I'm down to my last eight cents and the landlady's brother is sitting in the parlor brandishing a baseball bat." Such letters were especially painful when mom and dad were working-class people who earned their living by the sweat of their brow. Until that day when you made it big in show business, you were widely regarded as a bum, the family loser.

Most young vaudevillians quickly learned how to be sharp themselves, so as not to lose the little stake they had. For example, as a young coronet player, Jesse Lasky learned to carry his money in a secret pocket in his shirt to keep it safe. His Aunt Jenny had warned him about the people he'd be consorting with in his new career: "Vaudeville people live on trains . . . They're gypsies without homes."

The lack of a home and its attendant comforts—a hot meal, a clean bed, a quiet place to relax—was perhaps the vaudevillian's greatest sacrifice. The freedom of the road came at the cost of those little conveniences that more settled individuals take for granted. Food, for example, was generally gotten on the run and often terrible. Performers

Is there a problem, fellah?
Vaudeville comedians such as Jack Haley frequently worked with a stooge, or audience plant, for comic effect. (Billy Rose Theatre Collection, The New York Public Library for the Performing Arts, Astor, Lenox and Tilden Foundations)

BELOW: **I got a million of 'em!** The ragtime piano player and singer/comedian Jimmy Durante was such a cutup he needed two straight men to keep him in line. They flank him in this photo. Left to right in the foreground, the team consisted of Lou Clayton, Durante, and Eddie Jackson. (Billy Rose Theatre Collection, The New York Public Library for the Performing Arts, Astor, Lenox and Tilden Foundations)

ABOVE: **Vaudevillian at work.** The comedian Bert Lahr prepares to go on. A grammar school dropout, there is little doubt that his prospects for success would have been very different if not for show business. (Billy Rose Theatre Collection, The New York Public Library for the Performing Arts, Astor, Lenox and Tilden Foundations)

The ladder to legitimacy. George Jessel (left) gladhands Chicago mayor William Hale Thompson. Through such ingratiation of the political powers that be, Jessel was to rise to the post of Toastmaster General, an honorary position that kept him in the good graces of nine American presidents. (Billy Rose Theatre Collection, The New York Public Library for the Performing Arts, Astor, Lenox and Tilden Foundations)

Ed Wynn performs another of stardom's tedious chores. The smile on his face suggests the task was not without its satisfactions. (Shubert Archive)

This young man doesn't know it yet, but he's about to become the most famous performer in the world. Steaming toward the U.S. for the first time with the Fred Karno troupe is its star, a twenty-year-old kid named Charlie Chaplin (center). He was discovered on the vaudeville stage by agents working for Mack Sennett's Keystone Company, and the rest is history. (Roy Export, Ltd.)

Another young comic acrobat from England who came to the U.S. on tour and stayed was one Archibald Leach (bottom, far right), who found steady work as an all-around vaudeville utility man. He honed his persona within an inch of its life, renamed himself **Cary Grant,** and conquered talkies. (Margaret Herrick Library, Academy of Motion Picture Arts and Sciences)

The Russian actress **Alla Nazimova** was revered as a great artist for her definitive portrayals of Ibsen's heroines, but also had a real knack for show business, displaying her histrionics in vaudeville playlets and later in silent pictures. Here, we see the rebellious tendency that went over so much better in America than in her native country. (Billy Rose Theatre Collection, The New York Public Library for the Performing Arts, Astor, Lenox and Tilden Foundations)

For a while, the most popular duo in vaudeville was also its most popular song. **Ed Gallagher and Al Shean** built their whole act around that one song, "Oh! Mister Gallagher and Mister Shean." Its popularity was extended immeasurably by the fact that it was also a hit record. (Billy Rose Theatre Collection, The New York Public Library for the Performing Arts, Astor, Lenox and Tilden Foundations)

The singer and bandleader **Rudy Vallee** had been a radio star for several months before embarking on his first real vaudeville tour in 1929. Thanks to the power of the new medium, he was already a top headliner without having to climb the traditional rungs of the vaudeville ladder. (Billy Rose Theatre Collection, The New York Public Library for the Performing Arts, Astor, Lenox and Tilden Foundations)

Bob Hope was just a couple of years out of vaudeville when he made this publicity still for his NBC radio program. He was to hug that NBC mike for another five decades. (Billy Rose Theatre Collection, The New York Public Library for the Performing Arts, Astor, Lenox and Tilden Foundations)

Riding off into the future (but looking back with a laugh). The comedy team of Chic Johnson and Ole Olsen were among the first to make the jump into talkies. But it was the Broadway success of their vaudeville-inspired extravaganza *Hellzapoppin* a few years later that truly cemented their place in show-business history. (Billy Rose Theatre Collection, The New York Public Library for the Performing Arts, Astor, Lenox and Tilden Foundations)

Changing of the guard.
Vaudeville's top comic Frank Fay must little suspect that he is about to become a footnote in the biography of his new bride, a chorus girl and actress named Barbara Stanwyck. Some say his ignominious fall, combined with her meteoric rise, was the inspiration for the film *A Star Is Born.* The breakup of their marriage told an eloquent story: Hollywood was in, vaudeville was out. (Billy Rose Theatre Collection, The New York Public Library for the Performing Arts, Astor, Lenox and Tilden Foundations)

Vaudeville got a second wind in the late forties thanks to television. Here, **Edgar Bergen and Mortimer Snerd** fool around on *The Ed Sullivan Show.* (Photograph courtesy of Ann Shanks)

ABOVE: This behind-the-scenes photograph taken as part of a *Life* magazine profile gives some perspective of **The Ed Sullivan Show in progress,** circa 1959. Sullivan stands off to the left watching the unidentified acrobats work their hearts out. (Photograph courtesy of Ann Shanks)

The contemporary sideshow artist, clown, magician, and ragtime piano player **Todd Robbins** proves beyond a shadow of a doubt that vaudeville is not dead—it's just been very, very sick.

stayed at special boarding houses that catered to theatrical people. Hot plates were *verboten* in the rooms, but meals came with the package, as in today's bed-and-breakfasts. There was small incentive for a struggling landlady to play Julia Child to a lot of transient lunatics, however. You ate your plate of cold mashed potatoes and liked it. Likewise, the rooms were generally shabby affairs. They were typically equipped with a bed and a bureau—a wash basin if you were lucky. Harpo Marx described one place where the ants were so bad, each bedpost was placed in a dish of oxalic acid to keep the little varmints from reaching the sleeper. Bathrooms were generally shared by the whole floor.

Outside the theater and your hotel, there wasn't much you could do in the small towns. People still harbored prejudices from the variety days. You were a social pariah in East Whatchamacallit. Just try and talk to a local girl. The Marx Brothers did, and often found themselves taking it on the lam, chased by angry fathers with shotguns.

Flash was everything. Wardrobe was an important part of the professional tool kit. "In show business," Sophie Tucker once said, "clothes matter." Joey Adams claims former New York City mayor and erstwhile songwriter Jimmy Walker "taught me the importance of dressing well at all times." In a small town, the vaudevillian was instantly conspicuous by his loud, expensive clothes and his diamond jewelry. (Even the poorest—if he could afford nothing else—wore a diamond ring, as insurance for a day when he might get stranded someplace with no money. A very hockable little item is a diamond.) The flashy and attractive vaudevillian was like an emissary from Oz in the drear desert of the sticks . . . inspiring imaginative little townies, who would in turn become the next generation of vaudevillians. It was an endless cycle. Yet, at the same time such ostentation could inspire envy and resentment in barefoot locals. Walker and Williams were crossing Texas with a medicine show when a lynch mob, offended by their flashy duds, tore off their clothes and gave them burlap sacks to wear. They were left naked and penniless to make their way to the next town. After this incident, the team vowed never to work the South again.

George M. Cohan summed up life on the road this way: "The only thing I'm proud of about vaudeville is that I got out of it. The houses are not all Orpheums and Keith—not by a long way. There are only a few good houses and the others I wouldn't like to talk about—right out loud."

The two great vaudeville hubs were New York and Chicago. Keith-Albee, Proctor, and others ran the Eastern Vaudeville Managers Association from New York, but the city also was the base of operations for Loew's and other important vaudeville circuits. Martin Beck, Kohl and Castle, and others ran the Western Vaudeville Managers Association from Chicago, but again, one could also find there the headquarters for Pantages, Sullivan and Considine, and Gus Sun, among others. There was enough work in either city (without leaving the city limits) to keep an act busy for months.

"Once you leave New York," Joe Frisco sniffed, "every other town is Bridgeport."

Manhattan's vaudeville houses were both fabled and legion. We have discussed some of the most important ones: Tony Pastor's Music Hall, Koster and Bial's Music Hall, Proctor's Twenty-third Street, Keith's Union Square, Proctor's Pleasure Palace, Hammerstein's Olympia, Hammerstein's Victoria, Proctor's Fifth Avenue, Proctor's 125th Street, the Harlem Opera House, the Circle, the Colonial, the Alhambra, the American Music Hall, the Palace, Loew's State, and the Hippodrome. These big-time theaters were just like today's Broadway houses. In fact, some of them, such as the Palace, *are* today's Broadway houses. Enough remain in place for the reader to have a clear picture of the environment. The theater generally seated anywhere from a thousand to two thousand people, although some of the more ambitious ones sat up to five thousand (think of Radio City Music Hall). The atmosphere in big time was semiformal. People got dressed up to come to these shows, particularly at the "flagship" theaters, such as the Victoria, the Hippodrome, or the Palace. Ushers in fancy uniforms handed out printed programs. An orchestra pit accommodated a full orchestra; sets and props and all other production values would be of Broadway quality. The bill would have at least two stars. At the Victoria or the Palace nearly everyone on the bill would be a star. Other houses in Manhattan included Proctor's Fifty-eighth Street, Proctor's Eighty-sixth Street, Keith's Riverside, a number of Loew's small-time houses, such as the Delancey, the Avenue B, the Boulevard, the Lincoln Square, all the Yiddish houses around Second Avenue, and many others.

Brooklyn alone had fifty-three vaudeville theaters at its peak. Within that borough's proud precincts you could find the Orpheum, the Gotham, the Greenpoint, the Novelty, the Criterion, the Halsey, the Prospect, the Bushwick, the Flatbush, the Crescent, the Bay Ridge, the Bedford, the Hillside, the Metropolitan, and Fox's Folly. In Coney Island (which flourished during the summer, when the city theaters were dark due to heat in these days before air-conditioning) one found Henderson's Coney Island, the Manhattan Beach Theatre, the Brighton Beach Music Hall, and the New Brighton Beach. In 1909, Eddie Cantor became a singer at a Coney Island establishment called Carrie Walsh's Saloon. The pianist was sixteen-year-old Jimmy Durante.

Similar resort strips were found at North Beach in Queens, and South Beach in Staten Island. The Bronx, which was just starting to grow, thanks to the construction of the subway system, had the Bronx Theatre, the Royal, and the National.

A few of these houses, such as the Orpheum or the National, were regional flagships and hence big-time theaters, but most were what you might call regular small time, or medium time. Picture something on the scale of your local cinema. (Indeed, some of them did double as local cinemas.) It was an extremely common institution, for these theaters provided a cheaper alternative to the big-time theaters in the downtown areas. The industry affectionately nicknamed neighborhood theaters "the nabes." Locals would gather and socialize there. The atmosphere was rowdier than at a big-time house, and there is a reason a raspberry is also known as the "Bronx cheer." Most of the theaters could accommodate a few hundred people. The house "orchestra" might be more like four or five pieces, although at some joints you might just have a lone piano player (both Chico and Harpo Marx got their entrée into show business by serving such a function).

The structure of the show at this level would not be too different from that of the big time, with five or six acts (as compared to big time's nine or more) and three to six shows a day. Performers who were not yet major stars (or had fallen from their ranks, or were being punished by the managers) would provide the entertainment.

In Chicago, the next-largest vaudeville town, vaudeville fans went to the Palace, the Majestic, the Lincoln, the American, the State-Lake, the Chateau, the Rialto, the Trocadero, and many others. In 1903, a Windy

City theater was the site of one of the nation's worst disasters to date. During a performance of the Eddie Foy show *Mr. Bluebird* at the Iroquois Theatre, some sparks from a calcium lamp ignited the curtains. An asbestos fire curtain designed to contain such fires (which were common) wouldn't come down, and the flames, fueled by a draft from an opened stage door, engulfed the theater. The audience, composed mostly of women and children for the weekday matinee, began to panic. Six hundred audience members were either trampled or burnt to death. Public outcry was considerable, and the nation's first serious theater-safety regulations were drafted. Theaters nationwide were shut down for a time as managers got their houses in line with the new codes. As might be expected, Chicago's were shut down the longest. Vaudeville houses in that city did not reopen for business until 1906.

During Prohibition, bootlegging mobsters dominated Chicago's entertainment culture, not only the speakeasies and nightclubs, but also the vaudeville scene. Many are the comedians who told tales of stone-faced responses from sections of the house as they cracked unwise about local crooks, and even received intimidating visits backstage after the show. Eddie Cantor and perhaps half a dozen others spoke of being summoned into the back of a sedan by hoodlums and taken to a remote spot, fearful that each minute would be their last, only to arrive at the house of Al Capone, who would wine them, dine them, and express his admiration for their artistry. A fitting tribute to those same kids who learned to be funny to avoid getting beat up by street punks in the first place.

After Chicago and New York, San Francisco, Boston, and Philadelphia were the other major vaudeville towns. San Francisco's vaud history has two phases: before the earthquake and after. Prior to the 1906 shake-up and the ensuing conflagration, San Francisco could boast the Bella Union, the National, the Union Hall, the California, the Baldwin Academy of Music, the Unique, and the first Orpheum. The disaster destroyed all these and every other theater in town. Joe E. Brown, then a young acrobat performing with the Five Marvelous Ashtons, was unfortunate enough to be there at the time, as were a then unknown Fatty Arbuckle (who was playing the Pantages circuit), Australian funnyman Leon Errol, later to be a major star at the Palace as well as in the *Ziegfeld*

Follies, and Tod Browning, director of the movies *Dracula* and *Freaks*. In the aftermath, local vaudeville managers erected large canvas tents, cheering up beleaguered San Franciscans in the manner of the big circuses. Al Jolson arrived during this time and is said to have garnered his first notoriety—his ridiculously buoyant personality lifted the town's spirits. It was in one of these tents that he first uttered his catchphrase "You ain't seen nothing yet!" which is just what his audience needed to hear. Theater rebuilding began immediately, and soon the city had eleven theaters, including a new Orpheum.

Philadelphia was known as "the Cradle of Vaudeville," hosting an impressive number of vaud houses for a city of relatively modest population size. Nevertheless, vaudevillians who grew up there, such as W. C. Fields and Ed Wynn, found the post-Quaker atmosphere prudish and restrictive, and couldn't leave town fast enough.

Boston had Keith's Colonial and a whole bevy of theaters clustered around Scollay Square: The Beacon, the Palace, the Old Howard (formerly known as the Howard Athenaeum), Austin and Stone's Museum, the Scenic Temple, and others. Boston had a formidable reservoir of local talent, known as the "coast defenders" because they never left. (Among them Fred Allen, Ray Bolger, Jack Haley, and Benny Rubin.) Technically, Boston didn't have to look elsewhere for talent, but they did have to go out of the Hub for "names."

Jersey City and Hoboken were tough vaudeville towns, as anyone who is familiar with the career of Frank Sinatra can imagine. With a massive chip on their collective shoulders from being in the shadow of the town across the Hudson, audiences there were so rough that they booed Will Rogers for being a "dumb hick"!

Large patches of the country—particularly the Midwest, it seems—were notorious for unresponsive audiences. This is another form of "tough crowd," in many ways the worst—the type that never laughs, never claps. Do they like me? Hate me? Are they alive? Hello? One pictures Grant Wood's *American Gothic* four-hundredfold in the audience. W. C. Fields considered Washington, D.C., Kansas City, and St. Louis audiences to be especially tough in this regard. Eddie Cantor had the same feelings about Milwaukee and Cincinnati. Of Indianapolis Joe Frisco complained, "That audience was applauding with their knees. I don't think they ever took off their gloves." These men were big stars. How can this be? The answer is that this is a big country and there wasn't yet one big American audience. Much more so than today, with our homogenized, broadcast-based entertainment industry, regional prejudices existed. A midwestern audience on first encountering Eddie Cantor, a fast-talking, effeminate New York Jew, might think to themselves, "I don't understand—it's *funny* that this man is a coward? I think it's sad and rather contemptible!" Likewise with W. C. Fields. "Can't hear a word the man says! Why is he mumbling? If he took the marbles out of his mouth, maybe a person could hear what he's saying!" Some audiences couldn't understand the performers even when they enunciated clearly. Audiences in Scranton, Pennsylvania, were full of immigrant coal miners who couldn't speak English. Any act that talked would labor in vain for a reaction.

As you got farther out into "the sticks," or the countryside, the vaudeville theaters got smaller and cruder. A more modest small-time theater might consist of a storefront with benches or wooden folding chairs. In a dime museum, such a theater might be stashed in the backroom or upstairs. The seating capacity might be fifty to a hundred. The old joke was that such a place would feature a three-piece band: a piano, a piano player, and a stool. The show would consist of four or five acts, with massive turnover—maybe a dozen shows a day, just like a sideshow. After the turn of the century, "flickers" would be a key part of the lineup, but you'd also have song-and-dance acts, comedy teams, acrobats, and magicians. Anything too sophisticated—such as legitimate drama, a ballet dancer, or a smart-talking comic—would be hopelessly out of place in such an environment. It was in one such theater in Nagadoches, Texas, that the Marx Brothers claimed to have switched from being a singing group to a talking comedy act. During their performance, a local character burst into the audience and announced that a mule had escaped and was wreaking havoc on the street outside. The entire audience ran out to have a look. When they eventually returned, the team was so angry they let loose with all manner of craziness and insults—the patented anarchy that would become their stock-in-trade for the next fifty years.

In extremely rural places, there wasn't much distinction between a tent show, a minstrel show, a medicine show, and a vaudeville show. No stars made it out to these places. Like as not, blackface and the hawking of "Princess Iola's Tonic" or some similar stuff would accompany the juggling, music, and comedy exhibition. The show might be done out of the back of a wagon or truck, under canvas, or in some rented space, and usually featured a company of under half a dozen, some of them occasionally doubling as other characters to give the impression of a larger ensemble. And for many thousands of farmers with no radio, and who rarely got to a town of any size, this would be the only show of any kind all year.

Performers had to learn to alter their acts to account for local tastes. In rural areas (most of the country) an act like Chic Sale, with his repertoire of comic small-town characters, was surefire. But fast-talking urban acts like Ken Murray or Bob Hope had some adjusting (i.e., slowing down) to do. There was no TV, movies, or radio to prepare people in the hinterlands for the more sophisticated styles of the city. In effect, vaudevillians had to lay the groundwork for that national audience themselves.

Of course, if you were sufficiently fed up, you could just attack the audience, as did one Richard Bennett with the following tirade:

> For forty years I've been an actor on the American stage. My entire family is well represented in the entire field of show business. I've played this very city of Cincinnati for thirty or forty years. I've never had a decent reception here. I've been waiting all this time, ladies and gentlemen, to say to you that you, the people of Cincinnati, are the greatest morons, the most unintelligent, illiterate bastards I have ever appeared before in my entire life. Take a good look at me, because you'll never see me again.

They never did.

There was a saying in vaudeville: "Don't send your laundry out until after the first performance," meaning, when you come to a town, wait to see how the first show goes before settling in, for you may well be canceled. If the local theater manager (equivalent to an "overseer") didn't like what he saw in your performance during that first Monday matinee, he was well within his rights (as far as the circuits were concerned) to can you on the spot. There was no heart-to-heart talk, no "Sorry, I gotta let you go, kid," no severance pay. The way you would usually find out was the disposition of your publicity photos on the lobby wall. Maybe a "Canceled" sign would be plastered over them. Or the pictures would be shoved under your dressing room door. Some managers couldn't wait even that long. At Schindler's, in Chicago, the manager would walk down the aisle during your performance and say: "You are shut!" Writer Edwin Royle spoke of a manager who "used to stand in the wings with a whistle, and if he didn't like your act, he blew it, and a couple of stage-hands ran in and shut you out from your audience with two flats upon which were painted in huge letters 'N.G.'" (No good.)

Acts were thought of like cards in a poker hand, discarded with little remorse in the hopes of booking someone better. The house manager's power over performers was positively Dickensian. Rubbing one the wrong way could result in a setback potentially fatal to one's career. But while getting fired was always a blow, it was usually not an insurmountable obstacle to future booking. Fred Allen's strategy was fairly typical: he would change his name, go back to the small time, and work his heart out until the next big opportunity came along. Like a yo-yo, Allen went back and forth a half a dozen heartbreaking times until he finally achieved a secure hold at the top. In the meantime, he'd been known as John Sullivan (his real name), Paul Huckle, Fred St. James, and Benjamin Franklin before hitting it big with the moniker familiar to us. The only major star to top him—in name count—was George Burns, who at various times had been Eddie Delight, Billy Pierce, Captain Betts, Jed Jackson, Jimmy Malone, "Williams" of Brown and Williams, "Glide" of Golfie, Fields, and Glide, and, ironically, "Links" of Burns and Links.

Short of firing you, the local manager could also fine you for all manner of minor infractions, from using *verboten* material, to going overlong, to getting into fights with your fellow performers. Weekly reports were filed with the home office, and detailed records such as J. Edgar Hoover might have envied were kept on every performer.

The only other person besides the stage manager you didn't want to cross was . . . everybody else. Everyone had his hand out: stagehands, musicians, and so on down the line—all wanted tips, and if you didn't come across they were liable to miss a cue or misplace a prop. Stagehands were also known to put secret marks on the cases of acts that didn't tip so that their colleagues in the next town would know to give them "the treatment": "Aw, look what happened. All your props got broke into little tiny pieces."

Sophie Tucker described some of the theaters where she played as "drafty old firetraps, no toilets, filthy dirty cracked walls that let in the wind and the rain, old broken floors . . . One hard jump and down into the cellar you went. Never enough heat . . . I would borrow a hammer and nails, get a heavy cardboard to cover up the rat holes in the wall and ceiling of my dressing room."

Was it possible to have a normal life under such conditions? A surprising number tried. Since performers were on the road most of the year, any kind of family life was unlikely, unless the spouse and kids came along. The list of show-biz widows is long: the wives of Jimmy Durante, Groucho Marx, and Bob Hope spent their entire marriages waiting for their husbands to come home. The show-biz widower was not unheard of, either. Sophie Tucker bought her husband, Frank Westphal, a garage to occupy himself while she was away. However much you love cars, such an accommodation doesn't take the place of the charms of the opposite sex. The fact that Sophie made him call it the "Sophie Tucker Garage" couldn't have done much for his manhood, either. Before long old Frank was checking the headlights on some fairly nubile young sports models, and Sophie was minus one trophy husband.

Sadly, there were many show-business orphans, too. W. C. Fields constantly begged his wife (who'd been his assistant) to come back on the road with him after their son Claude was born. When she refused, Fields shut them both out of his life. As a teenager, Ken Murray was startled to learn that the kindly old folks he'd always known as his parents were actually his grandparents, and his older "brother"—a vaudeville performer—was really his father. The mother, another performer, was never heard from. Gracie Allen's father, a popular Irish clog dancer, ran out on his family, as did Charlie Chaplin's father, a fairly successful English music-hall performer. In some families, like those of child stars Elsie Janis and Clifton Webb, the father was *booted* out by a domineering stage mother. The reason is summed up by Maybelle Webb's answers to queries about her old man's whereabouts: "We never speak of him, he didn't care for the theater."

Although it was much rarer, some major stars made the ultimate sacrifice in order to support their spouses. English male-impersonator Vesta Tilley retired when her husband was elected to Parliament. And though she was the star of their act, Blossom Seeley retired for a while to give her husband, Bennie Fields, his own time in the spotlight.

Plenty of performers managed to have their cake and eat it, too, by bringing their spouses and families with them as they traveled. When such was the case, it was generally necessary for each member to pull his own weight, as passage and accommodations were costly. The obvious solution was to incorporate the whole clan right into the act. As the husband and wife were frequently both already performers, such a situation was a natural outcome. Many's the vaudeville couple who seemed blissfully happy to be both performing and living together: Vernon and Irene Castle, George Burns and Gracie Allen, Harry and Bess Houdini, Jessie Block and Eve Sully, Jimmy and Willie Cagney, William Demarest and Estelle Collete, Fred Allen and Portland Hoffa, and Paul and Grace Hartman. Groucho Marx recalled once being kept awake on a train by the sound of Walter Huston (father of director John Huston) making love to a woman in the berth below him. Groucho responded by dropping coat hangers on the couple, but they didn't seem to notice. The woman was Bayonne Whipple, Huston's wife and stage partner. (At least, I hope it was!)

Other couples were doomed. Songwriter-accompanist Jack Norworth managed to bag three of the hottest vaudeville stars of their day: Nora Bayes, Louise Dresser, and Trixie Friganza. None of them worked out. Bayes, who was vaudeville's biggest diva, truly pushed him to the limit, forcing him to walk her dog, to smoke outside (at the time a great indignity), and to accept the billing "Nora Bayes, Assisted and Admired by Jack Norworth." Norworth, among other things, had cowritten songs like "Shine On, Harvest Moon" and "Take Me Out to the Ball Game." He had little need to be Bayes's whipping boy, so he said sayonara. Stan Laurel and his common-law wife, Mae, bickered constantly. In their act, she played a battle-ax who browbeat Stan, humiliated him, kicked him, punched him, and broke crockery over his head. Unfortunately, she was the same woman back in the dressing room. Bert Lahr had an odd relationship with his common-law wife and partner, Mercedes Delpino. Constantly upbraided for her imperfections as part of the act, Delpino slowly lost her mind and was eventually hospitalized. It is by no means certain that Lahr's criticisms were the cause of her mental illness, but, according to Lahr *fils*'s account, the two of them were miserable together.

Meanwhile, some vaudeville couples were so blessedly happy they produced new baby vaudevillians. Donald O'Connor was born into "The O'Connors—The Royal Family of Vaudeville." Vaudeville cartoonist and silent-screen comedian Larry Semon was the son of a magician named Zera the Great. Pat Rooney passed his dance shoes on to his son, who passed them on to his. Joe Jackson passed his bicycle on to Joe Jackson, Jr. Comedian Frank Fay's parents were vaudeville actors in San Francisco. Josie and George Cohan joined their parents onstage at ages nine and eight, respectively, worked with them as a family act well into adulthood, and eventually became much bigger stars in their own right. Buster Keaton was born in a boardinghouse in Picah, Kansas, while his parents were on tour. He stayed with the act for the next twenty-two years. Eddie Foy turned his entire litter of seven children and his wife into an act. Judy Garland and her sisters joined their parents onstage in vaudeville. So, too, did her future costar Mickey Rooney, though back then he was known as Sonny Yule. Sammy Davis, Jr.'s, mother had run away with another vaudeville troupe, so little Sam joined Sammy Davis, Sr., onstage with the Will Mastin Trio. Martha Raye, "the Big Mouth," also started out in an act with her parents. Some vaudeville kids who were born too late to go into vaudeville themselves but managed to do all right in show business are Jerry Lewis, Steve Allen, Russ Tamblyn, Alan Alda, Teri Garr, Candice Bergen, and Dean Stockwell. The son of vaudeville comedian Doc Rockwell turned out to be a bigger clown than any of them—George Lincoln Rockwell was the founder of the American Nazi Party.

One of the major ironies of the vaudeville story was that the Society for the Prevention of Cruelty to Children (also known as the Gerry Society, after founder Elbridge T. Gerry) chose to crack down on the handful of underage entertainers—while allowing thousands of urchins to work lathes and assembly lines.

"What most burned up Pop," said Buster Keaton about his family's never-ending tussles with the Gerry people, "was that there were then thousands of homeless and hungry abandoned children of my age wandering around the streets of New York, selling newspapers, shining shoes, playing the fiddle on the Hudson River ferryboats, and thousands of other small children working with their parents in the tenement sweatshops on the Lower East Side. Pop couldn't understand why the S.P.C.C. people didn't devote all of their time, energy and money to helping them."

The discrepancy may have had something to do with the supposed "morality" (or lack thereof) in the show-business environment. And they may have had a point. As a teenager, Milton Berle was taken to his first prostitute by fellow child performer Phil Silvers. Charlie Foy picked up his lifelong gambling habit shooting craps backstage with grown performers. Gypsy Rose Lee's mother, "Mama Rose" Hovick, pushed her daughter into the sleezy world of burlesque. And some kids (like Buster Keaton), no doubt about it, were physically abused.

But such cases appear to have been the exception. While Buster only had one day of formal public schooling and was functionally illiterate, others, like the Seven Little Foys (an act devised by Eddie Foy in his twilight years, comprised of his large brood of children), traveled with their own private tutors. Fred and Adele Astaire's mother "home-schooled" them on the road. "I had a wonderful education," Rose Marie told me in a telephone interview. "Because we traveled from town to town, I got to visit all of the places I read about in school." Tourists to the Alamo will find her name etched in the wall—she signed it when she was six years old.

Book learning aside, vaudeville provided its own sort of education. Penny Singleton, best known as Blondie from her films of the 1940s and fifties, and also the cartoon voice of Jane Jetson, performed in vaudeville as "Baby Dorothy" (her real name was Mariana Dorothy Agnes Letitia McNulty): "I suppose it would be difficult for many people today to understand, but vaudeville was the most marvelous school for a child imaginable."

Stage mothers and fathers employed all sorts of subterfuges to get around the cabal of bluenose meddlers of the Gerry Society. (After all, their children *did* perform onstage.) Buster Keaton and Sammy Davis, Jr., were frequently given out to be midgets. To prove that she was *not* a midget, Baby Rose Marie (then a major NBC radio star) was given a vaudeville tour on the RKO circuit (successor to Keith's). To get around the Gerry regulations, she lip-synced to a record.

The Gerry people were no doubt well-intentioned, but in practice they generally did more harm than good. The fact that underage performers were being "exploited" also meant that they were the sole source of income for their poor and working-class families. Remove the underage talent and a lot of people would go hungry. The harshest illustration of this happened to the young Sammy Davis, Jr. In Michigan, a concerned woman complained to theater management about the fact that a child was performing. Because of the woman's intervention, the Will Mastin Trio (his act) was canceled, and Sam and his dad, penniless, were forced to sleep on park benches, starving and freezing in the Michigan winter, for several days. Thank God someone spoke up on behalf of the child's welfare!

Interestingly, the SPCC was founded *after* the better-known ASPCA, the Association for the Prevention of Cruelty to Animals. To compound the irony, vaudeville animals were much more harshly treated—and much less monitored. As Irene Castle recalled in her memoir, *Castles in the Air*:

> We saw dogs beaten unmercifully after the curtain fell and given the water cure in the alley, with the trainer holding a powerful hose close to the dog's nose and filling his lungs with water. We saw animals shocked with electricity, stuck with needles, and starved except for the few tid-bits reward which made them do the things they were afraid to do. There was little affection between the trainer and the animals. Affection might make a dog unpredictable on the stage. So the animals were cowed, afraid to make the slightest mistake.

What few animal-safety officers Castle saw she reports as having been corrupt. In the end, she and her husband, Vernon, would simply buy abused animals from their owners and give them more loving homes. When they realized that this habit was financially unsustainable, they simply wrote into their contracts that they would not appear on any bill with an animal act, as did many others (for similar reasons of conscience), including Sarah Bernhardt.

If child performers endured any "torture" at all, it was "suffocation" at the hands of their stage mothers. American vaudeville's premier impressionist Elsie Janis was so dependent on "Ma" that she remained in some sense a "child star" well into her forties. Ma Janis did everything for her: coached her on her performance, kept her schedule, made the bookings, selected her material, chose her wardrobe, and chaperoned her dates. Irene Castle called Ma Janis Elsie's "ringmaster" and "Svengali." "For pure drive and ambition," she said, "no mother manager . . . ever approached Ma Janis." The mothers of Milton Berle and Gypsy Rose Lee came awfully close, though.

"My childhood ended at the age of five," Berle recalled in his autobiography, but in some ways childhood for him extended well into middle age. Sadie Berle would be looking over Milton's shoulder long after he'd become "Mr. Television." Sadie was not only pushy but sort of crazy and desperate. She once finagled young Milton into Eddie Cantor's dressing room, where she forced him to do his Cantor impression. Cantor's response was reportedly something like "That's good, kid. So long." Even more brazenly, she bullied her way past a stage manager at the Wintergarden Theatre and pushed Milton onstage during a Jolson performance. Through gritted teeth, the entertainer permitted the apparently insane boy to do his Jolson impression before dismissing him, all to the hearty amusement of the audience. Most perversely, when Milton was cast in a prominent revival of *Floradora*, Sadie insisted he start off his dance number on the wrong foot on opening night, screwing up the routine. She said it would get him "attention." With attention like that, what's so bad about obscurity?

Among stage parents, Jerry Cohan seems to have been the exception, for his gentleness and his encouragement. To the day he died, George M. claimed to see Jerry's ghost sitting in the audience during rehearsals cheering him on—"Good boy, Georgie, put it over."

By the time child performers outgrew the interferences of the Gerry Society and hit puberty, they had a new problem. As hard as it may be to believe in our benighted era when everyone from five to fifty-five seems to aspire to be taken for an adolescent, in the vaudeville era there was little place for children once they found themselves "'twixt twelve and twenty." Teenage "cool" was not invented until the 1950s. In vaudeville, a teenager was seen either as a kid who was no longer cute, or a lamentably inexperienced and awkward proto-adult.

The Astaire kids, who'd had huge success early on as an adorable little bride and groom dancing atop a wedding cake, became lanky, ungainly, and unemployable when the growth spurt hit. A lot of child acts quit the game at this point, but dancing was all the Astaire kids knew and wanted. Their response was to work so insanely hard that they became in essence an entirely new act. As young adults it was their artistic excellence, not their adorableness, that made them a hit.

To survive the rough passage from childhood to adulthood without leaving the limelight it helped to be a prodigy of one sort or another. George M. Cohan was writing hit songs and sketches while still a teenager. His sister Josie was a dancer of unsurpassed grace. And Elsie Janis was still knocking them dead as vaudeville's greatest impressionist—just as impressive coming from a teenager as a tot. Most, however, eventually drowned, kicking and screaming, in a sea of obscurity. Think of Bette Davis in *What Ever Happened to Baby Jane?* and beware, *beware* the former child vaudeville star.

There was tremendous advantage in siblings performing together. Siblings look alike, they move alike, they sing with similar voices, they share the same sense of humor, and they generally don't double-cross one another. Five Marx Brothers worked together at various times, as did three Howard Brothers, who at different times made up the personnel of the Three Stooges. Two other Howard Brothers, Willie and Eugene (not related to Moe, Shemp, or Curly) were also a major comedy team. There were three Ritz Brothers. There were the Nicholas Brothers, who first danced with their sister Dorothy. Dance teams were often brother-and-sister acts: among them the Astaires, the Ebsens, and Fanchon and Marco. Sister acts were a vaudeville staple. Gracie Allen performed with her three sisters as the Four Colleens. Besides them, there were the Cherry Sisters, the Duncan Sisters, the Watson Sisters, and the Dolly Sisters, and hundreds of others. The Hilton Sisters had no choice but to work together—they were Siamese twins.

In one rare case, a professional spat tore apart a pair of brothers. In 1901 Harry and Al Jolson teamed up with one Joe Palmer as Jolson, Palmer, and Jolson in a sketch called "A Little Bit of Everything." Palmer, a former headliner who had written the lyrics to "In the Good Old Summertime," was now wheelchair-bound due to multiple sclerosis. In the bit, Harry played a doctor, Al a bellhop, and Palmer . . . a guy in a wheelchair. Offstage, part of the brothers' duties involved cleaning and dressing their disabled partner. One night they both wanted to go out on the town, and they got into a heated argument about who would stay home and take care of Mr. Palmer. This ridiculous (and rather cruel) argument seems to have been the source of a rift that Al and Harry never managed to patch up. Al went on to become one of the most popular entertainers of his generation. Harry was sort of the Frank Sinatra, Jr., of his time. To get bookings, he would have to endure the billing "Al Jolson's Brother."

One can see why having close family nearby would be important to a vaudevillian. With so much travel, maintaining deep friendships was difficult, if not impossible. "Vaudeville friendships were temporary," recalled singer and comedian Jack Haley. "You played a whole week with someone, went out to dinner with him every night. Then you never saw him again." As time went on, however, professional relationships could blossom into friendships. Maybe you only saw someone a couple of times a year, but a lot of vaudevillians did enjoy decades-long friendships in the business. "Vaudeville was an exhilarating, great new world for me," said Phil Silvers. "It had its share of deadbeats and egocentric maniacs and joke-snatchers. But we had warmth and camaraderie and time for laughs."

The sidewalk in front of the Palace Theatre became a popular hangout (nicknamed "the beach"), as did a lot of the surrounding Times Square eateries, such as Rector's, Lindy's, and Child's. In these gathering places, George Burns, Jack Benny, Georgie Jessel, Eddie Cantor, and scores of others got to know one another when they weren't performing. These old vaudeville friends stayed friends until they died. Milton Berle and Phil Silvers helped their old pal Rose Marie get work after she hit puberty and could no longer plausibly attach "Baby" to the front of her name. She, in turn, suggested her old friend the vaudeville comedy writer Morey Amsterdam when *The Dick Van Dyke Show* was in preproduction. The ones who stayed big tended to remember with generosity the ones who had faded. Jack Benny made room for walk-ons by his old pal Benny Rubin on his TV show. Twenty years earlier, Rubin had starred in his own films.

Despite camaraderie, some people were just too horrible to be-friend. Though almost all of the great vaud comedians speak with rever-ence about Frank Fay's talent ("Of all the great vaudevillians," James Cagney recalled, "I admired Frank the most"), offstage he was a notori-ous scoundrel and a mean drunk, and nary a single benign anecdote survives him. As Milton Berle once observed, "Fay's friends could be counted on the missing arm of a one-armed man."

An example of the arrogance that was to overshadow Fay's reputation occurred early in his career. In this incident, which became notorious throughout theatrical circles, Frank Fay let the audience wait several minutes while he struggled to tie his tie in the dressing room. "Let 'em wait!" he reportedly snapped to the stage manager, establishing a theatri-cal attitude that would not be revived until rock-and-roll was invented forty years later. When we compare Fay's behavior with that of his fellow vaudevillians, who literally worshipped the audience as a kind of collec-tive God, and when we remember the premium the managers placed on time, we understand that his conduct transcended arrogance and bor-dered on the realm of heresy.

Fay didn't go in for slapstick. He used to taunt Bert Lahr with barbs like, "Well, well, well, what's the low comedian doing today?" Fay's bag was verbal wit, and he gave no quarter, offstage or on. To Berle's chal-lenge to a battle of wits on one occasion, Fay famously replied, "I never attack an unarmed man."

Apparently Fay had one of those smirking faces that's just begging to be smacked. On one occasion, he attempted to humiliate comedian Bert Wheeler (later of the movie comedy team Wheeler and Woolsey) by dragging him onto the stage unprepared, and firing off a bunch of previously unrehearsed lines at him, to which he was supposed to at-tempt rejoinders. Tired of such treatment, Wheeler unnerved Fay by re-maining silent the whole time. Fay finally cracked and asked, "What's the matter? Why don't you say something?" Wheeler responded, "You call these laughs? I can top these titters without saying a word," and proved it by smacking him in the face. The audience howled, simulta-neously vindicating Wheeler and, in the process, demonstrating the ef-ficacy of low comedy.

Even when Fay tried to be nice he was rotten. Introducing Edgar

Bergen for his first Palace date, he said, "The next young man never played here before, so let's be nice to him." As any stage performer will tell you, such an introduction is patronizing at best, sabotage at worst.

Fay somehow managed to charm Barbara Stanwyck, and the two married and headed out to Hollywood to make pictures. In Tinseltown, as everywhere he went, Fay did not make a lot of friends. A standard joke of the time went as follows—Question: Who's got the biggest prick in Hollywood? Answer: Barbara Stanwyck. While the womanizing, wife-beating, and alcoholic Fay's career floundered, Stanwyck's flourished for decades; it is said that the marriage was one of the inspirations for the movie *A Star Is Born*. As Fred Allen recalled: "The last time I saw Frank Fay he was walking down Lover's Lane holding his own hand."

Another fairly unlikable character in vaudeville was Al Jolson. Consider: in 1910, he turned down an offer to audition for Ziegfeld ("Jolie don't audition for nobody"). And in 1911 he placed this appalling holiday message in *Variety* for no particular reason: "Everybody likes me. Those who don't are jealous. Anyhow, here's wishing those that do and those that don't a Merry Christmas and a Happy New Year—Al Jolson." Thanks for nothing! Once he saw some empty seats in the house and had to be coerced into performing. Another favorite trick of his was to stop in the middle of a performance and say, "Do you want me or do you want the show?" If the audience chose "him" he would proceed to do a song set, and the rest of the other performers could go home.

Many vaudeville friendships grew out of, or led to, professional partnerships. Some teams were inseparable. For example, when Olsen and Johnson died, they were buried next to each other in a cemetery in Las Vegas. Most partnerships, however, were more volatile. Comedians, with their special insecurities, were especially susceptible to breakups. A tension exists in all comedy teams between the "funny" member(s) and the straight man or stooge. One gets all the glory and is everyone's favorite—the other remains an unsung hero, appreciated fully by only a few aficionados. The situation can lead to strife, and there are numerous examples of the straight man turning to drink, exploding, or just quitting in disgust: Bud Abbot, Ed Gallagher, and Zeppo Marx come immediately to mind. But perhaps the most extreme and tragic example comes from Clark and McCullough.

The team had been together since boyhood. Originally Paul McCullough had been the "funny" member of the duo, as evidenced by his name being last in the billing. (It was traditional with comedy teams for the straight man's name to run first.) But Bobby Clark was a scene stealer who hogged all the attention wherever he went. Gradually, their positions became reversed. Over time, McCullough became a sort of mixture of straight man and stooge, feeding Clark the setups for all the laugh lines. In later years, Clark literally stole the show, and McCullough had less and less to do. By the 1930s, McCullough was hardly in their shows at all, and was barely missed. Following a nervous breakdown and a sanatorium stay, he committed suicide in 1936.

Other teams were more contentious, if less tragic. Alcohol abuse by the straight man was almost always the culprit.

One of the most famous teams of the vaudeville age was Gallagher and Shean, who in 1922 introduced what may have been vaudeville's most popular comic song, "Oh! Mr. Gallagher! Mr. Shean!" The song was such a hit it became the focal point of their act, and was one of America's first hit records, still sung and parodied the world over. Yet their relationship was especially acrimonious; in fact, it was the basis for the more bilious aspects of Neil Simon's play *The Sunshine Boys*. In reality, Gallagher and Shean were apart far more than they were together. The team first split up in 1914, then Minnie Marx (the Marx Brothers' mother and Al Shean's sister) got them back together again in 1920, and they became a bigger hit than ever. The team broke up again in 1925. Alcohol abuse took Gallagher four years later.*

In their last years, the blackface team of McIntyre and Heath didn't speak offstage, mostly on account of McIntyre's drinking problem, which necessitated the frequent services of an understudy. Bud Abbot's drinking problem, too, was well-known. The great team of Duffy and Sweeney never broke up, but perhaps that's because *both* were drunks!

Ted Healy's drinking came with tragic results. Healy was a drunk— a mean drunk. Contrary to commonly accepted practice in slapstick, Healy pulled no punches, and his Stooges wore no padding. (Besides, how do you pad your face?) When he was drunk, he got sloppy and care-

---

*Gallagher left us a legacy beyond the funny song, however. With her inheritance, his widow started the Gallagher's Steak House chain, still with us today.

less, and the act's stooges got hurt. This, plus the fact that Healy took the lion's share of the team's rather hefty salary, caused the Stooges to drop him like a hot potato the moment film opportunities arose. Healy was to die a few years later in a drunken barroom brawl while celebrating the birth of his son.

Sad, too, was the breakup of the Three Keatons. Ed Wynn called Joe, the father, "a totally undisciplined Irish drunk." As previously mentioned, the knockabout slapstick routine was particularly violent and called for split-second timing. Keaton's drunken misjudgments frequently resulted in serious injury for Buster, on one occasion leaving the young performer in a coma. The final nail in the act's coffin was an incident in Providence, Rhode Island. Joe Keaton, enraged by some cheap prop furniture the act had been given by a stingy stage manager, proceeded to smash every stick of furniture in the theater he could find. Martin Beck, the Keith-Orpheum booker, had it in for the act from that day on. In fact, Beck was backstage when the Keatons were about to go on in New York a few days later. "Make *me* laugh, Keaton," Beck is reported to have taunted. True to form, the pugnacious Keaton chased Beck out of the theater and halfway down the street. It's a hot-tempered vaudevillian indeed who tries to punch out the most important booker in vaudeville. They were finished in big time. Buster quit and went into films. His folks went into retirement.

As with Healy and the Stooges, sometimes a team broke up when one of the partners got a break that didn't include the others. In 1911, Eddie Cantor was the unbilled third man in a juggling act called Bedini and Arthur. At first, Cantor was little more than a glorified assistant with no stage time. After he passed this test for a few weeks, he was given a walk-on part in the show. His job was simply to stroll across the stage and hand a plate to Bedini, yet somehow Cantor managed to get a laugh, walking on with an "attitude." Bedini, the boss of the act, gradually expanded Cantor's part with spoken lines, bits of business, and even juggling, and before long Cantor's comic mugging had made him the star of the act. But still no raise and no billing. When an offer came to star with the Gus Edwards Company, Cantor left Bedini and Arthur holding their own plates.

While vaudeville was undoubtedly the most liberal institution of its day, prejudice was known to cause some backstage tension. Milton

Berle recalled having watched Frank Fay perform from the wings (a real no-no with some performers). According to Berle, he heard Fay say, "Get that little Jew bastard out of the wings," and something about "that little kike." If Berle's account is to be believed, he grabbed a stage brace and busted open Fay's nose with it. Ed Wynn (also Jewish) had the nerve to marry the daughter of legitimate stage actor and sometime vaudevillian Frank Keenan, a Christian. Keenan wouldn't speak to them for years, although he eventually softened. The fact that they named their firstborn Keenan Wynn (who became a well-known character actor in movies and television) may have had something to do with it.

Bert Williams, vaudeville's greatest African-American star—a singer, songwriter, dancer, mime, and comedian—suffered perhaps more than any artist from racism. I say this not because the indignities were any worse than those suffered by other African-Americans, but because he was widely considered one of the towering geniuses of the footlights and yet he *still* was treated by some as a second-class citizen. You could fill a chapter with raves about Williams from his white contemporaries. Remarks by song publisher Edward Marks are typical: "No Negro comedian ever reached his heights, and no white comedian ever surpassed him. In facial expression and pantomime he equaled the greatest clowns. In the . . . delivery of his songs he was a *diseur* without parallel." Yet even this was not enough to prevent painful incidents of racism. "He's a good nigger," he overheard one stage manager say. "Knows his place." Grace Kelly's uncle, Walter C. Kelly (who had a racist act known as "The Virginia Judge"), refused to play on the same stage with him.

Yet such attitudes in show business were rare. Far more representative of the trouper's attitude was Joe Keaton, who finding himself at the opposite end of a bar from Williams, beckoned for him to join him. But the bar was segregated and Williams was at the black end, so he mumbled an embarrassed but polite refusal. Keaton, realizing the situation, came down to the other end of the bar to join Williams. Interracial friendship in vaudeville was common. Fayard Nicholas spoke of having a "mutual admiration society" with Fred Astaire, while Astaire writes glowingly about an early encounter with Bill Robinson. Eleanor Powell got Willie Covan his job as head dance instructor at MGM. Eddie Cantor turned Sammy Davis, Jr., on to Judaism.

This sort of tolerance extended to other groups as well. Lou Holtz on the team of Savoy and Brennan:

> Sure, I knew they were supposed to be fags. But who cared? They didn't bother me. I knew women in this business who were lesbians. Again, who cared? So she's a lesbian one hour a day. The rest of the day she's charming, a great performer, and a pleasure to work with.

Does this amount to complete acceptance of homosexuality? No. But Holtz's is about as progressive an attitude as you're going to get in the 1920s. Maybe his language is out of line, but the sentiment is unimpeachable. Holtz harbors no ill will. He doesn't shriek, "This is unnatural," or "This must be stopped." If pressed on the subject he might say, "This isn't for me," or "I'd rather not hear about it." But the bottom line is, the melting pot of show business has placed him into a working relationship with homosexuals. They are his colleagues, and colleagues become friends.

Blacks, whites, men, women, gays, straights, old, young, Jews, gentiles, people from dozens of different nations worked together, shared dressing rooms, traveled together, ate and drank together, cooked for one another, slept together, socialized, gambled together, watched one another's performances, swapped pointers and new material, baby-sat one another's kids, loaned one another money, stuck up for one another—and sometimes, as people do, insulted and fought with one another. Over the decades, show business would continue to expand the philosophy of tolerance forged in the dressing rooms of vaudeville theaters. In the television era, their good example would come to have an influence on the entire country. Ironically, this unlooked-for outcome of "polite vaudeville" would result in a moral gain far greater than hypocritical attempts to ban foul language and naked bodies.

For those who could stick it out, the compensations of vaudeville could far outweigh its many indignities and inconveniences. The delicious moments of triumph could be measured as great spikes on a graph that included countless tiny troughs. After all, was the ceaseless grind of the travel, and the bad food and accommodations any worse than a life spent slaving away on an adding machine, a jack hammer, or a sewing machine? Sophie Tucker, after abandoning her child, had left Hartford, Connecticut, a pariah. She returned a few years later to find enormous billboards adorning the local Poli house, advertising HARTFORD'S OWN SOPHIE TUCKER. For a long time, Lew Fields had been afraid to tell his father he was in show business. It was years before the elder Fields ever attended a performance. In the end, the entire family changed their last name from Schoenfeld to Lew's stage name, Fields. And, on one occasion, Bert Williams walked into a St. Louis bar and ordered a glass of gin. The white bartender, in a transparent attempt to send him on his way, told him the drink would cost him $50. Williams laid a $500 bill down on the bar and said, "I'll have ten of them." In today's money that would be about $8,000. Now, if that's not empowerment, I'll eat my stovepipe hat.

But, of course, what goes up must come down. Nora Bayes had been washed up for years when she invited Palace booker Eddie Darling to her house for a midnight party in 1928. He arrived but, eerily, she was the only one there. She proceeded to sing her old songs to him, climaxing with a request that he put her publicity photos up in the Palace lobby for a few hours, as though she had an upcoming booking, just for old times' sake. He did as she requested, and she had her chauffeur drive her to the theater so she could see them there once more. Two days later, she was dead of cancer at age fifty. Eva Tanguay, who at one time had been the highest paid woman in vaudeville, and a "cyclonic dervish" of energy, died in 1947. She had been living on a fixed income, blind and bedridden for decades.

A number of vaudevillians died theatrical, appropriately symbolic deaths. Some died right in the theater. Trick cyclist Joe Jackson died of a heart attack following a 1942 performance at the Roxy after which he had taken five curtain calls. His last words were "My, they're still applauding." Strong man Eugene Sandow died of a brain rupture in 1925 as he single-handedly pulled a car out of a ditch. There is poetic justice to the death of W. E. Robinson (Chung Ling Soo). After making a career out of stealing the act of Ching Ling Foo, Robinson died onstage at London's Wood Green Empire in 1918, when a gun misfired during his bullet-catching act.

Female-impersonator Bert Savoy died tragically young in 1923. His last words are perhaps the richest that were ever spoken, and predictably blasphemous. While walking on a Long Island beach with friends during a violent lightning storm, he turned to the person next to him and said, "Mercy, ain't Miss God cutting up something awful?" There was a blue flash, a crack—and that was the end of Bert Savoy.

7

THE MARCH OF PROGRESS

On the whole, there is nothing wrong with vaudeville, except that it is dead.
—*Brooks Atkinson,* Billboard, *April 1939*

If somebody had told you in 1920 that vaudeville would be well nigh kaput in a decade you would have accused him of drinking too much bathtub gin. Vaudeville was at that date a well-established American institution. While most of the factors that would kill it off were in fact already in place, no one at the time saw it coming. Only with the benefit of hindsight do we retrofit this tale with storm clouds and read the warning signs for what they were. Furthermore, vaudeville died a-borning. It had only recently been created. How was it possible for it to be torn down and replaced by an entirely new industry practically overnight?

The vaudeville business, it turns out, was a phase—an important chapter in show-business history, but a middle chapter, a way station between Miss Kitty's Saloon and your local Time-Warner-AOL-Disney-ABC-Heinz-Ketchup-Googolplex. Just as the development of the railroad made the "revolutionary" (for a while) canal system in the United States quickly obsolete, so was vaudeville rendered obsolete by the mass-production technologies of the music, film, and broadcasting industries that it made possible.

He who lives by the sword, dies by the sword. "Survival of the fittest" had been the watchword of the Gilded Age capitalists. In vaudeville, that philosophy had been a ruling principle, as managers and artists vied for advantage in a never-ending scramble to be top dog. Now that very same principle had rendered the entire industry obsolete, along with many others. Vaudeville was not the only entertainment form to be smacked down by the Invisible Hand. Eventually, so, too, were showboats, dime museums, minstrel shows, medicine shows, old-style burlesque, the Broadway revue, silent films, and radio drama.

By and large, when the smoke cleared, the managers—wily devils—emerged from the bloodbath unscathed. Many, like Sylvester Poli, F. F. Proctor, and Percy Williams, cashed in their chips, sold off their interests, and retired rich. Others merely changed focus, concentrating their efforts exclusively on the exhibition and production of films. Martin Beck went on to become a successful producer of Broadway theatricals (as late as 2003 a prominent Times Square theater bore his name). These gentlemen were men of business, remember. For them, when one angle ceased to be profitable, they tried another.

But how could an industry so strong, so vital, cease to be profitable so suddenly? In the second half of the 1920s, receipts declined a stunning 70 percent. Whodunit? There were numerous culprits, so many in fact that this mystery plays out like *Murder on the Orient Express*. Everyone seems to have been guilty.

THE PHONOGRAPH

As we have seen, the phonograph had brought vaudevillians into people's homes as early as 1902. During the first two decades of the twentieth century, the Edison company even produced a special Vaudeville series, recording scores of comedy sketches, songs, and monologues on cylinders that can still be heard today.

In the teens and twenties, the floodgates opened, with a whole bevy of singers, comedians, and bands recording to disk, including Gallagher and Shean, Weber and Fields, the Avon Comedy Four, Al Jolson, Sophie Tucker, Nora Bayes, Eddie Cantor, Miss Patricola, Will Rogers, Waring's Pennsylvanians, Lou Holtz, Belle Baker, Sissle and Blake, Fanny Brice, Walter C. Kelly, Jimmy Durante, the Paul Whiteman Orchestra, Rudy

Vallee, and Ruth Etting, among scores of others. By 1919, Americans were buying 25 million records a year. In the thirties, this process only accelerated, and today, with the proliferation of iPods, Internet file-sharing, and the like, it is experiencing yet another revolution.

Did phonographs keep the entire audience home? No . . . but they provided the first of a thousand cuts that would accumulate to bleed the mighty beast to death.

NEW LIVE COMPETITION

Inspired by vaudeville's success, other forms of live competition emerged early in the twentieth century. This hurt vaudeville less at the box office than it did on the payroll end. Broadway producers and nightclub managers hired away some of vaudeville's top talent at unheard-of salaries. To remain competitive, the vaudeville managers had to match those salaries if they wanted to hold on to the big names. This cut into profits, making the vaudeville industry still more vulnerable.

Starting in the late aughts, the producers of Broadway revues began raiding vaudeville's talent pool. As we have seen, the pioneer of the field was Florenz Ziegfeld, whose *Follies* were inaugurated in 1907, and persisted in various editions posthumously as late as the 1950s. But Ziegfeld was not the only revue impresario. Others sprang up over the years: the *Passing Show* series presented by the Shuberts (1912–34), *George White's Scandals* (1919–39), *Earl Carroll's Vanities* (1923–31), the *Greenwich Village Follies* (1920–28), and Irving Berlin's *Music Box Revues* (1921–24). All of these annual revues (plus many other "one-shot" productions) employed the top vaudeville stars of the day.

To graduate to a Broadway revue, for many artists, was the true measure of "making it." Some stars continued to work in both vaudeville and revues at the same time, but many said "s'long" to the grind of the circuits for the greater prestige and remuneration to be had on the revue stage. The differences in working conditions were marked. Even a big-time vaudevillian was obligated to do two shows a day, while the revues were strictly prime-time. In addition, the revues were specifically a New York phenomenon. Some of them did tour, but for the most part the revue performer could go to work right from his home, bypassing the bad food, harsh travel, and dumpy accommodations that were part of the ordeal of traveling the vaudeville circuit.

One by one, they made the jump: Leon Errol and Bert Williams (1911), Willie and Eugene Howard (1912), Ed Wynn (1914), W. C. Fields and Will Rogers (1915), and Eddie Cantor (1917). Women singers like Nora Bayes, Belle Baker, Eva Tanguay, and Ruth Etting worked sometimes here, sometimes there, switching vaudeville and revues like so many pairs of stockings.

Some stars were so big or so lucky, they built entire revues around themselves. The series of revues Ed Wynn produced through the twenties and early thirties were his highest realization as a performing artist. To this day, despite ample record of Wynn's comic genius on film, radio, and TV, this string of Broadway smashes is regarded as the pinnacle of Wynn's career. Each was based around the familiar character Wynn had developed in vaudeville. Among the most successful of these tailor-made vehicles were *Ed Wynn's Carnival* (1920), *The Perfect Fool* (1921), *The Grab Bag* (1924), *Simple Simon* (1930), and *The Laugh Parade* (1931).

Other high-profile revues built around a single vaudeville star included Raymond Hitchcock's successful *Hitchy Koo* series, the Marx Brothers' 1924 hit *I'll Say She Is!* and *Frank Fay's Fables*, which flopped. In many ways these revues were *better* than vaudeville. No animal acts or acrobats to sit through . . . just the top singers and comedy stars, framed by beautiful women wearing opulent—and occasionally negligible—costumes. In fact, these revues drained off a lot of the top talent from vaudeville, while contributing to dramatic salary increases for many of the performers.

It is the opinion of some that the influence of the revue helped to kill vaudeville by introducing the concept of "class." All of a sudden, everything in the teens and twenties had to have "class." The comedians had to wear tuxedos or business suits; the women wore evening gowns. In 1913 the Palace opened, the first vaudeville house that appears to have been influenced by the revue culture as opposed to the other way around. A sort of bland and uniform glamour prevailed, eclipsing some of vaudeville's distinctive democratic flavor, which had been handed down from the variety days. Instead of clownish comedians in greasepaint, wearing battered top hats and derbies with checked vests, you had a lot of smart-talking nightclub-style comics like Bob Hope and Ken Murray. That's all right for some, but in 1930 it might well have been too la-di-da for Joe the Plumber, who just wanted to plunk down his dime and watch two baggy-pants comics beat each other with a slapstick.

Broadway's plunder of vaudeville talent didn't stop at revues, however. Many artists also abandoned the circuits for starring roles in book musicals.

A template of sorts had been established by Harrigan and Hart, who had grown their variety afterpieces into full-blown musicals, such as their productions in the "Mulligan Guard" series, at the Theatre Comique in the 1880s. Thus was the idea planted that vaudeville was a sort of stepping stone to "legitimacy." To be a star of a "show"—that was the summit. Weber and Fields followed Harrigan and Hart's lead around the turn of the century, gradually transforming the vaudeville revues they had been presenting at their music hall into full-length burlesques of popular Broadway shows—the *Forbidden Broadway* of its day.

George M. Cohan was thrust onto the musical stage by his falling-out with Keith. So, like his hero Ned Harrigan, he expanded one of his sketches, "The Governor's Son," into a full-length play. Over the next couple of decades he would virtually invent the Broadway musical. Important Cohan shows included *Little Johnny Jones* (1905); *Forty-five Minutes from Broadway* (1906); *Popularity* (1906); *The Talk of New York* (1907); *Fifty Miles from Boston* (1908); *The Yankee Prince* (1908); *The Man Who Owns Broadway* (1909); *Get-Rich-Quick Wallingford* (1910); and *Seven Keys to Baldpate* (1913). For them he penned the classic songs "Yankee Doodle Dandy," "Give My Regards to Broadway," "Life's a Very Funny Proposition After All," "Forty-five Minutes from Broadway," "Mary's a Grand Old Name," "You're a Grand Old Flag," "Harrigan," and "Over There."

Of course, most performers didn't open their own theaters and write and produce their own musicals. Most were content merely to star in them. From the first, vaudeville soubrettes like Lillian Russell, Fay Templeton, and May Irwin had done operetta and musicals in addition to vaudeville. Al Jolson only stayed in vaudeville for a couple of years. Once the Shuberts picked him up, he became the biggest thing that ever happened to Broadway. Other vaudeville stars who distinguished themselves in book musicals included Vernon and Irene Castle, Fred and Adele Astaire, Ray Bolger, Bert Lahr, Jack Haley, and Bobby Clark.

Mae West only discovered who she was in full-length vehicles. In the mid-1920s, she followed the pattern of Harrigan and Hart, Weber and Fields, and George M. Cohan by writing and producing her own plays. In vehicles like *Sex* (1926), *The Drag* (1927), *The Wicked Age* (1927), *Diamond Lil* (1928), *The Pleasure Man* (1929), and *The Constant Sinner* (1930) she discovered her talent for the witty epigram, and found that audiences would accept raciness in the form of a *character in a play* that they never would have stood for if she delivered it *as herself.*

Yet another new sort of venue entered the entertainment fray during the later years of vaudeville. With the concert saloon virtually extinct since the turn of the century, and always ill-regarded, a niche opened up for a classy French import, the cabaret, or nightclub. In 1911, Jesse Lasky built his own version of the Folies Bergeres in Times Square, where the likes of Olga Petrova and Mae West found early employment. (The building, renamed the Helen Hayes Theatre, still stands today.) The dance craze started by the Castles (1912), the advent of jazz (1915), and then Prohibition (1919) added to the allure of this exciting resurrection of the old saloon idea. Harlem, Times Square, and Greenwich Village all became locales for numerous speakeasies, and for a time, the city seemed to turn into a big party. Most of vaudeville's top singers, dancers, and musicians, and some of the stand-up comedians and two-acts, found lucrative work in illegal booze joints, rendering them less available to the formerly exclusive precincts of vaudeville. Some, like Jimmy Durante, Texas Guinan, and Helen Morgan, were more famous as co-owners and hosts at their own speakeasies than they were for their vaudeville turns.

Prohibition not only robbed vaudeville of its performers, it also took away something of its reason for being. The speakeasies were all owned and frequented by gangsters like Owney Madden, Al Capone, and Arnold Rothstein.* This had the side effect of thrusting vaudeville performers back into the discredited company that had been the traveling

---

*You could make the case that vaudeville had corrupted Rothstein, and not the other way around. He had played his first crap game in the prop room of the Victoria, and his mentors included Tammany Hall crook and vaud manager "Big Tim" Sullivan and Fanny Brice's husband, Nick Arnstein, a professional gambler.

companions of show folk since time immemorial. This time was a little different, however. Prohibition forced practically everyone else into the company of crooks, too. In the Jazz Age, audiences and performers were no longer inclined to frown on elbow-bending and premarital sex. Increasingly, the values of the nightclub, the revue, and the burlesque stage were creeping into vaudeville. This left vaudeville managers in something of a bind in terms of marketing their product. After all, if it wasn't the "polite" alternative anymore, what precisely was it?

MOVIES

Vaudeville, as we have said, was a flexible form, embracing elements of circus, minstrelsy, music hall, legit, freak show, and, for half of its existence, film. Managers and vaudeville performers did not feel threatened by the new medium initially. Rather, cinema was absorbed into the vaudeville show, just another attraction on the bill, same as a juggler or a man who played the violin with his feet. They had no reason to suspect that over time film would become like a parasite that swallowed up and spit out the bill around it until only the flicker remained. Yet if you were to plot on a graph the rise of cinema against the fall of vaudeville, the result might look something like this: X.

The popularity of films was hard for the vaudeville managers to deny. One by one, the big-time managers succumbed to including them on the bills. The short film (approximately ten minutes) rounded out a vaudeville bill nicely. Initially it served as a perfect chaser: any walk-outs would happen on your weakest attraction. But now something amazing was happening: people stayed in their seats! Soon, like machine-age junkies, they were impatient for the film to start. Au revoir, vaudeville.

It was Marcus Loew more than any other man who helped that come to pass. He opened his first New York movie theater on Twenty-third Street in 1906. Within six months he had forty of them. The Schenk Brothers, Joseph and Nicholas, owners of the Palisades Amusement Company of New Jersey, were brought in as partners and bookers. The company went from presenting films in little storefronts to acquiring and building full-fledged theaters to rival those of the big time. But while the big-time theaters might charge two dollars to see a show, the top Loew's ticket was fifty cents (and the bottom a dime). Turnover, and the fact that salaries were kept low, kept it profitable.

In 1910 the Loews chain in New York had eleven of these large theaters, including William Morris's old American Music Hall at Eighth Avenue and Forty-second Street, Loew's flagship house until the Loew's State Theatre was built eleven years later.

Four of the five major Hollywood studios of the studio era had historic ties to the vaudeville industry. There's William Fox, originally a furrier like Zukor and Loew, who, like them both, opened a chain of vaudeville and movie houses. He bought out most of the Poli chain in 1913, and two years later went into production, forming the Fox Film Corporation, which would merge with the Twentieth Century Films Company twenty years later.

In 1912, Adolph Zukor had begun producing his own films with a company called Famous Players. Jesse Lasky, fresh from the failure of his Folies Bergeres enterprise, formed the Jesse L. Lasky Feature Play Company the following year with his brother-in-law, Samuel Goldfish (who soon changed his name to Goldwyn), producing the first real American feature, *The Squaw Man*, directed by Cecil B. DeMille. In 1916, the two companies merged to form Famous Players-Lasky, which later adopted the name of yet another company it had acquired: Paramount.

In 1920, Loew acquired Metro Pictures, so that he, too, could produce and distribute his own products for his theater chain. In 1924 he merged his company with Goldwyn Pictures (founded by Sam) and Louis B. Mayer Productions to create Metro-Goldwyn-Mayer, or MGM.

The fourth major Hollywood studio with roots in vaudeville was RKO (Radio-Keith-Orpheum), which was created under entirely different circumstances. All of these companies kept their vaudeville interests going throughout their early years; for decades the same companies that produced, distributed, and exhibited motion pictures hedged their bets by continuing to present live entertainment—almost as though they were afraid film would turn out to be a fad and vaudeville would come back. That's how unthinkable the death of vaud was.

The mid-teens saw several developments in the film world that were to have a profound impact on vaudeville. First, in 1912, Mack Sennett (who himself had been in vaudeville) hired numerous minor vaudevillians to perform in his Keystone comedies, among them Fred Mace, Ford Sterling, and Roscoe "Fatty" Arbuckle. When Sennett hired Charlie Chaplin away from the Karno Troupe in 1913 and he became an overnight sensation, an explosion of talented vaudevillians followed his path to film: W. C. Fields, Buster Keaton, Larry Semon, Will Rogers, Toto, Harry Houdini, Harry Langdon, Alla Nazimova, Bert Williams, Weber and Fields, Eddie Foy, Moran and Mack, the Duncan Sisters, and the Dolly Sisters. Some artists who had been struggling far from the top of the vaudeville heap made big successes in silent films, such as Rudolph Valentino, Tod Browning, Lon Chaney, Stan Laurel, Charlie Chase, Mack Swain, Ben Turpin, Chester Conklin, and Clyde Cook. Eager for the big bucks being made in the new industry, the Marx Brothers self-financed their own celluloid debut, the reportedly atrocious *Humorisk* (1920), all copies of which are reportedly either lost or destroyed. Keith and Albee tried to forestall all this perfidious flight by blacklisting performers who did films; but it was to no avail.

More devastating still to the vaudeville industry was the introduction in the mid-teens of the feature-length film. Middle-class audiences took kindly to full-length movies, because in format they were roughly analogous to a legit play. Until then, for many, movies were in a class with comic books and amusement park rides—strictly for kids and the uneducated. When a movie was shown on the stage of a Keith theater in 1913, the audience actually booed! They thought it was a gyp—strictly small time—and associated it with those crummy storefronts with the wooden benches.

The impact of the feature-length film on straight vaudeville was clearly measurable. One by one, theaters started going over to the enemy. In 1907, Proctor's Twenty-third Street became the Bijoux Dream, concentrating on films. In 1912, Proctor's Fifth Avenue switched over to a movie format. In 1915, Hammerstein's Victoria was renamed the Rialto and made into a cinema. The convention was to still include variety acts, but there weren't many slots for performers around a feature-length show and the package of shorts that would surround it.

In 1919 there were close to a thousand vaudeville houses in the country. By 1921 it is estimated that a quarter of theaters that had played both films and vaudeville dropped the vaudeville shows. The new vogue was for "presentation houses"—large movie palaces that would also present live entertainment, such as big bands and popular comedy acts, on the same bill.

Such places were huge: the Capitol Theatre (1919) sat 5,300 people. Loew's State, the Loew's chain's 1921 flagship, had 3,500 seats. Others included the Paramount, the Strand, and the Roxy. "Don't get caught on the Roxy Stage without bread and water," Joe Frisco joked. George Burns joked that he couldn't see the audience across the orchestra of one of these houses it was so large.

At the Capitol Theatre in 1932 you might see a film surrounded by a bill that included Burns and Allen, Arthur Tracy, Cab Calloway, and six other acts. In time, all but the big bands and their singers (and the movie, of course) were phased out of most of the big presentation houses. Through the 1940s you could see the likes of Bing Crosby, Frank Sinatra, Kate Smith, and Judy Garland (and the big swing bands that accompanied them) at the presentation houses. Nothing else would fill the room! They were all shut down by 1948, as the trend toward specialization continued. The big bands played in dance halls and nightclubs, and movie theaters evolved into the specialized venue we know today, with no stage, just a flat screen on the wall in front of the audience. Built in 1932, Radio City Music Hall, home of the Rockettes, is the last remaining presentation house.

By 1925, there were only a hundred straight (no flickers) vaudeville theaters, and *Billboard* was editorializing about "the decline of the road." Jobs were truly drying up for performers by this point. The big-time theaters (only twelve of them left without films as the main attraction) had to drop their generous two-a-day policies, forcing their performers to do three and four shows a day to keep afloat. In 1926, film replaced vaudeville as the central focus of *Variety* magazine. This was a swift revolution, and we haven't even gotten to talkies yet.

Yet can we blame theater managers for booking "automatic vaudeville" over the flesh-and-blood variety? Films don't argue over dressing rooms. They are much cheaper to ship than a comedy team. They don't get sick, and they don't have an "off" night. For people who like to centralize, organize, and control, they're the perfect show-business product. By the 1930s, human performers in theaters were becoming an obsolete technology.

RADIO

In 1921 *Billboard* ran this headline: "Radiophone Cuts Into Show Business: Vaudeville Exchanges First to Realize That Their Value Diminished by Wireless Appearances." Surprisingly, this article was written in the days of independent stations—the nationwide networks hadn't even been created yet. Sensing the threat from this new competition, Albee forbade acts from appearing on radio, or from even mentioning radio on-stage unless the remarks were disparaging. Technically these were "suggestions," but, like every Albee suggestion, it was an order: "It would be a good idea for you to do this (if you'd like to keep working for me)." But there was also a pathos to such an order that Albee never suspected. After all, once one was a big enough star to work in revues, nightclubs, films, records, and radio, who gave a damn if vaudeville work was unavailable? A new sort of industry was being born, one that made the old vaudeville circuits (new as they were) seem quaint by comparison. Vaudeville was horse-and-buggy. A true national audience for vaudevillians was about to be forged, one in which millions of Americans would listen to their songs, quips, and routines simultaneously.

On NBC's maiden broadcast on November 14, 1926, listeners heard Will Rogers, Weber and Fields, Eddie Cantor, the Ben Bernie Orchestra, and opera singer Mary Garden. Day in, day out, this was business as usual, with scores of vaudeville performers being booked to fill the airtime. The following year, CBS was launched, increasing the demand for radio talent yet again. Audiences for the new product grew exponentially. Three million American homes already had radios in 1927. By the end of the 1930s, the number had grown tenfold.

Radio elaborated on the breakthrough of the phonograph by providing home entertainment by all of your favorite stars of the time. In the 1930s, vaudeville stars like Eddie Cantor, Burns and Allen, Fred Allen, Jack Benny, Ed Wynn, Fanny Brice, Edgar Bergen and Charlie McCarthy, and all of the big-band leaders of the day became major radio stars. And you could enjoy them in your bathrobe. You didn't even have to get out of bed. Going to a vaudeville theater to see stars is kind of illogical when all the vaudevillians are coming to you through your own furniture.

The Great Depression magnified the force of this argument. In

1932 a radio cost $19.95, the equivalent of twenty to forty vaudeville shows, only you could listen to it all day, every day, for years. If something was going to yank people off their sofas and get them buying theater tickets again it would have to be pretty spectacular. It was. Of course it wasn't vaudeville that did it, but the increasingly novel confections of Hollywood.

TALKIES

In 1926, another revolution occurred in cinema, one that seems to have put the coup de grâce to vaud. Warner Bros. had come out with Vitaphone that year, a means of syncing up sound recording with films. Experimental talking shorts (most of them starring vaudevillians) followed. In 1927, the first sound feature, *The Jazz Singer*, starring Al Jolson (preceded by a short featuring Baby Rose Marie), was released. That was all she wrote. Now all the big singers and comedians started making Vitaphone shorts. (Ironic, as Warner Bros. was the only one of the "Big Five" Hollywood studios that wasn't hatched by vaudeville entrepeneurs.)

Albee responded as he always had. "Vitaphone Declared on Opposition List," *Billboard* reported that year. "Contracts Prohibit Appearing in Talkies." His injunction had the usual effectiveness. There was no way of competing with movies.

Yet Edward F. Albee, perversely, couldn't see it. "I am vaudeville," he had once boasted. Perhaps, but now vaudeville was dying. You do the syllogism. Albee had won the vaudeville wars, but it was a hollow victory. He was king of a mountain that was dissolving beneath him. A younger man (a Loew, a Lasky, a Zukor, a Fox) would simply have gone on to become the king of movies, but Albee had spent fifty years putting all his eggs in the vaudeville basket, and he wasn't about to start life anew at age seventy. Eventually Father Time eats even the strongest of his children. I bet Albee tasted terrible.

While it would not be 100 percent accurate to say that film killed vaudeville, it would be fair to say that it killed Albee. The death blow was delivered by Albee's right-hand man, J. J. Murdock. Albee had given Murdock a present of Keith-Albee-Orpheum stock as a reward for his part in the acquisition of the Kohl and Castle properties. In 1928, Murdock turned around and sold that stock to one Joseph P. Kennedy. For sheer ruthlessness in business, Albee had nothing on the father of the thirty-fifth president of the United States. Murdock's stock was the last piece Kennedy needed to gain a controlling interest in the Keith chain. Albee had finally, and fatally, been outmaneuvered. Without his consent, Keith-Orpheum would now go the way of Loew's, Lasky's, Goldwyn's, and Fox's various enterprises and specialize in movie creation, distribution, and exhibition. The company was merged with RCA (parent company of NBC radio) and an entity called the Film Booking Office, forming Radio-Keith-Orpheum (RKO). Those hundreds of Keith houses across the country became RKO houses.

As RKO, the former Keith chain continued to grow past all precedent. Immediately after it was founded in 1928, the company gobbled up both the Pantages and Proctor circuits, making its monopoly on vaudeville (or what was left of it) literal. RCA purchased the Victor Talking Machine Company that same year. In 1929, RKO started turning out its first pictures. The Clear Channel of its day, the conglomerate was now in the enviable position of producing and selling records, radio, and motion pictures, and possessing a theater chain in which to present and promote all of its electronic stars. On the RKO stage you could see Arthur Tracy, Baby Rose Marie, Rudy Vallee, and countless others, many of whom just happened to be NBC radio stars or Victor recording artists.

One bad thing about monopoly, ironically, is that it is vulnerable. If anything happens to that corporation—that one corporation—it happens to the entire industry. If one man is the protector of an industry, and something happens to that man, it happens to everyone in the industry. Edward Albee was that man. It can be asserted with justice that, more than any other figure, he invented big-time vaudeville. In its waning days, he fought to protect it from radio and film. In the view of many he was a son of a bitch, yet he was *vaudeville's* son of a bitch. With him in the driver's seat, vaudevillians still had jobs. But he was about to be unseated.

The dropping of Albee's name from "Keith-Albee-Orpheum" in the switch to "Radio-Keith-Orpheum" should have been the tipoff. It is reported that when Albee tried to make a suggestion to Kennedy soon after the takeover, Kennedy told him: "Don't you know, Ed? You're washed up. You're through." Who knew there were human beings who actually talked like that? One could scarcely believe such behavior was possible but for the fact that these accounts have been corroborated again and again. At least Kennedy talked to Albee in a language he could understand.

Fatally flummoxed, Albee retired to Florida to die. He managed to do so before the Palace played its last two-a-day, before the RKO triumphs of *King Kong*, *Top Hat*, and *Citizen Kane*, little suspecting the previously untapped potential of the corporate leviathan he had grown from a single storefront freak show.

By 1929, the biggest vaudeville stars, such as the Marx Brothers, Joe E. Brown, and Eddie Cantor, were making sound features. Soon they were joined on the silver screen by Bill Robinson, Will Rogers, the Three Stooges, Wheeler and Woolsey, Mae West, the Ritz Brothers, Bob Hope, and many others. Joe Frisco said it seemed like half the Friar's Club had gone west. Even the Hilton sisters had their shot, appearing in Tod Browning's bizarre thriller *Freaks* (1932). "I made so many talkies, I got film on my teeth," quipped Willie Howard. W. C. Fields launched his third career in talkies, making his first thirty years in show business a curious footnote to most film fans. As the thirties wore on, minor vaudevillians, such as James Cagney, Cary Grant, Walter Pigeon, Walter Huston, and Henry Fonda began to make their mark.

By 1932, the Palace was the only straight two-a-day big-time house left in New York. RKO was by now a chain of movie theaters. That last Palace two-a-day is considered by some to be the symbolic end point of vaudeville. For my part, I prefer not to give a definitive date for when the industry went belly up. Properly speaking, there is none. It's like any organism—different parts fail at different times. First your eyes go, then you've got arthritis, then you need a hip replacement. Vaudeville definitely had been waning in such a fashion. Over a twenty-five-year period (roughly 1905 to 1930) you had a situation of films and other competition gradually displacing live vaudeville. On May 7, 1932, the Palace switched to a four-a-day format, interspersed with short films, bumping the former pinnacle of vaudeville down to something along the lines of small time. In July, they added their first feature film (Eddie Cantor's *The Kid from Spain*), and from then on continued experimenting with various combinations of live performance and film until 1935, when they dropped the vaudeville format altogether (although it would be re-vived sporadically as late as the 1950s).

The obvious irony is that it is only through films that later genera-tions became vaudeville buffs. Films did vaudeville a service even as they were killing it: by preserving it. In addition to the original flood of Vitaphone shorts in the late twenties and early thirties, Warner Bros. did a series called Vitaphone Vaudeville from 1934 to 1936 that captured small bills of four or five acts for distribution to cinemas. Between these two series, the studio (probably without meaning to) made it possible for us to sit down today and look at a record of many of the major (and some of the minor) acts of late vaudeville.

Throughout the thirties and forties, Hollywood put out countless "revue" films—skimpy plots punctuated with vaudeville turns created expressly for the cinema. These included the *Gold Diggers* series, the *Fox Movietone Follies*, the *Broadway Melody* series, *The Big Broadcast* se-ries, the *Hollywood Revue* of 1929, *College Swing*, *International House*, *Stage Door Canteen*, and dozens of others.

DEPRESSION

It is surely no coincidence that vaudeville collapsed in the wake of the stock market crash, falling into the depths of the Great Depression. "Wall Street Lays an Egg" read *Variety*'s famous headline. Boom and bust times are more influential in our social and cultural lives than we some-times acknowledge. For example, it's interesting to note that Messrs. Pastor, Keith, and Proctor had started their enterprises in the early 1880s, just as the nation was starting to pull out of the depression of 1873. The depression of 1892 is sometimes credited with finishing off some of vaudeville's weaker competitors, the minstrel show, the dime museums, and the last of the concert saloons, while also hurting legit theater (with its high ticket price) by driving audiences to the cheaper 10-20-30. Then, in the prosperity that followed that depression, we see the introduction of the phonograph and cinema. Radio takes off in the prosperity that followed the depression of 1914.

Vaudeville was able to weather the storms of 1892 and 1914, but the one in 1929 was particularly devastating because those hit by it could now turn to cheaper (or even free) alternatives to lighten their spirits. Also the Great Depression was the most severe of the three, and lasted much longer. Salaries of vaudeville headliners had by this time become prohibitively high, driven up by competing entertainment media. Yet ticket demand didn't warrant the high payout. Plenty of rank-and-file vaudevillians would have been glad to work cheap in their place, but there wasn't enough demand to warrant hiring them, either.

It's hard to imagine what a Depression-era vaudeville would have been like. Vaudeville's signature had been optimism, a spirit of "universal progress." Like Harold Lloyd's silent-movie characters—those Horatio Alger–esque go-getters of the 1920s who aspired to make good by working ever-so-much-harder than the next fellow—vaudeville (which radiated the same energy) did not speak to the spirit of the Depression.

NOT DEAD YET

Perhaps the vaudeville researcher can be forgiven for being a little confused as he enters the dark and crowded alley where vaudeville finally met its end. On the one hand, nearly every commentator, historian, journalist, critic, and even many performers give the date of vaudeville's demise as that last Palace two-a-day in 1932. On the other hand, many artists and fans too young to have participated in vaudeville during that period claim to have done so. Biographies of Lucille Ball, Danny Kaye, Jackie Gleason, Joey Adams, and others often say that they began their careers in vaudeville, even though they started out in the late thirties, forties, and even fifties. This is due to the fact that, while big-time and small-time circuits were gone by 1932, live variety, romantically still dubbed vaudeville, persisted for decades, especially in New York.

Some disputants claim that the last true vaudeville show was at Loew's State in 1947, but then there is the complicating fact that the Palace went back to a live vaudeville policy (with Hollywood films interspersed) from 1949 to 1957. The film-and-vaudeville offerings at Loew's and the Palace were not so different from what was offered at the presentation houses. Singer Molly Peirce, who performed at the Palace in the 1950s, recalls sharing the bill with the Nicholas Brothers, Louie

Armstrong, Cozy Cole, a French dog act called The Botes, and a trampoline act. A typical five-act bill would do five shows a day, alternating with the feature film, which might be anything from *The Ten Commandments* to *Rebel Without a Cause*.

Farther afield, there were still vaudeville engagements to be had abroad. If you didn't mind traveling very far for an engagement, for example, a vaudevillian could still get a job in Australia, on the Tivoli Circuit. Probably because of its location at the farthest corner of the planet, vaudeville didn't die there until the 1950s. Comedian Will Mahoney managed to buy himself another couple of decades in this fashion. Likewise, English music hall lasted a bit longer. Major stars like Sophie Tucker and Arthur Tracy extended their careers by performing under the Union Jack.

Burlesque was bumping and grinding on Broadway stages until the late thirties, when reformers finally closed the curtain. As vaudeville receded, Gypsy Rose Lee, for example, found her niche in the world of burlesque. Abbot and Costello, often thought of by the public as vaudevillians, were actually strictly burlesque men who came to prominence in that industry's final years. Others included Phil Silvers (who immortalized the genre in his musical *Top Banana*), Stubby Kaye, and Joey Fay. Some, like Lou Jacobs, Buster Keaton, and trick cyclist Joe Jackson, found work in the circus.

Broadway revues like the *Ziegfeld Follies* kept a semi-vaudeville format going through the late 1930s. After 1939, the war in Europe brought out a serious new spirit on Broadway, and tastes shifted during the next decade to more "adult" musicals featuring dramatic plots, with integrated songs, and complexly orchestrated scores. Revues became associated with simpler, more carefree times, and so became passé. A sign of the changing mood was the revue called *Priorities of 1942*—one imagines tap dancers and crooners interspersed with exhortations to ration gasoline.

Changing times didn't prevent several high-profile efforts to "revive" vaudeville. Even as the last two-a-day closed at the Palace, Lou Holtz put his savings into the *Lou Holtz 1932 Vaudeville Revue*. He lost his shirt. In 1936, songwriter and former kiddie-act producer Gus Edwards produced *Gus Edwards' Broadway Sho-Window-Revusical-Vaudeville*.

Same fate. In the 1938–39 season, the Shuberts presented a show called *Vaudeville Marches On*, featuring Molly Picon and Fats Waller. Ed Wynn's last Broadway vehicle was a wartime effort to revive vaudeville, 1942's *Laugh, Town, Laugh*. The show didn't do well, but some of his contemporaries had better luck. In the thirties and forties, columnists Ed Sullivan and Walter Winchell independently presented vaudeville shows at major venues like Loew's State and the Paramount Theatre. Sullivan, as we shall soon see, took his act to television. Winchell, on the other hand, was instrumental in making a hit of a show that had been panned by every other New York critic, *Hellzapoppin*. This nonsensical revue by the team of Olsen and Johnson represented the culmination of their twenty-five years in vaudeville as comedians and musicians. It opened in 1938, was a smash with audiences, stayed on the boards for years, and was made into a 1941 movie, costarring Shemp Howard and Martha Raye. Other Broadway shows followed: *Laffing Room Only* (1945), *Funzapoppin* (1949), and *Pardon My French* (1950)—all basically extensions of *Hellzapoppin*. You might say the various versions of *Hellzapoppin* were on stage continuously for over ten years. In 1942, an out-of-work Ken Murray launched *Ken Murray's Blackouts* in Los Angeles, where it played for seven years. A 1949 attempt to bring the show to New York, however, went over like a lead balloon.

In the late thirties, the Federal Theatre Project, a division of the Works Progress Administration, had a vaudeville unit. But the dates were largely makework, the units mostly booked to entertain the employees of other government agencies, such as the Civilian Conservation Corps. A far more successful federal vaudeville was the United Service Organization (USO). During the Second World War, former vaudevillians swelled the USO ranks at bases all over the world, not only stars like Al Jolson, Bob Hope, Irving Berlin, and Martha Raye, but also scores of lesser-known singers, dancers, comedians, magicians, and acrobats. The World War II–era USO was called the world's largest entertainment circuit up to that time, with five hundred separate shows running simultaneously.

On the home front, resort hotels continued to book live talent. In the Catskill Mountains, a constellation of large hotels and campgrounds catered to the vacationing needs of New York's growing Jewish population. In the salad days of the so-called Borscht Belt, there were five hundred hotels up in the region, most notably: Brown's, the Concord, and Grossinger's. In addition to such top headliners from the Palace as Milton Berle and Phil Silvers, a few years later you might have seen Henny Youngman, Jerry Lewis, Alan King, Danny Kaye, Joey Bishop, Red Buttons, or Jackie Gleason on a Borscht Belt stage. All are performers but a single remove from vaudeville.

As performer-scholar Monroe Lippman once observed, "Old entertainers never die, they just move to Las Vegas or Miami or Hollywood." Outside the Catskills, Miami, Atlantic City, and Las Vegas all became havens for displaced vaudevillians. And an ossified form of vaudeville lives on in these sunset metropolises.

In Manhattan, the nightclub scene flourished through the 1950s. It was survived by countless tiny "cabarets," rooms where music and stand-up were presented on elevator-sized stages, a type of venue that persists to this day. In the smoky little bars of New York during the Korean War era, you might catch an act like the young Tony Bennett, comedienne Judy Holliday, or singer-pianist Bobby Short.

Stage and television performer "Uncle Floyd" Vivino contends that amusement parks, at least in the summer, remained a viable venue for ex-vaudevillians until the bitter end. (In this context, recall that Chuck Barris, creator of *The Gong Show*, also penned the tune "Palisades Park.") At Gaslight Village, near Lake George, Floyd emceed a regular vaudeville show at a seven-hundred-seat theater called the Opera House in the late sixties and early seventies. The show featured continuous vaudeville from two to eleven p.m. daily. As late as the Nixon years, the Opera House was booking genuine vaudeville talent. Among the artists Floyd got to know well were trick cyclist Joe Jackson, Jr. (son and successor to vaudeville's Joe Jackson); the husband-and-wife song-and-dance act Morris and Reeve; the Royal Lilliputians (a midget act); a husband-wife escape-artist team called the Manzinis; and a banjo player named Warren Bowdoin (the son of the act Bowdoin and Bowdoin).

Yet, as attractive and opportunity-filled as all this may sound, it still didn't add up to the live entertainment factory that was vaudeville. As workers in all industries know, advances in technological efficiency usually mean a concomitant elimination of jobs. This was no less true when hundreds of vaudeville theaters (at least one in almost every town) switched to pictures. The end of live vaudeville amounted to a massive "downsizing," in which an estimated ten thousand workers were given the hook.

Oddly, when people discuss the fate of the old vaudevillians, you'll often hear a tone of generalized blame: "Oh, those poor vaudevillians! They should have done something for those people." Don't cry for them, Argentina. By entering show business they were taking a voluntary risk. They expressly chose not to become haberdashers and save 5 percent of their weekly paycheck. In fact *everybody* warned them *not* to go into show business in the first place; their parents, their teachers, their priests, ministers, or rabbis, certainly the managers, and maybe even the audiences. They gambled—and lost. So weep for them as you would for Don Quixote, or Ed Wood, or as you'd weep for your own dumb mistakes. But do not decry the injustice done them, for there was none. Times changed, and a few thousand people found themselves unwilling or unable to change with them.

Should there have been perpetual employment for "The Vagges— World Champion Bag Punchers"? *They made a living punching bags!* Thousands had acts as strange or specialized. Others may have been more conventional but were simply lame. What are we to make of "Harry L. Webb—The Man Who Talks and Sings in Vaudeville"? Rotten name—there were at least ten thousand men who answered the very same description. Raymond Wilbert was "The Unusual Fellow—Unusual Personality, Unusual Act, Unusual Material, Unusual Novelty." Mr. Wilbert has gone to great lengths to convince us he is unusual, but we get no sense that means unusually funny or talented.

As we have seen, within society at large, among their families, and in the world of straight jobs, vaudevillians were often considered misfits. Many were lucky enough to carve a niche for themselves on the stage, where they could belong and excel. Sadly, however, many others weren't so fortunate and remained, in society's cruel accounting, losers. When vaudeville died, America never felt their absence. The audience cared about the stars, and the stars went right on working in the new and higher-profile entertainment industries that superseded vaudeville. Show business, like any other, is at bottom guided by consumer choice, and live vaudeville eventually failed to make the cut. Yet this proved to be far from vaud's last gasp, and it wasn't long before it rose again, phoenix-like, from the ashes.

Only one year after the last show at Loew's State in 1947, *Variety* ran an ad proclaiming, "Vaudeville Is Back! The Golden Era of Variety begins with the Premiere of *Texaco Star Theatre* on Television." Milton Berle's hit program was joined that year by Ed Sullivan's *Toast of the Town*; the next year by *The Admiral Broadway Revue*, starring Sid Caesar; and *Cavalcade of Stars*, featuring first Jack Carter, and later Jackie Gleason. Nineteen fifty saw the debut of *The Ken Murray Show*, *The Colgate Comedy Hour* (with guest hosts such as Eddie Cantor, Bob Hope, and Jimmy Durante), and *The Four Star Revue* (with Durante, Ed Wynn, Danny Thomas, and Jack Carson alternating as hosts). *The Red Skelton Show* was launched in 1951, and the critically acclaimed *Red Buttons Show* in 1952. The *Tonight* show, starring Steve Allen, the son of two vaudevillians, began in 1954. In 1964 a variety show called *The Hollywood Palace*, specifically modeled on the old vaud format of its Times Square namesake, debuted on ABC, and held its own in the ratings until it went off in 1970.

Vaudeville dead? Performances on the old *Ed Sullivan Show* preserved at the Museum of Television and Radio in New York included comedy duo Wayne and Schuster; ukulele freak Tiny Tim; a star-studded Irving Berlin tribute; Maurice Chevalier; Sophie Tucker; Carl Sandburg reading poems; a Russian dance troupe; stars of the Metropolitan Opera (featuring Joan Sutherland); Bert Lahr; Smith and Dale; ballet dancers; plate spinners; fire eaters; teeterboard tumblers; trick cyclists; trampoline artists; trained elephants, tigers, and dogs; a piano recital by Van Kliburn; Judy Garland singing Chaplin's song "Smile." If vaudeville died during this period then the networks never got the funeral notice. The *Ed Sullivan Show*, for one, didn't go gentle into that good night until 1972.

Clearly, the form had survived intact; all that had changed was the platform from which it was delivered to the audience. Not only did vaudeville dominate television, but so did vaudevillians. Jack Benny, Burns and Allen, Abbot and Costello, and Phil Silvers all had their own sitcoms. Bob Hope and Jack Benny did countless TV "specials" with a variety format. Groucho Marx and Fred Allen had their own quiz shows (*You Bet Your Life* and *What's My Line?* respectively). Practically every former vaudevillian mentioned in this book who was alive and not retired in the television era did guest shots on variety shows, dramas, and situation comedies. A second, even greater, burst of fame for Laurel and Hardy and the Three Stooges occurred when their film shorts began to be shown regularly on television in the 1950s. The evergreen success of the Stooges is a testament, above all, to the power of television. By comparison, their old partner Ted Healy was no slouch. In his salad days, he was as well-known as anyone in vaudeville. He was there along with Ken Murray to give encouragement to the neophyte Bob Hope when he made his Palace debut. He was also a familiar face in films. Billy Rose considered him his favorite comedian. Yet today he is a footnote, while his stooges live on in cultural memory. Why the disparity? Healy was never on TV.

As late as the mid-1960s, ex-vaudevillians were still holding jobs in television's top situation comedies. Three of the stars of *My Three Sons* were in vaudeville. William Demarest ("Uncle Charlie") was a comedian, dancer, and musician, and long had a popular act with his wife, Estelle Collette. Fred MacMurray ("Steve Douglas") started out as a saxophonist in a group called the California Collegiates. And William Frawley, who played Uncle Charlie's predecessor Uncle Bub from 1960 to 1964, was in comedy teams on the West Coast with his brother Paul and his wife, Edna. Frawley is perhaps better known for his role as Fred Mertz in *I Love Lucy* (1951–57). Buddy and Sally from *The Dick Van Dyke Show,* Rose Marie and Morey Amsterdam, were both former vaudevillians, as were *The Munsters'* Al Lewis (Grandpa), *The Addams Family's* Jackie Coogan (Uncle Fester), and *The Beverly Hillbillies'* Buddy Ebsen (Jed Clampett). *Hogan's Heroes* employed French music-hall star Robert Clary (who was also Eddie Cantor's son-in-law) in the role of LeBeau. Emmet, a recurring character on *The Andy Griffith Show,* was played by Paul Hartman, who with his wife, Grace, had formed vaudeville's most popular comedy dance team.

Ironically, for most of America the death of live vaudeville meant not less vaudeville but more. As far as America was concerned, vaudeville was the new hearth in the family homestead.

VAUDEVILLE DIES ITS "SECOND DEATH"

But if Vaudeville was not completely extinct at this juncture, at best it was being kept on life support. In 1946, New York City radio personality Joe Franklin launched his first radio show, called, semi-optimistically,

Vaudeville Is Not Dead. But methinks Franklin doth protest too much. If you have to tell us it's not dead, you have to admit you're at least worried. While people were still using that word "vaudeville," by the 1940s it no longer had the same glimmer of magic. Before the Great Depression, vaudeville had been identified with the very height of modernism. A performer took the Twentieth Century Limited from New York to Chicago, and marveled at the speed with which he made the journey (fifteen hours). In the age of broadcasting, a performer could play Chicago and New York and everywhere else simultaneously, and yet electrons would make the journey for him in a split second.

An ominous portent of things to come was impresario Billy Rose's Gay Nineties–themed nightclub, the Diamond Horseshoe, which opened in 1938. Chorus girls and waitstaff were dressed in turn-of-the-century attire, while aging, second-rate vaudevillians provided the floor show. In the years to come, vaudeville was to be increasingly the sort of entertainment presented at theme parks and tourist attractions (like Uncle Floyd's venue at Lake George) with the apologetic modifer "old-time" affixed to it. Yes, it was fun. But it was also the past, a museum piece.

Television, with its intrinsic overkill, helped to reinforce that fatal impression. As one of the premier staples of this new entertainment medium, TV variety also became one of the first casualties of what has become a familiar pattern in the 24/7/365 landscape of dawn-to-dusk electronic engorgement. The old proverb holds true: familiarity breeds contempt. Once something is deemed popular, there is the tendency in television to inundate the viewer with it to a degree unmatched in any other medium but radio. In essence, the viewer, bombarded with too much of a good thing, becomes nauseated and moves on to some new fad . . . until he becomes sick of that, too.

By 1970, "vaudeville" had become a code word for the ultimate in unhip. Tap, for example, which had been one of the deepest sources of pride for African-Americans during the first half of the twentieth century (when it was one of the areas where blacks enjoyed national prestige), had come to be seen as the ultimate reactionary gesture. Now that blacks were making inroads in most other fields as well, the once universally popular tap became associated with the Uncle Tomism of Bill Robinson's many screen characters. Its last major exponent (prior to a revival a decade later) was Sammy Davis, Jr., a multitalented performer who, despite strenuous efforts to remain au courant, seemed fatally out of step with the times.

Another skill of Davis's, "impressions" of other celebrities, also fell out of favor. Indeed, the facile mimicry of stars by Sammy and contemporaries like Steve Lawrence pretty much represented the death knell of "impressionism" as a separate show-business discipline. Just the memory of one of this breed, long about 1975, beginning his *Tonight* show set with "And now, Mr. James Cagney . . ." makes me reach for the channel changer right now, and I'm not even watching TV.

Yes, "vaudeville" had become synonymous with "corny." Reduced to its least praiseworthy elements, it became sanitized, formulaic. A particularly embarrassing *Brady Bunch* episode finds Carol and daughter Marcia putting on a "vaudeville act" in the school talent show, wearing cute little tramp outfits, with bright little patches, doing cross-talk lifted from Bazooka Joe comics and singing "Together, Wherever We Go" until even the laugh track is laughing through gritted teeth. It's one thing to be dead. It's another order of tragedy to have your corpse exhumed and defiled by Munchkins.

Variety is nothing if not flexible, however. One reason it lasted twenty-five years on television is that its format allowed it to incorporate elements that made it appear at least nominally current. Its greatest achievement in this regard in the late fifties and sixties was the long overdue mainstreaming of African-American talent into U.S. culture. As it had done for the Irish and Germans in the nineteenth century and for the Jews and Italians in the early twentieth, vaudeville (in this case TV variety) was a prime mover in introducing black entertainers into the forefront of American consciousness. As we have seen, whites had long appropriated black music and dance and incorporated it into their minstrel and variety shows. By the 1920s a number of black artists themselves had achieved national name recognition. But still, theirs was a kind of second-class success. A few were famous, a few had lots of money, but aside from Bert Williams in some early silents, none got starring roles in films (they rarely got any at all), and those given radio or TV vehicles could be counted on the fingers of one hand. Without a doubt, stars like Bill Robinson and Eddie "Rochester" Anderson were beloved ensemble players, but usually they were relegated to the third, fourth, or fifth spot in the billing, and always playing a decidedly subservient role. Brilliant, if nonthreatening singers and musicians like Louis Armstrong, Pearl Bailey, Count Basie, and Ethel Waters were prominent in the culture, but only as supporting players. Yet, with the continued momentum of the Great Migration in the 1940s and fifties, and the Civil Rights movement of the fifties and sixties, a distinct change becomes apparent. Newly empowered, blacks start to bring a more raucous and confident energy into the mix, on a par with, or perhaps greater than, that introduced by the Irish, Italians, and Jews decades and decades earlier. In essence, the long-closeted aesthetic values of TOBA and the other all-black vaudeville circuits were brought out into the sunlight, exploding on millions of television screens. The low-down classic blues of Mamie Smith, Bessie Smith (no relation), Ma Rainey, and Big Mama Thornton, so long restricted to the black circuits, was now being adapted and interpreted for America on TV variety shows by Little Richard, Chuck Berry, Sam Cooke, and many others. The subversive and risqué comedy of Moms Mabley, Dick Gregory, Redd Foxx, Richard Pryor, and Godfrey Cambridge was making it to the little screen overturning long-held prejudices. And centuries after those first calamitous encounters between black and white, the descendants of the Africans were teaching the descendants of the Europeans how to do the Watusi.

Rock-and-roll acts—largely young white kids heavily influenced by black blues music—became an exciting new feature of TV variety. Elvis Presley, the Beatles, and the Doors all debuted on the *Ed Sullivan Show*, right alongside the trained tigers, the acrobats, and Topo Gigio. Though Mr. Sullivan and the suits up in network headquarters didn't know it, Mr. Presley's debut was the first broadside in a battle that would rage for two decades. The battle, fought between two generations, would not be definitively won until the older generation passed on, allowing some of the young generation into the power structure. Before then, the friction made for some weird, and sometimes tense, TV.

At the time Elvis came along, mainstream show business had been dominated by the Keith-Albee philosophy for some seventy years. It was literally unthinkable to knowingly present an act deemed "unclean" or "impolite." When the success of rock acts on radio made television bookings unavoidable, variety producers seemed not so much censorious as completely bewildered about what even to say about them. The humiliations of Elvis Presley during his first personal television appearances are now legendary: being shot from the waist up on the *Ed Sullivan Show*; being made to sing "Hound Dog" to an actual bloodhound on the *Steve Allen Show*. Some elements within the older generation were overtly hostile toward this style of entertainment. As late as 1965, Dean Martin blatantly ridiculed an appearance by the Rolling Stones on his own television program as though they had been booked as sideshow freaks. As late as 1972, Mike Douglas felt obliged to roll his eyes on camera while interviewing John Lennon and Yoko Ono.

While dissident voices were making it to the big time, they still weren't running the show. If anything, the presence of Jimi Hendrix or Tina Turner alongside Andy Williams and Dinah Shore pointed up the creakiness of "straight, clean" vaudeville in an era otherwise characterized by the sexual revolution, psychotherapy, experimental drug use, and political activism. The aesthetic values being embraced by younger people—openness, freedom, honesty, egalitarianism—were in direct opposition to the prevailing culture of enforced and restricted norms of behavior that dominated television. Small wonder, then, that baby boomers hated such expressions of Establishment values as vaudeville, show business, and Las Vegas.

This clash of values was in progress just as the last generation of original vaudevillians was beginning to pass on. Many who'd been staples of TV variety began to die off in the late sixties and early seventies: Sophie Tucker (died 1966), Charlie Dale of Smith and Dale (1971), Jimmy Durante (felled by a stroke in 1972, he died in 1980), Blossom Seeley (1974), Jack Benny (1974), Edgar Bergen (1978). By the late seventies the form was on its last legs. Attempts to be "hip" ultimately backfired as increasingly unhip pop acts were given their own variety programs. The descent into squareness progressed with a dismayingly straight trajectory: from Sonny and Cher . . . to Tony Orlando and Dawn to . . . the Captain and Teneille to . . . the ignominious end of the line: Pink Lady and Jeff. Along the way, the tuxedoes got pinker and bluer, the lapels and ties got wider, the shirts grew frillier. But they were still tuxedoes. The whole trend stank of an unbecoming querulousness and a lack of imagination on the part of studio executives.

By 1975, baby boomers had seen their own countercultural values repressed and ridiculed by the television industry for two decades. Coasting along on a standard laid down in 1881, TV variety was taking an exceptionally long time to become genuinely current. Record companies, concert promoters, and FM radio supplied the kids' music; nightclubs and record albums showcased their comedy. But television continued to be dominated by big-band music and Borscht Belt comedians.

But inevitably, as Willie Howard used to put it in his famous bit, "comes the revolution." Temporary glimmers of possibility had shown themselves. *The Smothers Brothers Comedy Hour* (1967–69) had attempted politically subversive content; *Rowan and Martin's Laugh-In* (1968–73) was, among other things, an hour-long celebration of sex and (by virtue of its faux-psychedelic format) drugs. But the network had censored and eventually canceled the Smothers Brothers, and *Laugh-In* ultimately became a platform for squares yearning to be hip, like Sammy Davis, Jr., and Tom Jones. The Who and Bob Dylan were never on *Laugh-In*.

Nevertheless, one *Laugh-In* alumnus, writer Lorne Michaels, was to cook up a television variety program that would finally put a bullet in the old way of making show business. As creator and executive producer of *Saturday Night Live*, he developed a program for younger adults that set all sorts of new precedents, by (*a*) booking rock musical acts, as opposed to safe pop acts; (*b*) doing mostly risky, satirical comedy, as opposed to safe, corny comedy; and (*c*) dispensing with phony trappings like tuxedoes—jeans and a T-shirt were just fine for the guest host. The vaudeville format was abandoned; *Saturday Night Live* was to be a sketch-comedy revue, punctuated by the occasional monologue or rock number. Because it was scheduled for 11:30 p.m. on a Saturday night, these experiments were permitted.

The show was an instant and immediate success, making stars out of John Belushi, Chevy Chase, Dan Aykroyd, Gilda Radner, Jane Curtin, Bill Murray, and even some of the bit players like Andy Kaufman and Albert Brooks. An illustration of the turnaround in the power dynamic: when Milton Berle was booked as the guest host in 1977, it was *he* who was the fish out of water. Backstage, the cast could barely contain their contempt for him, and many, such as John Belushi and Bill Murray, openly ridiculed him during rehearsal.

By the 1980s, television variety in any recognizable sense was truly dead. Shows like *Monty Python's Flying Circus*, *Saturday Night Live*, and *SCTV*, while superficially related to variety shows, were satirical sketch-comedy revues—a rather different form. In time, the revolution in taste made itself felt throughout American popular culture. MTV followed *Saturday Night Live*'s lead by creating an entire rock-and-roll television network. These days, theme music for television programs, commercials, and so forth today are frequently rock- or rap-oriented. Everyone on television is pretty much free to wear whatever they like. The medium is far more reflective of the way people are in their daily lives, and that's a good thing.

Yet while the restrictions of politesse that governed vaudeville and "Golden Era" television had been a dogma, it's difficult to say unequivocally that all that has followed has been an improvement. In the present age, we find our televised spectacle descending to near Roman levels. Vomit, snot, and feces regularly intrude into our comedy now—often on the children's shows. The Farrelly Brothers have added semen to the litany of comic liquids. "Reality television" and Jerry Springer and his legion of imitators host cruel forums for contrived confrontations and mean-spirited head games played as popular entertainment—usually at the expense of the economic underclass. Flip the channels: it seems impossible to avoid an exploding fireball or some teenage pop star tricked out like a Tenth Avenue hooker humping a lamppost. The American audience now seems to have far more in common with the gang who frequented concert saloons or even a Roman amphitheater. The wheel has come full circle.

Ultimately it emerges that the governing principle of show business, that old vaudeville saw "Give the people what they want," is by no means synonymous with "clean." Modern television and film producers, the "new managers," operate according to the same principle as had vaudeville's originators. Just as Pastor, Keith, Proctor, and company had sought to reach out to the double audience, courting not just men but also women and children, by making their product pure, screen producers of the late twentieth century sought to reach out to baby boomers (the largest generation in American history) and subsequent generations by going for edginess and scandal. In 1881, propriety was what sold tickets;

in 2005, the opposite holds true. But show business management never changed its philosophy—the audience did.

Once, audiences saw in all performers evidence of the devil, and were terrified. Today, an influential faction of them delight in watching performers ape Satan and spew blood all over the stage at a rock concert. And just who is the devil, anyway? The horns and hooves should give us a clue. It's the beast in us, a beast both science and religion acknowledge, although from different perspectives. It is the corporeal part, the passionate part, the part that thirsts for amusements. The question has always been: To what degree do we let that beast rule us? Euripides captured the human dilemma best in *The Bacchae*. We seem to be a species that vacillates in its identity between Puritans who burn dancers at the stake . . . and dancers who tear Puritans limb from limb. It would be nice if we could find a happy medium.

8

THE PHOENIX
IN FOOLSCAP

In 1881, the same year that Tony Pastor opened his music hall, a painter name Rudolphe Salis started the first *cabaret artistique* in Paris, called the Chat Noir, after an Edgar Allan Poe story. *Cabaret* is French for "tavern," and Salis used the term to suggest that his entertainments took the form of a menu, or a bill of fare, offering songs, sketches, poetry readings, shadow plays, and the like. Before long, the cabaret movement had spread to all the major European cities. In 1901, several influential cabarets opened in Berlin, thus inaugurating the cultural scene familiar to readers of Christopher Isherwood's *Berlin Stories* (and its stage adaptations, *I Am a Camera* and *Cabaret*). Opening that same year in Munich was the Elf Scharfrichter (the "Eleven Executioners"), where Frank Wedekind (author of the *Lulu* plays) sang songs to his guitar, and where one-act plays, songs, dances, puppet dramas, and music performers were presented. In 1916, Hans Arp and Tristan Tzara founded the Cabaret Voltaire in Zurich, where Dada (the cultural movement that was the precursor to Surrealism) was born. At their events, someone might scream poems from inside a large sack, insult the audience, growl like a bear, draw a mustache on a copy of the *Mona Lisa*, or perform other senseless, random acts of violence. In 1935 the Nazis banned cabaret in Germany, and later in all their conquered territories. They preferred to perform all the senseless acts of violence themselves.

Interestingly, the original cabaret movement never caught hold in the

English-speaking world, presumably because the prevailing Puritanism frowned heavily on anything so overtly antiestablishment. Nowhere is there an Anglo or American equivalent to Colette, both a performer in French *café-concert* and a highbrow novelist. The closest vaudeville came was in modern dance's Ruth St. Denis, who managed to find an audience for her art in popular and discriminating venues alike. Not that there was nothing artistic about American variety and British music hall—quite the contrary. But the English and Americans were never self-conscious about it. Vaudeville never declared itself to be "art," and it was never bohemian. While it produced many fine writers, such as George M. Cohan, Fred Allen, Groucho Marx, Mae West, W. C. Fields, and even Gypsy Rose Lee, none had any ambition beyond creating an intelligent popular art. Far from allying itself with an elitist or outsider stance, vaudeville was the very channel thousands sought for mainstream fame and acceptance.

Nevertheless, vaudeville and its relatives in the variety family came to be highly influential for Europe's avant-garde. In 1913 the Italian Futurist F. T. Marinetti wrote a manifesto titled "In Praise of the Variety Theater" in which he extolled the form: "The authors, the actors, and the machinists of the Theater of Variety have one sole motive to exist and to triumph—that of incessantly inventing new elements of wonder. Hence the absolute impossibility of stagnation or repetition . . ."

In Russia, Lenin borrowed the idea of party-sponsored political pageantry from the example of Robespierre, who had adapted France's own medieval carnival traditions, employing puppetry, makeup, costumes, songs, and street drama to serve the cause. In the era of Soviet ferment that preceded Stalin's purges of the 1930s, theater director Vsevolod Meyerhold infused his productions with all the variety forms that had fed and enriched vaudeville, as a means of forging a true "people's theater," one that would stand in rebuke to the bourgeois straw man of "high art." These forms included the medieval carnival, the commedia dell'arte, the Elizabethan theater—all those forms in which variety arts (in particular the physical art of the clown) played a key role.

Sergei Eisenstein, who was a theater artist before going into films, wrote in a 1923 article about creating a "montage of attractions," modeled on the modus operandi of the music hall and the circus and making use of the "chatter of Ostuzhev no more than the pink tights of the primadonna, a roll on the kettledrums as much as Romeo's soliloquy, the cricket on the hearth no less than the cannon fired over the heads of the audience." In Weimar-era Berlin, playwright Bertolt Brecht would follow Eisenstein down this path with his "alienation effect," an aesthetic of clashing moments, designed to jar the spectator out of his stupor and summon him to a critical awareness of the moment at hand. His "Epic Theater" broke his plays into disjointed fragments with disorienting leaps between scenes. Title cards and slide projections aided the proceedings. Brecht performed his own poems in clubs to a banjo or harmonium accompaniment, considered the Munich beer-hall comedian Karl Valentine an important influence, and said time and time again that he considered the most important ingredient in theater to be *spass* (fun, or joking).

Socialists like Meyerhold, Eisenstein, and Brecht were fascinated by vaudeville's relation to the Hegelian dialectic, a theory of history and philology taken up by Karl Marx that asserted that history constantly pendulates between oppositional periods, each new phase being a sort of break with what came before. Variety, for them, was a way of representing that principle theatrically to educate the masses about revolution.

The Surrealists, on the other hand, prized vaudeville more for the clown's aesthetic of dreamlike grotesquerie. In 1920, the poet Ivan Goll published a volume of poetry inspired by Charlie Chaplin called *Chaplinade*. In 1926, Spanish poet and playwright Federico García Lorca wrote *El Paseo de Buster Keaton* ("Buster Keaton's Walk"). Salvador Dalí wrote a screenplay for the Marx Brothers titled *Giraffe on Horseback Salad* and did the 1935 painting *Face of Mae West*.

In the postwar period, the playwrights known collectively as the Absurdists revealed that they, too, were inspired by vaudeville. Samuel Beckett's affection was explicit in his best known play, *Waiting for Godot* (1953), wherein the two main characters, Didi and Gogo, accoutred as tramp comedians in bowler hats, moldy suits, and hole-ridden shoes, engage in comic crosstalk and take pratfalls. The name Godot itself appears to reference "Charlot," the French diminutive nickname for Chaplin. The American debut (1955) of the play even starred the great vaudeville and burlesque comedian Bert Lahr. In 1965, when it came time to cast the lead (and only) actor for his avant-garde movie *Film*, Beckett selected Buster Keaton.

Another Absurdist playwright inspired by vaudevillians was Eugene Ionesco, who frequently acknowledged a debt to the Marx Brothers with their aesthetic of senseless anarchy. His enthusiasm for the team is most obvious in *The Chairs*, a one-act play that combines elements of scenes from *Animal Crackers* and *A Night at the Opera*. Antonin Artaud, the influential French theater theorist of the same period, cited the Marx Brothers film *The Cocoanuts* in his major work *The Theater and Its Double*. Jean Genet's 1957 play *The Blacks: A Clown Show* referenced minstrelsy.

The American theatrical avant-garde picked up these various threads and wove them like so many strands of hemp into its own unique homegrown cord. In America in the 1960s, San Francisco and New York's Off-Off-Broadway became thriving loci for experimental theaters that helped popularize the European avant-garde's interest in traditional variety arts in the United States. Particularly influential was the San Francisco Mime Troupe (formed in 1959), which made commedia dell'arte training an underpinning of their performance and presented controversial minstrel and vaudeville shows in the mid-sixties. In 1965, the company "radicalized" and joined San Francisco's burgeoning protest movement against the Vietnam War and for civil rights, bringing their artistry to the streets in the form of clownish pranks with a political message.

Similarly, the Bread and Puppet Theater (formed in New York City in 1962), followed the medievalist course as brought into the modern age by Lenin, presenting outdoor pageants featuring large puppets, stilt-walking, and similar techniques to protest nuclear proliferation and the war in Vietnam. Largely through their influence, a carnivalesque atmosphere would be a factor in many American political protests throughout the 1960s and early seventies.

The protest movement famously had begun on college campuses (Berkeley, in particular) in the late 1950s. When the baby-boom generation came of age, there was an explosion of college enrollment. The hugest generation in American history was now in college, and the nation's media seemed to focus exclusively on the surprising things they said and did. Meanwhile, their faculty were largely of the generation that had come of age during the 1930s, an era when, in reaction to the Great Depression, the nation's intelligentsia had experienced its greatest leftward shift.

Socialism was in vogue, as was a cultural tributary that has been very closely allied with it over the centuries, the folk movement. Trade unionism had its origins in the Middle Ages, at the very same time strolling troubadours were making up love songs, and jugglers and fire-eaters were busking for coin in the medieval marketplace. The commedia dell'arte itself originally had to do with unionism, the name referring to the fact that comedy was performed by those who were recognized as professional artists by the authorities. In early America, the two ideas had gotten neatly separated.

"Two great principles divide the world and contend for mastery," said Lord Acton, "antiquity and the Middle Ages. These are the two civilizations that have preceded us, the two elements of which ours is composed. All political as well as religious questions reduce themselves practically to this. This is the great dualism that runs through our society."

America was founded at a time of turning away from the values of the Middle Ages. The Roman Republic and the Athenian democracy were its models. In America, "We the People" were cherished, but more along the lines of a *demos* (a reasoned, enlightened, voting populace of landowners) than as a *folk* (a boisterous mob of messy humanity). This is not to say that at such times of upheaval as the American Revolution, or various domestic riots in our national history, that "the people" didn't more resemble the latter than the former. But those were momentary outbursts. Above all, America's brand of theatrical populism was a highly nationalist version, firmly married to the concept of democracy as economic opportunity for all. This way of looking at things lasted a long time, from the Jeffersonian "pursuit of happiness" that helped rationalize America's theater into being . . . to the Jacksonian-era populism of P. T. Barnum . . . to the "popular" prices and "people's palaces" of vaudeville . . . to the great fortunes made by vaudeville's formerly working-class managers and performers.

But faith in a "bootstraps" populism rapidly eroded in the wake of the Great Depression. For the next few decades in America, appeals to "the people" now meant a call from the left. One aspect of this movement was a renewed interest in folk culture. The ennobling of the common man was paramount. Homely, down-to-earth former vaudevillian Will Rogers was lionized for saying that he never met a man he didn't like. His fellow Oklahoman Woody Guthrie, with pals like Sonny Frisco, Pete Seeger, Burl Ives, and others, brought about a renaissance in American folk music. Poet Carl Sandburg compiled the country's best-loved folk songs in his *American Songbag*. Starting in the 1930s, folklorist Alan Lomax, working for the Library of Congress, began traveling the world with a tape recorder, capturing the people's songs and stories wherever he found them.*

In the late 1950s, this movement was revived, becoming inextricably linked with the campus protest movement throughout the 1960s as Bob Dylan, Phil Ochs, Joan Baez, and scores of others married the bard tradition to new topical message songs inspired by the daily headlines. Others, however, were content to interpret the often anonymous folk music and art of the past. On college campuses, thousands picked up traditional instruments and learned how to play. In 1963, the first Renaissance festival was established in southern California. The movement rapidly spread across the country, creating a new market for minstrels, jesters, and jongleurs—as juggling, clowning, and fire-eating became skills cultivated by a new generation of iconoclasts, one even more outré than their forebears.

In academia, interest in folk traditions extended itself to the first popular culture studies departments being established, such as the one at Bowling Green State University in 1973. This, combined with the establishment of film departments at major universities, resulted in the first scholarly books about vaudeville and related arts, such as Bowling Green professor John DiMeglio's 1973 book *Vaudeville U.S.A.*

College campuses and cinema art houses started showing old Hollywood movies, and as a result, the younger generation became exposed to the work of a number of key vaudevillians. Three "subversive" vaudeville comedians in particular enjoyed major revivals in the late 1960s and early seventies: the Marx Brothers, W. C. Fields, and Mae West. As the civil rights and antiwar movements were gathering steam, the anarchistic films of the Marx Brothers, (especially *Horsefeathers* and *Duck Soup*) gained new appeal, and were screened frequently. Groucho, who died in 1977 (at the age of eighty-six), enjoyed the second major revival of his

---

*While best known for capturing the sounds of American Folk and blues artists, Lomax also recorded extensively in the Bahamas and West Indies, the British Isles, and Spain.

long career. Wearing a groovy black beret and a turtleneck, he was in demand as a speaker at college campuses, worked the talk-show circuit, and filled concert halls with new comedy shows. In 1968, he acted in the LSD-inspired movie *Skidoo*, directed by Otto Preminger. In 1972, he caused a great commotion by remarking publicly that Richard Nixon ought to be assassinated.

W. C. Fields had been dead for over twenty years by the late sixties, but he, too, was held up as an antiestablishment icon, largely on account of his uncompromising individualism, his surrealistic sense of humor (especially in his later movies), and the drastic hedonism evinced by his worshipful relationship with alcohol.

Mae West, like Groucho, lived to enjoy the fruits of her revival. Gays had rediscovered her as early as the 1950s and prized her for her camp sensibility. As a result of the sexual revolution, the rest of the country finally caught up with the libidinous philosophy she had been living and espousing thirty years earlier. Not only were her films revived, but she made new ones, such as *Myra Breckinridge* (1970) and *Sextette* (1978). She even cut several rock records, such as *Way Out West* (1966), *Wild Christmas* (1966), and *Great Balls of Fire* (1968).

In addition, a flood of coffee-table picture books about the movies and careers of these three "classic" comedians, as well as others, like Charlie Chaplin and Laurel and Hardy, hit the bookstores in the early seventies, fueling still more interest in vaudeville. This is how your author, and many others, no doubt, first discovered that world in the lamentable days before home video.

Contemporaneous with the interest in old movies was an interest on the part of pop musicians in old records. The generation of rock-and-rollers who came up in the sixties (many of whom were art-school dropouts) had developed eclectic listening tastes in their never-ending quest for "new sounds." While they had begun their careers aping the latest records of Elvis Presley and Chuck Berry, many began to branch off in new directions. Some began to explore the folk revival that was also taking place, while others delved into old blues records, and their diverse journeys eventually led many of them to the realm of vaudeville-era pop.

This would include not only the voe-di-oh-doe croonings of the early big-band era, but a weird genre of music that has its origins in the 1940s and fifties. In 1942, Walt Disney hired a musician named Spike Jones to come up with a special song to accompany an anti-Nazi Donald Duck cartoon. The novelty number he came up with, "Der Fuehrer's Face," which combined elements of old-style Dutch comedy and a recurring Bronx cheer, became a surprise hit on the pop charts. This launched Jones on a career recording countless wacky "vaudevillian" albums, with sound effects and weird instruments like kazoos, slide whistles, and duck calls. His live stage show featured former vaudeville midget Billy Barty on drums.

In the fifties, slightly more serious groups reviving a 1920s shtick emerged in Britain, among them the Alberts and the Temperance Seven, who—to foreshadow—were produced by Beatles producer George Martin. In 1967, a U.K. outfit called the New Vaudeville Band had a monster hit in the United States with "Winchester Cathedral." Going back to a Spike Jones–type approach, but with a much more psychedelic flavor, was the Bonzo Dog Doo Dah Band, contemporaries of, and sometime collaborators with, members of Monty Python's Flying Circus (whose theme song, a march by John Philip Sousa, evokes the era perfectly). Such musical ferment began to put ideas in the heads of a generation of pop stars who were growing bored with the same old boy-and-girl songwriting formula and, perhaps not incidentally, had begun to experiment with drugs.

Paul McCartney, whose father had been a piano player in a ragtime band, is a good example of someone who would have been just as happy making music in 1917 as 1967. The fact that he played in a rock group was an accident of timing, not of temperament. (The Beatles' John Lennon was the true rock-and-roller of the band.) When McCartney was still a teenager he wrote "When I'm Sixty-four," which could easily have been penned twenty years before he was born. Over the years, he revisited the style (reminiscent of Paul Whiteman) many times: "Your Mother Should Know" (1967); "Honey Pie" (1968); "Maxwell's Silver Hammer" (1969); and "You Gave Me the Answer" (1974). It was at his urging that the album *Sgt. Pepper's Lonely Hearts Club Band* was structured like a vaudeville show, and that in their *Magical Mystery Tour* movie the band, dressed in white tie and tails, comes kick-stepping down a big Ziegfeld-style staircase. On the other hand, John Lennon was responsible for songs like "Being for the Benefit of Mr. Kite," the resurrection of World War I–era "granny glasses," and the *Sgt. Pepper* album-cover collage with pictures of Mae West, W. C. Fields, and other "cool" vaudevillians.

For a couple of years, this infatuation with vaudeville and music hall crept into mainstream pop. Ray Davies of the Kinks evoked old-time music hall on countless numbers: "God Bless Donald Duck, Vaudeville, and Variety," he sang in the title song of their 1967 album *Village Green Preservation Society*. The Rolling Stones sang antique-sounding songs like "On with the Show" and "Something Happened to Me Yesterday" and produced a TV show called *Rock and Roll Circus*, which alternated rock acts with fire-eaters, jugglers, performing midgets, and the like. Herman's Hermits had hits with the 1911 Harry Chapman music-hall song "I'm Henry VIII I Am" and the ukulele-driven "Mrs. Brown, You've Got a Lovely Daughter." The Monkees also had several such numbers, usually sung by the treacly-voiced Davy Jones, frequently sporting hat and cane ("Cuddly Toy," "Daddy's Song," "Magnolia Simms"). The Lovin' Spoonful had a hit with the vaudevillian "Daydream" and "Did You Ever Have to Make Up Your Mind?"—an old TV clip shows them lip-syncing the tune in straw boaters and striped jackets. The Beach Boys' aborted masterpiece *Smile* has old-timey vaud-inspired themes throughout, especially the main theme, "Heroes and Villains," which evokes saloons in the Old West. Country Joe and the Fish's "I Feel Like I'm Fixin' to Die Rag" qualifies as vaudeville. Then there was the ubiquitous anomaly Tiny Tim, with his enthusiasm for "Mr. Rudy Vallee," singing songs like "Tip-toe Through the Tulips" to his own ukulele accompaniment. Janis Joplin idolized Bessie Smith, dressed like her, sang like her, drank like her. The Mamas and the Papas had a hit in 1966 with the 1931 classic "Dream a Little Dream of Me," and the vaudevillian "Words of Love." Moreover, the plus-sized Mama Cass evoked the great large women of the vaudeville era, like Sophie Tucker and Trixie Friganza.

The era of psychedelic vaudevillianism proved to be just a fad, however, and by the late 1960s it had burned itself out, as its proponents moved on to new sounds and other fields of interest. Then, just as vaudeville was dying its second death in the form of television variety, some young artists began to hatch a most Quixotic dream—to become traditional variety entertainers in an era without vaudeville. The corporate descendants of the vaudeville circuits—the film studios, broadcast networks, and record companies—had long since hypertrophied into multinational conglomerates. It was becoming harder all the time for performers of any sort to participate in show business. In the new giant entertainment machine the artist was a much smaller cog than he had been in the vaudeville industry. Furthermore, the new system chewed up and spat out performers. Stars like David Steinberg, Three Dog Night, or Raymond J. Johnson, Jr. ("Eh, you can call me Ray . . ."), would be hot for a very short time and then jettisoned. It was this era that inspired Andy Warhol to say that in the future everyone would be famous for fifteen minutes. In the mid-to-late twentieth century you were lucky to be a star for fifteen months. By contrast, those who'd gotten in on the ground floor in vaudeville and did well could remain stars for sixty or seventy years.

Some of them stuck around perhaps too long. Years ago, a baby boomer friend spotted a copy of *Don't Shoot, It's Only Me, Bob Hope* on my bookshelf. "In that case," he said, "I'll be sure to take careful aim." No doubt, for this scraggly ex-hippie, Hope was the enemy—a mummified square who performed for the troops in Vietnam, and staged unbelievably unhip variety shows for which he booked acts ranging from the bodacious Barbara Feldon to the U.S. Marine Corps Glee Club. Hope is the epitome of the rah-rah flag-waver. He was America's premier *pro patria* stand-up comedian, whose subject matter tended to be girls and sports. In him one can glean much that is characteristic of the successful vaudevillian: the breezy self-confidence, the brashness, the unapologetic affluence—all of which was pretty consistent with the essence of conservative postwar America. In the late sixties there were plenty of archconservative ex-vaudevillians floating around for the counterculture to hate: George Jessel, Jack Haley, Martha Raye, Walter Winchell.

If you think about it, this is an amazing development. For more than two thousand years, variety performers were noncomformists, rebels, and social outcasts. Now they formed the very bedrock of the establishment, dues-paying Elks who socialized with presidents and potentates, had millions in the bank, lived in mansions, and sneered at the scraggly vagabonds of the younger generation. In essence, the nation's most successful vaudevillians had become traitors to the troupers' way of life.

The main trunk of the vaudeville story now shifts away from the old guard, and onto those in the succeeding generations who felt an urge to get back to basics.

The sixties were an era of individualism and rebellion. As thousands of young people were "dropping out" and "taking it to the streets," a number of them began to realize that they could circumvent the entertainment machine entirely. If you have a performer and an audience in a room together, a multinational conglomerate becomes irrelevant. In places like New York or San Francisco, there arose a real proliferation of long-haired, rainbow-suspender-wearing, face-painted, *Godspell*-looking freaks who did mime, juggled, and walked on stilts at protests, in the parks, and on sidewalks, not to mention at rock festivals, coffeehouses, and Renaissance fairs.

In the mid-1960s, a circus performer named Hovey Burgess (who'd been taught juggling and stilt-walking by his parents) was teaching circus skills at New York University. While performing at one of New York's top psychedelic rock clubs, the Electric Circus, he met a spotlight operator named Larry Pisoni whose grandparents had been performers in *varieta*, also known as *caffe-concerto*, or Italian vaudeville.* Pisoni took classes with Burgess, learning tumbling, trapeze, wire-walking, clowning, and juggling. After a few years of performing with Burgess's Circo dell'Arte, Pisoni went out west and joined the San Francisco Mime Troupe. Less interested in experimental theater than in simple, straightforward popular art, he split off in 1974, forming the Pickle Family Circus with his wife, kids, and several friends. No less politically radical (perhaps more) than the street theater of its day, the Pickles' message was expressed entirely through the medium of traditional circus arts: tumbling, wire-walking, clowning, juggling, and so forth.

In an atmosphere of renewed respect for clowning as an art form, in 1968 the Ringling Brothers, Barnum and Bailey Circus formed its famous Clown College. Ostensibly established to develop talent for its shows, the Clown College had the unintended effect of releasing hun-

*More modest in scope and less well-known than black or Yiddish vaudeville, this circuit began in New York's and Hoboken's Italian neighborhoods early in the twentieth century and continued on into the thirties and forties, and in some ways continues in cafés, restaurants, social halls, fraternal lodges, churches, and street fairs in the region.

dreds of talented and trained vaudeville-lovers back into the population. Within a few years, Clown College alumni peppered the country, comprising one of numerous talent streams that would feed into the renewed vaudeville movement. Among them was the clown Bill Irwin, who was also a veteran of the Pickle Family Circus. Like nearly all of the first-generation (so-called) variety revivalists I interviewed for this book, Irwin dislikes the label "New Vaudeville." Such performers take great pride in their craft and don't wish to see themselves pigeonholed as nostalgia acts, particularly when they, as baby boomers, are not particularly nostalgic for an era when vaudevillians wore blackface, made mother-in-law jokes, and boasted of the fact that they were only in it for the money.

"I don't see much point in a romanticized view of another era," says Irwin, who goes on to observe that working in the original vaudeville "was probably ghastly." When pressed, he names Chaplin and Keaton as influences, alone of all the dozens of mimes and knockabout acts a true vaudeville freak might name.

The impetus to clown, in Irwin's case, came not from admiration for any particular vaudeville performer but from a need for creative freedom and a need for a way and a place to perform in an industry with increasingly few opportunities. "Most of us wanted to be performers for the most noble—and ignoble—reasons. Rather than waiting around for a part in a play, we created our own stuff. It was a way of getting out of the straitjacket of the times."

His motivations, then, were practical, and not too different, in some ways, from those of the original vaudevillians. He just wanted to be seen. The derby-hatted, big-suited Irwin was to become nationally famous for his silent clowning in his Broadway shows *Largely New York* and *Fool Moon* (with David Shiner and the Red Clay Ramblers), as well as for numerous film and television roles.

Self-professed con man and magician Harry Anderson, too, spent his formative years in San Francisco, and was dubbed part of the New Vaudeville movement. But, says Anderson, "I never considered myself part of anything." He describes the crucial moment in his life as being an occasion when he was around nine years old and saw Blackstone the magician perform. "Why would anyone want any other job?" he asks. So he began hanging out at the magic shop across the street from where he lived, went into street performing, then stage performing, and finally went on to become a fixture on television throughout the 1980s and nineties via regular appearances on *Cheers* and *Saturday Night Live* and starring roles on *Night Court* and *Dave's World*. Tall, bespectacled, and invariably wearing a fedora, loud tie, and suspenders, Anderson seemed as though he had stepped out of a time machine. While an accomplished close magic artist, he has always been more cherished for his persona as a lovable rogue. The character he developed resembled Ryan O'Neal's in the 1973 film *Paper Moon*, a charming grifter who'd produce a coin from behind a kid's ear with one hand even while stealing his lunch money with the other.

Anderson's work has never in any way been political, and, truth to tell, there is nothing "new" about his vaudeville. He just happens to be doing his act at a certain point in time, and so finds himself being placed by the press in that category.

Howard Patterson, of the Flying Karamazov Brothers, says, "The only thing the New Vaudeville acts share in common is that they all insist they are not part of 'New Vaudeville.'" As a kid, Patterson played recorder in the 1963 Renaissance fair mentioned above. After taking up juggling in college, and working up a humorous act with his buddies, Patterson played the emerging Renaissance fair circuit and performed on the streets for years before the team landed their first Broadway show in 1983. As an act, the Karamazovs are a sort of cross between the Marx Brothers and W. C. Fields: a top-notch juggling team that keeps the audience laughing with an incessant stream of quips, puns, and gags even as it amazes them with their complicated juggling patterns. (My favorite exchange of theirs is: "Watch your language!"—"English! What's yours?") More than most others, the Karamazovs, with their long hair, beards, and occasional quips about the right wing, continue to evoke the heyday of sixties street performing.

Of his years of busking, Patterson says, "Had there been a vaudeville infrastructure like there was in the teens and twenties, where there was a series of gradations from the bottom all the way to the Palace, we would have gone that route. But there wasn't. So there was this urge to take control of the situation. We don't have to be a part of the international corporate conspiracy. All we need is us and other people. When civilization collapses, we can still eat."

Their allegiance, then, is to the soul, not the body, of vaudeville, which, after all, laid the foundations for the present entertainment machine. These performers hearken back still further, to the medieval environment where variety germinated in the first place. Vaudeville? We don't need no stinking vaudeville! We're jugglers, and jugglers were around when B. F. Keith wasn't even a twinkle in Adam Smith's eye.

Teller, of the team Penn & Teller, says he was "not even slightly interested" in the original vaudeville. The silent half of the well-known magic and comedy duo turns out to be every bit as articulate as his husky-voiced colleague. Like the others, Penn & Teller also spent many formative years in San Francisco, although they actually got their performing start in New Jersey in the mid-seventies with an act called the Othmar Schoek Memorial Society for the Preservation of Unusual and Disgusting Music. They became Penn & Teller in 1981.

For Teller, as for Bill Irwin, performing has never been about nostalgia, but about the essence of theater. He says he ascribes his philosophy of performance to a high school teacher who taught him magic, drama, and Aristotle's *Poetics*. Aristotle famously taught that "A is A," therefore a painting is a painting, a house is a house, and a performer is a performer—the implication being that a performer had better perform. For Teller, practically all contemporary magic was "insulting and stupid," but, above all, it failed as theater. It was "motion" without "action." As Penn put it, "If Eddie Van Halen had played his guitar the way most magicians do magic, he never would have gotten laid." According to Teller, the high level of skill was the only aspect of the old vaudevillianism that was of interest to him, an aspect, one might add, that is hardly unique to vaudeville. He describes a pilgrimage he and Penn had made to the great juggler Bobby May and being blown away by old films of May's show-stopping act in the twenties and thirties. One example should suffice: May could throw an unlit cigarette and a lit match into the air and catch them in his mouth at the same time. Then he would light the cigarette with the match, using only his mouth. "That [trick] was so fucking cool. It has nothing to do with vaudeville per se. A fourteen-year-old skateboard punk would be just as impressed. It's just amazing human flesh."

I have used the term "New Vaudeville" in this discussion because it is widely used and many readers will understand what group of entertainers I mean when I use it. But I dislike the label as much as the artists do, although for a completely different reason. When it comes down to it, the label is misleading. Most of the performers who have been placed in that category are circus-based acts, which in the original vaudeville would have been but a single stripe of a very broad spectrum. Instead of fifteen clowns, magicians, and jugglers, a fantasy modern big-time vaudeville bill might feature such diverse performers as Bette Midler, David Blaine, Savion Glover, Drew Carey, Daniel Day-Lewis, Gary Coleman, and Wynton Marsalis and the Lincoln Center Jazz Ensemble. One slot and one slot only would be available for the clownish likes of Irwin or the Karamazovs. Taking an entire bill of New Vaudeville acts and calling it vaudeville would be sort of like presenting a show of percussionists and calling it "New Wave Symphony Orchestra."

Another obvious difference between the original and the "New" vaudevillians is their level of book smarts. A "collegiate" like Rudy Vallee was quite rare in vaudeville. Most of the performers had dropped out of school at a young age. Furthermore, outside of a few remarkable autodidacts like W. C. Fields, Groucho Marx, and Fred Allen, most vaudevillians usually referred to books and education with a kind of sneering condescension as "egghead stuff." Like most Americans, vaudevillians valued practical know-how; they didn't have much use for theory, poetry, art, or context. (Their defensiveness on the topic, however, may have been an indication of a certain insecurity on their part. They knew they were smart, but their humble origins had prevented them from getting the benefits of a college education.) Fanny Brice, for example, once referred to Ernest Hemingway as a "schmendrick." George Jessel is said to have dazzled Cardinal Spellman in conversation with biblical quotes. Spellman was floored: "You're a Jew, you never went to school. Where'd you learn all that?" Jessel's answer was that in his vaudeville days, while waiting around in hotels for his nightly assignation with a hooker, he'd thumbed through the Gideon Bible.

By contrast, the New Vaudevillians are conspicuous in the flaunting of their gray matter. Those who talk evince erudition in their patter; those who don't have tipped their hands in interviews that explain their work. Harry Anderson was valedictorian of his high school graduating class. Bill Irwin went to Yale. Teller was a Latin instructor. Howard Patterson was an archaeologist.

The original run of American vaudeville had been nothing if not modernist (or pop modernist). It resembled the industrial design that characterized the biplane, the Empire State Building, and the Model T Ford. No one in vaudeville would ever have said that, however, nor, more than likely, would even have *thought* to say it. Conversely, for all their talk of meat and potatoes, the New Vaudevillians possess that potentially fatal self-knowledge: they have eaten the forbidden apple and know they are making art.

New Vaudeville, as a restatement, as a quotation, is what the eggheads call postmodern. It is infused with "attitude," "edge," "subtext." It is self-reflexive, self-reflective, and self-conscious. It often seems to be saying subtly, "I am really smarter than this thing I'm doing." Of all the thousands of vaudevillians, perhaps only the comedian Fred Allen had taken such an approach during vaudeville's heyday. Billed as "The World's Worst Juggler," his act was a parody of all the bad vaudeville acts he had seen, and incorporated not only bad juggling, but bad ventriloquism, bad singing, and bad banjo playing. Allen was decades ahead of his time. His act was about the fact that it was an act—similar to the goal of many modern painters: to point out that their paintings were just paint on canvas.

The camp sensibility helped play a role in the modern rehabilitation of vaudeville. In the 1960s, the pressure in show business was to create material that was "relevant," that seemed to provide some sort of social or cultural critique. Anything that was old school was suspect. Yet there were plenty in the younger generation who were attracted to traditional show business. To make it viable in the new era, a strategy had to be devised to make the old way of doing things seem relevant. The strategy became camp: a means of inoculating a seemingly reactionary tendency with a layer of subversive irony that carried with it an unspoken message of revolt. The camp performer puts "quotes" around his performance— he indicates that what he is doing is ridiculous, is to be laughed at. New York's gay community, with its drag subculture, led the way in developing this nuanced sensibility. The king (or queen) of the movement was Charles Ludlam of New York's Ridiculous Theatrical Company, who employed not only drag, but quick-change, impressions, ventriloquism, and Borscht Belt one-liners to put across his now classic stage comedies. Starting in the mid-seventies, the camp aesthetic began to influence television variety: *The Uncle Floyd Show*, Jim Henson's *The Muppet Show*, Chuck Barris's *Gong Show*, *Late Night with David Letterman*, and Penn and Teller's *Sin City Spectacular* all functioned as simultaneous tribute to, and comment upon, old-school show biz.

That said, a great number of performers came of age in the 1970s, and became famous in plainly vaudevillian disciplines, but without ever being lassoed into a movement. Ventriloquists, for example, such as Jay Johnson and "Bob" (of the ABC sitcom *Soap*), Willie Tyler and "Lester," and Wayland Flowers and "Madame" were constant fixtures on television for years, yet their appearances were somehow show business as usual.

Countless acts were merely "carrying on the family business" in the traditional show-biz way. The descendants of vaudeville trick-rider Poodles Hanneford are still international circus stars. Judy Garland's daughters, Liza Minelli and Lorna Luft, could lay as great a claim to performing within the vaudeville tradition as any juggler.

Likewise, the late Gregory Hines broke into show business at the knee of his jazz-drummer dad. He started to learn tap at age two from master teacher Henry Letang and at age five formed an act with his brother Maurice that toured the country and made frequent appearances at Harlem's famous Apollo Theater. In 1973, the film *The Sting*, with its Scott Joplin sound track resulted in a major revival of interest in ragtime. This paved the way for the 1978 Broadway show *Eubie!* featuring the music of Eubie Blake, and the tap-dancing talent of the then thirty-two-year-old Gregory Hines. Over the next couple of decades, the funky, sincere Hines almost single-handedly rehabilitated tap's foundering reputation and made it creditable again as a mainstream entertainment. Along the way he did the Broadway shows *Comin' Uptown* (1979), *Sophisticated Ladies* (1981), and *Jelly's Last Jam* (1992), and such films as *Tap* (1988) and *The Cotton Club* (1984). Hines's foremost protégé, Savion Glover, has done even more to rejuvenate the art form. Glover burst onto the scene in 1996 with the show *Bring in 'Da Noise, Bring in 'Da Funk*, in which he debuted a highly original, aggressive dance style that incorporated elements of hip-hop and contemporary movement. Some consider him the best tapper who ever lived.

Also upholding a legacy that extends back to the vaudeville days is cult favorite "Uncle Floyd" Vivino. Vivino comes from a line of several generations of Italian actors, singers, and musicians, many of whom, like Larry Pisoni's grandparents, performed in *varieta*. An accomplished piano player and singer, after years of gigging at places like Gaslight Village in Lake George, Floyd got the opportunity to produce and star in a local New Jersey children's television program in 1974.

Children's television was one of the last places left where the old spirit of the original vaudeville might be sustained. Vaudeville, as we know, had initially been invented to appeal to children (and women, and polite society generally). Now the children's market had branched off entirely on its own. In children's programming alone could you still find the mismatched plaid jackets, the slide whistles, the funny hats, and the puppets that one might once have found on a vaudeville bill or television variety program. The granddaddies of TV's golden era were of course the marionette Howdy Doody and Buffalo Bob, both of whom were on the air from 1947 through 1960. Bob Keeshan, who had played Clarabell the Clown on *Howdy Doody*, branched off on his own in 1955 to launch *Captain Kangaroo*, which brought Mr. Moose, Bunny Rabbit, and Mr. Green Jeans to young fans until 1984.

Floyd's kids' program had more in common with *The Soupy Sales Show*, which aired from 1955 through 1979, than it did with the straight, simple kids' fare like *Captain Kangaroo*. Sales, in a battered hat, big bow tie, and loud checked jacket, was the archetypal kids' show host, his material very much hearkening back to the days of vaudeville, with jokes, puns, silent movies, and, above all, pies in the face. *The Uncle Floyd Show* upped the ante. Floyd himself could do anything. He'd sit at the piano and do an old standard like "Ain't She Sweet" in a manner reminiscent of Chico Marx. Then he would do a ventriloquism bit with his "partner," Oogie (his hand with a face drawn on, as vaudeville ventriloquist Señor Wences used to do). And, of course, he was a human encyclopedia of jokes. As it became apparent that a certain percentage of his ad-libs went over the kids' heads, the show became an instant cult favorite with grown-ups. Still retaining the children's show format, *The Uncle Floyd Show* became an insane sketch-comedy show on par with the weirdest video artistry of Ernie Kovacs. He assembled a company of fat, possibly drunk, cohorts with names like Mugsy, Looney Skip Rooney, and Netto. The cigar-smoking Floyd would read letters from the "kids at home" (often peppered with sly double entendres), and the cast would do parodies of popular movies and songs, with offstage cast members filling in for the audience by laughing as hard as they could. The show became a cult favorite in New York City (counting John Lennon, Paul Simon, David Bowie, and Terry Gilliam among its influential fans) and for a brief time in the early eighties it was syndicated nationally. Today Floyd performs with a live lounge act. Though a baby boomer, he gives the impression that he is ninety years old.

At the end of the seventies, New York began to join San Francisco as a major breeding ground for vaudevillians. In 1977, two jugglers and former members of the San Francisco Mime Troupe, Paul Binder and Michael Christensen, founded the Big Apple Circus, a "one ring classical circus," in an attempt to restore some of the intimacy that had been lost in the more bloated three-ring variety. Despite that mission, Big Apple counted many Ringling Brothers Clown College graduates among those it nurtured through its New York School for Circus Acts. In Big Apple's wake, countless new vaudeville theaters and groups were founded, many started by Ringling Brothers Clown College alums.

In 1980, Yale drama graduate Dick Zigun revived the art of the sideshow at Brooklyn's Coney Island. His "Sideshows by the Seashore" features the occasional freak like an armless, legless "Human Cigarette Factory" and a dwarf named Koko the Killer Klown, while relying more consistently on skill-based acts: contortionists, escape artists, snake charmers, fire-eaters, sword swallowers, and fakirs who could lie on a bed of nails and walk on broken glass.

I think it would be safe to say that between them, the two previously mentioned institutions have produced and inspired hundreds of new variety artists in the last quarter-century. And at this point, it does get rather senseless to speak of New Vaudevillians, for vaudeville no longer exists in its pure form. We have an enormous amount of circus, burlesque, sideshow, and vaudeville-like activity happening across the country: hundreds and hundreds of outré performers working in scores of shows at dozens of locations. A good deal of these productions have elements of all of the variety forms. Most of them take place in the modern equivalent of the concert saloon, in the nightclubs and bars of New York, Chicago, San

Francisco, and most of the other major cities. What's new is that "clean" is now a dirty word. Variety is rowdy again.

In the early nineties, Seattle spewed forth the *Jim Rose Circus Sideshow*, which became closely associated with the grunge movement. For the first time since the advent of rock-and-roll, a traditional variety form developed a widespread following among young people. In imitation of the fire-eaters, sword swallowers, and human blockheads in Rose's show (which just happened to tour with Seattle rock bands), teenagers across the country began appalling their parents by getting tattoos and piercing their bodies.

Coney Island alumni began to branch off and establish their own organizations and careers. Bearded lady Jennifer Miller (a radical feminist who prefers to be called a "woman with a beard") formed Circus Amok in 1989. The hirsute and hypertalented Miller sings and clowns, juggles sharp swords, and performs any number of other tricks while hosting her Brechtian circus in which traditional variety stunts are presented with an anti-globalist message and a klezmer sound track. Also in 1989 anarchists Keith Nelson and Stephanie Monseau formed the Bindlestiff Family Cirkus in a former Williamsburg (Brooklyn) speakeasy. The pair, performing as Kinko and Philomena Bindlestiff, did all the traditional sideshow stunts, and gradually expanded their repertoire to include other specialties, such as bullwhip cracking and trick roping. The group mounts a new show annually that features elements of circus, sideshow, burlesque, and vaudeville. Another Coney Island alum, Todd Robbins (an amazing performer who can play ragtime piano, do magic tricks, and eat lightbulbs), had a hit Off-Broadway show called *Carnival Knowledge*, which opened in 2003 and remains on the boards at the time of this writing.

The hottest ticket at the moment appears to be the burlesque revival. The movement began in 1993, when Berlin expatriate Ute Hanna did the impossible by rehabilitating the long-discredited institution of New York burlesque. Hanna was smart enough to marry the art of the striptease to the feminist performance art pioneered by Karen Finley, Holly Hughes, Annie Sprinkle, Penny Arcade, and others, creating the long-running Blue Angel Cabaret (which still exists under the name Le Scandal at a club called the Cutting Room). In 1995, Michelle Carr founded the Velvet

Hammer Burlesque in Los Angeles, a postfeminist homage to stripping's glory days. This highly influential show was joined in 1998 by New York's Va Va Voom Room, helmed by L.A. expat Kate Valentine in her persona "Miss Astrid." By the turn of the twenty-first century, dozens of clubs around the country were offering classic burlesque shows, featuring strips, bawdy songs, snappy comics, and dancers.

Numerous neovaudeville troupes and individuals live the old vaude-villian dream by touring the country on a sort of loose proto-circuit. The Bindlestiff Family Cirkus has been touring annually since 1998, for example. Co-director Keith Nelson describes piecing together a wheel of diverse sorts of venues, including local fringe theaters (the regional equivalent of Off-Off-Broadway), rock clubs, and, on occasion, even authentic old vaudeville houses. Some of their stops include the Coolidge Corner Theatre (Brookline, Mass.), the Vortex (Austin), AS220 (Providence), the Dark Horse (Nashville), the Autobahn Hotel (New Orleans), and the King Opera House (Van Buren, Arkansas). In Des Moines, you can find the Vaudeville Mews. In Tucson, the Vaudeville Cabaret. At each stop along the way, the touring companies collaborate with the local talent, with the understanding that the outreach will be reciprocated when the local hosts come to their own town.

My own show, the American Vaudeville Theatre, was founded in 1995, and I bring it up only to illustrate the scope and breadth of the talent that is available today without even going outside of New York. In almost ten years of production I have been able to present banjoists, harp players, bagpipers, brass bands, rock bands, country bands, folk singers, yodelers, jazz singers, music-hall singers, ragtime piano players, sword swallowers, glass-eaters, jugglers, a unicyclist, bullwhip and lariat artists, a bearded lady, clowns, monologists, two-man comedy teams, female impressionists, sketch-comedy troupes, legit actors in one-act plays, impressionists, sister acts, kid acts, tap dancers, belly dancers, fan dancers, magicians, mind readers, ventriloquists, a man who played the spoons, a flea circus, and a Russian poodle act. I've even presented a blackface act (albeit a politically correct one—a Harlem mime troupe's tribute to Bert Williams). The oldest act I've presented was undoubtedly the Rappin' Granny (known to some from the *Howard Stern Show*); the youngest, my son, Charlie, who was still in his mother's womb.

Why is all this going on now? I have my theories.

Ironically, and maybe counterintuitively, new technology actually encourages and facilitates the study of the past. There is a precedent for this. In the centuries after the printing press was invented, recently rediscovered plays from the ancient world began to be disseminated throughout Europe, helping to spark an explosion of theater in the Renaissance. Similarly, by the 1980s, video- and audiotape technology, combined with the multifarious choices offered by cable television, combined to expose a generation of young people to a flood of "new" entertainment from the first half of the twentieth century. In stores and over the Internet, one could now buy audiotapes and CDs of old radio programs and jazz-era music recordings, along with videotapes and DVDs of silent films, early talkies, and early television programs. Cable allowed viewers to choose diverse programs, which now included previously obscure old films and television shows. This has allowed for greater exposure to old-time vaudevillians and their aesthetic, spreading their influence.

Of course, all the exposure in the world will not affect an audience that is not receptive. The fact is, a pendulum swing in generational outlooks was under way. In place of the slovenly stage presence of the rock-and-roll generation, vaudeville offers a more formal presentationalism. Rock acts and modern stand-up comedians show up in street clothes. Vaudevillians take great care with their costumes. Rock acts show up late to play, and then tune their instruments for an hour before playing. Vaudevillians don't waste the audience's time. Stand-up comedians frequently seem satisfied with weak material or no material at all, relying on their personal charm to carry them through. Vaudevillians obsessively hone their act to perfection. Stand-up comedians talk about their personal lives; vaudevillians assume grotesque, larger-than-life characters.

In 1957, Smith and Dale appeared on the *Ed Sullivan Show* dressed as Weber and Fields and proceeded to enact a routine that was somewhere in the neighborhood of seventy years old. It wasn't presented as a history lesson—it was the entertainment. Even at that late date, there was still an unbroken continuum with the humor of the McKinley era. As much as I enjoy rock-and-roll, the sad aspect of its influence is how remorselessly it has eviscerated and buried all that has come before it.

The overwhelming influence of broadcast and recording arts enabled an unprecedented attack on more traditional approaches to mass entertainment. All that was "old, corny, square" was disposed of. To me, this instinct of selective purgation resembles the one that launched Mao's Cultural Revolution. Destruction is always bad.

Straddling the line between the wild joie de vivre of variety and the greater formalism and care of vaudeville, the current generation seeks to reconnect with the religious element of live theater, the combination of ritual and the expectation of the unexpected that can be a transcendent experience—in short, magic.

But this is not its only virtue. As The Who sang, "Meet the new boss. / Same as the old boss." By the 1990s, baby boomers began to assume positions of leadership in the media, academia, and politics. Boomers in power revealed themselves to be vaguely Victorian in their outlook, turning their back on their own sexual revolution, banning smoking, and enforcing codes of "acceptable speech" on college campuses.

The vaudeville, burlesque, and sideshow subcultures express the younger generation's resistance to such restrictions. They are reliving, in a way, the career of the great Mae West. From 1924, when she created her Diamond Lil character, through the rest of her career, West embodied the 1890s. Though she pushed the boundaries of what it was acceptable to say and do onstage and on screen, she did so through a veil of nostalgia. The era of Bowery saloons—the heyday of pre-vaudeville variety—were an ideal for her. Mind you, she wasn't for returning to those times, which was also the era of Comstockery, after all (a term coined by Shaw to describe the prudish activities of Victorian reformer Anthony Comstock). Mae wanted only the good parts of the past. Similarly, second-wave New Vaudeville emulates the same era, filtered largely through a post-punk aesthetic that privileges an antisocial stance. It is reminiscent of that vaguely illicit, semicriminal phase of variety, where the audience is good and drunk, the performers foul-mouthed and earthy. In reaction to a splinter faction of prudish feminists who think all heterosexual sex is rape, new burlesque artists offer a positive expression of women in control of their bodies. For these women, Mae West is a deity.

This newest wave of vaudeville also seeks to counteract the unfortunate effects of market segmentation in the entertainment industry, which creates cultural subgroups that are often at odds with one another. Such target marketing has brought on an age of hyperspecialization. Nightclubs devote themselves entirely to a single branch of show business: stand-up comedy, improv, jazz, folk, and so on. Record labels, radio stations, cable channels, and websites do the same. While vaudeville was about uniting diverse factions to create one big American audience, modern show business does the opposite, encouraging factionalism in order to better fleece the isolated consumer. Divide and conquer.

Vaudeville was a transitional moment in the technological history of the performing arts, representing a midpoint between the era of the single hometown playhouse with a stock company and that of the global electronic entertainment Web. We are still in the midst of the revolution. Yet that midpoint was a nice place, wasn't it? Vaudeville was live. You mingled. You rubbed elbows with the great unwashed—in fact, you were probably one of them. I know I am.

Yet the vaudeville lifestyle presaged a modern disconnect that has become quite common. Today we are all wanderers with few meaningful ties to geography or family. There is little bond between employer and employee. The past means nothing. Pure materialism leads to ruthlessness. We are all accustomed to constant motion, bad food, superficial relationships, impersonal accommodations. We are, as Dylan sang, "Birds chained to the skyway."

The disconnect we all feel today used to be a feature only of dysfunctional individuals—people like our beloved but troubled vaudevillians. But now, with the interstate highway system, cell phones, and the Web, we can go wherever we want, and communicate with whomever we want, at any time. Superficial connections have increased; strong, lasting, significant bonds are a thing of the past.

"Nothing in excess" wrote the Greek philosopher Chilon (not Pantages!). The current nostalgia for a lost era seems to be a longing for a time when show business was neither prohibited by witch-burning, black-hatted killjoys, nor an all-encompassing, soul-deadening, violent alienation machine. One would hope it might be possible for us, like the ancient Greeks, to acknowledge the passions, live in harmony with them—yet rule them from a position of strength.

The vaudeville rebirth in some ways seems to be a movement to restore values the Puritans would have understood: connections between people, community, and a rejection of a corporate value system in which we are economically and technologically connected to everything but emotionally connected to nothing. In the summer 2003 edition of their show, Circus Amok climaxed with a riff on "Homeland Security." The things that made the Amokers feel secure included "food, shelter, healthcare, good art, love, no deception, sequins, no killer cops, good shoes, cup cakes, Arundhati Roy, small businesses, solar energy, free rent, no detention, [and] the B61 bus." Whether or not you are in sympathy with every aspect of their politics, these are vaudevillians who care about their community, who are not, in the Sex Pistols' phrase, "only in it for the money." Their show is mounted in public parks, and it is free (although in the finest busking tradition, they do pass the hat).

When people don't interact and form bonds, they become depressed (as 10 percent of Americans are) or violent (the other 90 percent). Today, people are trying to bond with machinery. You know what? It's just not working out. It's a little unrequited. "I want my MTV" but it doesn't seem to particularly want me. Well, the vaudevillian wants you. In fact, he needs you. From the stage, he practically makes love to you, and he probably would—right then and there—if the law and customs of public propriety did not forbid it.

We long for a place where individuals can shine on the strength of their individuality. Where being far out is seen as a strength and not a handicap. For a world of magic and of elbow room, of freedom and nature and adventure: of horses, gypsy wagons, campfires, hoppable freight trains; long walks down dirt roads, of meeting a constant stream of strange, eccentric characters—"fellow travelers"—other ungovernable, perverse, and willful idealists for whom town life is simply too bleak. We need escape from our "shiny metal boxes," from superhighways (where towns are passed through at eighty miles an hour and never savored, never cherished), from cages, cubicles, phones that ring no matter where we are, and jobs at "One Industrial Park Boulevard."

This is why vaudeville will always triumph, for it is merely an expression of people's longing for surprise, invention, joy, laughter, tears, transcendence. It is the theatrical embodiment of freedom, tolerance, opportunity, diversity, democracy, and optimism. The Russian literary critic Mikhail Bakhtin called this tendency to break out, to laugh, to enjoy living in one's body "carnival"; but there is another name for it, a tremendous word: vaudeville. A syllogism lies before us. Vaudeville is the life spirit itself, it is our very humanity. And this is why vaudeville can never be "dead." For the day vaudeville flatlines is the day you can also write the epitaph for the human race.

9

THE CHASER

Photo: Evan Fairbanks

PROF. JOHN GOLDEN POND
"Eats Frogs"

BIBLIOGRAPHY

VAUDEVILLE AND VARIETY

Caroline Caffin. *Vaudeville*. New York: Mitchell Kennerly, 1914.

Frank Cullen, ed. *Vaudeville Times* (quarterly periodical). Boston: American Vaudeville Museum, 1998–present.

Michael Marks Davis. *The Exploitation of Pleasure*. New York: Russell Sage Foundation, 1911.

John DiMeglio. *Vaudeville U.S.A.* Bowling Green, Kentucky: Bowling Green University Popular Press, 1973.

Andrew L. Erdman. *Blue Vaudeville: Sex, Morals and the Mass Marketing of Amusement 1895–1915*. Jefferson, North Carolina: McFarland & Co., 2004.

Douglas Gilbert. *American Vaudeville, Its Life and Times*. New York: Dover Books, 1940.

Susan Kattwinkel. *Tony Pastor Presents*. Westport, Connecticut: Greenwood Publishing Group, 1998.

Joe Laurie, Jr. *Vaudeville, from the Honky Tonks to the Palace*. New York: Henry Holt & Co., 1953.

Joe Laurie, Jr., and Abel Green. *Show Biz: From Vaude to Video*. New York: Henry Holt & Co., 1951.

Albert F. McClean. *American Vaudeville as Ritual*. Lexington: University of Kentucky Press, 1965.

Charles Norman. *When Vaudeville Was King: A Soft Shoe Stroll Down Forget-me-not Lane*. Victoria (Australia): Spectrum Publications, 1984.

Brett Page. *Writing for Vaudeville*. Springfield, Massachusetts: Home Correspondence, 1915.

Frank Rose. *The Agency: William Morris and the Hidden History of Show Business*. New York: HarperCollins, 1995.

Charles Samuels and Louise Samuels. *Once Upon a Stage: The Merry World of Vaudeville*. New York: Dodd, Mead & Co., 1974.

Anthony Slide. *The Encyclopedia of Vaudeville*. Westport, Connecticut: Greenwood
     Press, 1994.
———. *Selected Vaudeville Criticism*. Lanham, Maryland: Scarecrow Press, 1988.
———. *The Vaudevillians*. Westport, Connecticut: Arlington House, 1981.
William Smith. *The Vaudevillians*. New York: MacMillan & Co., 1976.
Robert W. Snyder. *Voice of the City*. Chicago: Ivan R. Dee, 2000 ed.
Marian Spitzer. *The Palace*. New York: Antheneum, 1969.
Shirley Staples. *Male-Female Comedy Teams in American Vaudeville: 1865–1932*. Ann
     Arbor, Michigan: UMI Research Press, 1984.
Charles W. Stein. *American Vaudeville as Seen by Its Contemporaries*. New York: Alfred
     A. Knopf, 1984.

SOCIAL MILIEU OF VARIETY
Tyler Anbinder. *Five Points: The 19th-Century New York City Neighborhood That In-
     vented Tap Dance, Stole Elections, and Became the World's Most Notorious Slum*.
     New York: The Free Press, 2001.
Herbert Asbury. *The Gangs of Chicago*. New York: Alfred A. Knopf, 1940.
———. *The French Quarter*. New York: Alfred A. Knopf, 1936.
———. *The Barbary Coast: An Informal History of the San Francisco Underworld*. New
     York: Alfred A. Knopf, 1933.
———. *The Gangs of New York: An Informal History of the Underworld*. New York: Alfred
     A. Knopf, 1927.
Gunther Booth. *City People: The Rise of Modern City Culture in 19th Century America*.
     New York: Oxford University Press, 1980.
Edwin G. Burrows and Mike Wallace. *Gotham: A History of New York City to 1898*. New
     York: Oxford University Press, 1999.
Kenneth T. Jackson, ed. *Encyclopedia of New York City*. New York: Yale University Press/
     New-York Historical Society, 1995.
Lloyd Morris. *Incredible New York*. New York: Random House, 1951.
Luc Sante. *Low Life*. New York: Vintage, 1991.

IMMIGRATION, ETHNICITY, AND RACE
John W. Blassingame. *The Slave Community: Plantation Life in the Antebellum South*.
     New York: Oxford University Press, 1972.
Lawrence J. Epstein. *The Haunted Smile: The Story of Jewish Comedians in America*.
     New York: Public Affairs, 2001.
Irving Howe. *World of Our Fathers: The Journey of the East European Jews to America and
     the Life They Found and Made*. New York: Galahad Books, 1976.
William Pencak, Selma Berrol, and Randall M. Miller, eds. *Immigration to New York*.
     A New York Historical Society Book. Philadelphia: The Balch Institute Press,
     1991.

Ronald Sanders. *The Lower East Side Jews: An Immigrant Generation.* Mineola, New York: Dover Publications, 1969.

Mel Watkins. *On the Real Side: Laughing, Lying and Signifying—The Underground Humor Tradition of African-American Humor That Transformed American Culture, from Slavery to Richard Pryor.* New York: Simon and Schuster, 1994.

SEX AND GENDER

Nel Bodding. *Women and Evil.* Berkeley: University of California Press, 1989.

Timothy J. Gilfoyle. *City of Eros: New York City Prostitution and the Commercialization of Sex, 1790–1920.* New York: W. W. Norton & Co., 1992.

Marilynn Wood Hill. *Their Sisters' Keepers: Prostitution in New York City, 1830–1870.* Berkeley: University of California Press, 1993.

Fergus Linnane. *London: The Wicked City.* London: Robson, 2003.

Marty Williams and Anne Echols. *Between Pit and Pedestal: Women in the Middle Ages.* Princeton, New Jersey: Markus Wiener Publishers, 1994.

GENERAL THEATER

Sheldon Cheney. *The Theatre: 3,000 Years of Drama, Acting and Stagecraft.* New York: Tudor Publishing Co., 1929.

The Cambridge History of English and American Literature. New York: Putnam, 1907–1921 (eighteen vols.).

GENERAL SHOW BUSINESS

Joseph Csida and June Bundy Csida. *American Entertainment.* New York: Watson Guptill, 1978.

Robert Grau. *The Business Man in the Amusement World: A Volume of Progress in the Field of the Theatre.* New York: Broadway Publishing Company, 1910.

Robert M. Lewis, ed. *From Traveling Show to Vaudeville: Theatrical Spectacle in America, 1830–1910.* Baltimore: Johns Hopkins University Press, 2003.

Brooks McNamara, ed. *American Popular Entertainments.* New York: Performing Arts Journal Publications, 1983.

Myron Matlon, ed. *American Popular Entertainment: Papers and Proceedings of the Conference on the History of American Popular Entertainment.* Westport, Connecticut: Greenwood Press, 1977.

David Nassaw. *Going Out: The Rise and Fall of Public Amusements.* New York: Basic Books, 1993.

Russell Nye. *The Unembarrassed Muse: The Popular Arts in America.* New York: Dial Press, 1970.

Kathy Peiss. *Cheap Amusements: Working Women and Leisure in Turn-of-the-Century New York.* Philadelphia: Temple University Press, 1986.

Tom Prendergrast and Sarah Prendergrast. *The St. James Encyclopedia of Popular Culture*. Chicago: St. James Press, 2000.

Don B. Wilmeth. *American and English Popular Entertainment*. Detroit: Gale Research Company, 1980.

————. *Variety Entertainment and Outdoor Amusements: A Reference Guide*. Westport, Connecticut: Greenwood Press, 1982.

William Winter. *The American Stage of To-day*. New York: E. F. Collier & Sons, 1910.

EARLY AMERICAN THEATER

Rosemarie K. Bank. *Theatre Culture in America, 1825–1860*. New York: Cambridge University Press, 1997.

Arthur Hornblow. *A History of the Theatre in America*. Philadelphia: J. B. Lippincott Company, 1919.

Reese Davis James. *Cradle of Culture 1800–1810, the Philadelphia Stage*. Philadelphia: University of Pennsylvania Press, 1957.

Lawrence W. Levine. *Highbrow/Lowbrow: The Emergence of Cultural Hierarchy in America*. Cambridge, Massachusetts: Harvard University Press, 1988.

George C. D. Odell. *Annals of the New York Stage*. New York: Columbia University Press, 1931.

Thomas Clark Pollock. *The Philadelphia Theatre in the 18th Century*. Westport, Connecticut: Greenwood Press, 1968.

MINSTRELSY

Dave Cockrell. *Demons of Disorder: Early Blackface Minstrels and Their World*. New York: Cambridge University Press, 1997.

Eric Lott. *Love and Theft: Blackface Minstrelsy and the American Working Class*. New York: Oxford University Press, 1993.

Jack Haverby. *Negro Minstrels: A Complete Guide*. Upper Saddle River, New Jersey: Literature House, 1969.

Robert C. Toll. *Blacking Up: The Minstrel Show in Nineteenth Century America*. New York: Oxford University Press, 1974.

Carl Wittke. *Tambo and Bones: A History of the American Minstrel Stage*. Westport, Connecticut: Greenwood Press, 1968.

BARNUM, CIRCUS, DIME MUSEUM, MEDICINE SHOW, AND SIDESHOW

Bluford Adams. *E Pluribus Barnums: The Great Showman and the Making of American Popular Culture*. Minneapolis: University of Minnesota Press, 1997.

P. T. Barnum. *Struggles and Triumphs*. New York: Penguin American Library, 1981 (reprint).

David Carlyon. *Dan Rice: The Most Famous Man You've Never Heard Of.* New York: Public Affairs Books, 2002.

John Culhane. *The American Circus: An Illustrated History.* New York: Henry Holt & Co., 1990.

Neil Harris. *Humbug: The Art of P. T. Barnum.* Chicago: University of Chicago Press, 1973.

Philip B. Kunhardt, Jr., Philip B. Kunhardt III, and Peter W. Kunhardt. *P.T. Barnum: America's Greatest Showman.* New York: Alfred A. Knopf, 1995.

Brooks McNamara. *Step Right Up.* Jackson: University Press of Mississippi, 1995 ed.

Jim Rose. *Freak Like Me: Inside the Jim Rose Circus Sideshow.* New York: Dell, 1995.

A. H. Saxon. *P. T. Barnum: The Legend and the Man.* New York: Columbia University Press, 1989.

BRITISH MUSIC HALL

Roy Busby. *British Music Hall: An Illustrated Who's Who from 1850 to the Present Day.* London: Paul Elek, Ltd., 1976.

Pete Collins. *No People Like Show People.* London: Frederick Muller, Ltd., 1957.

BURLESQUE, DRAG, NIGHTCLUB, REVUE

Robert C. Allen. *Horrible Prettiness: Burlesque and American Culture.* Chapel Hill: University of North Carolina Press, 1991.

Jerome Charyn. *Gangsters & Gold Diggers: Old New York, the Jazz Age, and the Birth of Broadway.* New York: Four Walls Eight Windows, 2003.

James Gavin. *Intimate Nights: The Golden Age of New York Cabaret.* New York: Grove Weidenfeld, 1991.

Morton Minsky and Milt Machlin. *Minsky's Burlesque.* New York: Arbor House, 1986.

F. Michael Moore. *Drag! Male and Female Impersonators on Stage, Screen, and Television.* Jefferson, North Carolina: McFarland & Co., 1994.

Laurence Senelick. *The Changing Room: Sex, Drag and the Theatre.* London and New York: Routledge, 2000.

Irving Zeidman. *The American Burlesque Show.* New York: Hawthorne Books, 1967.

Richard Ziegfeld and Paulette Ziegfeld. *The Ziegfeld Touch: The Life and Times of Florenz Ziegfeld, Jr.* New York: Harry N. Abrams, 1993.

BROADWAY, MUSICAL COMEDY, AND TAP

Rusty E. Frank. *Tap! The Greatest Tap Dance Stars and Their Stories, 1900–1955.* New York: Da Capo Press, 1990.

Stanley Green. *The Great Clowns of Broadway.* New York: Oxford University Press, 1984.

James Haskins. *Black Dance in America: A History Through Its People.* New York: Harper Trophy, 1990.

William Morrison. *Broadway Theatres: History and Architecture*. Mineola, New York: Dover Publications, 1999.

Cecil Smith and Glenn Litton. *Musical Comedy in America*. London and New York: Routledge, 1991 (reprint).

William R. Taylor, ed. *Inventing Times Square*. Baltimore: Johns Hopkins University Press, 1991.

Nicholas Van Hoogstraten. *Lost Broadway Theatres*. New York: Princeton Architectural Press, 1991.

CLOWNING, MAGIC, AND NEW VAUDEVILLE

Milbourne Christopher. *An Illustrated History of Magic*. New York: Thomas Y. Crowell & Co., 1973.

R. G. Davis. *The San Francisco Mime Troupe: The First Ten Years*. San Francisco: Ramparts Press, 1975.

Henry Ridgly Evans. "The Mysteries of Modern Magic." Introductory essay to *Magic: Stage Illusions, Special Effects and Trick Photography*, ed. Albert A. Hopkins. New York: Dover Publications, 1976.

Ron Jenkins. *Acrobats of the Soul: Comedy and Virtuosity in Contemporary American Theatre*. New York: Theater Communications Group, 1988.

John Rudlin. *Commedia dell'Arte: An Actor's Handbook*. London and New York: Routledge, 1994.

Tony Staveacre. *Slapstick! The Illustrated History*. Sydney: Angus and Roberston, 1987.

MUSIC AND THE RECORDING ARTS

Donald Clarke. *The Rise and Fall of Popular Music*. New York: St. Martin's Press, 1995.

Roland Gelatt. *The Fabulous Phonograph: From Tin Foil to High Fidelity*. Philadelphia: J. B. Lippincott Company, 1954.

David A. Jasen. *Tin Pan Alley: The Composers, the Songs, the Performers, and Their Times*. New York: Donald I. Fine, 1998.

Edward B. Marks (as told to Abbot J. Liebling). *They All Sang: From Tony Pastor to Rudy Vallee*. New York: Viking Press, 1934.

George T. Simon. *The Big Bands*. New York: Schirmer Books, 1967.

FILM AND TV

David A. Cook. *A History of Narrative Film*. New York: W.W. Norton & Co., 1990.

Neal Gabler. *An Empire of Their Own: How the Jews Invented Hollywood*. New York: Doubleday, 1988.

Michael Davis Harris. *Always on Sunday: Ed Sullivan: An Inside View*. New York: New American Library, 1969.

Doug Hill and Jeff Weingrad. *Saturday Night: A Backstage History of Saturday Night Live*. New York: William Morrow & Co., 1989.

Henry Jenkins. *What Made Pistachio Nuts?* New York: Columbia University Press, 1992.

Alex McNeil. *Total Television*. New York: Penguin Books, 1997.

David J. Skal. *The Monster Show: A Cultural History of Horror*. New York: Penguin Books, 1993.

VAUDEVILLE BIOGRAPHIES (ALPHABETICAL BY SUBJECT)

Joey Adams. *From Gags to Riches*. Hollywood, Flordia: Frederick Fell, 1946.

Fred Allen. *Much Ado About Me*. Boston: Little, Brown & Co., 1955.

Robert Taylor. *Fred Allen: His Life and Wit*. Boston: Little, Brown & Co., 1989.

George Burns. *Gracie: A Love Story*. New York: Putnam, 1988.

Fred Astaire. *Steps in Time*. New York: Cooper Square Press, 1959.

David Grisman. "Dave Apollon," in *Mandolin World News*, vol. II, no. III (1977) and vol. V, no. III (1980).

Ethel Barrymore. *Memories: An Autobiography*. New York: Harper and Brothers, 1955.

James Kotsilibas-Davis. *The Barrymores: The Royal Family in Hollywood*. New York: Crown Publishers, 1981.

Joe Collura. "Billy Barty: Born a Giant," in *Classic Images*. March 1999.

Milt Josefsberg. *The Jack Benny Show: The Life and Times of Ameria's Best Loved Entertainer*. Westport, Connecticut: Arlington House, 1977.

Mary Ellen Barrett. *Irving Berlin: A Daughter's Memoir*. New York: Limelight Editions, 1996.

Sarah Bernhardt. *My Double Life: Memoirs of Sarah Bernhardt*. Albany: State University of New York Press, 1999 (reprint).

Arthur Gold and Robert Fizdale. *The Divine Sarah: A Life of Sarah Bernhardt*. New York: Alfred A. Knopf, 1991.

Cornelia Otis Skinner. *Madam Sarah*. St. Paul: Paragon House Publishers, 1966.

Herbert G. Goldman. *Fanny Brice: The Original Funny Girl*. New York: Oxford University Press, 1992.

Barbara W. Grossman. *Funny Woman: The Life and Times of Fanny Brice*. Bloomington: Indiana University Press, 1991.

Joe E. Brown and Ralph Hancock. *Laughter Is a Wonderful Thing*. New York: A. S. Barnes & Co., 1956.

John McCabe. *Cagney*. New York: Alfred A. Knopf, 1997.

Eddie Cantor with David Freedman and Jane Kesner Ardmore. *"My Life Is in Your Hands" and "Take My Life": The Autobiography of Eddie Cantor*. New York: Cooper Square Press, 2000.

Herbert G. Goldman. *Banjo Eyes: Eddie Cantor and the Birth of Modern Stardom*. New York: Oxford University Press, 1997.

Charles Chaplin. *My Autobiography*. New York: Simon and Schuster, 1964.

Theodore Huff. *Charlie Chaplin*. New York: Henry Shuman, 1951.

Kenneth S. Lynn. *Charlie Chaplin and His Times*. New York: Simon and Schuster, 1997.

Joyce Milton. *Tramp: The Life of Charlie Chaplin*. New York: De Capo Press, 1998.

David Robinson. *Chaplin: His Life and Art*. New York: McGraw-Hill, 1987.

Irwin Chusid. "Cherry Bomb: 100 Years of Ineptitude." *NY Press*, November 13–19, 1998.

Edwin Behr. *The Good Frenchman: The True Story and Life and Times of Maurice Chevalier*. New York: Villard Books, 1993.

John McCabe. *George M. Cohan: The Man Who Owned Broadway*. New York: Da Capo Press, 1973.

Lawrence J. Quirk and William Schoell. *The Rat Pack: Neon Lights with the Kings of Cool*. New York: Avon Books, 1998 (for information on Sammy Davis, Jr.).

Max Pierce. "The Dolly Sisters: Glamour, Real to Reel," in *Classic Images*, 2000.

Marie Dressler. *The Life Story of an Ugly Duckling*. New York: William M. McBride Publications, 1924.

David Bakish. *Jimmy Durante: His Show Business Career*. Jefferson, North Carolina: McFarland & Co., 1995.

Than Robbins. *Inka Dinka Doo: The Life of Jimmy Durante*. St. Paul: Paragon House, 1991.

Buddy Ebsen. *The Other Side of Oz*. Newport Beach, California: Donovan, 1993.

Axel Madsen. *Stanwyck*. New York: HarperCollins, 1994 (for material on Frank Fay).

Armond Fields and Marc L. Fields. *From the Bowery to Broadway: Lew Fields and the Roots of American Popular Theatre*. New York: Oxford University Press, 1993.

James R. Curtis. *W. C. Fields: A Biography*. New York: Alfred A. Knopf, 2003.

W.C. Fields and Ronald J. Fields. *W.C. Fields by Himself: His Intended Autobiography*. Englewood Cliffs, New Jersey: Prentice-Hall, 1973.

Simon Louvish. *The Man on the Flying Trapeze: The Life and Times of W. C. Fields*. New York: W.W. Norton & Co., 1997.

Robert L. Taylor. *W. C. Fields, His Follies and Fortunes*. New York: Amereon Ltd., 1978.

Armond Fields. *Eddie Foy, A Biography*. Jefferson, North Carolina: McFarland & Co., 1999.

Ed Lowry with Charlie Foy; ed. by Paul M. Levitt. *Joe Frisco: Comic, Jazz Dancer and Railbird*. Carbondale: Southern Illinois University Press, 1999.

Paul "Mousie" Garner with Sharon F. Kissane. *Mousie Garner: Autobiography of a Vaudeville Stooge*. Jefferson, North Carolina: McFarland & Co., 1999.

George Fuller Golden. *My Lady Vaudeville and Her White Rats*. New York: White Rats of America, 1909.

Nat Goodwin. *Nat Goodwin's Book*. Boston: R. G. Badger, 1914.

Graham McCann. *Cary Grant: A Class Apart*. New York: Columbia University Press, 1996.

Glenn Shiley. *Hello Sucker! The Story of Texas Guinan*. Austin: Eakin Press, 1989.

Mitchell Cohen, ed. *Heart of the Tin Man: The Collected Writings of Jack Haley*. New York: R.J. Communications, 2000.

E. J. Kahn, Jr. *The Merry Partners: The Age and Stage of Harrigan and Hart*. New York: Random House, 1955.

Lawrence Quint. *Bob Hope: The Road Well Traveled.* New York: Applause Books, 2000.

Arthur Marx. *The Secret Life of Bob Hope.* Fort Lee, New Jersey: Barricade Books, 1993.

Raymond Strait. *Bob Hope: A Tribute.* New York: Pinnacle Books, 2003.

Ruth Brandon. *The Life and Many Deaths of Harry Houdini.* New York: Random House, 1993.

Milbourne Christopher. *Houdini: The Untold Story.* New York: Aeonian Press, 1969.

Raymond Fitzsimons. *Death and the Magician.* New York: Atheneum, 1980.

Kenneth Silverman. *Houdini!!!* New York: HarperCollins, 1996.

Lawrence Grobel. *The Hustons.* New York: Avon Books, 1989.

Elsie Janis. *So Far, So Good!* New York: E. P. Dutton & Co., 1932.

Michael Freedland. *Jolson.* New York: Stein and Day, 1972.

Herbert Goldman. *Jolson: The Legend Come to Life.* New York: Oxford University Press, 1988.

Rudi Blesch. *Keaton.* New York: Macmillan, 1966.

Tom Dardis. *Keaton: The Man Who Wouldn't Lie Down.* New York: Limelight Editions, 1979.

Marion Meade. *Buster Keaton: Cut to the Chase.* New York: HarperCollins, 1995.

David Robinson. *Keaton.* Bloomington: University of Indiana Press, 1969.

Jesse Louis Lasky. *I Blow My Own Horn.* New York: Doubleday, 1957.

Fred Lawrence Guiles. *Stan: The Life of Stan Laurel.* Chelsea, Michigan: Scarborough House, 1991.

John McCabe. *The Comedy World of Stan Laurel.* New York: Doubleday & Company, 1974.

Beatrice Lillie, aided and abetted by John Philip, written with James Brough. *Every Other Inch a Lady.* New York: Doubleday, 1972.

Joe Adamson. *Groucho, Chico, Harpo and Sometimes Zeppo: A History of the Marx Brothers and a Satire on the Rest of the World.* New York: Simon and Schuster, 1973.

Stefan Kanfer. *Groucho: The Life and Times of Julius Henry Marx.* New York: Vintage, 2000.

Simon Louvish. *Monkey Business: The Lives and Legends of the Marx Brothers.* New York: Thomas Dunne Books, 1999.

Arthur Marx. *My Life with Groucho.* Fort Lee, New Jersey: Barricade Books, 1992 ed.

Harpo Marx. *Harpo Speaks!* New York: Limelight Editions, 1962.

Ken Murray. *Life on a Pogo Stick: Autobiography of a Comedian.* Philadelphia and Toronto: John C. Winston Co., 1960.

Constance Valis Hill. *Brotherhood in Rhythm: The Jazz Tap Dancing of the Nicholas Brothers.* New York: Oxford University Press, 2000.

Parker Zeller. *Tony Pastor: Dean of the Vaudeville Stage.* Ypsilanti: Eastern Michigan University Press, 1971.

Donald C. King. "S.Z. Poli, from Wax to Riches," in *Marquee*, vol. 11, no. 2 (1979).

Moulton Marston and John Henry Feller. *F.F. Proctor: Vaudeville Pioneer.* New York: Richard R. Smith, 1943.

Jim Haskins and N. R. Mitgang. *Mr. Bojangles: The Biography of Bill Robinson*. New York: Welcome Rain, 1988.

E. Paul Alworth. *Will Rogers*. New York: Twayne Publishers, 1974.

Richard M. Ketchum. *Will Rogers: His Life and Times*. New York: American Heritage Pub. Co., 1973.

Bryan B. Sterling. *The Will Rogers Scrapbook*. New York: Grosset and Dunlap, 1976.

Ray Robinson. *An American Original: A Life of Will Rogers*. New York: Oxford University Press, 1996.

Ben Yagoda. *Will Rogers: A Biography*. Norman: University of Oklahoma Press, 1993.

Rose Marie. *Hold the Roses*. Lexington: University Press of Kentucky, 2002.

Benny Rubin. *Come Backstage with Me*. Bowling Green, Ohio: Bowling Green University Popular Press, 1972.

Richard M. Roberts. "Larry Semon: The Cartoonist as Comic," in *Classic Images*, April 1999.

Phil Silvers with Robert Saffron. *This Laugh Is on Me: The Phil Silvers Story*. Englewood Cliffs, New Jersey: Prentice-Hall, 1973.

Robert Kimball and William Bolcom. *Reminiscing with Sissle and Blake*. New York: Cooper Square Press, 1973.

Armond Fields. *Fred Stone: Circus Performer and Musical Comedy Star*. Jefferson, North Carolina: McFarland & Co., 2002.

Michael Fleming. *The Three Stooges: An Illustrated History*. New York: Doubleday, 1999.

"Interview with Mr. Al Parado [Eva Tanguay's husband]," New York: Columbia University Oral History Research Office, 1957.

Sara Maitland. *Vesta Tilley*. London: Virago Press, 1986.

Sophie Tucker. *Some of These Days: The Autobiography of Sophie Tucker*. New York: Doubleday Doran & Co., 1945.

Jill Watts. *Mae West: An Icon in Black and White*. New York: Oxford University Press, 2001.

Emily Wortis Leider. *Becoming Mae West*. New York: Da Capo Press, 1997.

Mae West. *Goodness Had Nothing to Do with It*. Englewood Cliffs, New Jersey: Prentice-Hall, 1959.

Ann Charters. *Nobody: The Story of Bert Williams*. New York: Macmillan & Co., 1970.

Eric Ledell Smith. *Bert Williams: A Biography of the Pioneer Black Comedian*. Jefferson, North Carolina: McFarland & Co., 1992.

Ned Wynn. *We Will Always Live in Beverly Hills: Growing Up Crazy in Hollywood*. New York: Wm. Morrow & Co., 1990.

ACKNOWLEDGMENTS

Sir Isaac Newton famously said that if he had seen any further it was because he had stood on the shoulders of giants. I don't know if my long-distance vision is any better than anyone else's, but in putting this book together I must admit I've stood on more shoulders than the Six Rockets, the Four Flames, and the Three Melvin Brothers combined.

As in the freak show, where the only real royalty are the honest-to-god freaks, in the writing of historical nonfiction, the real heroes are the historians. I confess that until I began this enterprise, my idea of a scholar was those fat guys in the caps and gowns in *Horsefeathers*. I stand corrected. If you want to see a vaudeville slapstick routine, I invite you to watch me try to thread the microfilm machine in a library—and witness the "slow burn" of the librarian in the bargain. The caretakers of our cultural heritage are saints. This is their town; I've just been passing through.

So let me begin by thanking the many professional historians, archivists, and librarians who helped guide me through this process: my former colleagues at the New-York Historical Society, in particular Ellen Denker, Stewart Desmond, Paul Gunther, Holly Hinman, Kathleen Hulser, Kenneth T. Jackson, Steve Jaffe, Mary Beth Kavanagh, Nina Nazionale, Jan Ramirez, Eric Robinson, Denny Stone, Mariam Touba, Grady Turner, and Mina Weiner; the staff in the Research Department at the New York Public Library for the Performing Arts (in particular the caretakers of the Billy Rose Collection); Joseph Sciorra at the John D.

Calandra Institute for Italian American Studies; Robert W. Snyder of the Journalism and Media Studies Program at Rutgers-Newark; Mary Ann Chach at the Shubert Archives; John Scherer at the New York State Museum; Ray Weblinger at the Hampden-Booth Library and the staffs at the Harvard Theater Collection, the Library of Congress, the Lilly Library at Indiana State University, the Museum of Television & Radio, and the Museum of the City of New York. Independent scholars Andy Davis, John McCabe, Caraid O'Brien, and Elyse Singer were generous with their time, advice, help, and attention.

Several fellow enthusiasts and aficionados (many of whom also double as performers) were also invaluable, notably: Rich Conaty of WFUV's *The Big Broadcast*; Frank Cullen of the American Vaudeville Museum; Dale Davidson; Howard Fishman; Laura and Rob Fleder; Viveca Gardiner and Rod Kimball; Andy Hammerstein; Ron Hutchison of the Vitaphone Project; Jay Johnson; Milt Larsen of the Magic Castle; Ben Model of the Silent Clowns; Todd Robbins; Ann Shanks; Raven Snook; and Dick Zigun of Coney Island, U.S.A.

Muchas gracias to all of the troupers who were so generous with their time in granting interviews: Harry Anderson, Joe Franklin, Sylvia Froos, Bill Irwin, Rose Marie, Jennifer Miller, Keith Nelson and Stephanie Monseu of Bindlestiff Family Cirkus, Fayard Nicholas, Howard Patterson of the Flying Karamazov Brothers, Molly and Dick Pierce, Teller of Penn & Teller, and Floyd Vivino. Thanks also to the families and estates of Jack Benny, James Cagney, Charlie Chaplin, W. C. Fields, Cary Grant, and Phil Silvers for their help in securing photos of their famous kin.

Word up to the following for their hot tips: Becki Barnwell; Joe Bevilacqua of Comedy-O-Rama.com; Matt Cohen; Kathy Ham of the Laurel and Hardy Museum; John Hulett III; Laura Leff of the International Jack Benny Fan Club; Patricia Tobias of the Damfinos; and Ted Wioncek, president of the W. C. Fields Fan Club.

Special commendation and eternal love and gratitude to Lisa Ferber for nursing me through the peaks and valleys of the process.

Huge thanks to my family, who supported me in so many ways throughout: John, Rosemary, and Susie Monagan; and Cashel, Charlie, Don, and Peg Stewart.

A special shout-out to Susan DeCarava for making the connection, and to Denise Oswald and Sarah Almond, whose blood, sweat, tears, and little gray cells helped me wrestle this unwieldy sucker to the mat. As any author will tell you, the editors ain't just checking the grammar; they're collaborators in a very real sense.

A nostalgic thank-you to my high school sweetheart, Lisa Sisson, who turned this former geeky teenager on to vaudeville in the first place.

And, finally, thanks most of all to the army of ten thousand troupers who contributed to this story in the most important way of all: by living it.

Goodnight, Mrs. Kalabash, wherever you are.

INDEX